SH?#!
Happens AGAIN!
TRAVELING WITH JOHN AND LESLIE

John Turzer

ISBN:

Ebook: 978-1-969066-30-6

Paperback: 978-1-969066-31-3

Hardcover: 978-1-969066-32-0

Travel, Essays & Travelogues

ACKNOWLEDGEMENT

I'd like to thank my good friend and golfing partner Doug Bradford for reading and editing the manuscript. I have a tendency to write as I speak. Sometimes it takes me hundreds of words just to say hello. Doug meticulously *'cleaned up'* my language and eliminated redundancies. He made sure the sentence structures were solid and included the correct verbs, adverbs, and adjectives. Friends now tell me Doug now talks and sounds like me! Many thanks Doug. Without you, this future New York Times Best Seller would never have happened!

John

Table of Contents

OUR 78 DAY EUROPEAN HOLIDAY
April — June 2024

FOREWORD

I've had the privilege of knowing John and Leslie Turzer for many years, and if there's one thing I've learned about them, it's that they have a knack for turning life into an adventure. So when they shared their plans for this trip—a 2.5-month journey through Europe as part of their bucket list—I knew it would be nothing short of extraordinary. What I didn't expect, though, was how much I would learn from their experiences, even from afar.

John, ever meticulous and deliberate, spent eight months mapping out every detail of this trip. From booking reservations and planning transportation to creating a logical and seamless progression of destinations, he took on the challenge with the precision of a seasoned cartographer. Leslie, with her easy-going charm, brought balance to the equation—embracing every twist and turn with a sense of adventure and trust. Together, they crafted a journey that was as much about the joy of discovery as it was about meticulous preparation.

As I read about their travels, it was clear this wasn't just a vacation—it was a masterclass in living life to the fullest. From the scenic splendor of Switzerland and Norway to the vibrant people and cuisine they encountered along the way, every stop became a story. Each plate of food, each conversation, and every breathtaking view added to the rich tapestry of their adventure.

What stood out most was how they handled setbacks. No trip of this magnitude is without its share of hiccups, but John and Leslie showed remarkable resilience and adaptability. When things didn't go as planned, they didn't let it derail the experience. Instead, they recalibrated, found solutions, and continued forward, often finding unexpected joys along the way.

Readers will find this story as inspiring as it is entertaining. The thoughtfulness in how they sequenced their travels is a testament to John's planning, but the spontaneity and connection they found along the way highlight Leslie's openness to life's surprises. This journey wasn't just about seeing the world—it was about experiencing it together, in all its beauty and unpredictability.

As their friend, I've always admired their zest for life, but this journey has deepened my appreciation for their partnership. It's a reminder that life is meant to be lived fully—through careful planning, yes, but also by embracing the unplanned moments that make it truly unforgettable.

So as you turn the page, prepare to be inspired. John and Leslie's story isn't just about places on a map—it's about how they made the most of a dream, together.

- Dale Andrews

INTRODUCTION

To get away from Las Vegas, and experience the trip of a lifetime, we planned a 30-day European land trip and 21-day Baltic cruise for the spring of 2023.

However, thanks to Covid 19 travel restrictions and John tearing his left Achilles tendon on January 16 and March 22, 2023, our travel plans were put on hold for three years.

While John was recovering from surgery, he meticulously planned a *'Let's catch up, let's go for it, we are not getting any younger'* 78-day European holiday starting on March 26, 2024. He booked all the hotels, scheduled rental cars, bought train tickets, and researched things to do and see each day. A four-page Excel spreadsheet listed the daily details of the 78-day trip.

Three months prior to beginning our journey, John had to learn how to walk again. Wearing an ankle wrap and over the ankle hiking boots, he walked more than 300 miles to strengthen his Achilles for the countless kilometers of walking ahead of us.

Starting in Milan, we used our Eurail Passes to visit various cities in Italy, Germany, France, Switzerland, Amsterdam, and Stockholm. We traveled to Bergen, Norway to begin the 14-day Viking Mars cruise along the western coast of Norway, finishing in Reykjavik, Iceland. We closed the adventure with 3-days in Reykjavik before heading back to reality (Henderson, NV) on June 11, 2024.

During the trip, we celebrated John's 75th birthday, our 41st wedding anniversary, and Leslie's upcoming 76th birthday. John also plans to play the *'trip card'* to cover Christmas, birthdays, and anniversaries through at least 2026! For 78 days, we roamed through nine European countries visited over 36 cities, stayed in 16 hotels, and spent 14 nights on the Viking Mars cruise ship. Seventy of those 78 mornings included a free breakfast in the price of our reservations.

To keep the local authorities guessing—and to avoid being recognized as *"those darn Americans"*—we changed our names at every stop along the journey.

When writing the daily recollections and adventures, we decided to give our reading audience a *'feel'* for the places we visited. So, the book includes information about each city obtained from Wikipedia and other websites cited in the stories.

We have a history of crazy things happening every time we travel. To properly present the inspiration for this book, it is essential for the reader to understand that each chapter is a coherent, detailed, and (we hope) entertaining presentation of our excursions, a compilation of our many adventures ranging from *'what a great time we had'* to *'I can't believe that happened'* and ***'SH?#! Happens'*** situations that just seem to follow us wherever we go. Many of our *'experiences'* mirror the slapstick comedy of the "I Love Lucy" TV series.

On this nearly two-and-a-half month holiday, we visited many wonderful cities and venues, experienced the *'local scene,'* met some truly great people, ate local food, drank many local adult beverages, and took many photos and videos. Our traveling motto has always simply been *'Live Like a Local.'*

We sincerely hope you will enjoy *'our experiences.'* So, *come along with us on an adventurous and exciting 78 days in Europe.*

The Turzers

OUR 78 DAY EUROPEAN HOLIDAY

March — June 2024

Tuesday, March 26 — Day 1
Las Vegas, Nevada to Jamaica, Queens, New York City

Welcome to the beginning of John and Leslie Turzer's March 26 to June 11, 2024, 78-day European holiday. In February and April 2023, I went *'under the knife'* twice to repair my torn Achilles tendon. During the Spring and Summer of 2023, my mobility was severely limited. So, while in a cast and using a knee scooter to get around and go to physical therapy three times a week, I had lots of *'free time'* to diligently research and plan the trip from airplane travel to hotels, rental cars, and European train travel. Also, I created a *'day by day list of things to do'* at each stop along the journey. My backpack holds six inches of file folders containing every travel detail and all the *'cool places'* to visit.

Today, our journey takes us from Henderson, NV to New York City (NYC). Thanks to our extensive nest egg of American Airlines' (AA) Frequent Flyer Miles, today's seven hour flight through Charlotte, NC required a total of only 20,000 miles; don't you just love **FREE** flights?

Some of you may have read our 2013 *"SH?#! Happens, Traveling With John and Leslie"* book about our 38-day European vacation. That book made the New York Times best seller list for seven minutes and 27 seconds!! While it seemed pandemonium rained during our last excursion, we were hoping this two-and-a half month sojourn will be more relaxing and uneventful, especially because of the extensive and comprehensive planning done beforehand. **BUT**... one never knows until one goes! So, sit back, pour yourself a favorite beverage, and see what if anything out of the ordinary happens to us. We hope you enjoy our latest European vacation.

Living in Sun City Anthem, we like to use a local transportation company called *"All About Time"*. Our driver picked us up before the sun rose at 5:30 a.m. for the 20-minute ride to Harry Reid International Airport. The airport is **NOT** crowded at that ungodly hour, thank goodness. We checked two bags curbside and took two carry-on bags and the backpack aboard the plane. Luckily, or maybe with just some divine intervention, *'nothing stupid or out of the ordinary'* happened from the time we left home until we boarded the flight. That's *'very unusual'* for us. Why? We are very susceptible to *'shit happens'* whenever we travel! But hold on valued readers, the day was **NOT** over yet. We just needed some time to get our *'shit happens legs'* under us!

First stop, Charlotte, North Carolina. Our plane arrived on time and without incident. (We were not lucky enough to get a direct flight to NYC). We leave the plane and walk to the departure gate for our flight to John F. Kennedy Airport (JFK)....again, so far, so good. After boarding our new plane, and just before taking off, the flight attendant taps me on the shoulder and asks, "Are you John Turzer?" Startled and confused, my brain *'goes bonkers.'* I wonder, *'Are you kicking me off the flight? What's up? Did TSA, the FBI, or Interpol put a hold and detain notice on me?'* Luckily, none of these situations were in play. She said, "You are being upgraded, at **NO** charge, to First Class because of the hundreds of thousands of American Airlines' Frequent Flyer Miles you have in your account." Befuddled, Leslie looked over at me and asked, "What is going on? Are they kicking you off the plane? What did you **DO** or **SAY** this time?" "No Leslie, all is good," I said. "I am getting a **FREE** First Class upgrade!" Leslie had that *'why are you SO special look?'* on her face, which really meant... "Why must I sit in coach with the other passengers while **YOU** get to *'move up'?*" I looked at her, evaluated her body language, the situation, and the ramifications of what would happen if I made a **POOR** decision. Being the gentleman that I am, (and not born yesterday), I decline the attendant's invitation and suggested that Leslie *'move up'* to First Class. However, I remind her that should I be upgraded again, the **NEXT** one is mine.

Our plane arrives on time at JFK. The airport is located in the Jamaica, Queens Section of NYC. It is an **OLD** airport. It opened 76 years ago on July 1, 1948. The airport clearly shows its age. We quickly notice significant construction going on as the airport was undergoing rehabilitation. To reach baggage claim, and hotel ground transportation, we hike about what seemed like a mile up and down two sets of escalators and through numerous corridors.

Surprisingly, our bags arrived without much delay! We located the hotel transportation pickup phone and call the hotel we are staying at overnight to let them know we were at the airport and are waiting to be picked up. The hotel front desk clerk instructs us to follow the signs to Air Tram, an inter-terminal people mover Tram System, exit at the Car Rental pick up location, follow the signs to Ground Transportation Passenger Pick Up, and call the hotel again when we got there. The walk to the Tram is long, arduous, and included more up and down jaunts using escalators and stairs. Unfortunately for us, some of the directional signs are missing. Confused, frustrated, and lost, I asked a janitor for directions. His body language conveyed that he thought we are two old, stupid people who cannot read the signs. Waving his hand, he points, "That way!!"

The traveling duo board the Tram and exit at Car Rental pick-up and hotel shuttle vans. When we exit, there is another twisting, turning walk to our designated destination.

Upon arrival, I call the hotel and was immediately placed on *'hold'* for nearly five minutes. I tell the desk clerk we are at the *'pick-up spot.'* She replies someone would be there in 15 minutes. **Are you kidding me??** The hotel was only minutes away!

Finally, the hotel van arrives. It was old, needed new seats, and a good interior and exterior cleaning. Within minutes, we were dropped off at the hotel, along with another couple.

We check into the *Marriott Fairfield Inn*, located on Rockaway Boulevard in Jamaica, Queens. The hotel has no onsite restaurant. Starving, it is time to search for something to eat. To say the least, the neighborhood is *'sketchy.'*

Now, Rockaway Boulevard is a four-lane highway full of *'east coast size'* potholes, you know, the big ones that look like they could severely damage a car's undercarriage. The lighting is less than desirable, i.e., it is **REALLY DARK!** After J-walking across the highway, where pedestrians are *'fair game,'* we looked at a Chinese restaurant's menu that uses MSG in the cooking process. We pass on eating there and instead head to the *'corner store.'* We squeeze past *'three neighborhood watch locals'* wearing blue jeans, black hoodies, baseball caps, and sharing a doobie. The sweet smell of burning MJ fills the air. The cashier stands behind thick, bullet proof glass. While the store offers a full array of *'made to order'* sandwiches, we *'move on'* because the store does not sell wine or beer, a *'must have'* staple after our long day.

Across the street, we see a *'corner grocery store.'* The entrance door *'safety glass'* bears the remnants of multiple bullet holes, which shattered the glass into hundreds of tiny spider webs. This door is **NOT** like the doors on convenience stores in Vegas. The clerk standing behind the bullet proof glass counter also tells us he does not sell beer or wine. Leslie says, "But the sign out front reads beer and wine." "We used to sell it, but not now."

Undeterred, we headed back towards the hotel. Despite my pleas of *"this neighborhood is NOT safe,"* Leslie is *'on a mission'* to find food and the desperately needed alcoholic beverages. Turning to me she says, "The hotel clerk said there is a liquor store next to the *Burger King* on the other side of the street one block up, but we must walk underneath the freeway." I counter and say, "No, I think it's next to the *7-11* under the freeway on **THIS** side of the street." Giving me that *'John, you have NO idea what you're talking about'* look...the same one that has ended countless minor *'I am right, you are wrong'* disagreements in the past...she unanimously *'wins'* the one sided debate. So, we cross the street and walk under the freeway onto a poorly lit and very dirty sidewalk. It is *'plain as day'* that this section of town has avoided cleaning since Rudy Giuliani was Mayor! We spot the *7-11* and discover **I was right!** So, we crossed the street again. The liquor store clerk walks Leslie to the individual sized wine bottles shelf. To her dismay he says, "Sorry, sold out" and removes an empty four-pack container. She settles for a small, individual sized bottle of Johnny Walker Red, you know, the kind they serve on plane flights and charge eight bucks for. I asked if the store sells beer. He says, *"7-11"*. He is definitely a man of few words. Standing behind the bullet proof glass counter, he takes my $2 for the bottle of scotch. Next, we head down to the *7-11* just two stores to the right.

At the *7-11*, I grab a 16-ounce can of Coors Light. The clerk, who is also standing behind bullet proof glass, takes my $2.50. The Mega Millions jackpot is over $1B. So, we decide to buy some lottery tickets. **BUT**, it seems there is **ALWAYS** a **BUT**, we must stand in a *'different line'* to test our luck and hopefully invest in our future. Unfortunately, the customer ahead of us calls out number after number while investing his paycheck in various daily lottery drawings. Then, to make matters worse, the lottery ticket printing machine runs out of paper...son of a gun....another delay! The clerk reloaded the machine, **FINALLY** it's our turn. We invest $10 for five Mega Million *'Quick Pick'* tickets. After spending 45 minutes wandering the *'mean streets of Queens Jamaica'*, we head back to the hotel, periodically glancing over our shoulders to see if we're being followed (We felt like we were in a *Law and Order episode* and the bad guys were on our tail.)

Anyway, back at the hotel, we place an order for a pizza delivery; **BUT** we are told delivery would take 45 minutes! "Too late, forget it," I bellow. Still hungry, and undeterred, we head to the hotel lobby where Leslie buys two bags of *Sun Chips* and a meat, cheese, and crackers snack pack. I choose a *Chicken Ramon Noodles* cup of soup. I use the in-room, one cup coffee machine to heat water that activates the freeze dried noodles. Yum, yum, two bags of chips, *Ramon Noodles*, a cheese and mystery meat with crackers snack pack, and an apple completes our five star dining experience at the *Marriott Fairfield Hotel*! Good thing checkout time is noon. Our bodies are still on West Coast time. It takes us a while to fall asleep and dream about the upcoming adventures, starting with tomorrow night's 7:15 p.m. overnight flight to Milan. Our room door is triple locked.

Good night from Queens New York, the former home of the King of Queens Doug Heffernan, his lovely wife Carrie, and her father Arthur Spooner.

*****

Wednesday, March 27 — Day 2
Jamaica, Queens, New York City to Milan, Italy

We take advantage of the late checkout to catch up on our sleep and almost miss the *'free' Fairfield Inn* breakfast buffet of oatmeal, toast, coffee, juice, powered eggs, burnt sausage, fruit, and bagels. Around noon, we bid ado to the hotel staff and catch the hotel shuttle van back to JFK.

At the airport, we did not see the Business Class check-in line, so we settled, instead, standing in line with the *'back of the plane common folks.'* But they don't have the same perks as those of us who have thousands of American Airlines travel miles that gives us **FREE** access to the two AA preferred customer lounges. Since we have nearly six hours to kill prior to boarding our flight to Milan, we visit the new, more private lounge which offers multiple seating options, a hot and cold buffet, beer, wine, soft drinks, tea, and coffee...plus a comfy seating area with a fireplace that *'sets the mood'* for a relaxing afternoon. I say to Leslie, "Act like we have been here before!" She reminds me *"we were there before"*...11 years ago. The lounge was a wonderful place to *'chill'* until our 7:15 PM flight to Milan. We enjoy virtually *'one of everything'* on the hot and cold buffet and desert bar. Before we know it, it's time to gather our belongings and head to the boarding gate.

The boarding process goes smoothly. We are in Group One Business Class. We settle in, play with all the buttons on the seat that converts into a bed, and sip on pre-dinner drinks, (Leslie wine, me **TOP SHELF** bourbon). We enjoy our meal and an ice cream sundae for dessert. Flicking on the TV, I decide to watch the first two episodes of a Netflix eight part series about the mafia controlled port of Barcelona. Even though the seat converts to a bed, *'quarters are tight.'* Leslie reads and plays with her iPhone. Falling asleep is *'more of a wish than a reality.'* We do manage to catch a *' few winks'* before landing in Milan on Thursday, March 28. We're really excited because the Turzer holiday is now officially on!

*****

Thursday, March 28 — Day 3
Milan, Italy

American Airlines Flight 198 arrives on time at 08:00 in Milan. According to the latest weather reports, rain is forecast for our three day stay. Starting today, we will use the '*24-hour clock*' (also known as the '*military*' clock) which is quite common in Europe. So, I will not be designating time as a.m. or p.m. One of our '*traveling traditions*' is changing our names in each country we visit. Arriving in Milan, John becomes Giovanni or Gio, while Leslie is Sophia or Sophie.

During the planning process, Giovanni booked a limousine service to pick us up at the airport and deliver us to *Innside by Melia Milano*, our Milan hotel. Shortly after arriving, Gio gets a text from Salvatore. He is our ride to the hotel, and he will meet us outside Baggage Claim Door 8. We quickly pass through customs, pick up our luggage, and head to meet Salvatore. We are a little jet lagged, but still excited. Although Salvatore is holding up an iPad displaying our names, Sophia approaches a '*studly*' Italian man who is sporting what looks like a two-day, dark, and thick beard. To round out his Italian mystique, he is wearing a black leather jacket. Sophie asks, "Are you here to pick me up?" Immediately, he becomes flustered. I can only think he's saying to himself, "*This must be my lucky day, an American cougar!*" Fortunately, or unfortunately (pick one), we will **NEVER** know. I tap Sophia on the shoulder and point to the iPad displaying our names.

In reality, Salvatore is barely 5'4" tall and speaks little or no English. He loads our bags, and we climb into a Mercedes mini station wagon. It is about an hour's drive to the hotel. Occasionally, light rain falls. The roadway is packed with traffic. I am sure most people were heading to work or dropping their kids off at school.

Here are some of the things we observe during the ride:

- Gasoline costs $7.11/gallon.

- Graffiti plays a major part in the city's beatification program. Budding artists who want to be like our friend Thom Metcalf (one of our Sun City Anthem friends) express their creative talents and inner feelings on the sides of walls and buildings.

- Cars park everywhere. There are no open parking spots. I wonder what happens when someone moves their car. Where do they park upon return?

- The streets are lined with high rise housing units.

- Raking leaves is clearly **NOT** a priority in Milan. The tree lined streets look like the city's landscaping maintenance department were on a break or they forgot rakes when they left the shop this morning. Also, most of the trees need pruning.

- It also looks like the city's lawn maintenance department took the fall and winter off. Uncut grass and an abundance of weeds populate the tree lined streets. That is not to say Milan is not a beautiful city!

About 45 minutes into the ride, we enter local city traffic. Salvatore makes a right hand turn down a narrow, one way street. Cars are parked on both sides. He abruptly stops the car and drops us, and our bags, off in the middle of the street! This sudden **STOP** creates a massive, 18-car and truck backup whose irritated drivers are honking, non-stop and waving at us with inappropriate hand gestures. Just like you see in the movies!

Standing in the middle of the street, we **CANNOT** see the hotel entrance. We ask Salvatore, "Where is the hotel?" He points up the street towards the left where a number of high rise buildings stand. He jumps into the mini station wagon and hurriedly drives off, leaving us standing in the middle of the street with our suitcases, wondering, **HOLY SHIT**, where are we?

Dark clouds menacingly hover above us. There is a nip in the air. The wind is kicking up. Adding to our bewilderment, a light rain starts to fall. Our heads and outer clothing are taking on water! It takes two trips to relocate our belongings to the sidewalk and alleviate the traffic jam. Our body language screams out, *'Where the hell are we?'* A shopkeeper standing nearby senses our plight and directs us into *Petrarca Café*. We quickly learn they speak English. For the price of a cappuccino, an Americano coffee, and a fresh Danish pastry, we learn the hotel is across the street and up at the corner in a building with no visible signage. We quickly remember our last trip to Europe 11 years ago.....coffee cups are **VERY SMALL**, and there are no **FREE** refills.

Two wet, cold, and tired Americano tourists, with luggage in tow, saunter up the street and check into our hotel, *Innside by Melia Milano*. The lobby is very modern and has present day amenities. The front desk person offers us a 25 Euros/per person/per day breakfast option; however, we pass, preferring to support the local, small restaurants and coffee shops. Our room is very modern. Floor to ceiling windows provide long range city views. Tired, we settle in and enjoy a two-hour nap.

The rain has stopped. It is time to start exploring! Our first stop is the Milan Central Train Station, which is only three blocks from our hotel. We are on a mission to validate our three month Eurail paper train passes. We go up and down stairs and walk the corridors looking for assistance to locate the **RIGHT** office to activate the passes. Spotting a security guard, we ask him. He has *'no clue'* where there is an office that can validate the passes. All he *'handles'* is security. Finally, on our fourth try, someone with intimate knowledge of where we need to go directs us **BACK DOWN** to the first floor train office. However, *'shit happens'*...we enter the **WRONG** train office. The customer service agent unceremoniously chases us out and tells us, in no uncertain terms, to go three doors down to the right! We locate the correct office and get in a long line, similar to what Nevada residents experience at the DMV. The *'control the line'* person tells us to take a ticket and wait until our number is called. The validation process is quick. It is now 17:22. The sun is out so it is now time to begin exploring Milan.

We walk to *Duomo di Milano*, the main cathedral in Milan. It is the fifth largest Christian church in the world. It is the seat of the Archbishop of Milan, is the largest church in Italy, and is the most impressive structure in Milan. Construction started in 1386 and after six centuries and 579 years, was completed in 1965. There are 136 spires and 3,500 statues. It houses works of art collected over centuries.

Our next stop is the largest shopping mall in Milan...*Galleria Vittorio Emanuele II*. It is the oldest active shopping gallery and a major landmark in Milan. The *Galleria* was designed in 1861, built between 1865 and 1877, and houses some of the oldest shops in Milan. There you will find luxury, high end retailers selling clothing, jewelry, books, and paintings. It is also home to cafes, bars, a hotel, and some of the oldest restaurants in Milan. Today's jaunt around Milan took 12,815 steps (according to my iPod). So glad we are both in great shape.

Still fighting jet lag, we spy a large Italian restaurant, *Cafe Panzera*, on the corner near the central train station. The establishment opened in 1931. The tables are small and tightly set up to maximize seating capacity. The waiters are professionally dressed in black pants, black shoes, white shirts, and black ties. Our waiter offers suggestions on local beers and wines. Since we are in Italy, we start our 28-day Mediterranean diet with what else... pizza, spaghetti with a seafood medley, salad, and local beer and wine. Our meals are excellent and *hit the spot*. After dinner, we forgo additional sightseeing and adventures, purchase a few postcards, and head to the hotel to enjoy a good night's sleep. Gio is under the influence of *'jet lag'* and retires at 19:00. Sophia is close behind, drifting into never, never land shortly thereafter.

*****

Friday, March 29 — Day 4
Milan, Italy

Gio and Sophie's body clocks are still not sure where we are and what time it is. Gio wakes up at 4:00. I see our various phone chargers are not charging and immediately take action to correct this.

March Madness is in full swing back home. I check the ESPN App on my iPhone and learn that my two championship game finalists, North Carolina and Arizona, have lost, thus ending their championship dreams. While reading the Las Vegas Review Journal on my phone, I learn *Walgreens's* is **CLOSING** all in-store medical clinics nationwide. So, at 4:30, I learn we lost our new primary physician as he is one of the casualties of the clinic's closing. When we get back, we need to find out where he is moving his practice because we like his medical professionalism.

Sophia is now up. While enjoying her freshly brewed coffee, we develop a Milan assault plan for the day and fall back to sleep at 06:00. Waking up two hours later, we each take a shower and get properly dressed for the expected rainy day. We leave the hotel and enjoy breakfast at a local café. Today's plan calls for purchasing two-day *'Hop On Hop Off'* bus tickets, giving us 48-hours of riding the Blue and Yellow route buses to gain an overview of the city.

The daring, dynamic duo sets out on a quest to purchase post card stamps so we can send notes back home. Thinking locals would know where the closest post office is, we ask our café waitress.

Unbelievably, she is clueless and so are all members of the café staff. Rumor has it, however, that a post office is located in the basement of the central train station. I wonder if putting a post office in a train station and not knowing where it is, is a *'European thing'*. Eleven years ago, while vacationing in Brussels, we asked locals the same question, "Where is the closest post office?" Some people shrugged their shoulders indicating *'no clue'* while others directed us to the Brussels Central Train Station. After an exhaustive, unsuccessful search, we learned the Brussels post office, previously located in the train station, closed six months earlier; however, word never reached the locals. Go figure!

Deciding not to look for the post office, we hop on the Yellow route bus for the first of our day's destinations — the *Pinacoteca di Brera*, one of the most famous art museums in Milan. It houses some of the country's most famous historical Italian art works. The bus drops us off where the museum is supposedly located; however, there are no signs directing us to the museum. So, we duck into a coffee shop for two Americano coffees with cold milk and a fruit croissant. I ask our waitress the big three questions: where is a bank, a post office, and how do we get to the museum? We get the proverbial blank *'I do not know about post office and bank locations'* stare; however, we get directions to *Pinacoteca di Brera*. I guess one out of three isn't bad. For our baseball fans out there, we would be batting a solid .333.

We enter an old open air building. The central courtyard is under construction. We walk the hallways and locate the *Braidense National Library*. Built back in 1770, this library is one of the oldest and largest in Italy. In 1880, the library became a national public treasure. There are thousands of books here, some dating back to the 1500's. We fail to realize that the *Pinacoteca di Brera Art Museum* we plan to visit later is in the **SAME** complex. This turns out to be a **FATAL** error. So, we head off to our next destination — the

Castello Sforzesco. We walk a mile or so adding plenty of steps to our Friday step count. Along the way, we stop at local businesses and ask for the location of a bank and a post office. Apparently that is a *'national secret.'* No one has a clue.

Glancing around the plaza, we see a sign *'Stamps for Sale'* on a sidewalk news stand and head that way. **FINALLY**, we can buy stamps!! Not so fast, sports fans! The clerk tells us he does not sell stamps. We decline to challenge him based on what the sign says. Why start a potential international incident? **BUT**, and there's always room for a **BUT**, he *'comes through'* and directs us to a post office a mere two blocks away! The post office is on our way to the castle. Low and behold, there it is! I bought a dozen Italian post card stamps to the United States and mail two postcards. Sophie and I resume our journey to the castle. Stopping at a major intersection red light, I ask two bicycle food delivery men for directions to the castle. One has the confused *'castle, what castle look?'* while the other points straight ahead.

Castello Sforzesco, or *Sforza's Castle*, is a 15th century medieval fortification that, at one point during the 17th century, was one of the largest citadels in Europe. We walk the grounds and decide to head to stop number three on today's itinerary...the *Pinacoteca di Brera Art Museum*. Totally confused and turned around, we get on a *'Yellow Hop On Hop Off Bus'* thinking this will take us to the art museum. We wind up on a **LONG** bus ride and, lo and behold, after consulting the bus ticket taker, learn where to get off. The bus lady points out the path to the museum. After leaving the bus, I experience Deja' Vu and say, "We've been here today." This is the first stop where we got off the bus. There is the cafe we enjoyed coffee and a croissant." Son of a bitch, we are back at the same building we were at four hours ago!!!! What the f?!?ck!! How did we screw this up? Now to make matters worse, the ticket machines to enter *Pinacoteca di Brera* are **NOT** working. So, I make an executive decision, "It's time to eat lunch!!" We find a local café and share a pizza and one-half bottle of an Italian cabernet sauvignon. After lunch, we *give up* on visiting the museum deciding to try again tomorrow. We get on a *'Hop On, Hop Off Bus'*, watch the sites of Milan go by, and return to the central train station area. We *'kill time'* walking up and down the streets window shopping and taking in the sites.

Later that night, we try another café and continue our Mediterranean diet. Unfortunately, tonight's pizza was made with a pre-packaged pizza crust vs hand tossed. The result, not so good; however, we survive and locate a grocery store. Google Maps has the store near the central train station; however, it fails to take us to the location. Sophia is ready to give up, so we head to the central train station and on the lower level...bingo, we find the grocery store! We pick up some snacks, water, and fruit. Our hotel is a short three block walk. It is now 21:00, time for the dynamic duo to hit the sack. Our final step count today was 12,063. Nighty night from Milan.

Milan

According to Wikipedia, Milan is the regional capital of Italy's northern Lombardy region. Founded in 590 BC by a Celtic tribe, it is the second most populous city in Italy, after Rome. The city proper has a population of about 1.4 million people, while the metropolitan area is home to 3.22 million residents. Milan is the economic capital of Italy and one of Europe's economic leaders. It is one of the best international tourist destinations, appearing among the most visited cities in the world, ranking second in Italy after Rome, fifth in Europe and sixteenth in the world. Milan is recognized as one of the world's top fashion capitals, too. Many of the most famous luxury fashion brands in the world have their headquarters in the city including Armani, Prada, Versace, Moschino, Valentino, and

Zegna. The city also hosts several international events and fairs, including *Milan Fashion Week* and the *Milan Furniture Fair,* which are among the worlds' biggest in terms of revenue, visitors and growth. The city is served by many luxury hotels that are ranked fifth worldwide in four and five star categories.

Milan is home to Italy's national stock exchange. It is a financial hub that is also known for its high-end restaurants and shops. The gothic *Duomo di Milano Cathedral* and the *Santa Maria Delle Grazie Convent,* housing Leonardo da Vinci's world famous mural *"The Last Supper,"* are a testament to centuries of art and culture.

*****

Saturday March 30 — Day 5
Milan, Italy

Today is our last full day in Milan. We now know the location of the famous art museum *Pinacoteca di Brera*. It's our number one priority today to visit and enjoy the fine Italian paintings and artwork.

The first Hop On, Hop Off bus rolls out at 09:30 from the stop across the street from the central train station. Our bodies are getting acclimated to being nine time zones ahead of Las Vegas time. After showering and dressing, we head out early on a rainy day. Today's breakfast stop is *Pasccucci,* a local café located near the bus stop. We catch the first bus to *Pinacoteca di Brera*, pay the entrance fee, and spend hours roaming the hallways, observing magnificent cultural and historical works of art.

Brera Art Gallery di Brera is the main public gallery for paintings in Milan. The gallery opened in 1776. It houses one of the foremost collections of Italian paintings from the 13th to the 20th century. It features works from *Rembrandt, Peter Rubens, Anthony Van Dyck, Caravaggio, Hayez, Londonio, Boccati, Spanzotti, Gozzoli, Visconti, Casella, Menzocchi, Orioli, Contarini,* and *Sironi.* Visiting art museums has never been a top tourist attraction and *'must see thing'* for me; however, I thoroughly enjoy our time taking in famous Italian works of art.

Physically, our bodies are starting to fade. It is still raining. So, we decide to spend the next few hours riding the Hop On, Hop Off Bus. Later, we will pack up and get ready for the train ride to Salerno and the Amalfi Coast on Easter Sunday March 31.

Impressed with the dinner we enjoyed on night one, we head back to *Cafe Panzera*. Our Thursday night waiter remembers us (must have been the nice tip we left) and brings out the adult beverages we enjoyed the other night. Dinner is superb and hits the spot. We retreat three blocks to the hotel, pack, set our iPhone alarm for 07:30, and leave a wake-up call with the front desk for the same time, just in case. Our train departs at 10:40. We allow plenty of time to get ready, get to the station, and enjoy breakfast. Milan is **ALMOST** in our rearview mirror. Sunday's journey begins our all-out assault on the Amalfi Coast in southern Italy.

*****

Sunday, March 31 — Day 6
Milan to Amalfi, Italy

Today is Easter Sunday, March 31, our last morning in Milan. We are taking the train from Milan to Salerno. I made arrangements with a transportation company to pick us up in Salerno and take us to our hotel, *Belleview Suite* in the town of Amalfi. When we wake up, we discover that the time **MOVED AHEAD** one hour in this time zone. No one told us to move our clocks ahead one hour! I guess the front desk staff thinks **EVERYONE KNOWS THAT!** Luckily, I set up a wake-up call last night with the front desk before retiring. After quickly getting *'ready to roll,'* I ask the front desk to call us a cab. While it's only a three block walk to the Milan Central Train Station, hauling our luggage and stuff in the rain is *'not in the cards today.'*

We have over an hour to eat breakfast and board the train. Moseying through the central train station, we find a high top table in the *Food Court*. The air is filled with the aroma of freshly brewed coffee and freshly baked croissants, pastries, and breads. Vendors offer a wide variety of breakfast choices. Undoubtedly, we have many *'difficult'* culinary choices to choose from. Sophia goes first and grabs coffee, a freshly baked croissant, and a blueberry muffin. When she returns, I roam the *Food Court* and order an egg, bacon, and cheese breakfast sandwich and coffee. After breakfast, it's time to make a bathroom stop and head up to the train departure level.

It costs one Euro to enter the bathroom. Sophie and I use our credit cards to pay the entrance fee; however, the entrance door doesn't open for me. Three swipes later, the door finally opens. Sophie gets lucky. The door opens on her first try. Other restroom patrons use a one Euro coin that grants them entrance on the first try. Right now, we have five Euros invested in potty. Adding insult to injury, despite my best efforts, '*here I sit broken hearted, paid four Euros and only farted!!!!*'

Arriving at the departure floor, Sophie and I find two seats and wait for our train's platform notification to be posted on the large departure board. When I go to get our Eurail passes and reserved seat tickets from my backpack, the worst feeling *'short of death'* comes over me. **WHERE IS THE BACKPACK? My adrenaline and blood pressure rise to dangerous levels as panic overwhelms and consumes me. WHERE IS THE BACKPACK?** Immediately, I retrace my steps, first heading to the men's rest room and then back to the *Food Court*. Frantically, I scour the area but *'come up empty.'* **NO LUCK, NOTHING, NO BACKPACK!** I ask around; however, no one has seen it. One more trip through the men's room yields the same result; **NOTHING, NO BACKPACK!** Meanwhile, the clock is ticking on our train's departure time. I go to the Trenitalia train office seeking assistance for the lost Eurail passes and train tickets. A customer service agent reissues today's reserved seat tickets: however, she warns me the conductor may **NOT** accept photo copies of the Eurail passes thus rendering the reserved seat reservations useless. There is **NOTHING** she can do about the stolen Eurail passes.

Eurail conducts all of its business, including customer service **ONLY** through email. Emergency telephone lines to customer service.....forget it! I instantly send an email to Eurail customer service explaining what happened and asked for replacement passes.

Emphatically, I remind them we have **NOT** used our three-month passes. Today is our **FIRST** train ride.

We then head to the Milan Police Station located on the ground floor of the train station. I press the entrance door button. An *'annoyed'* on-duty Police Officer gruffly asks me, "What you need assistance with?" After listening to the stolen backpack story, begrudgingly, he presses the security buzzer granting us entry. He parks Sophia in the lobby and escorts me into his workspace. Frustrated, frantic, pissed off, and upset, I explain what happened and what's missing. The officer is extremely *'nonchalant'* and informs me I can file a police report at **ANY** police station in Italy. The officer's *'matter of fact this shit happens all the time in Milan attitude'* doesn't ease the pain of our loss. He explains thieves *'grab and run, go outside, search for valuables, and toss the bag.'* So, I head back to street level and check **ALL** trash cans outside the train station. **NOTHING, NO BACKPACK.**

We head back to the Trenitalia ticket office. The customer service lady **STRONGLY** recommends I get the police report **TODAY**. So, Sophie and I head back to the police station. I press the entrance button again, announce our presence, and hear an obviously irritated police officer say, **"YOU HERE AGAIN?"** "I need a police report **NOW** in English and Italian." After buzzing us in, he parks Sophia in the lobby again and takes me inside the station to his desk. Mr. Easter Sunday *'why am I working today when I could be home stuffing my face with candy'* on-duty officer asks for my passport and driver's license.

VISIBLY ANNOYED, he leaves the room and returns 15 or so minutes later. Undoubtedly, he *'checks me out'* through Interpol, FBI, CIA, and other police databases. My profile comes back **CLEAN**, no warrants or *'hold and detain'* alerts. Mr. Italian police officer is **CLEARLY** in **NO** hurry to complete the incident report. He is one of these *'hunt and peck'* typists who uses his left and right index fingers to type a ½ page double spaced report. A partial list of the items in the backpack include our three-month Eurail passes, 90 days' supply of three prescription drugs, prescription sun glasses, $1,000 in cash, iPod, two phone chargers, a rain coat, and two baseball caps. Plus, we lost a four inch thick folder with the details of our hotel stays, reserved seat train tickets, car rental information, international driving permits, airplane reservations, and planned activities. The officer and I sign three copies. He keeps two and gives me one. I ask for a second copy and hear, "Sorry, you only get one, sorry can't make you a photocopy." The entire process took the better part of one hour. I guess Milan police, especially officers working holidays and weekends, get paid by the hour, not by the written report. Most likely, he is a *'holiday weekend relief officer'* who lacks sympathy and empathy for what happened to us.

Eurail customer service replies to my email and informs me they **CANNOT** issue replacement passes. I **MUST**, *(emphasis added)*, purchase **NEW** passes for our holiday travel. **Are you shitting me?** I have copies of the passes. Each rail pass has a unique identification number on it. No one can use the stolen passes **WITHOUT** the proper picture ID. What's the big deal?? They simply reply, **"Company Policy!"** *'Company policy my ass. Are you shitting me? This is bullshit.'* When Sophie and I complete our last train ride, I plan to contact our credit card company and file a dispute for the charge to purchase replacement tickets. (October 2024 update, we **WON** the dispute and were **NOT** charged for the replacement passes.....don't screw with me, Eurail!!!) Much to my chagrin, I later learn that Eurail has an office in the Milan Central Train Station; however, none of the Trenitalia customer service agents knew this!! What else is new?

The number one priority is replacing the prescription drugs. I send an email to our primary care doctor, Dr. Fraga, asking for ideas on how to fill the prescriptions in Italy. Next, I call our neighbors, Thom and Marie, who have a key to our house. I explain the situation, ask them to go into the night stand on the right side of the master bedroom, grab the extra supply of drugs, and go to *Walgreens* to pick up the rest of the drugs I need. Without hesitation, Thom and Marie immediately *'jump into action.'* I call *Walgreens*, explain the situation, order the drugs I need, and let them know Thom and Marie will pick up the prescriptions soon. After picking up the drugs, Thom and Marie head north on Eastern Avenue to the Federal Express office at St. Rose Parkway and ship the drugs to me at the Amalfi hotel address. I have a Federal Express account. They bill me the $196 charge. However, it takes four days for the package to arrive in Amalfi. Whatever. Right now, that is the only solution on the table. Later that day, the family doctor sends me an email instructing me to go to an *Amalfi Walk-In Clinic* in the morning and explain *'what happened.'* That is a **GREAT** doctor....how many people can reach out to their family physician on a Sunday and get a quick reply? Many of you are now wondering how we will replace the 90 days' supply of prescription drugs ASAP and handle the Federal Express package expected to arrive at the hotel on Thursday, April 4. Stay tuned, the answer to these questions will be revealed in the Monday, April 1 story. And trust me..... It will **NOT** be an April's Fool's joke!

Our **ONE AND ONLY** way to get to Salerno **TODAY** requires us to purchase tickets. I pay more than 300 Euros (about $325) for two business class tickets for the five-hour, twenty minute ride. You know it is not your day when we get on the 14:25 train and see we are one of a *'handful'* of travelers sitting in Business Class. We almost have an entire car to ourselves. If we had known this, we could have purchased open seating tickets for 50% of the price we paid! The conductor verifies our tickets, provides two bottles of water, and two ridiculously small snack boxes containing a bread-type cookie, and a piece of cake. Needless to say, the snacks are *'underwhelming.'*

Later during the journey, Gio learns there is a food and beverage car. So, I head that way walking between the cars. Various candy bars, chips, beer, wine, and a premade sandwich or two are available for purchase. I invest in the veggie sandwich and two bags of chips.

At 19:15, we arrive in Salerno. I contact the prearranged transportation company; however, **NO ONE SPEAKS ENGLISH!** What else could go wrong today? How are we going to get to the hotel? Alas, on Easter Sunday night, there is a God! A taxi van from Amalfi is dropping off travelers at the station. The driver hears me screaming for all to hear, "How the hell are we going to get to Amalfi tonight?" and says, "I am going to Amalfi, I can take you!" However, since the request for transportation **DID NOT** come through the taxi company switchboard, I must pay *'cash'* for the *'off the books'* trip. No problem, I gladly agree to the 150 Euros (about $160) fare for the hour plus long drive and ask the driver to stop at an ATM machine when we get to Amalfi.

Night has fallen. There are **NO** lights on the, *'at best,'* two lane roadway. Along the way, the driver occasionally **MUST STOP** to allow cars to pass from the other direction. The journey takes us through unnamed towns and villages. The driver stops at an ATM machine. Finally, around 21:30, Sophie and I arrive at our hotel, *Bellevue Suite*.

During the check-in process, the owner/manager *'comps'* the breakfast buffets for our seven night stay. That is a 40 Euros per day saving! We head to our room to drop off the bags before heading out for a very late dinner. We open the room door; however, we cannot find a light switch that works. Sophie chases me back to the lobby. To activate the room's electricity, I learn I must put the credit card size *'room entrance card'* into the slot on the wall to the right of the inside door. Magically, this feat turns on the electricity in our room. At future stops on the trip, many hotels **REQUIRE** guests to do this. Apparently, Italy does not believe in light switches.

After dropping off the bags and solving the electricity problem, the owner sends us **DOWN** a **VERY NARROW** and **DARK** road about 500 meters (we later learn that is what everyone says when asking directions.....about 500 meters....) to *La Preferita*, a local restaurant located in a neighboring hotel. **VERY NARROW** is an understatement. Some sections have 12" to 18" wide sidewalks while other sections require Sophie and me to walk on the roadway to get around parked cars. Clearly, we are *'sitting ducks'* and could easily become hood ornaments on fast moving cars, motorcycles, and scooters!

By 22:00, Sophie and I arrive, hungry and thirsty, at the second floor restaurant. We exchange pleasantries with the manager and waitress. We start our meal with an Italian red wine, a Nastro Azzurro very good draft Italian beer, and some Italian bread to dip into virgin olive oil and balsamic vinegar. We order fish and chicken, share a salad, eat, and pay the bill. I notice a ten Euro charge on the check and ask for an explanation. I learn restaurants in this part of Italy charge guests a two to five Euro per person *'seating charge'* to cover the napkins, silverware, and the bread! **You cannot make this shit up!** *'Should we bring our own napkins, silverware, and bread the next time we eat out?'* So, we *'suck it up,'* pay the charge, and move on.

The walk back to the hotel is all **UPHILL**. The weather is pleasant. We hear the ocean waves gently crashing on the rocks below. It is dark. Sidewalks are narrow. Along the route home, we are once again **FORCED** to walk into the street to get around parked cars and *'run the risk'* of becoming hood ornaments or road kill. Since we spent most of the day traveling, our step count today was less than 2,000.

Given today's setbacks, to say the least, the bed looks **REALLY** comfy to us weary travelers. It does not take the dynamic duo long to fall asleep. Tomorrow's first mission is to head to town, locate an *Amalfi Walk-In Clinic*, and get my prescriptions filled. Good night from *Bellevue Suite Hotel* in Amalfi, Italy!

*****

Monday, April 1 — Day 7
Amalfi, Italy

After a good night's sleep, Gio and Sophia woke up at 07:30. We are ready to tackle the world today. The top priority is purchasing the prescription drugs that were in the stolen backpack. After showering and dressing, we amble down to the breakfast room. The waiter brings coffee and a dish of mozzarella cheese balls and cherry tomatoes marinating in olive oil. This is definitely **NOT** a breakfast starter at home. The hot and cold buffet offers many choices to our liking including the *'to die for fresh croissants.'*

After breakfast, we start our assault on the town of Amalfi, a one mile walk **STRAIGHT DOWN** the narrow street filled with speeding cars, scooters, motorcycles, and busses. Like last night's adventure walk to a restaurant, pedestrian sidewalks are narrow and limited. Safely arriving in one piece in the town supersedes rushing down the hill. Just off the main *'road,'* we arrive in Amalfi's business district. We walk into a courtyard area surrounded by the Cathedral, outdoor restaurants, and retail stores, but no *Walk-In Medical Clinic*. I spot a *Farmacia* (Italian drug store), enter, tell the clerk the story about the stolen drugs, and ask is there **ANYWAY** the pharmacy can sell me a 90-day supply of each drug. Without hesitating, the gentleman relays the situation to the pharmacist. She looks at the pictures of the prescription bottles on my iPhone and proceeds to pull a 90-day supply of each drug off the shelf! **Are you**

shitting me? This could be one of the best days of my life! I use my credit card to pay and shower the staff with many **"Grazies!"** No more worries about replacing the drugs! We are back in the *'holiday game'* without a care in the world!

As a side note, on Wednesday April 3, I received a call from *Italian Customs in Milan*. The Federal Express package with the drugs arrived in Milan; however, since the contents are drugs, they must be screened and tested by Customs prior to their release and delivery. The agent told me the cost to test the drugs was 40 Euros, and there was no timetable for when the drugs would be tested and delivered. After thinking it over for *'seven seconds'* and recognizing we will be leaving Amalfi over the weekend, I tell the agent please send the drugs back to the United States. Low and behold, when we returned home in mid-June, the drugs were sitting in a Federal Express envelope in the man cave. Plus, Federal Express did **NOT** charge me for the return!

We celebrate replacing the prescription drugs at an outdoor cafe. For a *'mere'* 25 Euros, which includes a 4 Euros seating charge, we enjoy coffee and a very tasty lemon dessert. Last night, we paid 10 Euros to sit in a restaurant! It looks like we have to budget a few extra Euros every time we sit down to eat. Adjacent to the restaurant is a merchant selling suitcases and backpacks. I see one that *'will work'* and pay 35 Euros. We now have something to carry the junk we are about to buy.

Amalfi

Courtesy of Wikipedia: here is a little historical snapshot of this coastal Italian town. Amalfi is a town in a dramatic natural setting below steep cliffs on Italy's southwest coast. Between the 9th and 11th centuries, it was the seat of a powerful maritime republic. The *Amalfi Cathedral* was built in the ninth century. It is located in the *Piazza del Duomo* heart of town. With its striped Byzantine facade, it has survived since the ninth century. The town lies at the mouth of a deep ravine, at the foot of *Monte Cerreto* (1,315 meters, 4,314 feet), surrounded by dramatic cliffs and coastal scenery. The town of Amalfi was the capital of the maritime republic known as the *Duchy of Amalfi*, an important trading power in the Mediterranean between 839 and around 1200.

Amalfi became a popular seaside resort with members of the upper class spending their winters here. Amalfi is the main town of the coast on which it is located, named *Costiera Amalfitana* (Amalfi Coast), and is today an important tourist destination together with other towns on the same coast, such as Positano and Ravello. Amalfi is included in the UNESCO World Heritage Sites.

Let's get back to our day in Amalfi. A narrow, commercial pedestrian walkway runs for about one mile up the hill. Restaurants, retail stores selling men's, women's, and children's clothing, and a variety of *'just gotta have'* souvenirs including soap, towels, and liqueur focused on the region's top fruit lemons, line the pathway. It's a wonder how so many stores that sell **IDENTICAL** products can **ALL** stay in business. My favorite purchases are refrigerator magnets, lemon soap bars, and postcards. Sophia just window-shops. Near the top of the walkway, there are many three and four story housing buildings. Most units have outdoor clothes drying lines. Everything from bed sheets to pants, shirts, and underwear are on full display. Clothes dryers are not an everyday household item in this part of Italy.

It's time for lunch. We *'spy'* an outdoor café with large umbrellas to shade us from the warm sun. Every restaurant brings fresh Italian bread, virgin olive oil and balsamic vinegar to your table. Asking for butter is a *'no-no'* in Italy. We continue our daily Mediterranean diet by sharing a pizza and washing it down with an Italian beer and wine.

After lunch and more window shopping, we are back on the waterfront town square. We find a shady sitting area and consider panhandling to cover the lost $1,000 that was in the stolen backpack. Sophia meets a group of college age men and women from Minnesota who are members of a church choir. Using her Midwestern charm, Sophia conveniences them to sing a song for us. However, it only takes the local, ornery, no nonsense traffic control police lady 30 seconds to break up their *'gig'*, yelling, "No singing allowed along the streets. Stop it **NOW**!" I guess singing in the streets without a permit is a crime in Amalfi. Oh well, we gave them a chance to audition their talents.

The entire Amalfi town is jammed packed with locals and tourists. We learn Easter Monday is an Italian holiday. Rather than walk up the one mile hill on the narrow roadway and sidewalks to our hotel, we decide to take the bus. **NOW**, here is where the fun begins. There are buses parked in two locations. We try to ask the bus drivers and bus ticket sellers which bus heads up the hill. Rude and unprofessional is an *understatement*. They could *'give a shit'* about assisting old Americanos. Some use hand gestures to *'shoe us away'* while other play the "No speaka da English" card. However, being known for my tenacity and bulldog mentality, I am persistent and finally get answers. I buy the tickets and obtain the bus number we need to get on. Getting on the bus becomes another *'fiasco.'* It is jammed, standing room only. We now know what the tomatoes in the can *'feel like.'* As the bus approaches our hotel, we call out **"STOP;"** however, the bus **GAINS** speed, roars past our hotel, and rumbles up and around the mountainside on the very narrow, winding road! The road has many 90-degree hairpin turns where the bus must **STOP** to let cars pass by and where cars must stop to let the bus pass. Occasionally, cars or the bus must **BACK UP** to avoid a total road shutdown. This drive brings back memories of living in Maui, driving the road to Hana, and driving the northern narrow road around the mountains from Lahaina to Wailuku.

We **FINALLY** get the bus driver's attention. He **STOPS** the bus in a very remote area well over three miles past our hotel, lets us and a family of three get off, and tells us to wait by the sign on the other side of the road for a bus going to town. He has **NO** clue whether a bus will come by soon, tonight, tomorrow, or never! Sophia is ready to shoot me or at least beat me with a baseball bat. **YES**, to say the least, she is **REALLY** upset and pissed, gives me *'stink eye'* (a Maui thing), and screams out, "How the hell are we going to get back to the hotel? There is **NO WAY** I am walking back on this road!" A German couple and their child are also in the same boat. Apparently they got on the **WRONG** bus. Their hotel is on the opposite side of Amalfi! We cross the street, wait by the sign, get acquainted with our new friends from Germany, and try to come up with a plan to get us out of this mess. Thank goodness they speak English. The stranded group of five *'stews'* on the side of the road hoping and praying a bus will come by soon and stop. Then out of nowhere, a *'miracle happens.'* The cab driver who picked us up last night in Salerno came around the corner, saw our plight, recognized us, and stopped to help. **You can't make this shit up!** There is a God. We jump into the van and head home. Sophia negotiates the fare. However, the German man balks at the price. **Are you shitting me?** We just caught the *'break of a lifetime'!* Mr. German guy are you going to insult the driver by attempting to negotiate a lower fare?! **Really? Come on man!** Sophia turns to the gentleman and calmly says, "Our treat. We got this handled. Enjoy the ride to your hotel." If it were me, my language would have been slightly stronger and direct; however, there was a child in the van!

The driver drops us off at our hotel's doorstep! We toss out many "Grazis" to the life-saving driver. It's time to celebrate our good fortune. We purchase a bottle of wine from the hotel staff, grab two glasses, and chill in the expansive living room style lobby.

Not wanting to head back to town for dinner, we head up the street about a ¼ mile to a local convenience store with a second floor restaurant. Unfortunately, the food leaves a lot to be desired. Can anyone in Italy make a sandwich on a huge, thick roll with **MORE THAN** one slice of cheese and meat? I guess they have never heard of *Subway, Port of Subs, Firehouse Subs, Jersey Mike's,* or *Capriotti's*. I almost cried out, *'Where's the meat?'* but thought better of it.

Disappointed and filled with bread, beer, and wine, we head back down the narrow, dark sidewalk. Suddenly and without any warning, Sophia trips over a raised section of sidewalk, falls forward, hits the right side of her head on the metal railing, and lands very hard on her right knee. It's a *'down goes Frazier'* moment. She is clearly dazed and drops a few F-bombs. I pick her up and slowly walk her back to the hotel. We get some ice from the bar to ease the swelling on her head and knee. We *'hope'* by morning all will be well. Today's step count was 8,594.

I *'bite the bullet'* and purchase two new Eurail train passes and use the Eurail App on my iPhone to plan our train trips. Remember, Eurail would **NOT** replace the stolen passes and has no telephone customer service support. Email is the only method of contact. I struggle but finally install the passes on my iPhone. They are now ready to use. But now, I must enter all the reserved ticket numbers for every train trip on our holiday. It is going to be a long, frustrating night. Lastly, I need to finalize the two car rentals that require international driving permits which were in the stolen backpack.

That's enough work for tonight. It's time to *'shut it down, forget about it,'* and head to bed. Hopefully, tomorrow will be a better day. Good night from *Belleview Suite Hotel* in Amalfi, Italy!

*****

Tuesday, April 2 — Day 8
Amalfi, Minori, and Maiori, Italy

I spent a frustrating Monday night on my iPhone trying to learn how to use the Eurail App to add and manage our future train rides. My #1 challenge is learning how to add our reserved train seat tickets. The process is stressful since Eurail does not have a customer service phone line. Our wake up time of 07:00 comes too fast. The stress level is high. We get up, get ready, and head to the breakfast room. We pass on the dish of mozzarella cheese balls and cherry tomatoes marinating in olive oil and dive into the hot and cold breakfast buffet. After breakfast, I spend a few hours in the expansive hotel lobby learning how to use the Eurail App.

I am pleased to report that Sophia's injuries from her fall last night are minor and should not slow us down today. The knee's a little sore but a few Aleve's help with the pain and minor swelling. She *'sports'* a small black and blue bruise on her forehead just above her right eye where she contacted the metal fence. She deftly uses makeup to cover the bruise.

Getting the Eurail App up and running now becomes secondary. It's time to trek one mile down the hill, avoid becoming *'road kill'*, and walk down a long flight of steps (well over 100) that start to the right of the main tunnel and head to the main section of Amalfi.

Two small towns just south of Amalfi are accessible by bus, walking, or ferry. Being the boat enthusiasts that we are, we purchase the ferry tickets and enjoy a short ride to Minori and Maiori. The ferry drops us off at Maiori, a quaint, sleepy town. It has been a popular tourist resort since Roman times and is famous for having the largest unbroken stretch of beach on the Amalfi coastline. There are numerous affordable hotels and restaurants. Within an hour, we have seen everything. So, we head back to the dock and catch the ferry over to Minori. This small town is roughly one mile south of Amalfi. Minori is a beautiful small town on the Amalfi Coast, lesser known than some of its beautiful neighbors such as Positano or Amalfi itself, but very charming and welcoming. There is not a lot to see; however, we sit down on a seaside bench, relax, take in the sights, and enjoy some quiet time. I suggest we walk back to Amalfi through the one road tunnel; however, Sophia *'nixes'* this idea with a majority 1-0 *'no walk'* vote.

Back in Amalfi, we head up the main shopping pathway and select *La Taverna Del Duce*, a nice restaurant for dinner. The restaurant is charming. Our waiter is outgoing and nice. The food and adult beverages are excellent.

After 12,470 steps, it is time to head back to the ranch, rest, and keep learning how to add our reserved train tickets into the Eurail App. Cabs want 30 Euros to take us **ONE MERE MILE** up the hill. That's just **NOT** going to happen. So, we board the correct bus without tickets. This bus driver is very personable, gives us a **FREE RIDE** and drops us off right in front of our hotel! There is a nice bus driver in Amalfi!

I spend time in the living room style lobby entering reserved train ticket numbers into the App. Finally, after two days, I am getting the *'knack'* of correctly setting up our reserved seats train travel. It is time to hit the hay. Tomorrow, we plan to take a ferry to the town of Positano, a playground for the rich and famous. Nighty night from *Belleview Suite Hotel*!

*****

Wednesday, April 3 — Day 9
Amalfi and Positano, Italy

Our assault of the Amalfi Coast continues today. We plan to visit the seaside town of Positano. So, just like Monday and Tuesday, we walk down the hill to the town center. Today, we navigate a separate set of 100+ steps just past the tunnel. The steps lead us to the north end of town. 300 meters later (about 990 feet), we arrive at the ferry ticket office, purchase round trip tickets to Positano, and head to the ferry boat loading area. The weather report predicts clouds till 16:00 today. This confirms our decision to visit Positano today and the Isle of Capri tomorrow when the sun is forecast to be out all day.

Positano, Italy

According to Wikipedia, Positano is a cliff-side village on southern Italy's Amalfi Coast. It is a well-known holiday destination with beachfront and steep, narrow streets lined with boutiques and cafes. Its *Chiesa di Santa Maria Assunta* (Church of Santa Maria Assunta) features a majolica-tiled dome and a 13th-century Byzantine icon of the Virgin Mary. Positano is booked out months in advance and during peak season, it is usually completely full. Most hotels in Positano are situated on steep hills 200 plus steps up and are very expensive due to the limited supply. Famous for its spectacular setting, this vertical town is a resort destination and international fashion center. It's a playground for the rich and famous. The *Sentiero degli Dei* hiking trail links Positano to other coastal towns. Positano was a relatively poor fishing village during the first half of the twentieth century. It began to attract large number of tourists in the 1950s, especially after John Steinbeck published his essay about Positano in *Harper>s Bazaar* in May 1953: *"Positano Bites Deep"*. Steinbeck wrote, "It is a dream place that isn't quite real when you are there and becomes beckoningly real after you have gone."

Let's get back to our day in Positano. After getting off the ferry, we mosey along the main beachfront street. This is a **HIGH END** tourist town. The street is home to upscale restaurants and high end clothing stores. Next, we walk up and down the many narrow paths that lead to the hotels and spectacular long range ocean views. These paths are also home to takeaway snack bars, shops hawking those *'gotta have souvenirs,'* small shops selling lemon based products, and men's and women's clothing.

We settle into a seaside restaurant, *Ristorante La Pergola*, and sit at a table under an umbrella that keeps the sun off us. Today is day seven of our Mediterranean diet. We order and enjoy a pizza, salad, Italian beer and wine, and delicious cappuccinos.

We have exhausted our fill of Positano. Clearly we are **NOT** the target customer for this upscale town. So, we head to the dock to catch the 13:30 ferry back to Amalfi. On the dock, we see a sign that says, **"Amalfi."** But there is always a **BUT** for us. When we attempt to board, the ticket taker points us one slip over to the correct boat. Apparently, there are two ferry lines that travel between Amalfi and Positano. We make a mad dash to the correct dock and display our tickets for the ticket taker. Our return tickets are for 18:30, or last boat, back to Amalfi. The male ticket taker looks at the departure time and, in no uncertain terms, says, "Next time take the 18:30 boat!" I'm thinking, *'Hold on buddy, the lady who sold us* *the tickets said we could return ANYTIME that was convenient for us.'* Not wanting to get *'into it'* with him, we just hop on the boat versus tossing out a *'few choice comments'* that could incite a mini international confrontation. Whatever, odds are in my favor I will never run into this guy again.

It is time for dinner. Clouds are rolling in. The temperature is dropping. We select an outdoor café, *Bistro flli Pansa*. However, even with the restaurant providing blankets, it's too cold to sit outside. So, we find a two-person table inside and split a pizza, a fresh salad, and wash it down with our favorite Italian beer and wine.

It's another *'crap shoot'* where we stand to get on the bus to take us one mile up the hill. We purchase two tickets. The ticket seller directs us to the **WRONG** departure point. What else is new? Suddenly, we see our bus leaving from the other side of the town square. I run (or hobble with the repaired Achilles) in that direction and just as the bus pulls out, jump in front of the bus forcing the driver to jam on the brakes and stop. The bus driver opens the small window to his left. He is poised and ready to *'question my heritage with a few hand gestures and choice Italian words.'* A minute or two later, I finally convince him to open the door. The driver is *'more than slightly annoyed'* by my antics; however, he relents, lets us on, and drops us off at the hotel entrance! It's nice to finally win a battle with an Amalfi bus driver.

We have an early start on Thursday for our trip to the Isle of Capri. After 12,680 steps, it is time to relax, review the memories we created today, turn out the lights, and drift off to sleep in preparation for our next adventure in Italy.

*****

Thursday, April 4 — Day 10
Amalfi and Isle of Capri, Italy

No need to update everyone about getting up, showering, getting dressed and eating breakfast. That's what we do every day in Amalfi. Today, the dynamic duo plans to visit the Isle of Capri.

Sophia's made a strong recovery from her Monday night fall and is ready to take on the sites on the Isle of Capri. We embark on our usual walk down the hill, climb down 100+ steps and arrive at the town square in Amalfi. We catch the 09:10 ferry to the Isle of Capri. The trip takes one hour and 45 minutes, which includes a stop in Positano. The ride is smooth. The long range ocean views are spectacular. The Isle of Capri's harbor is home to numerous fishing and small tour boats as well as large, and obviously expensive, yachts owned by *the rich and famous* from all parts of the world.

Isle of Capri, Italy

Here is some info about Capri, courtesy of Wikipedia. Capri is an island located in the *Tyrrhenian Sea*, off the Sorrento Peninsula, on the south side of the *Gulf of Naples* in the Campania region of Italy. The largest settlement on the island is the town of Capri. The island has been a resort since the time of the Roman Republic. From the rock formations to the beaches to the delicious food, there's so much to love about the lavish Italian Island of Capri.

Capri is famous for its dramatic stretch of coastline peppered with grandiose villas. Capri is one of the world's most exclusive destinations. It makes you wonder who, if anyone, can afford it. The good news is almost anyone can afford a visit to Capri; but you may have to spend less in some areas, like hotels, so you can afford other things, like delicious seaside meals.

From *Goaheadtours.com*, Sally Dent's article "Five Things Not To Miss in Capri, Italy" provides us with more information about the Isle of Capri. The scenery around this remote island is incredibly beautiful. A must "to-do" is to take a tour boat ride. While sailing around the island, you will see the famous *Faraglionisea* stacks, as well as the iconic *Arco Natur*ale. Other notable sights to look for are the *Tiberiòs Leap, Grotta Bianca, Grotta del Corallo*, and of course, the exquisite *Blue Grotto*. Make sure to peek out over the side of the boat at the water as you cruise. "The water is so clear, you can see the jellyfish," said tour guide staffer Charlotta. While boating around the island, you'll also see dozens of colorful houses. "They're just like in the movies," said Charlotta. "Capri is a charming island, which encapsulates all of the rich culture of Italy while providing a peek at paradise. Seeing it in person is breathtaking."

That's enough overview of Capri. The 9:10 ferry from Amalfi drops us off in the Capri harbor at 10:45. We hustle and catch the 11:00 one-hour *'circle the Isle of Capri'* boat tour. Because of time constraints and long lines, we skip the two-hour plus wait to enter the *Blue Grotto*. As noted above, the hillsides, rock formations in the water, and the blue ocean waters are spectacular. We use the cameras on our iPhones to take picture after picture for our post trip album. We see a couple swimming in the light blue warm waters near a rock formation that has an opening on both ends. We sure wish we had more time to spend on the Isle, rent a private boat, and *'take a dip'* in the light blue warm waters. Maybe on our next trip!

If any reader visits Capri, taking one-hour *'circle the Isle of Capri'* boat tour is a *'must do'* activity.

We enjoy our Mediterranean diet lunch, seaside, overlooking the harbor. After lunch, we take a tram from the harbor area up the hill to the town center. The high end shopping reminds us of Beverly Hills and Milan. Sticker shock!! Without a doubt, we are **NOT** the target customer...**NOT** even close! The **BEST** we can do is window shop, it's **FREE.** We gaze at clothing, accessories, and shoes by *Pucci, Eres, Saint Laurent, Versace, Buccellati, Brunello Cucinelli, Louis Vuitton, Ralph Lauren, Bvlgardi, Valentino, Gucci, Swarovski, Ersilia, Pucci, Chantecler, Massa,* and *Ferragamo.* Did I miss anyone? White convertible *Mercedes Benz* cabs are a transportation option for those with deep pockets. We get a fantastic view of the entire island from this hillside perch and take many pictures for post trip memories. A movie production company is filming at one of the hotels. The area is secured by what looks like are many ex-NFL offensive and defensive linemen standing at least 6'5" tall and weighing in at a minimum 325 pounds. Any attempt to get past them to catch a glimpse of what's being filmed and who the actors and actresses are met with swift resistance. Trespassers are quickly subdued with Billy clubs, handcuffed, and laid out on the street in the hot sun awaiting a ride to the police station or being tossed into the ocean off one of the many high cliffs. (Just kidding.)

We are *'window shopped out.'* So, we decide to skip the tram ride down and add to our daily steps count by walking to the boat dock. Sophia realizes we are heading to the **WRONG** side of the island. Gio insists we are heading in the **RIGHT** direction; however, Sophia, in no uncertain terms, **KNOWS** she is correct. She starts walking back up the hill and telling me "You ungrateful pain in my ass, you are wrong and on your own. Good luck reaching the ferry boat." Rather than *'chance it'* by walking in the wrong direction, I follow her back up the hill to the tram car depot.

While Sophia makes a financial contribution to use the lady's room, I buy two return tram tickets. When we reach the tram entrance turnstile and insert our tickets, we get the **RED LIGHT** buzzer: **TICKETS NOT VALID.** "But I just bought them not five minutes ago!" I bellow in utter disbelief! "Too bad," the entrance supervisor says. "Go back up the steps and buy two more tickets." After feverishly tearing through the back pack, my pants pockets, and wallet, the tickets are still *'missing.'* Apparently, while waiting for Sophie to finish up in the lady's room, the tickets must have fallen out of my pocket while sitting on a bench. Or was I the victim of a local pick pocket or did a local pigeon swoop in and take the tickets if, and when, they fell out of my pocket? Where's Columbo when you need him? So, I head back up 40 stairs to the ticket booth and explain the situation to the ticket seller. She checks my tickets and says, "Expired, need to buy new ones." My but, but buts go nowhere. So, I am faced with: A: buy two new tickets or B: figure out how to walk down to the pier. I chose Option A — invest another five Euros for two tickets. I proceed back down to the tram entry, insert the new tickets, and **BINGO**, the gate opens allowing us to enter! The ferry back to Amalfi leaves in one hour. We park our bodies on cement steps next to a fountain and wait for the boat ride across the bay.

Back in Amalfi, the sun is covered by clouds and the temperature is dropping. We sit down at an outside café across from the cathedral and enjoy another Mediterranean dinner and gelato for dessert. It's time to head home to *Casa Hotel Belleview Suite.* The 30 Euro cab fare is **A CRAZY STUPID SCAM**. There's just **NO WAY** we would ever consider paying the **OUTRAGEOUS** fare... it's just **NOT** going to happen. So is walking one mile up the narrow road to the hotel. Luck is with us today. We get on the **RIGHT** bus with the **RIGHT** tickets. As the bus approaches our hotel, the driver **FINALLY** hears our **"STOP, LET US OFF"** cries and drops us off about 200 meters **PAST** the hotel. That's a **VERY SHORT** walk back to the hotel entrance compared to Monday's three miles down the road drop-off.

We decide to make Friday our last day in Amalfi and add an additional day to our stay in Florence. Frankly, we are *'done with'* the hikes down the hill, the same old—same old shops, restaurants, and the rude bus drivers. Back at the hotel, I go online and try to add one night to our three night hotel stay in Florence. Unfortunately, the B&B we are staying at is booked for Saturday night. On Booking. Com, I find availability at a hotel close to the Florence Central Train Station and just a few blocks from our Sunday to Wednesday B&B. Next, I change our train tickets from Sunday to Saturday and alert the hotel manager we will be checking out one night early. There is no refund for the prepaid booking; however, the manager comped us with the breakfast buffet during our stay so I guess we can't complain. He also arranges transportation to get us to the Naples Train Station on Saturday morning. We are looking forward to an exciting trip walking through the ancient ruins of Pompeii, even though it is going to be a long day. After a mere 8,650 steps today, it is time for bed and lights out!

*****

Friday, April 5 — Day 11
Amalfi to Pompeii, Italy

Today is our last day on the Amalfi Coast. We get an early start and take our last walk down the hill to the town square to catch a tour van that will be taking us on a two-hour ride up and over the mountains north to the city of Pompeii. Before we talk about our Pompeii tour, here are some observations from our six days along the Amalfi Coast:

- It would be really nice if the bus transportation company places signs in Italian and English in the town square bus depot indicating which buses go to the various places along the coastline. One day, we are instructed to get on a bus on one side of the square, and the next day, we are told to catch the same bus on the opposite side of the town square. Go figure.

- If we ever return to this area, we will stay in Central Amalfi or in the quaint villages of Minori or Majori. They are located close to Amalfi; but are away from the hustle and bustle of tourism and can be easily accessed by bus, ferry, or walking.

- Our hotel was located one mile north of town. There are no restaurants nearby. The comped breakfast at the hotel was the only local breakfast meal option.

- Public toilets cost one Euro to enter. Most of the bathrooms **DO NOT** have toilet seats. One must *'balance their tush'* on the ceramic toilet bowl.

- The Italian Postal Service does not deliver mail every day.

- The local roads are, in most places, very narrow and do not have shoulders, like here in the U.S. There are places, especially near tunnels, where traffic heading in one direction **MUST** yield to the oncoming traffic as the road narrows to one lane.

- There is no office supply, business center, electronics, large grocery stores, or big box stores like Walmart and Target.

- We **DID NOT** see one Amazon truck.

- You *'take your life in your hands'* walking on the narrow streets. There's a **HIGH PROBABILITY** of becoming *'road kill'* or *'a hood ornament.'*

- The area is a beautiful place to train for a triathlon.

- Cab service is extremely expensive and monopolized by one company.

- When on the bus, you better sit up front to let the bus driver know where you want to get off or you could wind up like we did 200 meters to three miles past your stop. Only 25% of the time we were dropped off at the bus stop steps from our hotel.

- Rather than book water excursion activities, use the ferry system to see the coastline and visit neighboring towns. You'll save lots of money.

On the road to Pompeii, the driver is taking us on the proverbial *'over the hill to grandmother's house'* route. Pompeii is north of Amalfi; however, he drives the twisting and turning, very narrow road **SOUTH** towards Salerno. It's like driving the very narrow,

1 1/2 lane 'road' to Hana or the North Shore of Maui. The narrow, 1 ½ - two lanes 'road' over the hill has no shoulder or 'stay on your side of the road lines' and '**NO PASSING**' signs. The narrow roads through small villages create 'near death experiences' for residents stepping out their front doors and failing to look both ways. Aggressive drivers who choose to pass another car take their lives in their hands, especially when passing around hairpin turns. I kid you not. After an hour or so, our driver gets on a four lane highway heading north. Our bus driver now becomes a Formula One race car driver with speeds exceeding 120 kilometers per hour (75 mph) and weaves in and out of traffic without signaling lane changes.

After the 'exciting' two hour 'excursion,' we arrive in Pompeii. With time 'to kill' before our tour starts. we walk around town, do some window shopping, stop for coffee, and have something to eat. We cannot locate the starting point of today's tour. A lady working for another tourist company directs us to go back to where we started, turn right, and go up the hill. Sophia does not buy these directions and directs me to ask at the tourist office across the street. A lady comes out and confirms the instructions to head up the hill. Score one for me while Sophia earns a minus one. Walking up another steep hill, we arrive at the tour starting point, and check in. Independent guides, who have extensive, authentic knowledge about Pompeii, lead the tours. We have a few minutes before the tour starts so I wander up the street, buy a few souvenirs, and a freshly squeezed orange juice to share with Sophia.

The tour leader provides everyone with head phones so we can listen to his narration. We enjoy the two hour small group tour; however, the walk, if you can call it that, has become **EXCEEDINGLY difficult** for my repaired Achilles and Sophia's back and knees. The route was **NOT** level and easy to transverse. We spend two and one-half hours walking on and over uneven, extremely large cobblestones, unearthed from thousands of years ago. Without a doubt, this makes walking a challenge for Gio and Sophia. Occasionally, we fall behind. So, the tour leader stops the group and says, "We have to wait for the Las Vegans to catch up." because of our respective ailments, we always 'bring up the rear' for our group.

It's hard to capture in words the vast array of unearthed ruins. Although two-thirds of the city has been excavated, the remnants of walls, houses, government buildings, and roadways are visibly deteriorating.

The two and one half hour tour is informative and physically challenging. During the 'adventure,' Sophia severely twists her right knee walking on the uneven paths and sidewalks. It is the same knee she fell on Monday night. Walking on the cobblestones further aggravates the injury. For the balance of the tour, she slowly hobbles along. Every step is difficult. We are hoping this does not turn out to be a huge setback for our trip, which is just 11 days in.

Before catching the 15:30 van back to Amalfi, we head to town and stop for a quick bite to eat to 'take the edge off.'

We arrive back at the Amalfi Town Square around 18:00 and select an open air restaurant, *C. Francese SNC Di Cola*, for our dinner last night. We sit down and wait and wait for a server to come to our table. Meanwhile, we observe five waiters standing by the entrance 'shooting the shit' while we sit for a good 10 to 15 minutes. Finally, 'one of them' decides to leave the group and get to work serving us. He comes to our table with menus and takes our drink and food order. We were famished and quickly ordered before he went to get our drinks. Why you ask?? We had ample time to read the menu beforehand!!

For our first course, we share a salad. When the waiter comes to clear our plates, I accidentally knock over a large, almost full bottle of virgin olive oil. It explodes into hundreds of pieces when it hits the stone floor. Glass flies in every direction and creates a raging river of virgin olive oil on the outdoor café stone floor. The disaster takes four tables out of service for at least two weeks. The cleanup continues while the owner waits for the hazmat and OSHA teams to ensure the clean-up is complete and the workplace is safe. We are fortunate they did not initially charge us for the damage to the tables, chairs, and six linen tablecloths now *out of service* after the cleanup. However, we observe the owner and clean-up crew huddle to assess and determine the cost plus 20% markup to clean up our mess and add it to our dinner bill. I anxiously await the bill to see the damage cost so I can figure out a way to explain the charge to our travel insurance company when I file a reimbursement claim.

There is no rhyme or reason why the city bus we take back to the hotel boards at two locations in the Amalfi Town Square. It is one of life's little mysteries that won't be solved in my lifetime. We catch the 20:00 bus up the hill and, despite our best efforts to have the driver stop **AT** our hotel, he continues on for another 200 meters. A short, downhill walk facing traffic gets us home. Today's step count is 9,061. Back in our room, we pack up and retire for the night. Tomorrow at 09:00, we will check out and take a taxi to Naples, about a 75-minute ride and a distance of about 28 miles. Good night from Amalfi.

The History of Pompeii

Here's what Wikipedia says about Pompeii.

- Pompeii is an ancient city in what is now the municipality of Pompeii, near Naples, in the Campania region of Italy. Along with Herculaneum, Stabiae, and many surrounding villas, the city was buried under 13 to 20 feet of volcanic ash and pumice during the eruption of Mount Vesuvius in 79 AD.

- Pompeii was built approximately 130 feet above sea level on a coastal lava plateau created by earlier eruptions of *Mount Vesuvius*. The plateau fell steeply to the south and partly to the west into the sea. Three layers of sediment from large landslides lie on top of the lava, perhaps triggered by extended rainfall. The city, once close to the shoreline, is today 2,300 feet inland.

- Pompeii covered a total of 160 to 170 acres. The first stable settlements on the site date to the 8th century BC when the Oscans, a population of central Italy, founded five villages in the area. By 79 AD, Pompeii had a population of 20,000 which prospered from the region's renowned agricultural fertility and favorable location, although more recent estimates are up to 11,500, based on household counts.

- The eruption of Mount Vesuvius around noon on August 24, 79 AD lasted for two days and buried the city under a thick carpet of volcanic ash. It was one of the deadliest volcanic eruptions in history. The first phase was of pumice rain lasting about 18 hours, allowing most inhabitants to escape. Approximately 1,150 bodies have been found on site, which seems to confirm the theory that most escapees probably managed to salvage some of their most valuable belongings. Many skeletons were found with jewelry, coins, and silverware.

- Mount Vesuvius violently spewed forth a cloud of superheated tephra and gases to a height of 33 km (21 mi), ejecting molten rock, pulverized pumice and hot ash at 1.5 million tons per second, ultimately releasing 100,000 times the thermal energy of the atomic bombings of Hiroshima and Nagasaki. Pyroclastic flows began near the volcano, consisting of high speed, dense, and scorching ash clouds, knocking down wholly or partly all structures in their path, incinerating or suffocating the remaining population, and altering the landscape, including the coastline. By the evening of the second day, the eruption was over, leaving only a haze in the atmosphere through which the sun shone weakly.

- Largely preserved under the ash, Pompeii offers a unique snapshot of Roman life frozen at the moment it was buried, as well as insight into ancient urban planning. It hosted many fine public buildings and luxurious private houses with lavish decorations, furnishings, and artworks which were the main attractions for early excavators. Subsequent excavations found hundreds of private homes and businesses reflecting various architectural styles and social classes, as well as numerous public buildings. Organic remains, including wooden objects and human bodies, were interred in the ash. Their eventual decay allowed archaeologists to create molds of figures in their last moments of life. The numerous graffiti carved on outside walls and inside rooms provide a wealth of examples of the largely lost Vulgar Latin spoken colloquially at the time, contrasting with the formal language of classical writers.

- Following its destruction, Pompeii remained largely undisturbed until its rediscovery in the late 16th century. Major excavations did not begin until the mid-18th century. Their efforts to unearth the city were haphazard and marred by looting. Many items or sites were damaged or destroyed. By 1960, most of Pompeii had been uncovered; but was left in decay. Further, major excavations were banned or limited to targeted, prioritized areas. Since 2018, these efforts have led to new discoveries in some previously unexplored areas of the city including a banquet hall adorned with rare, well preserved frescoes depicting various mythological scenes and figures.

- Objects buried beneath Pompeii were well-preserved for almost 2,000 years as the lack of air and moisture allowed little to no deterioration. However, Pompeii has been exposed to natural and anthropic deterioration following excavation. Erosion, light exposure, water damage, poor methods of excavation and reconstruction, along with tourism, vandalism, and theft have damaged the site in some way. The lack of adequate weather protection for all but the most interesting and important buildings has allowed original interior decoration to fade or be lost. Two-thirds of the city has been excavated; but the remnants of the city are rapidly deteriorating.

- A multidisciplinary volcano and bio-anthropological study of the eruption products and victims, merged with numerical simulations and experiments, indicates that at Pompeii and surrounding towns, heat was the main cause of death of people, previously believed to have died by ash suffocation. The results of the study, published in 2010, show that exposure to at least 480 °F hot pyroclastic flows, at a distance of six miles from the vent, was sufficient to cause instant death, even if people were sheltered within buildings. The people and buildings of Pompeii were covered in up to twelve different layers of tephra, in total, up to 19.7 feet deep. Archaeology in 2023 showed that some buildings collapsed due to one or more earthquakes during the eruption, killing the occupants.

- Today, funding is mostly directed into conservation of the site; however, due to the expanse of Pompeii and the scale of the problems, this is inadequate in halting the slow decay of the materials. A 2012 study recommended an improved strategy for interpretation and presentation of the site as a cost-effective method of improving its conservation and preservation in the short term.

- The severe earthquake of 1980 caused great destruction. Since then, work has been confined to the excavated areas except for targeted sites and excavations. Further excavations on a large scale are not planned. Today, archaeologists are more engaged in reconstructing, documenting, and slowing the decay of the ruins.

- Pompeii is a UNESCO World Heritage Site, owing to its status as "the only archaeological site in the world that provides a complete picture of an ancient Roman city." It is among the most popular tourist attractions in Italy, with approximately 2.5 million visitors annually.

*****

Saturday, April 6 — Day 12
Amalfi to Florence
thru Naples, Italy

Today marks the one year anniversary of the second surgery to repair Gio's torn left Achilles tendon. For 11 plus months, I was in a cast, used a knee scooter to get around, and endured 80 sessions of physical therapy. From December 2023 to March, 2024, I logged 300+ miles learning how to walk again. For added stability and support, I purchased and wore *'over the ankle'* hiking boots. In addition, I patiently assisted Sophia recover from leg and knee aches and pains. There is no way I could have embarked on the 78-day trip without getting as healthy as possible so I could become *'secure on my feet'*.

Today, we leave Amalfi and head to Florence. We check out of our Amalfi hotel one day early and add an additional day and night in Florence. Up at 06:00, we pack, get ready, eat, and prepare to head to Florence. Our laundry bill came to 120 Euros. Fortunately, the hotel owner *"comped"* us with six-40 Euros a day breakfast buffets during our six day/night stay. We were more than grateful for the comp we were given as there are no refunds for checking out a day early. Plus, he did not charge us the 20 Euros city tax.

The owner arranged transportation from the hotel to the *Naples Central Train Station*. While waiting for the 130 Euros (cash deal) ride, just to confuse the authorities, I search for new Italian names for our stay in Florence. Our *'taxi'* is an early model 2000's four door compact car owned by one of the hotel's staff! The 90-minute *'ride'* takes us up and over the mountains through numerous small villages. The roadway has numerous twists and 90-degree hairpin turns too many to count. The narrow roads through small villages create *'near death experiences'* for residents stepping out their front doors and failing to look both ways. The width of the roadway varies from a single lane, forcing oncoming cars to stop to let us pass, to two narrow lanes. Guard rails are nonexistent on the shoulder-less *'road'* through the mountains. One wrong turn or swerve would send any car or truck tumbling down hundreds of meters down cliffs that would lead to certain death.

Our prayers are answered. We arrive safely at the Naples Central Train Station in one place. However, I cannot find our tickets on the Eurail App. I *'park'* Sophia and head to the *Italia Rail* customer service office. The ticket counter agent **CANNOT** find our tickets. She recommends heading to the *Trenitalia* customer service hut in the center of the train station lobby. This agent also cannot find our tickets; however, she directs me to the *Trenitalia* customer service office. An experienced agent locates our tickets and prints them for me. He asks to see our train ticket confirmation email. **Son of a bitch, our tickets are located at the BOTTOM of the confirmation.** I am now in the running for *'dumb American of the day.'* If I win, the ticket agent promises to email me a prize! Just think, it only took 20 minutes and 826 steps from arriving at the train station to find a knowledgeable *Trenitalia* customer service agent who points out our tickets are attached to the confirmation email! It's just a *'huge senior moment'* for me.

We have a few minutes to kill before getting on the train. We share an Americano coffee with cold milk and a pastry. I was craving a soft pretzel. Sadly, no vendor in the train station sells them.

Ten minutes before leaving Naples, the departure board lists the platform for our train. Our tickets show the car number and seat numbers. Without any screw ups or missteps, we get on the **RIGHT** train car, find our reserved seats, store our bags, and enjoy a smooth three hour and eleven minute ride to Florence. I officially change my name to Marcello for our stay in Florence while Sophia sticks with Sophia.

We exit the Florence Central Train Station, and we think we're heading toward our hotel. Not so fast traveling friends: the address is incorrect. We call the hotel front desk; however, we have trouble understanding his directions. He tells us to stand in front of the large Italian flag pole and call him. He tells us he is outside the hotel waving at us; however, of course, we **DO NOT** see him. Finally, he instructs us to *'stand'* where we are and **NOT TO** move. He sends a hotel employee to *'fetch us.'*

The hotel front desk person is very enthusiastic. He has all the verbal skills to become a top notch timeshare salesman! He greets Sophia, "Hi, beautiful lady"! Now, she's telling stories and laughing with him for the next five minutes. He uses a city map to give us a 15-minute briefing showing us the location of the top attractions in the city. We cannot wait to explore Florence.

We head up to our room and settle in. Much to my astonishment, the credit card size plastic key not only opens the door but also actives the room's electrical system. Sophia decides to *'chill'* while I need a bite to eat to *'take the edge off.'* First, however, I speak to the desk clerk to learn where I can print out our car reservation, train tickets, and international driving permits. He instructs me to email the documents to the hotel and he promises to print them by Sunday morning.

I stroll around the neighborhood, *'get a lay of the land,'* and look for building landmarks that will guide me back to the hotel. I find a small café and enjoy half of a tuna sandwich, with the crusts cut off, and an Italian beer.

For dinner, Marcello and Sophia (that's us, remember?) walk to *Ristorante Sabatini*, a high-end eatery the front desk clerk highly recommends. This establishment supposedly makes the **BEST** *Steak Florentine* in Florence. We order drinks and peruse the menu. The recommended steak is priced based on the weight of the meat. The cost **STARTS** at over 100 Euros. We *'pass'* and start with a green salad. It's a clear *'Italian eating violation'* to eat salad **BEFORE** the main course; but we don't care. Marcello orders the wild boar and wide noodles in a nice red sauce while Sophia orders a ribeye steak. My meal is excellent; however, Sophia's steak is 60% fat and grizzle thus invoking an aged old question, "Where's the beef?" After finishing our meal, we meander around the touristy section of the city for about 30 minutes. Sophia locates an ice cream shop and orders her daily one scoop of gelato. Back at the hotel, we settle in after 8,824 steps and plot tomorrow's first day of *'checking out'* Florence. FYI, it's now been almost two weeks since we watched TV. It's amazing what you can do without if you don't think about it!! Nightie night.

Florence, Italy

More info from Wikipedia: Florence is the capital city of the Italian region of Tuscany. It is also the most populated city in Tuscany, with nearly 37,000 inhabitants and approximately 990,500 in the greater metropolitan area (2024 statistics).

Florence was a center of European trade and finance and one of the wealthiest cities of the medieval times It is considered by many academics to have been the birthplace of the *Renaissance*, becoming a major artistic, cultural, commercial, political, economic, and financial center.

The city attracts millions of tourists each year. In 1982, UNESCO (United Nations Educational, Scientific, and Cultural Organization) declared the Historic Centre of Florence a World Heritage Site. The city is noted for its culture, Renaissance art, architecture, and monuments. The city also contains numerous museums and art galleries that still exert an influence in the fields of art, culture, and politics. Due to Florence's artistic and architectural heritage, in 2010, *Forbes* ranked it as one of the most beautiful cities in the world.

Florence plays an important role in Italian fashion and ranks in the top 15 fashion capitals of the world by *Global Language Monitor*. Furthermore, it is a major national economic center as well as a tourist and industrial hub.

Florence, in the Italian language, is called Firenze. It comes from Florentiae, a name from Latin conveying good luck.

Tourism is, by far, the most important of all industries. Most of the Florentine economy relies on the money generated by international arrivals and students studying in the city. The value tourism brings to the city totaled 2.5 billion Euros in 2015 and the number of visitors had increased by 5.5% from the previous year.

In 2013, Florence was listed as the second best world city by *Condé Nast Traveler*. Florence is believed to have the greatest concentration of art (in proportion to its size) in the world. Thus, cultural tourism is particularly strong, with world-renowned museums such as the *Uffizi Gallery*. The city's convention center facilities were restructured during the 1990s and host exhibitions, conferences, meetings, social forums, concerts, and other events.

One of the bridges, in particular, stands out – the *Ponte Vecchio (<Old Bridge>)*. The most striking feature is the multitude of shops built upon their edges, held up by stilts. The original bridge was constructed by the *Etruscans* and the current bridge was rebuilt in the 14th century. It is the only bridge in the city to have survived World War II intact.

The *Uffizi Gallery,* one of the finest art museums in the world, was founded on a large bequest from the last member of the Medici family. It is located at the corner of *Piazza della Signoria,* a site important for being the center of Florence's civil life and government for centuries.

Florence Cathedral, formally the *Cattedrale di Santa Maria del Fiore,* is the Cathedral of Florence, Italy. Construction started in 1296, in the Gothic style, to a design of *Arnolfo di Cambio* and was structurally completed by 1436. Filippo Brunellesch designed the dome. The exterior of the basilica is faced with polychrome marble panels in various shades of green and pink, bordered by white, and has an elaborate 19th century Gothic Revival façade by *Emilio De Fabris.* The Cathedral complex, in *Piazza del Duomo,* includes the *Baptistery* and *Giotto's Campanile.* These three buildings are part of the UNESCO World Heritage Site covering the historic center of Florence and are a major tourist attraction of Tuscany. The *Basilica* is one of Italy's largest churches and its dome, when built back in the 15th century, was the largest ever built in Western Europe. In the Catholic world, it is now second only to *St. Peter's;* but it remains the largest brick dome ever constructed in the world. The *San Giovanni Baptistery* located in front of the Cathedral, is decorated by numerous artists, notably *Lorenzo Ghiberti,* who designed a pair of bronze doors in 1401.

*****

Sunday, April 7 — Day 13
Florence, Italy

Today is the one week anniversary of the Milan stolen backpack disaster. I am pleased to report we got through our misadventures relatively unscathed. We are recovering mentally and emotionally. Our new Eurail passes and reserved seat reservations are set up on the Eurail App on the iPhone. We confirm the car reservations for our trip to Tuscany. We email our Henderson insurance agent Mike about our predicament. He strongly suggests we document our losses and file a claim against our homeowners' policy when we return.

Our room has a 4.5' x 7' bathroom. The telephone booth sized shower and toilet (with toilet seat A++) fit into a 2.5' x 4.5' area. Let's just say the Italian people like **COZY** and efficient utilization of limited spaces.

For the eighth straight day, our stay includes a continental breakfast. The restaurant also offers a variety of *'American'* breakfast items at very reasonable prices. We enjoy croissants, coffee, juice, and order and share a bacon, ham, and cheese omelet. It's perfecto! (Interesting sidenote: The eggs are brightly colored yellow. I guess the Florence egg farms feed their chickens differently than on the Amalfi Coast.)

After breakfast, it's time to check out and relocate to our bed and breakfast (B&B) *La Nannina*. It's just a few blocks up the street.

We head towards the train station and turn left. Most buildings in Florence do not display address numbers. We stop at a retail clothing store and ask the clerk for directions. She looks confused but points and says, "Go left out the front door and look for number 21". A block up the street, we see 21A, 21B, 21C, and numbers getting higher. Where is plain old #21? We stop, call the B&B, and receive directions from the desk clerk. We turn around, make a right turn at the café, look for a locked gate with the B&B *La Nannina* sign, and press the button. The clerk opens the gate which lets us onto the property.

The B&B is located in a five story condo/apartment building. We have never stayed at a B&B in a high rise building. I guess there's a first time for everything. We walk to the building's front door and take the elevator up one floor. We check in and the desk clerk gives us a lesson on which keys will get us in and out of the building. We also get the Wi-Fi codes: the first code does not work; however, the second one connects us to the outside electronic world. I log into *Booking.Com* and pay for our three night stay. The clerk tells us our room will be ready in 30 minutes. So, we find a couple of comfortable chairs, chill, play with our iPhones, and enjoy a cup of coffee.

Marcello and Sophia are set to explore the city and decide to use the Hop On-Hop Off bus. We ask our hostess for directions to the nearest bus stop. She gives us a confused *'what are you asking me about'* look. Clearly, she has never heard of the Hop On-Hop Off tour bus system. Normally, one can find this tourist bus on main streets and near prominent places like the central train station. Luck is with us today. Just across the street from the train station, we see the bus stop we need to get to. We cross the street, find the ticket agent, and purchase two day bus passes.

The bus is running behind schedule because the *Florence Marathon* has many streets blocked off. I once considered training to run a 26 mile, 385 yards marathon; however, the desire and willpower quickly faded into a faint memory.

The bus takes us through the beautiful commercial and residential streets of Florence. We cross the river and take a winding route through tree lined upscale neighborhoods. We stop at a neighborhood square and walk around. Sophia stops at a local artists craft store searching for that *'just right souvenir'* unique to the area. When it's time for lunch, we settle into *Bistrot 5*, a sidewalk local culinary place with a contemporary flavor. The restaurant has its roots in traditional Italian dishes. Large white umbrellas shade patrons from the cloudless sky and warm sun. We share a bowl of the soup of the day...*"Pasta e Fagioli"*... a mixed green salad, freshly baked Italian bread, a local Italian Pinot Grigio wine, and a local beer. We are firm believers in going *'local'* when enjoying adult beverages.

Heading down the hill after lunch, we enjoy long range panoramic views of the city. To say the least, it's simply spectacular! Since it's not yet time for dinner, we stroll through the narrow streets of central Florence, window shop, and visit a historic Catholic Church. The weather is great. Temperatures are at least 10 degrees above normal. As the sun goes down, we agree to dine at *Cobreo Trattoria*, a ridiculously small sidewalk café located down a narrow alley. We do the Mediterranean thing (we really don't have much choice, LOL)...salad, pasta, pizza, and local adult beverages. On the way back to our room at the B&B, Sophia stops for her daily gelato. I've lost count of the number of consecutive days she enjoys her favorite Italian desert. P.S. From time to time, I also indulge in this delicious treat.

It's been a great first day in Florence. We added 7,538 steps today. Tomorrow, we plan to continue our exploring ways in one of Italy's beautiful cities. Arriving back at B&B *La Nannina*, we jump into bed for a good night's sleep. Nighty night from Florence.

*****

Monday, April 8 — Day 14
Florence, Italy

Good morning world from Florence, Italy.

We are up and *'at it'* at 08:00. The phone booth shower at B&B *La Nannina* is let's say, a cozy 28"x 34". Obviously, there's no room for two people showering together for the *'let's save water'* conservation movement. For me, because I'm 5'11", turning around in the petite shower is quite difficult and dropping the soap is disastrous.

Sitting on the balcony overlooking other buildings, and just steps outside of our room, we enjoy coffee and our continental breakfast.

Last night, the Trenitalia ticketing agent informed me I need to **CANCEL** and **REPURCHASE ALL** of our train tickets because they are *'somehow'* connected to our stolen rail passes. Not sure about this, but the agent cancels and refunds our tickets to the *Cinque Terre* next week and issues new ones. On the flip side, I recall an email from Eurail telling me all the purchased tickets **WILL WORK** with the Eurail iPhone App. So, what's the right answer to this seemingly easy question? I wait for a reply from Eurail customer service to determine if I must print out all of the reserved seat train tickets for the next two months. While I am in limbo, Rosanna, our hostess, is extremely helpful and patient with me. She locates a printing/copy center about a 25-minute walk from the B&B.

Sophia has her heart set on visiting the *Uffizi Gallery*, one of the finest art museums in the world. It is located at the corner of *Piazza Della Signoria*, a site important for being the center of Florence's civil life and government for centuries. Unfortunately, the *Uffizi Gallery* is closed on Monday and sold out on Tuesday. This is a **HUGE** disappointment for Marcello (just kidding). We stroll over to the high end retail area that leads to the *Ponte Vecchio* (<Old Bridge>). Well known jewelry stores including *Rolex, Frarelli, Puccini, Patek, Philippe, Carlo Piccini, L. Vettori, Dante Cardini, Tag Heuer, and Cassetti,* just to name a few, are located on both sides of the pedestrian walkway leading to the bridge. For the record, these retailers are *'way above our pay grade'* and budget. Plus, we are **NOT** the *'target demographic.'*

Today the weather is in the mid to high 70's. The unseasonably warm temperatures on most days—10-15 degrees above normal—make for enjoyable and comfortable strolling. It sure beats cold and rainy weather requiring hats, gloves, scarves, umbrellas, and coats. To get out of the heat, we locate a small café, sit down at an inside table, and *'take the edge off,'* sharing a pizza, and enjoying a beer and wine.

To be on the safe side, I want to print out our train itinerary and tickets. Granted, they are now available on the Eurail App on the iPhone; however, I am *'old school'* and more comfortable with *'pieces of paper'* documenting our train trips and hard copies of our reserved tickets. We set out to the copy service store our B&B hostess Roseanna recommends.

We pull out our iPhones, Google *"Copisteria Universale,"* and press *'directions.'* Google Maps tells us it's a 15-minute walk. **BUT,** and there is always a **BUT,** the GPS directs us in the right direction and then, for some unknown reason, changes the route three to four times while we're on our journey! Frustrated by technology, we aimlessly wander for at least 30 minutes. Finally, we find the **RIGHT** street and find a building marked #20; however, #20 is a residence, **NOT** a business. Frustration builds even more, what the hell is going on?? I ask a local merchant for assistance. He teaches me the most valuable lesson of the day. The numbers on the tiles on the buildings in **BLACK** are residences while the numbers on the tiles in **RED** are businesses. So, the building we are looking for is **RED 20**. Next to **RED 20**, there's a **BLACK 32** meaning it's a residential unit. He tells me this is how the street numbering system works in Florence. **Since we don't live in Florence, how are we supposed to know that?**

I spend an hour going through the iPad train ticket files, email the files to the print store, and watch staff print out the documents. The staff is **VERY** patient with me. I cannot figure out how to attach multiple **PDF** files to an email I create on the iPad. Therefore, I must send over 25 emails. After an hour, *'I am back in business.'* I have the train tickets and train itineraries in hand!

We catch the Red Hop On-Hop Off bus and exit at the best panoramic, scenic stop with an amazing view of Florence. Zig zag-ging across a four lane street like two All Pro running backs (**NOT**), we dodge cars and buses and grab an outside table at *Ristorante La Loggia del Piazzale Michelangelo* for happy hour, adult beverages, and snacks as we enjoy the view.

For dinner tonight, we agree on *Cobreo Trattoria*, a ridiculously small sidewalk café down a narrow alley. We do the Mediterranean *'thing,'* again and dine on salad, pasta, pizza, and local adult beverages. On the way home, we decide to check out the local McDonald's. We order two decaf coffees to go. Before heading up to our room, Sophia stops for her daily, *'must have'* gelato dessert. I've lost count of how many consecutive days she has enjoyed this delectable dessert.

We have a short walk back to the room and finish up today's step count at 10,131. When checking our travel files on the iPad, I notice I apparently made a car reservation with Eurocar for our Wednesday trip to Tuscany. I call the number on the email confirmation to cancel. The agent tells me he cannot cancel the reservation since it was made on their website! So, I log into their website and cancel the duplicate reservation.

Tomorrow is laundry day and our final day walking the streets of Florence. I also schedule a massage with one of the B&B owners. It's that time again.....lights out, sweet dreams.

Some quick Florence observations:

- McDonald's to-go cups have no protective sleeve or do not carry a **HOT** warning imprinted on the cups. They assume when you buy hot coffee, you know it's **HOT**! I guess no one in Italy has sued McDonald's for millions of Euros for burns from scalding hot coffee. Italians clearly understand and know to **BE CAREFUL** when handling hot cups of McDonald's coffee. Only in America is stupidity rewarded with tens of thousands of dollars when there's an accident handling a hot coffee cup!

- Italian restaurant menus offer a number of courses. We always order just *'one course.'* The portion size is perfect; just enough to *'hit the spot.'*

*****

Tuesday, April 9 — Day 15
Florence, Italy

Today, we begin our third week in Europe with the usual continental breakfast. We pass on the cheese and salami and enjoy a bowl of cornflakes, croissants, juice, and fresh coffee.

Our first order of business is to find a self-service laundromat and wash our clothes. Google Maps directs us 3/10ths of a mile to the laundromat. Sophia sees they offer two options. One - self-service or two, they do it for us. She opts for *'door two.'* The cost is only 25 Euros. Our clean clothes will be ready for pick up at 12:30. Sophia makes an excellent decision. Next, we set out to find the Green Motion Rental Car office to confirm *'all is good'* for our Wednesday pick-up. Luck is on our side today. Their office is another short 3/10ths of a mile walk. We are two for two getting the correct directions from Google Maps today. We are on a roll. With the car rental paperwork complete, we cross the street and enter *Gamberini*, a local corner cafe. They offer an outstanding array of pastries, candy, and sandwiches plus a dinner menu that **SCREAMS** *'we will eat here tonight'*!

We receive a disturbing email from Southwest Airlines indicating our June 11 return flight from Denver to Las Vegas has been moved up by one hour. We are scheduled to land at 7:00 PM in Denver on our non-stop flight from Iceland. The Southwest flight is now scheduled to depart at 9:00 PM. This schedule change is going to make it difficult to reach the Southwest departure gate on time to catch the flight home. We will have **JUST** two hours to get through customs, retrieve our luggage, get to the Southwest terminal, check our bags, get through TSA security, and arrive at our departure gate. Needless to say, the new timeline is very tight. But, that challenge is two months down the road, so more later.

Marcello has a massage on tap at 12:30 with one of the B&B owners. Before heading back to the room, I stop at the post office to mail a postcard and purchase more stamps. When I enter the post office, I see four postal clerks, three of whom are helping customers. The fourth worker at the far right counter is sitting there playing with his cell phone. I walk up and hand him a stamped postcard. He confirms I am using the correct amount of postage. Next, I ask to buy four stamps. His matter of fact reply is, "Take a number from the machine." Wait a minute buddy; you are **NOT** waiting on anyone. You are sitting here on government time playing with your phone! I just want to buy four stamps! Again, he says, "Take a number!" and returns to playing a video game on his phone. I locate the ticket dispensing machine and draw number 25. I feel like I am in a deli or bakery in America. Patiently, I wait for my number to be called. After a noticeably short wait, number 25 appears on a digital display board above another clerk's head. I call out, **"BINGO"** and purchase my stamps. Looking over at the first clerk, I notice he is **STILL** playing with his phone! Should I report him to the Italian Postal Clerks Union?

We have a few minutes to kill before we need to head back to the B&B for my massage. So, we *'take a lap'* around a long block to add steps to our daily total.

It's close to 12:30, time for my massage. I head to the B&B. Sophia strolls the local streets. Somehow, I get into a discussion with the masseuse about how the Italian medical system works when you visit a doctor's office, clinic, or hospital. Italy uses a color coding system to prioritize patient care. A black tag signifies the patient is dead (I guess that's obvious!!). A red tag tells the staff the patient is extremely critical, a yellow tag means the patient is moderately critical, a green tag signifies the patient is not overly critical, and a white tag means the patient is not critical. Patients categorized as green or white may have to wait up to one year to have non-essential surgery; but they have access to immediate surgery if something urgent happens. The cost of medical care is based on one's income and is mostly covered for by the Italian government.

I also learn about the ages to obtain an Italian driver's license and the types of vehicles a person can drive. At 14, you can drive a small scooter. At 16, you can drive a motorcycle and larger scooter. At 18, you can drive a car. Insurance is **MANDATORY**. Helmets are also **MANDATORY** when driving scooters and motorcycles.

Today's massage is great. My aches, pains, and tightness are gone.

It's time to retrieve the laundry. Unfortunately, we once again walk down the **WRONG** street. It's my fault. I got a well-earned *'bullet'* from Sophie. The five minute walk becomes 15 minutes. For the record, crossing the street at a red traffic light is a sport here. J-walking is also immensely popular. We quickly learn cars, scooters, and bikes will not stop if you are in their way.

With the laundry secure in our room, we flip a coin to determine if we should 1) get on a trolley car and ride around town or 2) continue walking the streets of downtown Florence. We are currently sitting at 9,200 steps today. Sophia feels energetic and chooses *'door two.'* Our two hour walking excursion gets us to over 12,150 steps for the day before dinner. This decision is a *'nearly fatal mistake'* for Sophia. Her knee is **BARKING** from the Pompeii tour. But, she's a trooper.

We navigate our way back to *Cafe Gamberini*, a locals' restaurant. How do we know? **NO ONE** speaks English and **EVERYONE** at the restaurant looks *'local.'* Clearly, the two old Americanos stand out. After a few minutes, the non-English speaking young water *'attempts'* to take our order. We must **POINT** to our selections on the menu. We try in vain to have the waiter bring the salad first. Our request falls on deaf ears. **CLEARLY** there is a language barrier. The burger, fries, club sandwich, and salad all arrive at the same time....oh well.

I decide to scan the extensive dessert counter for something decadent to finish off a great meal. Ladie, the young counter person and cashier, explains the various *'sinful looking'* deserts. Everything looks so tempting. I settle for my *'go to'* Italian dessert, Tiramisu. Sophia waits patiently for her nightly gelato.

When you finished eating, you do not pay the waiter. You go to a centrally located cashier (in small restaurants it's normally the owner). You point to the table you sat at. Each table has a unique number. Today's checkout person is Ladie, the young lady who assisted with my dessert selection. The bill is 77 Euros! I challenge the total and ask, "whoa, no senior discount, no happy hour prices, no AARP discount, no *'locals'* discount???" Ladie gets *'my drift, massages the numbers,'* and issues a 17 Euros **CREDIT**! The bill is now a reasonable 60 Euros!! It's my lucky day. Remember, you never know what can happen unless you ask!

After a slow 15-minute walk, we arrive at the B&B. Sophie stops for her last Florence gelato. It's now time to pack up and get ready for our next adventure starting on Wednesday, our assault on Tuscany.

Night, night!

*****

Wednesday, April 10 — Day 16
Florence to San Gimignano, Tuscany, Italy

Today, we leave Florence and drive to the Tuscany region for five days and nights of exploring the beautiful rolling countryside and small villages, many of which are surrounded by large walls that date back hundreds of years. We also plan to visit a winery or three.

Anxious to get started, we are up early, grab a bite to eat, check out, and walk four blocks to pick up the rental car. The morning air is cool, the aftermath of last night's rain. I guess I shouldn't be wearing shorts. Sophia is moving a bit slower due to *'overdoing it'* yesterday; however, she's a trooper. She is now using her cane, slowly moseys along, and rests as needed.

All goes well getting the car, obtaining directions to drive out of Florence, and then getting to our Tuscany destination. Sophia is an excellent navigator. She gets us out the city and going in the right direction; but; when we arrive in *San Gimignano*, we circle the city's narrow streets and look for the *'country road'* where the B&B is located. Luigi, my new name for our Tuscany stay, makes an *'almost fatal wrong turn'* into someone's **NARROW** driveway and parking lot. To say the least, I have trouble attempting to back out without hitting the stone wall and trees. So, I decide to pull forward and *'turn around.'* **Not so fast Luigi.** This turns out to be an **UNWISE** decision.

The area is **SO** tight. I am partially *'blocked in'* by a four foot high stone wall and a car parked in the narrow entranceway. A three point turn is out of the question. It takes me about 20+ *'back-ups and go forwards'* to get the car pointed in the right direction! On one of the backups, I hit the stone wall. After exiting *'jail,'* we see a narrow dirt road on the left side of the street. Bingo, this is the unmarked *'street'* we have been searching for. Our accommodations are ¼ mile down a dusty, extremely uneven dirt road. When we arrive at the B&B, I discover that the wall-car contact dislodged 50% of the license plate from the car. Houston, we have a minor problem.

Check-in time is 14:00; however, we arrive at 11:30. The B&B is a small family run operation. I cannot find the office, so I do the next best thing, call out **"HELLO, ANYONE HOME?"** In less than a minute, Francesca, our hostess and daughter of the owners, warmly greets us. She is a very enthusiastic, warm, and charming person who you instantly like. She leads us to our room for the next five nights. We unload our luggage and set up shop. Francesca's father provides some heavy duty tape to attach the rear license plate to the inside of the car's rear window. After settling in, we drive up the *'poor excuse for a road'* to the walled city center.

We leave the car in a parking lot very close to the walled city of San Gimignano. After entering the city, I walk the complete length of the city's narrow pedestrian path to the top while Sophia manages to walk half way up the path before she needs to take a break. Retail stores sell everything from souvenirs to clothing and leather products. Numerous restaurants line both sides of the steep ascent.

Sophia finally joins me, and we enjoy a late lunch at a restaurant recommended by Francesca, our host. Unfortunately, the meal is fair at best; but it provides the needed nourishment and alcohol.

As the advanced scout, I set out on a mission to check out what's ahead and search for some impressive views of the surrounding countryside. My journey is successful. Despite the 90 degree downhill path angle, I discover beautiful, long range views of the surrounding countryside! I also found another restaurant our hostess recommends.

Sophia and I hook up in the Main Town Square at the top of the hill. Here, after standing in a short line, we enjoy gelato from *'Europe's #1 Gelato Store.'* A few hours ago, the line was 60 to 70 people deep with tourists, most likely from a tour bus.

After enjoying our *'afternoon delight'* gelato, we slowly and carefully descend down the path towards the parking lot, stopping along the way to pick up a Panini to share for dinner. Although we are only minutes from the B&B, we drive around the town circle **TWICE** to find the *'road'* we need to turn onto. Not to worry, the rental car comes with unlimited miles!

Back at the ranch, Sophie ices her knee. We relax on our private patio, enjoy the late afternoon sun, and the sounds of birds holding conversations with their friends. Francesca brings us a bottle of a local red wine to enjoy with snacks and our Panini. This is without a doubt the most relaxing, peaceful stop on our journey to date. Francesca's father stops by with two small glasses filled with homemade Limoncello, an Italian liqueur. It's an excellent after dinner drink made from lemons grown on the property. I entertain myself with a Netflix mini-series about the criminal element controlling the port of Barcelona while Sophia enjoys reading from a pleasant book before falling asleep. I settle into our king size bed, dreaming about tomorrow's adventures. Until then..... good night from Tuscany!

Tuscany and San Gimignano

Time to learn a little about Tuscany and San Gimignano. According to Wikipedia, Tuscany is a region in central Italy with an area of about 8,900 square miles and a population of about 3.8 million inhabitants. Florence is the regional capital. Tuscany is the second-most-popular Italian region for travelers in Italy. The main tourist spots are Florence, Castiglione Della Pescaia, Pisa, San Gimignano, Lucca, Grosseto, and Siena.

Tuscany is known for its landscapes, history, artistic legacy, and its influence on high culture. It is regarded as the birthplace of the Italian Renaissance and the foundations of the Italian language. Having a strong linguistic and cultural identity, it is sometimes considered *"a nation within a nation."*

Eight Tuscan localities have been designated World Heritage Sites: *the Historic Center of Florence* (1982), the *Cathedral Square of Pisa* (1987), the *Historical Center of San Gimignano* (1990), the *Historical Center of Siena* (1995), the *Historical Center of Pienza* (1996), the *Val d'Orcia* (2004), the *Medici Villas and Gardens* (2013), and *Montecatini Terme* as part of the Great Spa Towns of Europe (2021).

Tuscany has many small and picturesque villages, 29 of which have been designated as the most beautiful villages in Italy.

Surrounded and crossed by major mountain chains and with few (but fertile) plains, the region is dominated by hilly country used for agriculture. Hills make up nearly two-thirds (66.5%) of the region's total area. The climate is fairly mild in the coastal areas, and is harsher and rainy in the interior, with considerable fluctuations in temperature between winter and summer giving the region a soil-building active freeze-thaw cycle. Tuscany is known for its wines, including *Chianti, Vino Nobile Montepulciano, Morellino di Scansano, Brunello di Montalcino,* and white *Vernaccia di San Gimignano.*

San Gimignano, our home base, is a small walled medieval hill town in Siena, Tuscany. Known as the Town of Fine Towers, San Gimignano is famous for its medieval architecture, unique in the preservation of about a dozen of its tower houses, which, with its hilltop setting and encircling walls, form *"an unforgettable skyline"*. Within the walls, the well-preserved buildings include notable examples of both Romanesque and *Gothic architecture*, with outstanding examples of secular buildings and churches. The *Palazzo Comunale*, the *Collegiate Church and Church of Sant> Agostino* contain frescos dating from the 14th and 15th centuries. The Historic Centre of San Gimignano is a UNESCO World Heritage Site.

Piazza Della Cisterna is the main square in town. It is triangular in shape and is surrounded by medieval houses of different dates, among them some fine examples of Romanesque and Gothic palazzos. At the center of the piazza stands a well which was the main source of water for the town's residents. The structure dates from 1346. Although much of the square has been renovated in the late 20th century, parts of the paving date from the 13th century.

*****

Thursday, April 11 — Day 17
Siena and Monteriggioni, Italy

Going to bed early last night gives us a good night's sleep and an early wake-up. After showering, dressing, and Sophia icing her knee, we head to the common breakfast room just outside our front door to the right and down six steps. Today's continental breakfast includes fruit, cereal, yogurt, croissants, juice, hard-boiled eggs salami, cheese, ham, and Francesca's mother's homemade sweet rolls. We enjoy a traditional American continental breakfast and avoid the salami and cheese. The coffee cups are small; however, I point to an American size cup on the shelf and convince Francesca to please use for my coffee during the rest of our stay.

Today's plan calls for a drive to the two small walled villages of *Monteriggioni* and *Siena*. Backing out of the parking lot, I run into the B&B sign post. It survives; however, the car's right quarter panel is *'slightly bruised.'* Sure, glad I purchased the additional rental car damage insurance. This incident will most likely result in a 500 Euros *'hickey.'* Nothing I can do about it now. So, let's get started on today's adventures.

The drive takes us through rolling hills covered with vineyards as far as the eye can see. I wonder how the farmers harvest acres and acres of grapes. Our hostess, Francesca, is very knowledgeable about the Tuscany area. At breakfast this morning, she created today's adventure and informs us local wine-masters use the grapes to create a variety of Italian red and white wines. Soil, temperatures, winds, and rain determine the growing location for distinct types of grapes.

Sophia is our crackerjack navigator. Using the Waze App, she flawlessly guides us through the countryside. For the record, Italy's 5G internet service works great even in hilly rural areas. Luigi misses a few crucial turns. Much to the dismay of the Waze directions lady, she reroutes us three times and gets us back on the correct route. Arriving at the walled city of Siena, it seems 99.99% of the free parking spots are spoken for. It appears **EVERYONE** in Italy comes to Siena on Thursday. Luckily, I spot someone pulling out of their space and cut through and around four other cars to secure the spot. While I didn't make any new friends, at least I secure a parking spot. All is fair in love, war, and claiming parking spots, too!

At a café overlooking the walled city, we enjoy coffee and a fat free, sugar free croissant. The sun is out and the balmy 70 degree temperature is ten degrees above normal. The weather continues to be fantastic on most days during our holiday.

Sophia passes on walking around the walled city. Her knee is still sore and not ready for walking up and down the hilly Siena pathways. She **GRANTS** me one hour to roam and return while she relaxes in the car. So, off I go. I have no idea where to start and how to get to the main part of town. I head down and up a 45 degree walkway and after 15 or so minutes, locate and enter the main town square.

Like most Italian towns, the town square has numerous dining establishments. Souvenir and gelato stores are commonplace and over 20 tables are set up in the middle of the square where vendors sell sweets including candy, cookies, and pastries. So far, I am 35 minutes into my one hour solo adventure. Leaving the square, I see three exits; but I cannot, for the life of me, remember which path to take. So, I take the middle fork in the road, see the church where I began my journey, and head down another 45 degree road-way. About half way down, I say to myself, "This doesn't look like the route I took to reach the square." I point and ask a *'local,'* "How do I get to that church?" He directs me to walk back up the path, turn left, and take the next alley. His directions are perfect. I follow the signs to the church and arrive 15 minutes early at our designated meeting point. I call Sophia and ask her to pick me up at the meeting location. Success! We are now on our way to our second destination.

Monteriggioni is a quaint, exceedingly small village. Around the town square, there are a few restaurants and an incredibly old church. It takes 10 to 15 minutes to walk around and window shop. We settle at a park where a large contingent of middle school aged children are playing soccer, talking, laughing, and running around after their lunch break. The teacher calls out in Italian, "It's time to go;" however, policing the area for trash is not a priority for these youngsters. The teacher then selects *'a few responsible honor roll students'* and tells them to "go pick up the trash and put it in the trash cans for your sloppy ungrateful classmates. When we return to school tomorrow, the rest of the class will use toothbrushes to clean the classrooms and bathrooms. Hopefully, they will *'get the message'* to next time, clean up their mess." Once the class has left, the local pigeons discover a *'gold mine'* and feast on the food items lying in the grass. It looks like a scene out of the movie, *The Birds*.

It's time for a late lunch. Three of the four restaurants in the town square close at 15:00 and reopen at 18:00. *Bar XXXI Canto* is currently the only restaurant open. We park ourselves at an outdoor table under a large umbrella and enjoy our Mediterranean style lunch of a mixed salad, pizza, a local beer, and wine.

On the way back to the B&B, we miss a few turns at the round-abouts driving the Waze App directions lady **CRAZY**! We hear more than *'a few choice words'* about our heritage, our country, and our *'smarts.'* There are a few times when I think she gave up on us. It didn't matter; the car rental includes unlimited kilometers.

Sophie and I decide to stop at the grocery store in the neighboring town of *Poggibonsi* to pick up some items for an evening picnic on our patio. We stop at an appliance store and get directions from the cashier. She tells us to "Go left, in front of the McDonald's. The grocery store's name is Palm." Off we go around three roundabouts. The directions are spot on.

As we enter the store, there are no shopping carts to use. I see carts in the cart collection area in the parking lot and walk back over to get one. However, they are chained together and locked up tight! *A sign indicates a customer must pay one Euro to unlock one cart!* Do you hear that??? If you want the privilege of using a cart to buy groceries, the cost is one Euro. But, and there's always a **BUT**...I have no change. I see a lady coming out of the store with a cart full of groceries. I beg her, **"PLEASE** allow me the privilege of using your cart. I have no coins on me." She gives me the **"YOU MUST PAY"** look. However, my *'help the lady'* instincts kick in and I load her groceries into her car, commandeer the cart, and head into the store. Lucky for me, there are no grocery cart police officers patrolling the parking lot.

Once inside, Sophia and I go up and down the aisles and grab some snacks, cheese, Coke Zero, sliced turkey, chicken, strawberries, and head to the self-checkout area. The head self-checkout clerk (a department of one) asks, "Cash or credit?" In unison, we say "Credit." She directs us to a specific checkout register. We pay a nominal charge for a plastic bag and head to the exit only to be stopped *'dead in our tracks'* by a **LOCKED** gate! I know we paid. I have the receipt. We are **NOT** shopping and dashing. What do we have to do to exit the store?? Seeing our plight, the *'top dog'* head self-checkout area clerk approaches, asks for our receipt, places the bar code on the receipt against a reader, and magically, the gate opens! We are out, home free, and head to our car. Sophia does her usual 100% excellent job navigating us back to our *'home away from home'*. The last stretch of the drive is two kilometers up the one way dirt road!

Time to relax, settle in, enjoy a glass of wine, and set up tonight's picnic. Francesca stops by to say hello, sees what we are doing, and brings us a basket with plates, silverware, and napkins. Francesca's father stops by again tonight with two small glasses of homemade Limoncello Italian liqueur. It's an excellent after dinner drink.

Today was a great, adventurous day! Sophia ices her knee while finishing her book. Luigi finishes the last two episodes of his Netflix eight-part series about the criminal element controlling the port of Barcelona.

Until the morning, night, night!

*****

Friday, April 12 — Day 18
Montepulciano, Italy

Our day starts with a hearty continental breakfast, including a small bowl of cold cereal, two croissants, one homemade egg bite, two homemade apple muffins, one banana, tomatoes, juice, and coffee served in my American sized coffee cup.

Today, we set out on our farthest Tuscany adventure, the town of *Montepulciano*. Our 90 minute drive takes us on various two lane country roads. The rolling green hills are full of rows and rows of vineyards, as far as the eye can see, in either direction. High up in the hills, we occasionally see large country farm houses overlooking the fields and vineyards. Thank goodness for the Waze lady. She speaks English and perfectly pronounces all names of the Italian roads and towns we pass thru. Sometimes, I miss her instructions. Yet, despite missing a few turns and two or three laps around some traffic circles searching for which exit to take, we climb the steep hills to the town of *Montepulciano*.

The higher we drive, the closer we get to the city entrance thus saving our legs for an all-out fun adventure at Rick Steves favorite Tuscany town. As many of you know, Rick is America's leading authority on European travel. He is the author of numerous books and creator of videos on the best ways to see Europe. We locate a parking spot and determine by looking at the dashboards in other parked cars, you must prepay for parking lest you run the risk of being towed to who knows where by God knows who.

The high noon sun beats down on the parking ticket machine screen, making it very difficult to read the instructions (in Italian) on how to buy a pass. After tapping every part of the screen, a message pops up saying *'press here to continue.'* The system wants me to enter the license plate number. No one told me I need to memorize it. So, back to car, I snap a picture of our now dangling license plate. The heat inside the car melts one side of the tape used to display the license plate in the rear window. Houston, we have a problem that we **MUST** deal with later today. With the aid of a local gentleman, who was also trying to buy a parking ticket, I figure out which buttons to press, enter the license plate number, purchase a four-hour pass, and place it on our dashboard.

We enter the walled, extremely hilly town. There doesn't appear to be a town center. The town offers **FREE** potty **WITH** toilet seats, a luxury since most other restrooms we used charge .50 to one Euro for the privilege of relieving oneself in bathrooms devoid of toilet seats!

Sophia is hungry. We select *RE AL Quadrato*, a small restaurant located on a narrow semi-steep, one lane road. Outdoor and indoor seating is available. Since the weather is warm, we choose an outside table under a large umbrella. We share, what else, a pizza, and plan our time in *Montepulciano*. Since her knee is sore and sometimes painful, Sophia chooses not to venture up and down the town's hilly roads. She sets out to find a bench in the park close to where we parked the car. Large shade trees provide a relaxing place to chill. I set out on foot looking for that *'just gotta have photo opportunity.'* Using my iPhone, I make various videos of the surrounding hillsides and vineyards.

Having seen *'all there is to see,'* I find Sophia engrossed in a novel. I settle onto the bench and check my email, Facebook,

ESPN sports scores, Fox News, the Las Vegas Review Journal, and watch a few mindless videos.

The park includes a small playground with two swings and a slide. The play equipment is set on a gravel rock base. I don't think the village is worried about a lawsuit. Why, there is a sign that clearly says *'Use at your own risk. The Village assumes no liability for any injuries!'*

It's now approaching 15:30. Time to begin the journey back to the B&B. When we arrive at the car, the taped on license plate has completely fallen off the back window. I lift the rear hatch and using what little strength this 75-year old body has left in it, press the license plate back on the window. As we drive away, the license plate falls off again. Luigi does not want to attract attention from the Italian police for driving a car without a license plate. It's time to find a hardware store that sells duct tape or something similar. A fruitless Google search reveals there are no Home Depots or Lowe's nearby or anywhere in Italy!

I pull into the first gas station that luckily for us has a mechanic on duty. He assesses our situation and informs us he cannot help us. I press for "Do you have any strong tape?" but get nowhere. However, he sends us to someone who can fix it! He uses my iPhone to enter directions, a two mile drive just up the road. Off we go; however, I miss an important turn and wander for 22 minutes to the destination, a full-size auto repair shop. After explaining the predicament to the owner, he assesses the situation, takes off the license plate, grabs four sheet metal screws, and reattaches the license plate!!! We are back in business. The cost is just five Euros! He also fills our empty windshield washer fluid reserve for four Euros. Off we go back to the B&B.

The 90-minute journey home turns into 2 plus hours as we continue to miss important turns the Waze App lady announces. The rerouting takes us through every small, quaint town and village in the area. Finally, at 18:00, we arrive back in San Gimignano. We are hungry. Tonight, we choose a dining establishment just outside the city's walled entrance.

I drop Sophie off at the restaurant entrance and head to the nearly parking lot. Most of the parking spaces in the lot are small. I spot a car about the size of our Jeep getting ready to leave. I patiently wait as they load their SUV and drive off. As I begin to carefully pull into the spot, an elderly Italian lady plants herself in the middle of the spot and indicates thru hand gestures and Italian that, in no uncertain terms, this is **HER** spot! She points to a large SUV unable to navigate a small parking space two rows over and gestures to her husband to bring their car around and park it here. She tells me to get out of here, get lost, move on, and find another spot you Americano shithead. **Are you kidding me??**

Luigi thinks twice—should I drive towards her and take my chances or avert an international confrontation and find another parking spot. Most likely, I will lose the argument and spend the night in jail. So, I drive away with my tail between my legs and locate two spots designed for **SMALL**, two seater Italian cars. The first spot does not work. I have no chance in hell of parking there. The angle is bad. The second spot shows promise. I inch my way in and don't hear the sound of bumpers on car doors. Success, I barely squeeze in at a horrific angle. So glad I put some Vaseline on the right side of the car! It helps me get into the parking spot. Getting out???? Forget about it now, it's time for dinner.

Sophia secures a table in *Caffe' Giardino*, a small, intimate, local restaurant. She dines on chicken cacciatore while I go with my Mediterranean dinner of a mixed salad and spaghetti. We finish off the meal by sharing Tiramisu. While Sophie stays at the restaurant, I head to the parking lot and decide to leave a *'thank you for taking my parking lot spot'* message on the dirty rear window on the vehicle of the rude Italians. Hope they can read English. "Fuck you for taking my parking spot!" I then walk to our car, back out of the tight parking spot without any difficulty, pay, go around the circle, pick up Sophie, and head for this week's home. What a day. Can't wait to see what happens on Saturday. Good night!

*****

Saturday, April 13 — Day 19
Staying Home in San Gimignano, Italy

Luigi awakens at 07:15, on a beautiful Saturday in San Gimignano. The sun the out, the birds are singing, and life is very good. I decide to call grandsons Brady and Tanner for a quick "Doggie, what's up?" conversation before they go to bed. All is well in Riverside, CA. Next, I text and call my friend and computer expert Roderick. He has successfully cracked my iCloud account and is downloading my pictures.

This morning, Francesca brings me a special breakfast treat: scrambled eggs along with the everyday offerings, and my American size cup of coffee.

Sophia proclaims in her best Italian, "I goa nowhereo todayo. I resta da body!!" So today, I set out for the laundro-mat, a mere six kilometers away to the quaint town of *Poggibonsi,* which is in the province of Siena, Tuscany. This will be my first solo driving adventure. Fortunately, I know the way to Poggibonsi like the back of my hand. Plus, the GPS generated directions are spot on **BUT**...I miss the turnoff. Lucky for me, I make a U-turn just before another traffic circle. I perfectly execute the turn and go left towards the laundromat. "You have arrived at your destination!"

bellows the Waze App lady. However, I do not see a sign for the laundromat. Maybe it's on the other side of the building.

So, I drive around and check it out. Unfortunately, I head the wrong way into a one-way alley and must pull over to allow a car to go in the correct direction. The driver gives me the fickle finger of fate... An Italian salute followed by violently shaking his left fist at me. I respond with a **"Gratz"** and Hawaiian Shaka. After this close encounter, there's the laundry! I exchange Euros for the special coins to operate both washers, load the clothes, insert the coins, press the right (I hope) buttons and son of a bitch, the machines start up and dispense the soap and water. We have the beginnings of clean clothes! It looks like a 40-minute cycle. The clothes only need 16 minutes in the dryer. Amazingly, 95% of our wardrobe comes out completely dried. With a basket full of folded clothes, I have one more stop before I head back to San Gimignano.

Prior to heading out, Sophia asks me to pick up some Aleve. My first stop is the Palm grocery store just down the street. I search the store, no Aleve anywhere. I need to find a local Farmacia. The checkout clerk provides directions. "Turn left out of the parking lot, left at the circle, go straight to the first light and turn right." Her directions are perfect! In a few minutes I park, go into the Farmacia, buy the Aleve generic brand (Aleve is not sold in Italy) and head home.

I return the neatly folded clean clothes to their correct place in our room while those slightly damp are spread out on the in room clothes drying rack.

Lunch consists of leftovers in the refrigerator. After charging my iPhone, I head out on a walk to town. I find a *'by the slice'* takeout pizza establishment and spoil myself with a slice covered in black and green olives. I climb up the hill to the town square, stop, and listen to a local musician playing the violin. On my way down the pathway, I pass on stopping at the world's best gelato stand.

Both sides of the downhill walkway include souvenir stores, what Americans would call delicatessens, clothing and jewelry stores, restaurants, pastry shops, and leather goods retailers. The smell of leather permeates the air. The weather remains unseasonably warm. Shorts and a short sleeve golf shirt embroidered *'Sentry Tournament Championship'* from my days working as a volunteer at this tournament in Maui, are the appropriate attire for the day. Two hours and 5,150 steps later, I return home and take a well needed nap.

We have 19:00 dinner reservations at *Ristorante Da Pode*. A quick shower revives this old body. Off we go. It's a mere two kilometer drive down the one lane dirt road. It seems like everything in this area is a mere two kilometers away when in reality, it's more like eight to ten kilometers. Locals have an extremely poor sense of distance.

We sit at an outdoor table under a large umbrella and gaze out at the hilly green countryside. This is by far the nicest restaurant of our holiday. Two waiters do their best to spoil us. Luigi and Sophia start the meal with a Chianti and Chardonnay, liver pate served on toasted bread (*da bomb*), and a bottle of Pellegrino. We graduate to a shared mixed green salad, lobster ravioli, spaghetti with meat sauce and black olives, and of course, the freshest, recently baked Italian bread, balsamic vinegar, and virgin olive oil. Vanilla ice cream with fresh strawberries, decaf coffee, and a cappuccino finish off a great and filling meal. The two waiters provide excellent service. We reward them with the equivalent of a $20 tip.

We return to our home away from home and settle in; however, we are unsuccessful trying to connect to Netflix or Amazon Prime on the iPad. The WIFI connection in the room is essentially non-existent. The walls of the converted barn are too thick to allow any signals to pass. I have a solution. I grab a jacket and move to the patio where the signal is strong, and the weather is delightful. After two episodes of a mindless eight episode Netflix mini-series, I retire for the night. Sophia ices the knee in bed and falls asleep with a book on her lap.

Some observations about the property:

- The views of the walled city San Gimignano and the surrounding hillsides are breathtaking.

- The property has small grassy areas. Someone cut the grass today; however, the edging and trimming is left for next week. No need to overwork oneself.

- Every time we open the door, the curtain on the inside of the door falls off.

- If we decide to watch TV, we will need two pairs of binoculars to see the small screen on the wall across the room.

*****

Sunday, April 14 — Day 20
Tuscany, Italy Small Towns and Villages

Today is our last day in Tuscany. Needless to say, this is, without a doubt, the best stop so far on our 78-day trip. The weather is unseasonably warm and sure beats cooler temperatures apparently heading our way later this week in the Cinque Terre. I prefer wearing shorts and a tee shirt or golf shirt versus loading up on layers of clothing.

This morning, we enjoy breakfast outside on the lawn. The temperature is perfect. The view of the walled city of San Gimignano in the distance makes the setting a memorable ending to a spectacular five day stay. We enjoy homemade pastries, coffee, juice, fruit, and cereal. Our hostess, Francesca, helps us plan our final day. She **STRONGLY** insists (u Musta go here you understando American tourists!) we visit the *'Chianti Region'* punctuated with many small towns and villages. We set out towards Badia, Castellina, Panzano, Greve, Radda, Gaiole, Cavriglia, and Montefioralle.

The roadways climb at least 3,500 feet above sea level and provide exceptional, long range views of the surrounding hills where farm houses, vineyards, and farms as far as the eye can see dot the landscape.

Let's talk about the **ROADS**. Not only are the climbs steep, but the roads are also narrow, 1.5 lanes, at best, in **BOTH** directions. Many sections are only one lane. Whoever gets there first gets to go first, while the other car pulls over and waits for their opening. Impatient Italian drivers in small, medium, and large cars, and daredevil teenagers and adults on motorcycles, love to tailgate and express frustration with this Americano senior citizen driver. Whenever possible, I pull over and let the *'locals'* pass. Never once did I see a *'thank you'* wave or *'thumbs up'* gesture. Our courtesy is usually met with a *'Get out of our way you stupid tourists. You are making us late for (fill in the blank).'* When I can't pull over, frustrated locals direct obscene gestures towards us and yell *'nasty words'* questioning our heritage and intelligence.

In some cases, there is less than six inches clearance between the cars going in opposite direction and the rock walls on the passenger side of our car. Motorcycles are frequently driven 100% over the speed limit. Most cyclists drive like they do on the pro motorcycle tours. Some of the homes in these small villages are perched *'right on the road.'* Stepping out your front door and not paying attention could result in you becoming a hood ornament or becoming crushed between the side of the house and the vehicle.

About 90 minutes into our journey, we see a small roadside restaurant. There are seven small outside tables; however, just two have customers enjoying lunch. We make an *'executive decision'* to stop, grab something to drink, share a salad or Panini, and use the facilities. I grab a Coke Zero. Sophie and I move outside and find a table. The hostess says, "You wanta eat?" I reply, "We'd like to split a small salad please." "Salad, you no eat (a meal)?" "No just split a salad, please." Sadly, our meal choice is **NOT** going to work. She mumbles something about a 20-minute wait. I said, "For a salad?" Obviously, she's not interested in our business. Maybe she's expecting a tour van to pull up soon with 10 hungry tourists.

Who knows? Wanting to avoid an international incident in God knows where we are, I pay 2.50 Euros for the Coke. We then go back to the car.

Back on the road, I lose count of the number of 90 and 180 degree hairpin turns. Let's leave it at **MANY.**

Locals and tourists crowd the small villages and towns and are out enjoying the great weather, local restaurants, and wineries. Parking is nonexistent. We enjoy the views as we drive on. After a few hours, the gas tank displays there's a quarter tank left. So, I pull into a self-service gas station and diligently study the instructions, which of course are in Italian. There are no buttons that say, *'press one for Italian and two for English.'* An Italian gentleman is filling his car; but, even when he senses I may not understand how to pay and dispense the gas, he fails to come to my aid. After carefully studying the display screen and payment options, I first try to use my credit card. Numerous attempts fail for who knows why. Then, I see an option to *'insert cash.'* I insert 20 Euros, select pump four, and son of gun, it works! I dispense 20 Euros worth of gas. Success, we have, I trust, enough gas to find our way back to the B&B.

Sophie and I drive through the hills for another 60 to 90 minutes. Thanks to the expertise and patience of the Waze App directions lady, we remain on course despite numerous attempts by Luigi to be adventurous and take a left or right down another country road. She nails me every time I do this essentially saying, "Hey buddy, stay on course, listen to my directions, or I could decide to delete your Waze App and leave you stranded in the hills of Tuscany. Last chance, you understando?"

Just before 15:00, we pass a cozy outdoor restaurant with long range views of the hills and vineyards. "Stop," I say? "Sophia says, "No, let's just keep going." A kilometer or so down the road, it's time to pull over and *'water the grasses.'* Sufficiently relieved, I suggest we return to the restaurant back up the hill. Sophia gives a *'thumbs up.'* We park along a dusty gravel country road and walk across the street to the entrance of *Poggio AL Sole*. The views are spectacular. We grab a table under an umbrella. A waiter greets us and says, "We're closed! Sorry." Sophie responds, "Can we at least get a glass of your best wine?" The waiter nods his head *'up and down.'* He brings two glasses of Chianti to our table. One of the owners stops by and offers us some homemade bread, olive oil, balsamic vinegar, and baked bread brushed with olive oil. The snacks are outstanding and pair well with our wine. One discussion with the owner leads to another. We learn this winery can ship a case of their wines, olive oil, and balsamic vinegar to the USA. The wine master, who also doubles as the shipping person, brings us samples of four other wines to taste. When it's all said and done, we make a large investment in wine, virgin olive oil, and balsamic vinegar. It takes about 30 days for the box to arrive at our Henderson home. I also buy a bottle of the top rated Chianti for our hostess, Francesca, in appreciation for making our stay the best!

By 17:30, we arrive back at the B&B, relax for a bit, and head to San Gimignano for a light dinner. Unbeknownst to us, the town shuts down at 19:00 on Sundays! Luckily, I find a sandwich and pastry shop and buy two paninis and two soft drinks. We have seven minutes to sit outside and devour the meal. We finish with a mere 9.32 seconds before staff scoops up the tables and chairs and puts them in the shop for the night!

We head back to the car; but first, we stop for, you guessed it, *'gelato for dessert.'*

It's now time to pack up for our 08:00 morning departure to Florence. After returning the rental car, we will head to the Florence Central Train Station and catch the noon train to *Monterosso*, one of the five towns in the *Cinque Terre*.

Just who is Francesca, our B&B hostess?

Francesca is a delightful, caring young lady. Her smile warms any room she walks into. She is always attentive and easy to laugh and converse with. She offered so many good suggestions of things to see and places to visit and explore. Francesca is the primary caretaker of bed and breakfast. She does it all, from booking reservations to setting up breakfast to cleaning the rooms. Many years ago, her parents converted an old family barn into a four-room B&B. Today, her father is the groundskeeper and maintenance man, and her mother is the baker of the delicious morning pastries.

Once in a while, you meet a person who is genuine and who makes you feel *'right at home.'* That's Francesca. Without a doubt, we will return because of the way we were treated while visiting. We are blessed to find their B&B in the San Gimignano countryside area of Tuscany. It's one of the most beautiful places one can experience.

*****

Monday, April 15 — Day 21
Monterosso, Italy

It is 06:30, time to rise, shine, and head to Florence to catch the train to *Monterosso*, one of the five villages in the *Cinque Terre*. Francesca and her father bring us breakfast which includes scrambled eggs, croissants, fruit, cereal, and coffee. We load the suitcases into the car. It's time to go. But first, we take a group photo and hug goodbye. For the last time, we drive down the dusty one lane dirt road and begin our journey to Florence.

Sophia does her usual fantastic job of getting us on the right roads to Florence. Before we enter the city limits, we need to fill the gas tank. Little did I know or factor into the equation, the instructions to pump the gas are in Italian. Seven, count them seven times I try to use my credit card. But I can't understand how to answer a question on the touch screen. The screen displays a message *'enter a code.'* What code? Or maybe it's asking how much gas I want to buy. In any event, I give up and go the *'cash money'* route. 20 Euros moves the fuel gauge needle to a half tank and another 20 Euros **ALMOST** gets the indicator just below the "Full" mark. Another five Euros later, we are *'in business.'* Off to the car rental return garage. Surprisingly, we arrive without getting lost or having any other incidents. We only miss one or two turns. The Waze App lady immediately corrects our route and gets us to the Green Motion Rental Car return garage. The rental car garage check-in clerk inspects the vehicle, notices the damage on the right quarter panel, and asks me to write down how it happened. Luckily, I bought the extra insurance coverage that has a 500 Euros deductible.

The front desk clerk confirms my purchase of the insurance policy and deductible. She tells me Green Motion needs to get an estimate of the body work to repair the car. Therefore, she cannot provide me with a final bill. She promises to email me the *'bad news'* later today! **GREAT**, another over budget trip cost. I can't wait to see the bill. Maybe I should just buy the car!

We have almost two hours to kill before our three hour journey to Monterosso. The train departs at 11:59. So, we walk across the street to *Cafe Gamberini*. We enjoy our final coffees in Florence and share a croissant. Purchasing refreshments gives us access to free, clean potty with an added bonus...toilet seats!

Ladi, the jack of all trades young counter clerk, is working today. She is the young lady who, five days ago, gave me a 17 Euros discount on our dinner bill! I try to talk to her and remind her about our earlier interactions. Unfortunately, she does not remember me. She has that, *'who the hell are you Americano tourista? Get out of my face look!'* "But, what about our plans and the promises we made to each other? Was it all just lies??", I quietly say to myself. With my tail between my legs, I pay our bill. I am devastated by the loss; but—another day, another adventure. It takes me 8.9 seconds to come back to reality.

Sophia is still hobbling and **STRONGLY SUGGESTS** that I "find a cab! There is no way in hell I can pull my suitcase and walk 3.5 blocks to the central train station." Luckily for us (i.e., me), there is a cab stand a mere half a block up the street. The cab driver places the suitcases and duffle bags in the back of the station wagon and drops us off (no long hauling thank you) at the train station entrance. We have about an hour to kill; however, the station is crowded with weekend travelers returning to who knows where. There's **NO PLACE** to sit and chill. We find a four foot section of a wall between a book store and a take-out restaurant. Sophia guards the luggage while I head to the post office to mail five postcards. I could use more Italy to America post card stamps; however, since it is Monday, the line to get service is long and wraps around the building. I'm sure I can buy stamps in Monterosso.

The large departure screen does not post the platform number until 15 minutes prior to the scheduled departure time. However, Antonio (my new name just to keep the authorities confused) notices the departure time has been moved up six minutes to 11:53. We did not receive a text or email that the departure time changed.

Sophia suggests I buy a sandwich that we can share on the train. So, off I go on a mission to buy the best Panini in the station. Upon returning, I am put in charge of guarding the luggage while Sophie heads to the bookstore for some new reading material.

The departures board shows the 11:53 train to *Pisa* leaves from track 1A. It's around the corner at the far end of the station. We enter a double deck *'local'* train that will stop 16 times in the next 75 minutes, until pulling into *Pisa*. After exiting the train in Pisa, we notice there are ten tracks at this station. Which track is the train to Monterosso leaving from? Of course, there are no signs. A slight amount of fear comes over me. Luckily, there is an elevator to take us down one level to the underground tunnel connecting the five platforms; however, there are still no signs.

The departure clock is ticking - tick, tick, tick. Do we go left or right? Sophia flips a coin and wants to go right. However, I notice travelers arriving in the tunnel from the left. So, I make an *'executive decision'*, plant Sophia in the tunnel, and go left looking for the station center and departure board. At the top of the ramp, I see the display board. Our train leaves on track five!

I head back, collect Sophia, and our luggage. We take the elevator up to the five/six platform. We have 26 minutes before we leave.

The platform is extremely long. Our reserved seats are in car two. So, the question is, will car two be at the front of the train where we are standing, or will it be at the back of the train about 300 meters down the platform? Fortunately for us, we see a message on the display board, *'First class cars are located at the back of the train.'*

Our train pulls into the station. We head down the platform towards the back of the train, push our way through many boarding passengers, and watch the train car numbers drop eight, seven, six, five, four...two more cars to go. By now, everyone but us is on the train. In unison, the conductors blow their specialty designed and unique sounding whistles signifying *'all aboard, we are leaving!'* We could be in trouble. I reach our car and lift my suitcase onto the train. Sophia is still one car behind me! Will she make it or is this another London train experience where I get on the subway, the door closes, and she is left standing on the platform just like the *'police officer/drug dealer'* subway scene in the movie French Connection? I hear the train engines start, lift her suitcase on the train, get her up the steps, just as the train door closes behind her, almost catching her left pant leg. No problem, *'piece of cake,'* we make it! We settle into our comfortable first class seats for the 90-minute ride to Monterosso.

Our hotel offers hourly van transportation from the city center. However, we just miss the 15:00 van. Plus, we have *'no clue'* where to catch the van. So, we hail a cab. If we thought the steep hilly roadways in Tuscany were challenging, the ride up the hill to the hotel breaks all kinds of fear and exciting experiences!

This is a two-lane road that is one lane wide and has at least six 180 degree hairpin turns. Formula One car drivers could not safely navigate this roadway! Finally, this 15 Euros *'A ticket ride'* ends at the entrance to our new home, *Hotel Bellevue Suisse*. We are at least 2,000 feet above sea level high. Spectacular, long range, 180-degree ocean and mountain views introduce us to Monterosso. Our room is on the second floor, has a balcony with two chairs, and a small table where we can sit and enjoy the views. Down at sea level, the weather is warm. On the balcony however, it's chilly. Tourists are lying on the beach catching some Italian rays, while others brave the 65-degree waters for a refreshing swim.

It's time for dinner. We catch the van down the hill and find a waterfront restaurant. The homemade soup and salad are great; but the deep fried calamari *'leaves a lot to be desired.'* A few glasses of wine and a bottle of beer wipe away the taste of the disappointing calamari. A short stroll down Main Street reveals the usual tourist souvenir shops and a few takeaway food counters. While waiting for the 19:30 van, Antonio, my name for the week in the Cinque Terre, checks out the main pedestrian road and finds a few restaurants we may try during our stay. Back in the room, I enjoy episodes six and seven of the eight part Netflix mini-series *"Outlaws."* Sophie finds peace and quiet in a paperback novel. Day 1 in the Cinque Terre comes to an end. Tomorrow at breakfast (which of course is included in the stay), we will develop a plan to conquer the five villages.

Cinque Terre

According to Wikipedia, the Cinque Terre, which means *'Five Lands'*, is a coastal area within Liguria, in the northwest of Italy. Along a beautifully isolated six-mile stretch of the northern Italian coast lie the five small, dramatically set villages, *Monterosso al Mare, Vernazza, Corniglia, Manarola,* and *Riomaggiore.* The five villages, the coastline, and the hillsides are all part of the Cinque Terre National Park, a UNESCO World Heritage Site. Vernazza is one of the most beautiful villages of Italy.

The Cinque Terre area is a popular tourist destination. Over the centuries, people built vineyard terraces on the rugged, steep landscape right up to the cliffs that overlook the *Ligurian Sea.* Paths, trains, and boats connect the villages as cars can only reach them with great difficulty from the outside via narrow and precarious mountain roads.

Access to Cinque Terre by car is possible, but parking is major issue. The best method of transportation is the train. Trains run from *La Spezia* to all five towns in the Cinque Terre, as well as to major regional and national destinations.

A scheduled passenger ferry runs between Monterosso and Levanto stopping at all of the main villages except Corniglia, which does not have a landing point, as it is not on the coast.

Each village is a variation on the same theme: a well-whittled, pastel jumble of homes some perched on steep hillsides, some sloping into ravines, clinging to their hillsides like crusty sea creatures in a tide pool. All five are nestled among the rocky vineyards that have allowed generations to quietly flourish here. With a traffic-free charm, a happy result of their natural isolation, these towns are the rugged alternative to the glitzy Riviera resorts nearby. This is the place to take a sightseeing breather, and inhale slower-paced Italian culture in perhaps its purest form.

Riomaggiore is the most substantial non-resort of the five towns and the farthest south. It is a fascinating tangle of colorful homes that lean on each other like drunken sailors. A cliff-hanging trail offers sweeping coastal views passing castle ruins and two churches before leading to the town's tiny harbor.

The next town up, tiny Manarola, is a picturesque tumble of buildings bunny-hopping down its ravine to a little harbor. The trail ringing the town's cemetery, on the peninsula north of the main harbor, affords some of the most strikingly beautiful town views anywhere in the region. Find a cliffside café and enjoy tasty treats born right here like pesto on your focaccia, washed down by a glass of crisp local wine that glistens with the reflection of the Mediterranean.

Talk about going local; Corniglia, with its mellow main square, is the quiet town and the only one of the five not on the water. From the train station, a footpath zigzags up nearly 400 stairs to the hilltop town. According to legend, a Roman farmer originally settled Corniglia, naming it for his mother, Cornelia (which is how Corniglia is pronounced). Locals claim that its ancient residents produced wine so widely exported that jars have been found at *Pompeii* stamped with the town name. Still today, wine is the town's lifeblood.

The fourth town up, Vernazza, is the jewel of the Cinque Terre. Its action is at the harbor, where you'll find restaurants, a bar hanging off the edge of a ruined castle, a breakwater with a promenade, and a tailgate-party street market every Tuesday morning.

Monterosso al Mare, the Cinque Terre's only resort town, is almost 'car less.' Very few cars are seen on the streets. There are lots of hotels, rentable beach umbrellas, crowds, and a thriving late-night scene. Its historic center cradles Old World charm within crooked lanes and hole-in-the-wall shops. Strolling the waterfront promenade, you can pick out each of the other Cinque Terre towns decorating the coast. After dark, hundreds of twinkling lights reflect off the water, making the town seemingly sparkle.

Vineyards, with their many terraces, fill the mountainsides beyond the towns. Someone probably, after too much local wine, calculated that the roughly 3,000 miles of terrace walls have the same amount of stonework as the Great Wall of China. We were told that wine production is down nowadays, as younger residents choose less physical work. But locals still maintain their tiny plots and proudly serve their family wines.

Hiking from village to village takes you up, down, over, and up and down the hillsides covered with grape vineyards and offers spectacular long range ocean views from high above the five villages.

Here's a brief overview of the hikes between the villages taken from local brochures explaining the trails.

Monterosso to Vernazza

The trail is easier with fewer steps if you walk from Vernazza to Monterosso. If you start in Monterosso, the trail begins with a very long and high staircase; but you will have magnificent views of the hillsides and ocean below.

The footpath is marked in white and red. If you start in Monterosso take the small pedestrian road leading to the Hotel Porto Roca. Many of the paths are narrow, uneven and have no guard rails. Vineyards dot the steep hillsides.

Vernazza to Corniglia

You can walk this path in both directions, but it is easier to start in Corniglia, taking the shuttle bus from the train station in Corniglia up to the village. After visiting Corniglia, with its lovely tiny streets with shops and restaurants, follow the signs to Vernazza. Starting in Corniglia the trail is relatively flat. Wonderful views await you as you descend towards Vernazza.

Manarola to Corniglia

If you start in Corniglia, the first part of the hiking trail has a very steep climb. To avoid the steps, you can start in Manarola by taking the shuttle bus up to Volastra. The trail starts behind the small church of Madonna della Salute in Volastra. Now the most beautiful part begins. The walk will lead you through ancient terraces that decline to the sea where grapes and olives grow thanks to heroic wine makers who produce limited quantities of quality grapes. The vineyard hike is moderately easy. You have wonderful views of the Mediterranean and the villages.

Manarola to Riomaggiore

This trail between Manarola and Riomaggiore can be done in either direction. Be warned that this hike is very strenuous. Being in very good physical condition is needed.

The villages of Riomaggiore and Manarola are very close to one another but have a very steep mountain separating them. Hikers have a half an hour challenging climb due to the number of steep stairs up over the ridge. They pass through a metal gate when crossing the high point then drop through terraced small-plot grape fields into the beautiful town for refreshments. The trail offers panoramic long range sea views.

*****

Tuesday, April 16 — Day 22
Monterosso and Hike
to Vernazza, Italy

Today, Antonio and Sophia begin week four of our journey. We are staying in Monterosso, one of the five villages in the Cinque Terre.

I can't believe we have been gone for four weeks. Seems like our European holiday *'just started.'* Maybe we will extend the trip and return to our favorite stops. Right now, Cinque Terre is leading the pack followed by San Gimignano in Tuscany. Milan and Florence have been removed from the future travel list. The Amalfi Coast, Milan, and Florence are nice; but *'been there, done that.'* They are therefore off futures travels.

We wake up to a hazy sky over the water. The sea is very active this morning. Waves aggressively crash against the shoreline and rocks tossing mist and water high in the air. It's a spectacular view to wake up to.

Our hotel bathroom has a full size shower thus ending our streak of eight days of *'showering in a phone booth.'* It's time for breakfast. So, I walk down two floors to the breakfast room. Sophia's knee is still barking so she rides the elevator down. Every guest room is assigned a table (with the room number placed on a table) for the stay. We sit down at a quaint, two-person table.

The breakfast buffet, which is included in the nightly rate, is hands down, without a doubt, the best so far on our journey. The breakfast buffet includes the usual continental breakfast items of croissants, cereal, fruit, juice, lunch meats, and cheese. It also includes Americano nourishment items such as scrambled eggs, bacon, and two types of quiche. Without *'overdoing it,'* it's time to start the day.

The hotel provides hourly van transportation to the center of town. Today's *'man behind the wheel'* drives like a retired Formula One race car driver. The one lane roadway is all **DOWNHILL** with many 180-degree hairpin turns. The driver **NEVER** blows the horn on the blind turns, choosing instead to be extremely aggressive, and not caring if a car might be coming up the hill at the same time. I time the journey— 3 minutes 12 seconds.

Sophia decides to stay at the hotel and enjoy a *'chill day'* reading, icing her knee, and enjoying the view from our room's balcony.

My plan today is to walk to and explore the Old Town section of Monterosso and later ride the train connecting the five villages to the last village, Riomaggiore. I plan to explore and learn about Riomaggiore and use the train to work my way back, stopping at each village to roam, explore, and learn what makes each village special. Little did I know that today's **EASY** exploring day would turn into something I definitely **DID NOT,** in my wildest dreams, expect.

Old Town is a combination of three and four store residential buildings, indoor and outdoor restaurants, clothing and souvenir shops, a bank, post office, drug store, and laundromat. At the ATM machine, I reload my wallet with Euros. Then, I visit the laundromat. The owner/attendant (another multitasker) recommends that I just drop off our dirty clothes. He washes, dries, and folds them. Then 24 hours later, you return, pay, and pick up your clothes. The attendant let me know the laundromat closes on Saturday and Sunday! Ok, so be it. Don't think that schedule will work for us. I am out of Italian postcard stamps to the United States, so I ask him for directions to the nearest post office. He points just up the walkway to the right; **BUT,** and there is always a **BUT** on our journeys, the post office is closed today! **CLOSED** on a Tuesday??? Why, I will never know.

The ATM machine next to the closed post office only disburses large denomination bills, so I need to get some change. I see a bank just two doors down the path. It takes me a few minutes to figure out how to navigate the bank's double locked doors security system and enter. How do I figure it out??? Easy, I squeeze in behind a local gentleman. (That's not easy to do for a fella who is 6' tall.) Upon entering, a female teller and her boss greet me with a *'Buongiorno'* and ask what brings me into the bank. I take four 50 Euro bills from my wallet and ask for smaller bills, and some Euro coins. Remember now, I **AM** in a bank that, I thought, is supposed to have money.

The teller and her boss, who is leaning on her right shoulder and lurching forward (trying to look down at her blouse, maybe???) in no uncertain hand gestures and in broken English tells me, "No givea change!" But I say, "Isn't this a bank? You don't have any money?" They repeat, "No givea change!" My first response is almost, *'you got to be shitting me!,'* this is a bank, right?!?!. All banks in the United States have money. Why the hell can't you change a few 50 Euro bills? But my discretion becomes the better part of valor and not wanting to meet the local police, I make *'new friends'* without causing an international incident knowing full well that Biden will never negotiate my release from an Italian jail or offer to trade 10 Italian bad guys for me. As I head to the door, I just can't resist dropping a parting shot—"I guess I will have to find an American bank. They have and change money!"

As mentioned earlier, today's plan calls for the train ride to Riomaggiore. Sophia is taking it easy today as her knee still troubles her. When leaving Old Town, I discover many restaurant options for dinners later in the week. As a side note, from our room balcony, we can see the next town, Vernazza. I am not sure what possesses me to follow others walking up a well-built paved path and thinking, maybe *'I will just follow the crowd and take a nice walk to Vernazza! It can't be **THAT** far.'* Well sports fans, the *'nicely paved path'* all of a sudden, without warning, turns into a hundred or so steps leading **WAY UP** the mountain.

The summit is at least a quarter mile above the clouds and just below heaven, it seems. No problem, the steps are well constructed, evenly spaced, and even with my repaired Achilles tendon, they are easy to navigate. There's even a solid wooden handrail to hold onto. This is going to be an **EASY, PIECE OF CAKE** jaunt! However, as I reach the top and turn left, I come upon a very, very steep walkway up to God knows where! Paved, even steps and the solid wooden handrail are *'a thing of the past.'* The new steps are very **UNEVEN** and the separation between each step varies in height. **REALLY**, are you shitting me?? Needless to say, this is not what I thought the walk would be like.

But, digging extra deep inside me for that *'don't give up attitude,'* I march on, hoping and praying this is the last ascent. **NOT EVEN CLOSE!** The ascent quickly turns into a steep **DOWNHILL** path. At the bottom of the hill, there is a ticket attendant. I show him my three day train and hiking pass. I politely ask him, "How far is the next town?" He replies, "Four to five kilometers and takes about two hours to hike." Using his right hand, he waves up and down to signify it's a very steep terrain. What??? I now have a **MAJOR DECISION** to make: do I **QUIT** and retreat back to Monterosso or do I *'dig deep, suck it up, take one for the team'* and go forward??? While my brain says take option one, *'retreat,'* my inner voice says—*'keep going, you can do this.'*

So, I make what I hope is a good decision and begin the assault up and down the mountainside pathway to Vernazza. Trying to accurately describe the **PATH** I travel is, to say the least, extremely difficult. There are a few level sections of the path only two feet wide and **NO** handrails. For most of the journey, I hold onto the rocky hillside that's on my left for support as I navigate over the rocks and uneven, steep rock steps. In some places, the path narrows to just 12" to 18" wide adding to the challenge! Plus, a misstep could result in tumbling hundreds of feet down the hillside to a certain death. Meanwhile, because of my slow pace I'm causing a hiker traffic jam. So, like a car, I find a place to pull over and hug the mountainside while allowing the real climbers to return to their normal, fast pace. Where do these men, women, and children of all ages train for this?

I have an interesting *'hiker'* encounter along the way. First, I run into a group of high school teenage ladies heading in the opposite direction. One says, *"Buongiorno, where you from?"* —"Las Vegas," I reply! "Las Vegas!!!!," she screams and spreads the news to her classmates. As they pass, I get a *'Las Vegas high five'* from each student! I guess I made their day.

Continuing the journey, I **MUST** stop for a large group heading towards me. I am about to descend down a long, one lane 18 inch path. A group of high school boys and girls are coming up the path towards me. I learn they are visiting from the Netherlands and are on a school trip! After I learn where they are from and why they are here, they ask me, *"Where are you from?"* — "Las Vegas," I reply. As they pass by, the large group of young men and women greet me with a chorus of *'Viva Las Vegas!'* I guess I just made their day, too.

I am amazed at how *'nonchalantly, quickly, and gracefully'* most people, both young and old, tackle this journey. Meanwhile, there's me, stumbling, bumbling, and clinging to the rocky mountainside that doesn't have very many handrails. Occasionally, I am down on all fours, crawling up *'steps,'* trying to reach the next level part of the *'path.'*

I see older people using walking sticks, men and women carrying babies and dogs, yes dogs in their backpacks, and a lady clutching her newborn baby in a *'child sack'* on her chest! Young kids bounce up and down the terrain like they are walking and running on level ground! One person is wearing flip flops (we are **NOT** in Hawaii) and another, pink clogs! **Are you serious?**

I break the record in the 75 years of age and over category for most times a senior climber pulls over and allows real hikers pass, a mere 243 stops. Occasionally, I pause and rest on flat, hillside rocks to drink some water to hydrate. My water bottle is in the right side pocket of my backpack. I cannot reach it and have zero desire to take it off. So, I do the next best thing—I ask a passerby to pluck my water bottle out of my pack and hand it to me! After refueling, I ask them to please put it back. A few souls are more than happy to help and earn their good deed badge for the day!

To my surprise, I encounter a young 20's-something couple **RUNNING**, yes **RUNNING,** down a very steep, extremely rocky path! I wonder if they are late for the train or maybe they are training for some crazy cross country, over the mountain, ultra-stupid trail race! They breeze past me without saying a word.

My journey down the rocky steps brings me into contact with two ladies from Quebec. Seeing me struggle at times, they express concern for my agility, safety, wellbeing, and mental health. "Are you ok? Are you traveling alone? Do you need help?" I assure them I am fine and can continue on my own. They mention they have walked this and other local trails before. In their opinion, this was an **EASY** trail, others are *'much harder'* and *'straight up and down'* hillsides. I also learn I had another 50+ minutes until the end of the trail! *Are you shitting me?* I just caught a glimpse of Vernazza! I bid them a *'ciao'* and offer to meet them at the end of the trail for a beer or three. I bet; however, they reach the bottom and head back before I reach the Vernazza Town Square.

On the positive side, the views are breathtaking and spectacular. I take many photos of the hillsides, the ocean, Vernazza, and the trail to prove it. There will be a nominal charge for the pictures; but, if you order now, you will get a *'good deal'!*

Just as the views of Vernazza become more spectacular, my iPhone battery dies. I didn't bring a back-up battery charger. I brought the charging cord and plug; but it doesn't take a rocket scientist to figure out there are no electric outlets on this trail. So, the remaining pictures are *'just memories.'*

The final descent into Vernazza is steep; however, I look ahead and tell myself that with every step down, I am one step closer to the end of the journey! Finally, I arrive in Vernazza tired, sweaty, hungry, and thirsty. And there's no one there to greet me, take my picture, and place a ribbon around my neck signifying I just completed the slowest walk from Monterosso to Vernazza in history! Turning right, I unsuccessfully look for someplace to eat, drink, and charge my iPhone. To my left is a small sandwich shop. I pick up a Panini and cold one then find an open seat on a bench in the town square. The Panini and beer *'hit the spot'* and fill me up. Without a doubt, my story covering this journey will become a best seller without any embellishment!

After my late lunch, I walk to the train station to head south to Riomaggiore. For whatever reason, all trains in both directions are running 18 to 30 minutes late today. Amtrak must have trained train operators, schedulers, engineers, and conductors! As the clock approaches 17:00, I decide to *'skip the ride'* to Riomaggiore for fear of getting stuck there with no possibility of getting home. So, I make an executive decision and catch the next train north to Monterosso hoping to find a place to plug in my dead iPhone. Success! I got on the train. It's packed with travelers returning home for the day. Alas, I am standing next to three electric outlets! I quickly plug in my IPhone trying to get a 10% charge and call Sophie to let her know where I am. Another success, two in a row! After exiting the train, I call Sophia, give her a *'Cliff Notes'* update on today's activities and ask about her dinner plans. She lets me know she ate a late lunch at the hotel. She tells me to eat dinner and let her know when I am heading back. I retrace my steps to Old Town looking for a restaurant that serves fresh fish.

While I find some eateries, they don't open until 18:30 and 19:00. I am not waiting 45 minutes to over an hour to eat. I recall passing a restaurant that advertised homemade pizza. Luck is now on my side. Not only do I locate the restaurant, but I also sit outside right next to an electric outlet! I *'kill'* two birds with one stone, eating and charging up! The local Italian beer is cold and refreshing. My custom order pizza includes sauce, mushrooms, black olives, garlic, and cheese. I go piggy and eat the whole pizza, along with enjoying one large and one small Moretti draft beer.

On the way back to the town square to catch the hotel van, I invest in a slice of berry crème pie to share with Sophia, a bottle of sparking (with gas) water, and a decaf Americano coffee to go. While waiting 40 minutes for the next van, I enjoy a small lemon gelato with my coffee. Don't tell Sophia I had gelato! The ride up the hill takes about three and a half minutes. My body is screaming *'that's enough abuse for today.'* I walked over 14,000 steps on my *'journey'* today, including the five kilometers up and over the *'hill'* from Monterosso to Vernazza. My *'dogs'* are barking. The Achilles tendon needs icing and resting. At the ground floor bar, the multitasking clerk, bartender, and cook fills my plastic bag with much needed ice for my tendon. During the icing process, I recount my day's journey with Sophia and show her all the pictures and videos. I finish the last episode of my eight part Netflix mini-series **"Outlaws."** I then *'brush my choppers,'* and quickly drift off to sleep as soon as my head hits the pillow. What a day...a day in my life like never before!

*****

Wednesday, April 17 — Day 23
Riomaggiore, Manarola, Corniglia, Italy

We wake up to a sunny, pleasant, warm day. There's not a cloud in the sky! The ocean is very calm. After a filling breakfast at the hotel, my mission today is to follow yesterday's plan which got sidetracked by the *'over the hill'* **DEATH MARCH** from Monterosso to Vernazza. Today, I plan to board the train in Monterosso and head south to visit Riomaggiore and on the ride back, stop at the villages of Manarola and Corniglia. Meanwhile, Sophie is still not 100%, so she decides to remain at the hotel, ice the knee, read a book, and enjoy the fantastic coastline view.

When I get to the train station, I find myself on the **WRONG** platform! So, what's new? Nobody is standing where I am. It seems all the tourists and security guards are on the platform across two train tracks. Security motions me to come over to that platform. Even though signs clearly say **DO NOT CROSS THE TRACKS**, I use three fingers on my right hand to motion like *'walk across the tracks.'* He emphatically shakes his head **NO**, adds a right index finger *'no, no, no wave,'* and points to the underground tunnel connecting the platforms. Another potential international incident is averted.

Arriving in Riomaggiore, I miss the sign pointing **RIGHT** to the main city shops and restaurants. Instead, I head **LEFT** up the street into a mostly residential area. Halfway up the path, I see a small outdoor café, hear loud music playing, and someone singing. I follow the music and see and hear the cafe counter lady dancing and energetically singing along with the music. For the memories file, I make a 12 second video. Looks like a beautiful place to *'chill'* and look at the very colorful homes built into the hillside. It's not yet noon; however, it must be noon somewhere in the world, so I order a tall cold beer. A couple sitting next to me are drinking coffee and devouring chocolate crème deserts smothered in whipped cream. While it looks like a fantastic treat, I don't think it goes well with beer, so I pass.

I settle up with the counter lady, take a *'selfie'* with her, and thank her for the great entertainment. I walk down the hill through the residential area and arrive in the center of town. Here, restaurants and shops fill both sides of the *'no cars allowed'* (except delivery vehicles) walkway. Arriving at the water's edge, the waves are crashing against the rocks sending ocean spray and water high into the boat dock area. The water is too rough today for the ferries to stop, the sunset cruises to run, and the local fishermen to fill their nets with fresh fish. The views are spectacular! The sun is glistening on the clear, light blue waters just like the waters in the Caribbean. I couldn't ask for better weather to enjoy this magnificent view.

Along the way, I come across a post office. My iPhone shows the time is 11:58 and 23 seconds. There is one customer ahead of me. When it's my turn, I calmly ask the postal clerk for six stamps to send postcards to the United States. (I **STRONGLY** recommend you sit down and *'fasten your seatbelt'* because her response is ***'off the charts and totally unbelievable.')*** **"Sorry, I can't help you!"** "What, hold on missy, isn't this a post office? Don't you sell stamps? Are you closing for lunch or forever?? I just want to buy six postcard stamps! They cost 1.50 Euros each. I'll give you ten Euros. You can keep the change." No matter what I say or how long I plead my case, her facial expression stays the same. "I can't help you" and politely asks me to leave before she calls security.

Was it my breath? Did she not like my four weeks facial hair growth? Did she have to use the toilet? Is it against union regulations to serve a customer after the noon time church bells ring out? Whatever, I stomp out without further comment or giving her the *fickle finger of fate gesture.* I made the *'wise decision'* to avoid a *'meeting'* with the Italian Postal Police.

Heading back to the train station, I look up at the hillside and see a straight up to heaven stairway for young and old alike to hike to the next village, Manarola. While my mind says, *'go for it'* and accept the challenge, my brain says *'don't even think of trying it'* — remember your hike of a lifetime yesterday? My one and only Cinque Terre, up and down and over the hillside hike from Monterosso to Vernazza ended my hiking career 24 hours ago.

Upon arriving at the train station for a no more than a three minute ride to Manarola, it's obvious that the trains today, just like yesterday, are running well behind schedule. The platforms are packed with tourists and locals heading in both directions. All of the bench seats are spoken for, so I gracefully and slowly sit down on the platform sidewalk and rest my back against a stone wall. I could easily take my hat off, place it by my ankles, sing songs, and beg for Euros! Instead, I use the 40 minute delay to finish yesterday's story. I hope to God that when the train pulls in, I can get up quickly without asking for aid. Time will tell. Next time, I might just jump down on the tracks and walk through the tunnel to the next town. I'm sure those actions will catch the attention of the local authorities who most likely will delay my return home but...

Finally, the train arrives, I board it and relax for the short train ride to Manarola. The platform there is overrun with travelers waiting to get on and off the train. The exit steps leading **DOWN** to the underground tunnel and street are jammed with people trying to walk **UP** to the platform to get on the train I just exited. My descent *'comes to a screeching halt'* for a good five minutes. Eventually, the steps and tunnel clear of passengers ascending and descending to get to where they are going.

Experiencing significant train delays during the past two days begs the question, "Did Amtrak personnel train the Italian train schedulers, engineers, conductors, and rail maintenance staff?" For a moment, I thought I was on the east coast of America, patiently waiting to board a train.

It's past 14:00 and before I set out to the next village, I decide to eat something other than pizza for lunch. I find a nice restaurant with fresh fish on the menu. I spy an inside table on the first (one floor up) floor and enjoy the sea bass seafood ravioli, indulge myself in the freshly baked bread dipped in olive oil and balsamic vinegar, and wash it all down with two cold draft beers. Desert? Why not!! The tiramisu looks decadent so, what the hell, I order it.

I slowly walk back to the train, get aboard, and travel the few minutes it takes to get to *Corniglia*, the only village with no sea access. I can't figure out what makes this village special. All I see is a long, uphill road to *'who knows where.'* About half way up, I decide to end the journey and return to the train station. Along the way, I see many lemon trees with ripe fruit dangling from the branches. I really want to grab a few lemons; however, every orchard is surrounded by fences with locked gates. So much for grabbing some souvenir fruit.

Because of the train delays, it's getting to be late afternoon. So, instead of getting off the train at Vernazza, which I briefly visited yesterday, I head back to Monterosso and check in with Sophia. She tells me she ate another late lunch, so just stop and eat dinner before heading back. So, I decide to head to Old Town Monterosso. Here, I hope to finish some writing, enjoy an adult beverage, and possibly eat a light dinner. I head to a large outdoor bar which is surprisingly empty. I grab a seat under the awnings hoping that a server will appear. After 30 minutes or so of relaxing, writing, and no waiter or waitress, I locate a *'locals'* bar for a beer and an appetizer or two. Success—I come across *El Sorago Wine Bar*. It's too cold to sit outside so, I head inside, find an empty high top table, sit down, order a tall cold draft, and a tomato, olive oil, and anchovies brochette. The light dinner is outstanding. The anchovies are fresh, with no lingering aftertaste or *'need for a breath mint.'*

It's time to get back to the town square and catch the van home. Today's step count is 11,702, about average for our trip. Sophia spent the day relaxing, reading, and enjoying the magnificent view of the mountains and ocean. We are both hoping by Saturday her knee will be stable enough to venture out for a few hours. Time will tell.

Night, night.

*****

Thursday, April 18 — Day 24
Levanto, Italy

We wake up to a weather forecast which suggest that there will be a *'significant drop in temperature'* with rain and wind. Today is going to be a nasty, unpleasant weather day. But, not to be deterred, Sophia has a *'honey do'* list for Antonio—take the dirty clothes to the laundromat, (wash, dry, and neatly fold, please), stop by the Farmacia for some Tylenol and mouthwash, find a shoe store for a can of shoe deodorant (your boots stinka), and stop at the post office for postcard stamps to America.

I have three options for the laundry chore: Option one - a *'do it yourself'* laundromat in Riomaggiore (use the train to get there and back). Option two - take the clothes to the laundromat in the Old Town section of Monterosso where they wash and dry your clothes. You *'picka up'* when done. It's not the cleanest place in Italy and the owner, operator, or the hourly counter clerk could use a shower, a shave, and a haircut. I drop this establishment for obvious reasons plus, there could be many baskets of dirty laundry ahead of us. That means it could take a day or two to wash and dry our clothes. **PLUS**, the laundry is **CLOSED** on Saturday and Sunday. Hotel front desk personnel recommend option three - a laundry only a block up and one block left from the town square where the hotel van drops passengers off. The owner washes, dries, and delivers your clothes to the hotel the same day! This makes an easy decision; I go with option three, drop off our laundry, and head to town to continue my *'honey do's.'*

Just as the rain begins to fall, *'out of nowhere,'* multiple street vendors appear selling umbrellas and rain ponchos. For a moment, I thought I was in New York City.

The cold winds are brisk and are blowing right in my face as I walk down the sidewalk, umbrella in hand, to the Farmacia. The clerk sells me Tylenol and mouthwash and sends me out the door with an *'Arrivederci.'* Next stop is the post office. I make my way through Old Town. I am an expert navigating the two narrow pathways in Old Town. I pass by restaurants with indoor and outdoor seating, shops, and gelato stores. Who in their right mind wants to sit **OUTSIDE** and eat in this weather? But some people do! Whatever! When I arrive at the post office, son of a gun, it's closed on Thursday! A sign on the door shows *'open and close times'* for each day; however, my Italian is bad. So, I shrug my shoulders, bang on and kick the door in frustration, and head back towards the train station.

Along the way, all of a sudden out of nowhere, I hear plastic snapping. The left strap on my replacement backpack breaks off! Now, if I were a one armed person, this wouldn't be a problem because I still have another strap. However, I have two arms, left and right, and Houston, *'NOW I have a problem!'* I bought the backpack in Amalfi the day after my original backpack was stolen in the Milan Central Train Station on Easter Sunday. Doing the math, this backpack served me well for three weeks and four days. I remember the vendor who sold me the backpack saying, "I make you **GOOD** deal 35 Euros! It comes with a one year money back guarantee. Should it fail for any reason, just bring it back and I give you a new one or replace it with an upgraded backpack no charge!" Unfortunately, I am now in Monterosso, in the Cinque Terre region hundreds of kilometers north of Amalfi.

Should I catch a train back to Amalfi and have it replaced? It should only take two days to make the trip down and back. With the Eurail pass, we get unlimited *'free train rides,'* so making the trip is a *'long shot'* possibility. If I had his name and phone number, I could call him for his address to mail it back; however, since it was a cash deal, I don't have a receipt or record verifying the transaction. Now, if I had a needle and thread, I could sew it back together; but I left my sewing kit at home in Henderson. So, I do the next best thing— tie the loose ends together and make it *'do for now.'*

Let's get back to today's plan. I have one day left (today) left on my three day rail and hiking pass. Hiking is a definite *'NO, NO, never again happening.'* So, like we did when it rained in Milan (we rode the Hop On Hop Off Bus all day), it's time for me to take the train up and down the five Cinque Terre villages. But first, the aroma of fresh coffee and pastries *'draws me'* into a cafe for an Americano coffee. To my surprise, the coffee comes with a small fruit pastry! No better time to catch up on my writing and enjoying locals bantering back and forth. I am not sure how this establishment makes money. It's clear that sitting at an indoor table is a prized possession given the weather outside. After 30 minutes of nursing a three ounce coffee and enjoying the pastry, I am the first to leave. Other patrons play with their phones, read the paper, or just *'hang out.'*

Back at the train station, the Cinque Terre *'local'* pulls in. Jumping on, I decide to extend today's trip one additional stop and head to Levanto, a large city of over 85,000 people. When I exit the train, the rain persists but does not discourage my *'adventurous spirit.'* The station is in a residential area of four and five story apartments, condos, and homes. I use the old *'tried and true method of getting somewhere;'* I follow the crowd. A map shows I should descend to street level, turn left and head to the town square. I am extremely aware of my surroundings because the pigeons are eating the breadcrumbs I drop to find my way back to the train station.

My first stop is at a Farmacia. I ask if they sell canes. Sophia is still **DOWN** and needs a cane to provide stability when walking. They sell one for 10.5 Euros; however, Sophia requests I send her a picture before I make a purchase. I snap a picture and text it to her. I inform the clerks I will stop on my way home to buy one if Sophia approves.

My next stop is a multi-cultured family souvenir shop. I select a few cold drinks and *'fall in love'* with a red Cinque Terre baseball hat. The hat costs 12 Euros. I hand the clerk 20 Euros; however, it appears I am the first customer of the day. The cash register only has one and two Euro coins. There are no five Euro bills in the register. He just shrugs his shoulders and appears totally confused. Then, he looks to the younger member of this family business for assistance. This man pulls out a large wad of bills and peels off a five Euro bill. Is the daily drug money haul now five Euros short? I am not *'hanging around'* to listen to their discussion. Lastly, I ask for directions to the post office. "Turn right out of the store and turn right at the first street. It's half way down the block."

Sure enough, the directions are *'spot on.'* And to my amazement, the post office is **OPEN**! Six customer service agents stand behind the counter to help people. The Italian Post Office *'system'* requires each customer take a number (like in the old days at a bakery or deli) for the service he/she requires. Given the instructions are in Italian, I look at the three choices and press the button that appears to signify *'I want to mail a letter.'* My number is P29. There are customers holding tickets with the letter *'A.'* Sure enough, three customers who enter after me have tickets A120 to A122. And as luck would have it, their numbers *'come up'* before mine. **PLEASE** don't close for lunch or the day, **PLEASE,** as one clerk shuts down Window Four and disappears. Twelve minutes later, P29 pops up on the *'next customer'* board. I let out a "**BINGO**" and confidently walk to Window Three. Using my fingers and voice, I request six postcard postage stamps to America. What could be easier? **HOWEVER** (a **BUT** is **NOT** strong enough) the clerk smiles and says (hold on to your hats now), **"WE DON'T SELL STAMPS AT THE POST OFFICE!!"**

Perplexed and caught off guard, and **NEVER** expecting to hear that, I lose it and let out a **BIG TIME** scream for all of Italy to hear, **"Hold on, this is a Post Office. You don't sell stamps!!! Are you kidding me? What do you sell here - drugs, groceries, cigarettes, lottery tickets, and train tickets???"** The clerk explains that she can *'run'* my postcards through their postage machine. However, I reply, "I don't have the postcards with me. They are in my hotel room in Monterosso!! Plus, the Monterosso Post Office in Old Town Monterosso is **ALWAYS CLOSED!!"** She senses my disappointment and frustration and asks the gentleman clerk at Window 1 if he might have a solution. He looks at me and says, "Don't you understand what the clerk at Window Three just told you??? Are you deaf or can't you hear and understand her message? We **DON'T** sell postage stamps here. Now get the hell out of here....get lost you Donald Trump loving homophobic American before I call the postal police who will lock your sorry ass up for months for disrespecting a member of the Italian government workforce! Go now, thanks for stopping by, and have a nice day! PS, you can buy stamps at a Tobacco Shop!" **Holy shit, how was I supposed to know that???** It's not covered in Cinque Terre tourist information articles. Even Rick Steves doesn't cover this in any of his travel videos and books!

So, I ask for directions to the nearest Tobacco Shop. "Turn right, go down the street other side." As I turn to leave, I see two clear exits. I am just about to press on the horizontal bar to open the door, when **ALL** the clerks in unison scream out, **"NO DO NOT PRESS THAT BAR!!"** Too bad I can't read Italian. **This door is an emergency only exit.** I wave and call out to my new besta friends, "I like to push on things!" and head out the other door. In hindsight, I should have pushed the emergency exit door. They would have had a *'story to tell.'* Plus, they would have to stay after work and spend a few hours documenting the situation for the national postal authority and local police. Press hard, you are making three copies.

Begrudgingly in the driving rain, I set out for the Tobacco Shop that is *'allegedly just down the street.'* But as luck would have it; after walking three blocks, I fail to locate the store. I duck into a *'locals'* bar that has that all important *'authentic smell of beer'* and red cracked plastic seat bar stools. Three older gentlemen are sitting in the far back left corner at a table. On their table, there's a stack of many empty beer bottles. It's not even noon; but their eyes are *'glassy and bloodshot.'* They probably wonder who the hell is this old, Americano stranger is who's entering their *'hangout.'* Clearly, he is **NOT** from around *'this neck of the woods.'* I ask the female bartender where I can find the tobacco shop on this block. She points right out the door and says, "One block up just past the restaurant." I thank her and continue on my journey. It just hasn't been my day. I find the Tobacco Shop; however, just my luck, it is **CLOSED! That's it. I give up, I surrender.** It's time to get out of this godforsaken town. They win; I lose. There is zero chance of my ever returning. Plus, this town earns and deserves a very poor review on Facebook, Instagram, and every Italian tourist website I can find. That will serve them right!.

I retrace my steps towards the train station. Passing by two very nice restaurants where pizza and Italian food dominate the menu, I thought about going in; however, I really want to *'just get out of this town.'* Just before stopping at the Farmacia to pick up Sophia's cane, I pass by what looks like a new gourmet pizza restaurant. What the heck, I decide to *'give it a try.'* The manager/owner seats me at table eight. I order a cold draft beer and the Napoli pizza with cheese, sauce, anchovies, and add black olives and mushrooms. I take some time to relax, enjoy the beer, and edit my hundreds of pictures. About 20 minutes later, I notice people who came in **AFTER** me are now eating. What happened to **MY** pizza? I flag down the manager/owner who took my order and ask, "Where's my pizza?" He says, "Napoli??" "Yes," I said. "I'll go check." Twelve minutes later, my lunch arrives. Someone apparently forgot to give my order to the pizza chef. I couldn't be angry because the pizza is great!

I recall passing a Tobacco Shop on my way into the city. Low and behold, it's still there and it's **OPEN**! I ask the 92 year old clerk who is wearing large hearing aids, for six postcard stamps to America. He pulls out a folder and counts off twelve stamps. At first, I thought he *'misheard'* me; however, I notice the value of each stamp is 50% of the value for the stamps bought in Amalfi. The owner walks over and confirms this. "Please put two stamps on each postcard." With stamps in hand, I stop at the Farmacia, buy the cane for Sophia, and head to the train station.

At the station, I learn the train to Monterosso will be leaving in five minutes. How about that valued readers and travel groupies - the train is **ON TIME**. When I am back in Monterosso, I need to kill 45 minutes before the hotel van makes its hourly pick up in the town square. To get out of the rain, I find a table in a bar/restaurant, order a glass of local red wine, and nurse it for 35 minutes. The van is on time; the ride is four minutes slower today due to the wet streets. I am home for the night. It's time to update Sophia on today's *'events,'* relax, and then head down to the lobby where a comfortable couch becomes my *'new home.'* I plan to finish writing yesterday and today's *'you are not going to believe what happened'* stories. Today's step count is 7,864. It's not bad considering the rain. Until tomorrow—good night.

*****

Friday, April 19 — Day 25
Cinque Terre Ferry Ride

I learned a valuable lesson last night—don't spend three to four hours writing Days 23 and 24 stories before bedtime. Even with the lights out and lying comfortably in bed, my mind continued to race, recanting, and visualizing the events and experiences making April 17 and 18 truly unique and memorable. To answer my friend Mike Gardner's question, I reply to his text: "Yes Mike, I am typing these stories into my iPhone Notes. Tell your wife, Debbie, the pool boy says hi."

Hotel personnel are true multi-taskers. The ladies manage the front desk, serve drinks at the lobby bar, and prepare light meals for lunch, dinner, and up till 02:00, late night snacks. No one complains or says, "That's not my job." With a smile on their faces, everyone cheerfully *'pitches in'* insuring memorable experiences for guests.

I'm up at 06:47. I see a magnificent sunrise cresting over the mountains and the ocean. The sky is a perfect aqua blue color. There's not a hint of clouds as far as the eye can see and there's not a breath of wind on this chilly 46 degree morning. The ocean is as *'still as still can be, frozen in time'* like a frozen pond in the upper peninsula of Michigan in winter and looking like *'that special moment'* magnificently captured by Thom Metcalf in one of his ocean scene paintings.

Birds, simulating the flight pattern of hang gliders, majestically and gracefully glide over the water and village. They are never in a hurry and probably understand just how lucky they are to live in Monterosso. After breakfast, I take the 09:30 van down the hill, walk to Old Town, buy an all-day ferry ticket for 41 Euros, cash only, and hop on the 10:30 boat. Meanwhile, Sophia's knee is still troubling her so she stays in the hotel room, reading a book on the balcony and enjoying the gorgeous, yet chilly day.

The ferry is full of tourists who, like me, will be exploring the coastline and the other four villages today. Luckily, I find the **LAST** seat on the upper deck. The journey offers spectacular views of each village and the hillsides. I clearly see some of the *'paths'* I navigated on Tuesday during my hike from Monterosso to Vernazza. Many of the steep hillsides are fertile farming areas where grape vineyards, vegetables, and fruit trees grow under the watchful eye of the local farmers. I see people pruning, hoeing, and weeding. There's only one person I know who would enjoy this lifestyle - our good friend, Cindy Feely. I visualize her working in the fields hours on end after finishing a two to three hour hike up and down the steep hillsides to who knows where. Back in Rockland Maine, she keeps a flourishing summer vegetable garden. She burns tree trimmings, trash, and garbage. She would be *'right at home'* here as open fires are common and do not require permission and an expensive government EPA clean air permit.

My plan is to take the ferry to the last stop, Riomaggiore, looking for things I did not see on my first visit there, and then take the ferry to Manarola.

After I depart the ferry, I head up the steps and narrow path to a great viewing area overlooking the village and the dock. Just across the way, I see a worker using a rope to pull himself up a steep, three-story stone wall. His mission is to repair and replace some of the damaged stones. Using straps, he somehow secures his body from slipping down the wall and pulls out a hammer and chisel to begin his artistry. There are **NO** safety nets three stories down. It's clear no OSHA required safety rules are in place.

Slowly, I walk the main pathway in Riomaggiore and see a lady on a fourth floor balcony hanging what appears to be a white queen size top bedsheet on a clothes line. She deftly maneuvers the clothes line left and right and uses red, green, yellow, and white clothes pins to secure the sheet. Her husband comes out with a large, white bath towel and two white hand towels to hang on the clothes line. The sheet and towels gently sway in the breezy, mid 60's, sunny day; they should be dry in an hour or two.

It's time for something to quench my thirst. A small store displays a sign, *'Fresh Squeezed Lemonade five Euros.'* While the price seems a little high, I pull out a five Euro bill and order. "No ice please," I say. I want a drink, not a glass of ice flavored with lemonade. The lemonade is cold, refreshing, and tart. My lips will be puckered for a few hours. This local, freshly squeezed drink puts frozen Minute Maid lemonade to shame.

For the second time, I stroll up and down the steep walkway passing souvenir stores, *'hole in the wall'* grocery stores, and restaurants serving you guessed it—pizza.

With nothing more to see or do in Riomaggiore, I head back to the dock and catch the 12:35 ferry one stop north to Manarola. The steps and the steep pathway from the ferry dock to the village center are *'wall to wall'* people. Why can't the people waiting to get on the ferry wait until the people exiting the ferry clear the area? Oh well. From my earlier visit to Manarola, there's not much to see and do other than hike up and down the steep pathways looking at restaurants, souvenir shops, and clothing stores.

It's just past 13:00. Without warning, my body *'fuel tank hits empty.'* I am *'out of gas, stamina, and energy.'* I dig deep for the strength to walk up the many steps and hilly paths. Above the dock, I see a large, u-shaped concrete bench. The bench becomes my home for the next 90 minutes. I *'get off my feet, try to nap, and let my body rest.'* The *'rest'* does not revive me. Clearly, it's time to end today's assault on the Cinque Terre villages and head home.

I can take the next ferry, or I can hop on the train. Not wanting to take the 100 steps down to the ferry dock, I head to the train station. My three day train pass expired yesterday. For the past three days, I only met one train conductor checking tickets, so I conclude that the odds are squarely *'in my favor to get a free ride.'* Worse case, if I see a conductor, I can duck into the bathroom and hide until the train reaches Monterosso. When I arrive at platform two, the sun beats down on the tourists patiently waiting for the next train to arrive. Unfortunately, the train is 35 minutes **BEHIND** schedule. Finally, the northbound train pulls into the station. I board and find a seat. It turns out to be my *'lucky day.'* There are no conductors checking tickets.

Arriving in Monterosso, I have 90 minutes to kill until the next hotel van arrives and takes me up the hill. Walking up the extremely steep hill to the hotel is **NOT** an option, even on a good day for a 25 year old.

I need to eat something **NOT** on the Mediterranean diet (pasta and pizza). I recall Sophie enjoying a bowl of soup at a waterfront cafe. I pour my tired and weary body into an outdoor booth and enjoy a large bowl of homemade vegetable soup and a can of Coke Zero. I still have 30 minutes to kill so I walk to the pickup point, find a bench, sit, and rest. Just behind me people of all ages sit on the beach and *'catch some Mediterranean sun.'* Spirited American and Italian music creates a festive afternoon *'beach day'* atmosphere.

It's 17:00 when I get back to the room. Sophie ate dinner at the hotel. She informs me her knee is feeling better. Hopefully, she will be able to get out and about on Saturday. Meanwhile, without hesitating, I strip down to my skivvies, jump in bed, and *'die.'* Hopefully, my body will recover with a good night's sleep, and I will wake up sometime on Saturday refreshed and ready for more exploration.

*****

Saturday, April 20 — Day 26
Old Town Monterosso, Italy

After 16-hours in bed reviving my *'worn out'* body, Antonio arises at 09:00. Today's plan is simple; *'hang out at the hotel and do nothing—just chill and recharge the body batteries.'* My goal is to get back to at least 80% or more energy level before tackling anymore *'adventures'*. Maybe I should head to town and buy a few 16-ounce Monster Energy drinks and a few sugar-free Red Bulls to get my energy back faster.

After a nourishing breakfast, I plant myself in the hotel lobby, relax on the comfortable sofa, and read three on-line newspapers to learn what's *'going on'* in Las Vegas, Philadelphia, and Maui. From what I read, nothing changes. It's the same old-same old news. I use the Fox News App to learn what's really happening in the United States and the world. Again, nothing is new...just lots of *'political noise'* and no solutions that benefit all Americans. I make a concerted effort **NOT** to discuss religion or politics in my daily writings. Sophia is happy to learn I am keeping my *'mouth shut'* and my personal beliefs to myself. On the flip side, if I start ranting, I could wind up taking a short, one-way trip straight down from our three story balcony, courtesy of my beloved wife!!

A one-hour early afternoon nap gets me over the 80% energy threshold. It's now time to do something. Sophia's right knee is feeling slightly better. So, we decide to take the hotel van down to the city center and take a cab or the local mini bus to the Old Town section of town, a place Sophia has yet to visit. It's our lucky day. As soon as we exit the van, the blue mini bus is right in front of us and is going to Old Town. The fare is 2.50 Euros per person each way; however, the bus driver asks if I have the Cinque Terre Pass Card, which I do, (but it expired two days ago but let's not let *'little details'* get in the way of a free ride) so he waves us on. When he sees Sophia taking her time to slowly climb the three steps onto the bus using her blue cane, he gives her a free ride. While on the bus, we see youngsters of all ages climbing a tall rock formation just off the shoreline. Maybe my eyes were deceiving me but I thought I see Hunter, Tanner, Brady, Christian, and Connor scaling the sharp rock formation, barefoot of course, and planning their first cliff dive. Good time to close the book on that thought.

Arriving in Old Town around 17:00, Sophia takes a few minutes to get blood flowing in her right leg. We stroll around for about 10 minutes. Not wanting to go too far into this section of Monterosso, we agree on a nice indoor/outdoor restaurant for dinner. The sun doesn't set until 20:00. So, the weather is *'just right'* thanks, in part, to no wind. *Ristorante Miretto* has a diverse menu meaning choices other than 30 varieties of pizza and 10 pasta dishes. We start with a glass of local red wine and follow by dipping the fresh, thinly sliced Italian bread in a perfect mixture of virgin olive oil and balsamic vinegar. After 20 plus days, we are getting very good at creating the *'just right mix'* of each ingredient. We share our daily mixed green salad with Italy's one and only salad dressing; you guessed it, virgin olive oil and balsamic vinegar. Don't even think of asking for ranch, thousand island, honey mustard, or blue cheese. None of these choices made it to any places we visit including Milan, Amalfi Coast, Florence, Tuscany, and the five villages of the Cinque Terre. Sophia selects the seafood ravioli while Antonio goes *'local'* selecting the anchovies stew. The local Italian anchovies are fresh and **DO NOT** give off lingering anchovies *'after taste and smell.'* We skip dessert (for now) but take our time to enjoy decaf Americano coffees. We know full well where our favorite gelato stand is right next to where we board the van back to the hotel.

We plan to take the blue mini-van bus back to the town's main square; but first, Sophia, who had not left the hotel room for four days until this excursion into town, decides to **SLOWLY** window shop. She fails to make it past one store, choosing instead to enter a jewelry store where, after 15 minutes, she purchases a *'I just have to have this'* bracelet.

Not wanting to *'overdo it'* on the first night out, we venture two more blocks before heading back to where we **HOPE** we can catch the mini-van bus. Unfortunately, after waiting 15 to 20 minutes, no bus shows up. We unsuccessfully try to locate an online bus schedule. As the sun begins to set, the air becomes cooler. It's time to *'forget about waiting for the bus'* and find a cab. Ten minutes later, I spy a cab which, for 15 Euros, takes us to where we catch the hotel van and buy a gelato to enjoy while we wait for *'our take us home'* chariot. While the cab ride price, in my opinion, is **STEEP**, I can easily rationalize the cost knowing full well the first part of tonight's journey was free. We saved five Euros getting the free bus ride to Old Town.

Watching a Netflix 91-minute movie wraps up our day. Tomorrow, we hope to use our Eurail passes and take a one-hour train to *Santa Margherita*. It is north of Monterosso on the Italian Riviera. We plan to enjoy a lakeside lunch and some sightseeing.

Today was my shortest walking day, only 2,575 steps. This will lower my daily average number of steps; but, what the heck, my body **NEEDED** the day off. So, until Sunday morning, night, night.

*****

Sunday, April 21 — Day 27
Santa Margherita, Italy

We wake to a bright, sunny, but chilly low-40 degree morning. The sea is very calm again today, like a *'sheet of ice'* with the sun glistening on it. After breakfast, I take the train to Santa Margherita, a seaside town located 50 minutes north. This area of Northern Italy is referred to as the *'Italian Riviera.'* Sophie decides to remain at the hotel, rest the knee, enjoy the view, read a book, and watch a movie on her iPad.

My Sunday morning van driver must be a part-time Formula One driver or *'wanta be.'* He casually accelerates down the steep and hairpin turn one lane road arriving at the town center in under three minutes, a new record since our arrival last Monday. Since the van schedule to town and the departing train times don't line-up, I have about an hour to kill. While seeking out a waterfront bench to sit on, I run into a preteen boy deftly dribbling a blue soccer ball. It's clear his *'feet to ball'* skills are very good. I can tell by his carefree attitude; he does not care he is in a high traffic pedestrian area. He probably thinks he is the next Renaldo or Messi. His mother calls out in Italian, "get out of the old Americano man's way. If you run into him and knock him down, he'll most likely hire one of Donald Trump's lawyers and sue us for millions of Euros, which we do not have."

I find a comfortable bench along the waterfront and spend time writing, reviewing, and editing photos. While killing time waiting for the train, I see a young man wearing a Los Angeles Dodgers baseball cap, my first siting of a non-New York Yankees baseball hat. Later in the day, I cross paths with a teenager wearing a Boston Red Sox cap.

While the sun is out, there is a mild breeze coming off the water. Today's temperatures will be in the low to mid 50's, not what I'd call a *'great beach day'*. However, even though it's not yet 11:00, people set up camp on the beach, and a few brave youngsters frolic in the clear, turquoise blue water. Ah youth!

My journey to Santa Margherita will take about 60 minutes. The train takes about 10 minutes to get to *Levanto*, where, after a 12-minute wait, I will board a second train to my final destination. As the train pulls into the Levanto Train Station, the head conductor, and what I gather is his young female assistant in training conductor, asks to see my ticket. Around her neck, the assistant carries a credit card processing machine and an electronic tablet that checks tickets. Here is where the *'you've got to be kidding me not so much fun part of my day starts.'* I show my Eurail Pass QR code and show a photo of today's schedule for the train I am on. The schedule clearly states, *'For pass holders, you don't have to buy a reserved seat. Just get on board the train.'* **That's exactly what I did!** However, when their hand held electronic device brings up my train travel records, they inform me my **NEXT TRIP** using the Eurail pass is not until Tuesday when we leave Monterosso and head to Tirano. "That's right," I say, that's the reserved seat I bought for the next segment of our European holiday.

However, since today's journey is **NOT** in my Eurail pass travel records, **they INSIST I MUST pay 60 Euros for the 10-minute trip from Monterosso.** Emphatically, I repeat my story over and over, adding some *'colorful language'* to make my point. **Facts fail**

to sway them. I think the head conductor is trying to impress his female trainee on how to be **tough** with American passengers. In my opinion, both fail to use *'common sense'* to assess this situation. After all, they can clearly see I have an active two month Eurail pass. Why would I try to sneak onto this train for a free ride? **When the train stops, I say, "I am not paying anything. This is (fill in the blank) _____ ridiculous," adding more colorful language for emphasis purposes only.**

I get off the train and attempt to distance myself from them. However, Mr. Big Shot train conductor and his young trainee follow me down the platform. They attempt to block my way. They also signal for a very large train security officer to *'join the party.'* Standing inches close to my left arm, he makes his presence known. **I am effectively surrounded.** Mr. Head Conductor emphatically, and very loudly, presents me with two alternatives: 1) Pay 60 Euros now (their train is pulling out in less than two minutes) or 2) the security officer will escort you to the police station where you will be forced to pay a 300 Euros fine and spend time in lockup. There is no negotiation, *'no give and take,'* or *'no common sense'* trying to deal with him. **He is close minded and emphatic, "pay or go to jail," period, paragraph, end of story.** He refuses to look at the facts. (I wonder to myself if he gets a % of this outrageous ticket price which is calculated from where the train **STARTED** its journey (**NOT** where I got on) to where we are standing.)

Our *'discussion'* gets even more heated. My language gets colorful, calling them every name in the book and telling them what I think of their *'customer service'* and *'common sense.'* I hope they understand, **"This is fucking bullshit!"** Adding insult to injury, my phone loses its weak internet connection. I reboot the phone twice trying to redisplay my evidence. **The clock is ticking down on their train's departure, tick, tick, tick.** People on both platforms use their iPhones to record a video of our *'discussion.'*

Who knows, I might find myself in a Facebook or Instagram video post. I hope they record my good side and get lots of '*likes*'! Time is running out. In my mind I have two options: 1) Fight Italy's largest train company Trenitalia, get hauled off to the police station, most likely get an Italian and Interpol police record, and be forced to pay a 300 Euros non-refundable fine. (I suspect that trying to explain my side of the story to the Italian police doesn't sound like a '*fair fight.*'); 2) Pay the assistant conductor 60 Euros, live to fight another day, and explain what happened to the train company weekend ticket agent in the train station. I just love dealing with weekend help! Finally, time is up. The conductors are blowing their '*get on the train now*' whistles.

The train is about to pull out of the station. It's D-day and H-hour. Tension mounts. If I get hauled off to jail, will Sophia come to rescue me? Will my good friends Dale and Griff post my bail if need be? Am I about to get hauled off to the police station in cuffs? The security guy has the cuffs out and ready to '*hook me up.*' Or do I relent and pay the outrageous 60 Euros? My brain quickly processes the options and ramifications of what my decision will be. **Pay or go to jail, get an international police record, and pay the 300 Euros fine.** '*Discretion and common sense become the better part of valor.*' So, I surrender, choose option two, and pay the 60 Euros, save the receipt, and reiterate, in no uncertain terms, what I think of their customer service and how they can sexually satisfy themselves. **I close by looking them right in the eye and saying, "I will have your jobs. This is bullshit!"**

The next train to Santa Margherita doesn't leave for another hour. So, I walk over to the Trenitalia ticket counter and calmly explain to the weekend ticket lady what just transpired. While she expresses sympathy and concern, **BUT**, yes another **BUT**, there is nothing, squat, zero 0, she can do to remedy the situation right now! However, I can fill out a Complaint Form and drop it off at any Trenitalia train station ticket office. After she hands me the form, I ask, "After I complete the form, will I be able to talk to someone about what happened and get the issue quickly resolved?" "No," she says. "All you can do is drop off the completed form. Someone will contact you with the final resolution." Great, I wonder how long that will take. But, I have a backup plan. Once I get out of Italy, I will call my credit card company and set up a **DO NOT PAY** dispute claim. Citibank is very good at handling my prior dispute claims so I feel semi-confident that this will work if Trenitalia refuses to refund my money. (**UPDATE: My DO NOT PAY request was approved by Trenitalia. They waived the bogus charge and emailed me a *'we are sorry this happened letter.'* HA!! DON'T MESS WITH THE BIG GUY!**)

My next question revolves around getting on the next train to Santa Margherita **WITHOUT** the journey listed in my Eurail travel account. The clerk sells me a three Euros reserved seat ticket and says, "good luck in trying to explain your *'story'* to the train conductor." She closes by saying, "Arrivederci, have a nice day sir and **THANKS** for choosing Trenitalia for your travel today, Next customer pleasea."

I still have a good 30 to 40 minutes to kill. I find *'just the right spot'* in the train station where the internet connection is *'barely working.'* It's *'just'* slightly better than the early 1990's AOL dialup connection, **BUT** I get a connection! After numerous attempts, I locate my Eurail pass travel plans and **FINALLY** figure out how to **ADD** today's journey into my account. I successfully press the *'magic button'* and **ADD** the first segment (which I paid 60 Euros for), then add the next segment to Santa Margherita. Lastly, I add two travel time choices (18:30 and 19:30) for my return trip to Monterosso. Just like that, all four trips are now in my account!

While standing on the platform waiting for the 13:00 train to Santa Margherita, an overweight elderly security guard starts talking to me (in Italian, of course) about the argument and confrontation with Mr. Big Shot train conductor 45-minutes ago. I could tell by his body language and hand gestures that he thoroughly disagrees with Mr. Big Shot and expresses sorrow for the unnecessary situation he put me through. All I could say was, "Thanks, I appreciate your concern, Arrivederci!"

The train to Santa Margherita arrives. I board and take my assigned seat. I am sharing a four seat *'face to face'* sitting area (I am in aisle seat 8-A) with an Italian couple. The gentleman is doing a crossword puzzle. "Sorry sir, no can helpa u."

My phone is running out of juice. I pull out my charging cord and plug it into four different outlets; but, to my dismay, none work! So, I resort to using my precious backup battery.

Here's something that will *'curl your hair.'* During the 40-minute ride to Santa Margherita, **NO** train conductor asks to see my Eurail pass and ticket! **You can't make this shit up!**

At 14:00, I finally arrive in Santa Margherita. The views are magnificent from the station platform high above the city. Colorful buildings line the right side of Main Street with the Mediterranean Sea on the left. After climbing down 40 or so steps, I arrive on Main Street and start snapping photos to share with Sophia. It feels like I am in *Newport Beach, Marina Del Ray,* or am strolling down *Rodeo Drive in Beverly Hills, California.*

In the distance, I see the ferry boat that travels to *Portofino,* a secluded village where the rich and famous *'hang out.'* The trip takes 30 or so minutes each way. After purchasing a 16 Euros round trip ticket, I board ferry and find a prime viewing seat on the upper deck. With iPhone in hand, I snap picture after picture and record multiple videos to share the landscape and journey with Sophia.

The ferry docks in a small, protected cove lined on two sides with restaurants and shops. Again, I snap picture after picture and scan the landscape to find *'just the right spot'* to enjoy lunch. The sun is out. The weather is just perfect on this Spring Sunday afternoon. I walk over to a high end waterfront restaurant on the far left end of the cove. There is no open table to sit down at. So, I patiently wait 15 to 20 minutes for a table to clear.

It really *'pisses me off'* when I see couples who have **CLEARLY** finished their meals just sitting there playing with their phones. They have no regard for the restaurant owner who likes to quickly *'turn tables'* for other customers. Finally, a table opens up. I order a beer and peruse the menu. Not only are the prices a little bit *'steep,'* but there is also nothing on the menu that *'suits my pallet.'* So, I call the waiter over, *'make up a story'* I have to leave, and pay the eight Euros beer tab (no seating charge!). I move from restaurant to restaurant checking out the menus for that just *'something special'* meal; however, nothing looks inviting. I have my heart set on fresh fish; however, I don't really want to dissect baked or grilled shrimp that have *'head to toe body parts and eyes'* attached. Plus, most whole fish grilled options come with the bones, tail, and head in place. So, I leave the waterfront area and stroll up the hill. I discover additional eating options. Not wanting to eat another pizza, I enter a small café, pass on a multitude of sandwich options, including hamburgers and hot dogs, and order a bowl of spaghetti with meat sauce. I wash it down with a tall, cold *Moretti* beer. The portion size was *'just enough'* to *'satisfy my appetite and take the edge off.'*

It's closing in on 16:00. Time to take the ferry back to Santa Margherita and work my way back to the train station. The weather is changing. It's getting dark and starting to cloud over. Rain is forecast for the late afternoon.

Back in the city, after a 30-minute boat ride, it starts to rain. The temperature drops. Glad I brought a light jacket. I need to find a *'gentlemen's lounge'* as my father used to call the men's room. Most of the restaurants are closed until 19:00 or don't serve a snack and a drink. Thus, I can't buy *'something'* and *'use their facilities.'* Finally, I come across a small indoor/outdoor cafe and settle into an inside corner table. Potty is **FREE** when ordering a drink. I order an Americano coffee and a piece of apple cake. Nourished and *'comfortable,'* it's time to head down the street and up the 40 plus steps to the train station.

A steady rain is falling now. My hoodie covers my head. Today, of course, I made a conscious decision **NOT** to bring my umbrella. I take the underground walkway to track three, sit on a bench, and watch rain steadily fall from the sky. I call my sister, Barbara, who is living in Ocean City, New Jersey, to let her know I sent eight postcards. Plus, I am alive, well, and enjoy watching rain fall while sitting on a train platform in Italy. Today is another Amtrak day, the train is six minutes late. But that's a lot better than the two 30 plus minute delays experienced this week on the Cinque Terre local that runs between the five villages.

My first class seat - A8 - is in car one. Thinking that the first car of the inbound 12 car train will be car one, I head to the far left end of the platform. **BUT**, and we know there is **ALWAYS** a **BUT,** I ask the conductor if the first car is car one. He points and replies, "Last Car!" Who would have thunk it? Only in Italy is car 12 first and car one last!

There is no way, even if I were 100-meter gold medal champion, and Olympian, Bob Hayes, could I get **CLOSE** to car one before the train pulls out. All of a sudden, everyone but me is on the train! The conductors, in unison, blow their special train conductor whistles meaning, *'get on now or forget it,'* the train is about to pull out. I scurry up the steps onto car 11 and as the train rolls towards the next stop, carefully scoot past people who, for whatever reason, are standing in the aisles. This is definitely another contact *'nice to* *meet you'* sport. Slowly, I work my way up to car six. When you pass between cars, you push a green button to open the floor-to-ceiling clear acrylic sliding door which allows entry/exit to the next car. No problem. I quickly work my way forward. Suddenly, the train stops. I hop off and dash as fast as I can towards the front car. Again, whistles blow signifying *'get on or see you later.'* I am now in car three. I have two more cars to navigate. I continually wedge myself between people heading to the rear of the train. However, there's always a **BUT** - the doors between car three and car two only open about two inches. There is no way in hell I can squeeze through even if I am a skinny kid like my grandson, Connor. I press the button that opens the door a few more times, without success. Since it is Sunday, there is no reason to go on a mission to find train maintenance. So, I push with *'all I got'* and force the doors open!

Thinking I am now in car one, I see someone sitting in my assigned seat! Is someone trying to get a free seat in the first class section? I motion, *'excuse me but that's my seat.'* The gentleman, who is bigger than Ben Labrador times two, pulls out his ticket and shows me he is sitting in the **RIGHT** seat. Mr. Americano, this is car two! Your seat is in the next car up! It's just another *'tail between my legs'* moment. I head to car one and settle into my seat with time to spare before the train stops in Monterosso. Within a few minutes, here comes Joe conductor wearing his official Trenitalia uniform, including a hat that appears to be one size too small. I am ready for him. I have my reserved seat, first class ticket QR code and my two month Eurail pass QR code on my phone ready for him to inspect. Son of a bitch, I did it right! No arguments like *'you are on the wrong train in the wrong car on the wrong day'* or any combination thereof. My pulse and heartbeat slow to normal ranges.

When I go back to the hotel in Monerosso later tonight, I will write my *'I want a 60 Euros refund for the first segment on this day trip'* story. I still maintain that the conductors could clearly see I possess an active, two month Eurail pass and could clearly see on the written train schedule that, *'Just board the train, no ticket needed.'* However, they insisted that my train pass travel plan *'did not'* show this trip.

Arriving in Monterosso, I have only 2-minutes to kill before the next hotel van stops in the town square. I hustle to the closest takeaway restaurant and purchase a Panini for dinner. It's raining so the streets are empty. Lucky for me, I get my order in **JUST** before the restaurant closes for the night. I am their last customer so I purchase a ham and cheese Panini. Right on schedule, the van arrives and takes me up the hill to the hotel. I call and ask Sophia to please open the room door.

I survived making it home alive and well after today's *'adventure.'* **You can't make this shit up!** There must be a movie or TV producer somewhere who could create a 30 minute comedy special about today's encounter.

P.S. When I tell Sophia about the incident on the first train ride, she thankfully commends me for my decision **NOT** to go to jail. If I chose to go that route, she half-heartedly told me she would have gathered up her belongings, got on a plane for Las Vegas, and left me behind to deal with the law.

P.S.S. While standing on the train platform in Santa Margherita, looking down at the tracks at the tunnel that runs thru the mountainside, the tunnel entrance/exit reminds me of one my favorite World War II movies made in 1965: Von Ryan's Express, starring Frank Sinatra. The film depicts a group of Allied prisoners of war (POWs) who conduct a daring escape by hijacking the freight train carrying the POWs and fleeing through German-occupied Italy to Switzerland. In the final scene when the Nazis were chasing down the train, Colonel Von Ryan (nicknamed "Von" because he allegedly helped the camp Commandant) races out of the tunnel and down the train tracks desperately trying to catch up to the train escaping to Switzerland.

The remaining Army commanders, standing on the rear train car landing are frantically encouraging him to *'Run Ryan Run'* as fast as he can while extending their arms and hands to help him get aboard the train. However, the Nazi commander, who is about 40 yards behind the train, grabs a machine gun and shoots him. Ryan falls dead on the railroad ties between the tracks. Sadly, and in stunned horror, the Allied POWs watch their leader die.

If you want to see the movie, it is available on Amazon Prime! I call Sophia and ask her to rent it for tonight's viewing pleasure. She succeeds. It's the best $3.00 we spend today. We finish the day lying in bed watching this all-time classic.

Today's 9,352 step count provides a full day of exercise and an unexpected encounter with Trenitalia train conductors. I wonder what could happen tomorrow?

*****

Monday, April 22 — Day 28
Monterosso, Italy

It's time to celebrate! We are four solid weeks into our European holiday! Today is also our final day in the Cinque Terre. During our stay—except for one day—the weather has been great. However, the previous night, a rain storm, complete with numerous flashes of lightning, loud thunder, and intense winds rolled in. Mike Gardner, you missed a *'good one.'*

Today, the forecast calls for *'off and on'* rain and wind with temperatures ranging from the mid 40's to the low 50's. It's definitely **NOT** a day for shorts and a tee shirt. The cold, blustery morning *'feels like'* a crisp, fall day. The ocean again is flat, no waves crash into the shoreline. Sophie decides that Antonio needs to make a final trip to the laundromat. She wants to make sure I *'no catcha coldo'* on this cold, blustery day, so I don a long sleeve, navy blue turtleneck, a heavy, rose colored Rio Secco (love dropping names) golf vest, a black and grey Under Amour hoodie, a navy blue sock hat, and black gloves. I am ready for whatever the early morning weather throws at me!.

To ensure I get to the laundry early since we're leaving Tuesday morning, I skip the breakfast buffet, catch the 09:30 van to town, walk one block up, and make a quick left at the local corner grocery—the kind of store that populated many corners in big American cities prior to the creation of the modern day large supermarkets and convenience stores—to the laundromat. There is a sign posted on the locked front door indicating the owner would be *'right back.'* Given it is Monday, as we have come to know, many establishments close on Mondays. I wonder how the owner defines *'I will be right back?'* Will it be a quick 15-minutes, one-hour, today, or this week? Great, I just **LOVE** sitting outside on a 43 degree overcast day on a *'bench'* that appears ready to *'give way'* if I suddenly shift my weight.

It's my lucky day. The owner returns in 13 minutes and determines I have one load. The cost is 17 Euros. The clean clothes will be delivered to the hotel by 16:30. I stop at the local grocery store and purchase some fresh fruit; two bananas, one apple and one plum. The store has an old fashioned produce scale. The clerk weighs each item and prints a cash resister type receipt, which I hand to the cashier when checking out.

I have 40-minutes to kill until the hotel van returns for the ride back. It's Monday and as I mentioned before, some stores and restaurants close. Plus, today's forecast of nasty, cold, windy, and rainy weather will limit foot traffic along the oceanfront walkway. Right now, it's cold, windy, and starting to rain. The hotel breakfast buffet will be closed before I return. So, I find a table inside our favorite *'locals hangout'* and order a lemon crème donut and an Americano coffee. Many locals, both young and old, order squares of deep dish pizza with a variety of toppings or a six-inch personal size pizza to enjoy with their espresso, Americano coffee, or cappuccinos. *'Whatever floats your boat to get your morning started is good by me.'*

When I return to the hotel, Sophie is lounging in our room. I hang out in the lobby on my favorite couch and finish writing Sunday's story. I use the iPad to complete the Trenitalia complaint form covering the *'incident'* with the train conductors and create five evidence attachments to back up *'my story.'* The front desk lady, Barbara, a German lady from Munich who married an Italian, suggests I email her the report and attachments. She graciously prints two sets for me. *"Grazie"* Barbara!

Now that the *'administrative'* work is done, I pull out the iPhone to catch up on reading three daily papers and Fox News. It's about 16:00 so I *'collect'* Sophia and we head down the hill for dinner. But first, Antonio goes over to the Trenitalia Train Station office to turn in the complaint form. Agent one directs me to agent two, the senior ticket agent on duty today. I hand her the documentation to review. The two young ticket agents speak very good English. After reading my *'what happened story,'* she is flabbergasted by the *'Joe Friday of Dragnet just the facts please sir'* report. She calls in the assistant customer service agent who works in the platform area. This agent is decked out in her official red Trenitalia company jacket embroidered with *'Assistant Customer Service Agent.'* After reading the report, she is also confused and says, "Did this **REALLY** happen? Why did the conductor charge you 60 Euros, which is the fare from where the train started, not where you said you got on in Monterosso?" Obviously, that was new news to me as I didn't know there were separate fees! The two ladies make a few phone calls and go over my story one more time. "Yes, I got on the train at 11:45 in Monterosso. Yes, the documentation from the train schedule says, *'just board'* and yes, I **FORGOT** to push the button to add the trip to my Eurail travel pass log."

The first agent adds her investigatory comments to the form and signs it. She explains she submits the report *'up chain of command.'* I understand. She further gives me a signed receipt indicating she read and understood the complaint. Finally, she informs me the company *'powers to be'* at the corporate customer service complaint department will email me their verdict within 30 days. I thank both ladies for their understanding, concern, and excellent service. I also receive a six Euros refund for two reserved train seats we do not need. Lastly, I ask the first agent on what track tomorrow's train IC

666 to Milan is scheduled to arrive on. She told me that this daily train normally arrives on track one; but check the TV monitors in the station just to be on the *'safe side.'* Also, there is an elevator from street level to platform at the end of the station. Hauling two suitcases and Sophia up 40 plus steps tomorrow is just *'not in the cards'*.

The walk to and from the Old Town section of Monterosso is just too far for Sophia. Her knee is bothering her again. So, we head, one last time, to our favorite *'locals'* place, find an inside table, enjoy a few adult beverages, and eat a light dinner. No gelato tonight. That establishment is closed; remember it's Monday. We catch the 19:30 van back to the hotel, pack up, and retire for the evening. When packing, we discover we have somehow, and somewhere, *'misplaced'* one umbrella, one pair of my favorite black pants, and one black electric outlet converter. Losing a few items is not bad for 28 days in Italy!

P.S. Shout to my grandson, Tanner. Here's something to consider for the DeMatteo's Woodcrest location in Riverside County—while it is already a top takeout and delivery pizza restaurant—expand the menu to include breakfast items like sliced pizza, coffee, and a small variety of pastries.

*****

Tuesday, April 23 — Day 29
Monterosso, Italy to Tirano, Italy

Today, we start week five of our holiday. It's a travel day. The weather is not good on getaway day. It's cloudy, raining, and cold. We are up at 07:15, shower, get dressed, close up the suitcases, hustle to breakfast, pay our bill, and local 13 Euros city tax (cash only please). This morning, I meet a nice gentleman at breakfast. He is a partner in a Nashville CPA firm. I mention I worked for Price Waterhouse in Philadelphia from 1971 to 1975. We discuss our European travels and adventures. I offer tips on *'things to do'* in the Cinque Terre, including the *'death march'* hikes between villages. He is heading to Switzerland later in the week. So, I promise to email him suggestions on where to stay and eat based on our journey to Switzerland, which we are starting today.

Sophie and Antonio say our *'good byes'* to the restaurant and office staff. Their professional service creates a fantastic experience for travelers. For the better part of the week, they took great care of Sophia as she rested her sore right knee.

We have two escape plans to get to the train station for our 10:32 train to Milan, then onto Tirano. Plan one calls for taking a cab from the hotel to the Monterosso Train Station. The hotel desk clerk arranges a 09:25 pickup. Plan two covers what to do if the cab *'no shows.'* Should the cab fail to arrive on time, which can happen based on the hotel's hilltop location, we will take the 09:30

van down the hill and walk or grab a cab to travel a quarter mile to the train station. It's 09:29, no cab.

So, we hop in the hotel van. Upon reaching the town square, Sophia says she can *'gut it out, take one for the team'* and walk to the train station as long as she can use the umbrella and I push the two suitcases. This works for me. We ride up the elevator to platform one and bump into many travelers standing undercover, out of the rain, waiting for their train to arrive. The Trenitalia ticket agent is the same young lady who handled my complaint yesterday afternoon. She confirms our train, which is 35-minutes behind schedule, will now depart at 11:07. We exchange *'Arrivederci.'* She remembers me, but then again, why would she *'ever, ever, ever'* forget me and my *'you won't believe what happened to me on Sunday on the train to Santa Margherita with the Macho train conductor and his trainee assistant!!!.'* (Go back and read the Sunday, April 21, Day 27 story for the complete details.)

Should Sophia and I *'act macho,'* stand outside under the roof, and expose our bodies to the chilly and wet elements? Or do we head over to the station's small cafe, park ourselves in a warm environment *'out of the elements,'* enjoy a coffee and cappuccino, and wait for train number IC666. This is really not a hard decision; we choose option two. I navigate down five steps dragging the suitcases one in each hard, execute a perfect 9.9 gymnastic like landing, and assist Sophia down. We squeeze into a small table for two and begin the wait. Sophia makes friends with a Southern California couple sitting next to us.

It's getting close to departure time, so we head back to the platform. With the assistance of a Good Samaritan, Antonio lifts the luggage up five steep steps to the platform and assists Sophia up as well. Our reserved seats to Milan are in car one. I ask the platform agent if car one is first or last. She points left towards the tunnel indicating car one is the **FIRST** car on this journey. The dispatcher comes over the loudspeaker and announces the train's pending arrival. Quickly, (two, 75 year olds *'moving'* quickly may **NOT** be considered quick **BUT**...) we head to the left end of the platform to *'beat the crowd rush'* hoping to climb aboard first. Mission accomplished! We get on, store the luggage, find our seats, take off wet jackets, and settle in for a two-hour ride to Milan. We know through experience that travelers only get seconds to board the train before the conductors blow their whistles meaning *'it's now or never—get on or get back.'* The train **MUST** get back on schedule no matter what!

There is a very good chance we will miss our connection in Milan to Tirano because our train from Monterosso departed over 30 minutes late. So, to be on the safe side, I book another train two hours later at 15:30. Reserved seats are not required for this local train. All we need to do is get on the 23 train to Tirano in northern Italy. Time will tell which train we will get on, either the 13:30 or the 15:30.

Once we get outside of Monterosso, It turns into a beautiful afternoon. The ride is smooth. We pass thru villages, small towns, and settlements perched on steep hillsides. Lake Como is visible on the right. The views are majestic. The train engineer makes up part of the 35-minute delay by not stopping at the first two stops in Milan. I guess those passengers will have to find another train, bus, or cab to their destination, or just walk.

Upon arriving in Milan, the station clock displays 14:14. Our connecting train to Tirano is scheduled to leave at 14:20. We have a chance to make a connection! Scanning the large Departure board, Antonio *'thinks'* he reads the train to Tirano leaves on track three. We are at track one. I alert Sophia. We zigzag thru masses of people getting off numerous arriving trains. We are like two salmon trying to swim **UPSTREAM** thru rapids flowing strongly **AGAINST** us. Again, the clock is ticking. We get to

track three, scamper to the last car, jump on and.....I quickly *'sense'*
..... **SOMETHING IS WRONG!** Why am I standing in front
of a door leading into a first class car? We have reservations on a 23
stop *'local train'* that has **NO** first class section and requires no seat
reservations. This train is about to pull out! All of a sudden, a conductor appears, senses our confusion, reads our body language, and
asks, "Where are you two going?" "Tirano," I reply. "Dissa traino
NO GOA Tirano, goa to Trano. You twoa Americanos have just
seconds to getta offa disa traino right nowa!"

I scramble down three steep steps, grab each suitcase, lift them
down to the platform, and help Sophia get off the train. We **JUST**
get off in the nick of time. If Sophia was three seconds slower, the
train door would have sandwiched her in the doorway. What the
hell just happened?? Clearly, I am going to take **BIG BULLETS**
from Sophia for this almost disastrous chain of events. Hey, "No
harm, no foul," I say. However, Sophia is **CLEARLY** upset with
me. I, on the other hand, feel completely *'OK.'* Why you ask? We
just avoided disaster!

We slowly walk back towards the Milan Central Train Station
area to recheck the departures board. I notice our train to **TIRANO**
is 30 minutes behind schedule! The departure track is not posted
until 15 minutes prior to leaving. *Just to take the edge off and calm
down the situation,'* we need a bite to eat and adult beverages. About
halfway down the departure waiting area, we spot a take away cafe
with seats on the expanded platform. The menu choices include
Paninis, salads, pastries, a variety of hot and cold drinks, beer, and
wine. Slowly, we maneuver towards a small table. There are two
empty chairs. In fact, these are the **ONLY** two open chairs in the
courtyard setting. We instantly become acquainted with two older
ladies, one who speaks no English and one who becomes Sophia's
'new bestie.' One of the ladies is from Tirano! She is on her way to

the Vatican Library in Vatican City to do some religious research....
IMPRESSIVE to say the least!

The departure board shows that our train (RE2828) to Tirano
departs from platform six. When we board the local train, most of
the seats are *'spoken for.'* However, a nice lady and her young son see
our predicament and give us their seats! Do we look that forlorn,
that old, that disheveled? Their *'good deed'* shows there is good in
the world! The train pulls out of the station. We have a 2.5 hour
ride to Tirano. For some strange reason, the train conductor doesn't
check our Eurail passes.

The train rolls through old towns with homes almost right on
the tracks! *'Up close and personal,'* if you know what I mean. Later
in the journey, we ride on the east side of lakes, part of the Lake
Como system. We see large estates lining the shoreline and hillsides.
This area is where the *'rich and famous'* live, we're told. This area of
Italy is definitely a potential vacation spot for us *'down the road.'* We
fondly remember our five days when we stayed lakeside, between
Bellagio and Como, 11 years ago.

During the train journey, Antonio makes a pit stop. While
searching for the flush button, I accidentally press the *'Need Help
in the Bathroom'* button. Before *'help'* arrives, I scamper back to
my seat before anyone knows that I was the culprit. I relax and
finish yesterday's journal notes for this story. Mike Gardner, this
is when I do some of my best writing, my friend.

We are getting close to our destination, only three or four
more stops to go. Suddenly, an announcement, in Italian of course,
comes over the loudspeaker. We fail to understand or compre-
hend the message. However, we notice **EVERYONE** is getting
OFF the train. **THAT SHOULD TELL US SOMETHING!**
What's going on? We are the only passengers remaining in our
train car! A conductor finally shows up and says, "You two going
to Milan?" "Milan?" I reply. "No, we are going to Tirano!" She

points to the train on the next track and says, "**THAT'S** the train to Tirano! **GET OFF!** You better **HURRY** as that train is about to leave the station!"

We scramble out of our seats, grab the bags and suitcases, hastily toss our luggage onto the platform and jump down. All of a sudden, the train door closes; however, Sophia is still on the train heading back to Milan! She frantically pushes the green *'open door'* button. Success— it opens! I help her down. Both of us then scamper across the platform dragging our luggage towards the other train. The conductor sees our plight and stops the door from closing or else we will not make it!!

Shaken up, but none the worse for wear, our new train **SLOWLY** starts the climb up the hill to Tirano. However, *'something'* seems strange. The original train schedule not only didn't have this train change, but it also shows Tirano is only two stops ahead! This train makes **FREQUENT** stops at places where there is **NO** station! What's going on? Are we dropping people off at their houses?? What kind of train is this? Is it really going to our destination? Sophia is **CLEARLY UPSET** and to say the least, '**NOT HAPPY**' with the situation and me! Panic overwhelms her; however, a passenger exiting the train points to the monitor and says, "Tirano next stop." The color returns to her face. Thankfully, we didn't have that *'almost unwanted bowel movement moment.'*

We exit the train, enter the town square, and see our hotel 100 meters straight ahead! Our prepaid check-in is delayed about 12 to 15 minutes by the guy ahead of us. **HE** doesn't have a reservation, and his credit card is not working. Let's go buddy, pay, or leave! We are tired, we want to check in and get to our room.

Finally, it is our turn to check in. We prepaid the night's stay through Booking.Com. The check-in clerk hands us our room key. We proceed to take the elevator up two floors. Our room, 201, is right next to the elevator. We don't have far to walk! The room is clean but *'compact.'* The bedroom consists of two twin beds pushed together leaving about six inches max on each side. Two, three-drawer night stands are placed **SIDEWAYS,** so they fit into the six inch space. Good luck trying to access the drawers! The shower is a *'miniature replica of a London phone booth,'* about 20" x 30" max. Don't try turning around or try to pick up the bar of soap if it drops to the shower floor. You will have a *'Houston, we have a problem moment!'* The Euro style room heating system moves hot water through the pipes. There is no thermostat in the room to control the temperature. Thermostats that control the temperature in each room are located at the front desk! In the morning, I learn if the room is too warm or cold, guests can call down to the front desk. There, someone can adjust the room temperature. I visualize a large electric display board, similar to a control board at central railway headquarters tracking all train movements, with up and down sliding switches for each room to adjust the room temperature.

Tired from a long day of travel delays and a few missteps, Sophia points to the hotel restaurant and says, "We are eating here. The menu looks very good." Well, *'hats off'* to Sophia. She makes an **EXCELLENT** decision. We haven't had beef since we left home on March 26. Since then, we have been on the Mediterranean diet, pasta, and pizza. Sophie orders the Chateaubriand for two. We share a house green salad. Wine and beer *'get us going.'* Our waitress, Victoria, is a young lady with dual Brazilian and Italian citizenship. Her grandfather was born in Italy before moving to Brazil. Her English is very good. She is poised, professional, and chose to move here to gain more experience speaking English as she plans to enroll in a university in England and study law. Her parents and brother live here. So, she has housing and *'banks'* her earnings for college. Both Sophia and I are fortunate to meet this goal oriented young lady.

The meal is better than advertised. The thin slices of medium rare beef garnished with béarnaise sauce melt in our mouths. Despite being *'stuffed,'* we order Victoria's desert recommendation, an apple crisp cake. She tops it off with a scoop of homemade vanilla ice cream and, of course, whipped cream. We finish the meal with decaf Americano coffees, one with hot milk, and one with cold milk. The price for this outstanding meal is a mere 102 Euros: very, very reasonable. We leave a 20 Euros tip for outstanding service.

Tomorrow, we will board the Bernina Express at 14:22 for the four-hour ride through the mountains and small villages into southern Switzerland. We will arrive in Chur, Switzerland for another *'one night stand.'* So, from Tirano, Italy, Sophia and I say good night and sweet dreams!

P.S. when this day started, I thought there would be **VERY LITTLE** to write about. Boy was I wrong. **You just can't make this stuff up!**

*****

Final Thoughts And Observations
After 27 Days In Italy

- Ashtrays are placed at every restaurant table even though there is a "No Smoking" sign.

- Walking down the street is a contact sport.....no one gives an inch.

- Our bowels have been in an uproar adjusting to the carb loading pasta, pizza, bread, balsamic vinegar and virgin olive oil, beer, wine, and gelato.

- We are seriously thinking of writing to the IOC (International Olympic Committee) suggesting that farting become an Olympic sport in 2028. Just like boxing, there could be men and women categories by weight. Team competition could be men, women, and mixed couples, like ice skating. The judges would evaluate the individuals and teams on four categories, including time, (length of time passing gas), sound, clarity, and fragrance. Right now, we are running far ahead in the mixed couple division and most likely will set an Olympic record that would be hard to beat in the coming years.

- Italians eat dinner starting at 19:00, way too late for us.

- Bus drivers could *'give a shit'* if they don't stop where you ask them to.

- When boarding a train, you better be **ON** the train when the conductors blow their whistles else you could be left on the platform or sandwiched between the closing doors.

- Salami and cheese are featured foods on a breakfast buffet.

- If you want milk in your coffee, be sure to specify **COLD MILK** or else you get a pot of hot foamy milk.

- When you stop and ask someone for directions, your destination is **ALWAYS** 2KM away.

- Map reading for Italians is a prehistoric event.

- Kleenex is non-existent in hotel and B&B rooms.

- Turning **ON** the electricity in most hotel rooms requires you to insert the room key into a slot by the front door.

- The speed limit on all roadways is clearly a **SUGGESTION** or **OPTIONAL** for cars, buses, scooters, and motorcycles.

- Hotel elevators are very small. There's room for max two people and two suitcases.

- Many USA prescription drugs are available *'over the counter'* without a doctor's prescription and are reasonably priced.

- When out and about, be aware of your surroundings and keep your possessions secure and safe. Leave valuables in the hotel safe.

- Italian sandwiches and Paninis **NEVER** include more than one very thin slice of meat and one slice of cheese between two and a half inch pieces of bread. They need to go to Subway, Port of Subs, Jersey Mikes, and other American sandwich stores to learn how to make a **REAL** sandwich. Italian Paninis beg the question??? Where's the meat?

- Toilet seats are **OPTIONAL** and are more often than not missing in public bathrooms.

- Toilet doors sometimes don't lock, so be prepared to meet a new friend while sitting there playing with your phone.

- People take their dogs everywhere—on trains, buses, subways, hiking trails, and around town. Some transport their animals in a back pack or baby carriage.

- No matter how large the glass, a glass of wine **NEVER** exceeds four ounces.

- Coffee comes in very **SMALL** cups. There are **NO** free refills.

- Open fires burning trimmings and whatever are allowed without permit or EPA approval.

- Tanner and Zack, there is no doubt in my mind both of you could get a job **TODAY** first making pizzas, then managing a chain of pizza establishments throughout Italy. At the restaurant I am looking at now, you would be required to wear a maroon Italian shirt and hat.

- New York Yankees baseball caps are the most popular MLB baseball caps worn in Italy.

- Luckily, the Cinque Terre villages sit right on the Ligurian Sea (which, as you didn't already know, is a part of the Mediterranean) so it's easy to take a dip and cool off.

- The Amalfi Coast (Italian: Costiera Amalfitana) is a stretch of coastline on the northern coast of the Salerno Gulf on the Tyrrhenian Sea, located in the Province of Salerno of southern Italy.

- I would not visit Milan or Florence again. Big cities have too many tourists. Only go if you want to shop, shop, shop.

- Tuscany is a very beautiful area. It's a wonderful place to drive through the countryside, visit walled cities and wineries, and is a restful place to chill. We would consider going back to San Gimignano.

- We could also consider going back to the Amalfi Coast and staying in the Amalfi city center or the two small villages: Minori and Maiori.

- We recommend to anyone visiting the Cinque Terre that you can see it all in four to five days unless you are an avid, in-shape hiker. You can stroll the four villages in two days, take the ferry to visit the Isle of Capri and Positano, and chill one day.

- In every restaurant, each table has a number. When it's time to pay, you go to the check-out person standing at the cash register and give him/her your table number. He/she finds your bill and runs your credit card.

Things I wanted to do but didn't:

1. Ring doorbells on apartment buildings or condos and say "*Buongiorno Amazon.*"

2. Stop at someone's home and say, "Buongiorno. I am Luigi, a third cousin on mother's side of the family and dis is my bride to be, Sophia! Chia! Can we stay with you for a week or two? Someone stole my backpack with all our train tickets and cash. I am sure u no minda helpa family members!"

3. In a restaurant, passing a table where people are eating while being led to our table, I would love to say, "What kind of pizza did you order? Looks very good. Can I have a piece?"

Business opportunities:

1. Selling pretzel nuggets, sticks, and regular good old American pretzels.

2. Portable disposable toilet seats.

*****

Wednesday, April 24 — Day 30
Tirano Italy, Bernina Express and Chur, Switzerland

We have been *'going hard'* the last few days, so we sleep in till 09:00. Then we shower, dress, and head to the breakfast buffet. First, here's a big **SHOUT OUT** to my son Bob, aka *'Bobby Hoops.'* Today is his 48th birthday. Happy birthday buddy: we love and miss you.

For the first time on this trip, real American butter pads are part of the breakfast offerings! We *'do'* the daily continental breakfast, check out as required at 10:30, store our luggage with the front desk clerk, and walk around the old section of Tirano. It's a pleasant, sunny morning. There's just a slight breeze that keeps things comfortable. The views of the surrounding mountains are outstanding. We take many photos, mosey about town, and discover a local bakery. Here, we *'invest in'* cookies and *'to die for'* desserts to enjoy later on as we continue our journey.

For lunch, I enjoy a small beer, and Sophia drinks ginger ale. We split a Panini. Our ham, cheese, lettuce, and tomato warmed up sandwich between two **THICK** pieces of bread beg the question, *'where's the stuff that makes a sandwich **GREAT**?'* The one ultra-thin slice of Parma ham and cheese, the **ONE** small lettuce leaf, and one thin slice of tomato clearly show why the sandwich costs only five Euros. The gross profit has to be 4.50 Euros or higher!

Someone needs to teach all Italian Panini sandwich makers how to make a **REAL** sandwich. Boy, do I miss Port of Subs, in my humble opinion, the **BEST** sandwich in Las Vegas.

After lunch, we finish our walk around town and land back at our hotel. We collect our bags and at 14:00, board car number one, and settle into our comfortable first class reserved seats on the Bernina Express, bound for Chur, Switzerland. At 14:22, the train pulls out. Our scenic journey begins.

The cars have large scenic windows. We share a four-seat area with retired school teachers from Sydney, Australia. They are world travelers. While Sophia and the retired Australian school teacher remain in their seats, her husband and I head to the back of the car (car one is the last car) and snap pictures of the country-side. A window is half open, allowing us to take photos without getting reflections off the glass windows. For four hours, we rotate positions at the rear window to allow each of us to take hundreds of pictures and numerous videos. The views of the snow covered mountains and countryside are *'hard to put into words.'* Let's leave it at everything is beautiful!

During the train ride, we pass thru numerous small towns, enter, and exit approximately 55 tunnels, travel over 196 bridges, and around six 360 loops (roundabouts). The best way to get a clear understanding of the ride is to Google *'Bernina Express'* videos.

Ciao Italy, hello Switzerland. At 18:30, the train pulls into Chur. Antonio is now Luca and Sophia is now known as Greta. Changing our names in every country we visit keeps the local authorities *'guessing'* (and our readers, too!) My iPhone shows three percent battery power left. Our backup battery is drained. I call the hotel for directions and the location of the nearest taxi stand. Something is missing during the conversation exchange. So, I head out the train station door searching for a cab. With one percent power left, I call the hotel again and learn we went out of the

WRONG train station exit. We retrace our steps and head back through the tunnel that takes us underneath the 14 track station. Twenty-six steps up to street level is not what Greta needs to climb. Fortunately, we locate an elevator, ride up to street level, and bingo, there's a cab waiting for us!

My iPhone is *'out of juice.'* The hotel name and address are in the files on the iPad. Fortunately, I retrieve the hotel name and address for the driver from the iPad. Less than five minutes later, we arrive at the hotel where the owner warmly greets us! She has owned the business for more than 40 years, lives with her husband on the hotel's 6th floor, and manages the day to day operations, including preparing the daily breakfast.

After settling in, our host recommends two restaurants for dinner. Both are less than one kilometer down the street. We walk down the street, review the menus, (the prices in Switzerland are twice that in Italy!!) and settle on the first recommendation, *Drei Könige (3 Kings)*. The restaurant is 225 years young and decorated like a hunting lodge. A variety of animal heads and antlers cover the walls. You *'feel'* like you are dining in a 200+ year old restaurant! I can only imagine what it was like back in the 18th and 19th Centuries when royal banquets were served here and the town's leaders could be found *'talking story'* in the smoke filled back room.

The manager/waiter/bartender, and busser (a multi-tasker to say the least) explains the menu and the list of ingredients. We have no clue about the ingredients. Greta selects the baked chicken breast smothered in tomato sauce, the seasonal veggies, and a potato pancake. Luca goes *'local'* ordering veal wrapped in something with a nice sauce (the menu says it's a sausage roll; but it bears no resemblance to a sausage), the seasonal veggies, and the potato pancake. We start the meal sharing a mixed green salad that, for the first time on this trip, comes with **REAL** salad dressing, **NOT** virgin olive oil and balsamic vinegar! We pass on desert, coffee, and *'waddle'* back to the hotel.

A light rain begins to fall. We run into the hotel owner and enjoy a decaf coffee in the small, five seat bar. The coffee is excellent. We think the owner brews Americano decaf coffees! We inquire about the coffee brand. To our surprise, she shows us a jar of **Nescafé Gold** instant decaf! It's made in Switzerland. We never would guess it is instant coffee because it sure didn't taste like it. Its 22:30, time for bed after a day of traveling through the mountains and small towns in Switzerland. Tomorrow at 12:14, our journey takes us from Chur to Zermatt, a six hour train ride through snow covered Swiss mountains! Good night from a quaint hotel in Chur.

*****

Friday, April 25 — Day 31
Chur to Zermatt Switzerland
Via The Glacier Express

Greta and Luca wake-up around 08:00 in Chur, Switzerland. Our room is on the fifth floor and offers a nice view of this section of town. Looking out our bedroom window, we see the mountains received a light dusting of snow last night.

Today is the second day of our two, *'one night stands.'* Unfortunately, our **POSSE** took off leaving us on our own. It's a nippy 34 degrees outside. Our cold weather clothes have spent most of the trip in our suitcases. Today, they are *'now in play'* and we will be dressed in them for at least the next three days in Zermatt, where the **HIGH** temperatures are predicted to be from the 20's to the mid-40's.

Shower time. After studying the various knobs on the five speed shower, I determine which one controls the hot and cold water and which one controls the rain shower or the hand held device. After dressing in our winter wardrobe, it's time to head to the breakfast buffet. Being on the fifth floor, we decide **NOT** to tackle the steep steps down to the lobby. So, we use the elevator.

The breakfast buffet is again included in the nightly room rate. Our streak of *'free breakfasts'* started on April 1. After trying *'one of everything'* on the buffet, it's time to check out and locate an ATM machine or a bank. I follow the hotel owner's directions and instead of walking left, I take a right. Realizing my mistake, I ask a local resident if he knows the location of an ATM machine. "To take out money?" he says. "Yes," I reply. He points down the walkway. "There's an ATM on the left." I head in that direction and, *'low and behold'*, find the ATM. I pull out my Wells Fargo ATM card and insert it into the machine.

After entering my pin number, *'Invalid Card'* appears on the screen. **No way Jack! So, I try again, same result! Is the magnetic strip or the chip damaged? This can't be happening!** The card worked a few days ago. Prior to sending out a **WTF** scream, I try the adjoining ATM machine and **BINGO**, the card works! The screen displays a message *'Do you want large or small bills'*? I thought I pressed *'small;'* however, the machine dispenses 20's and 50's, not exactly what I consider *'small'* bills. Okay, whatever, I now have some cash. Switzerland is not part of the European Union. They have their own currency — Swiss Francs.

Turning around, I see a bank right in front of me. Remembering my experience in Italy where I unsuccessfully tried to change large Euro bills into smaller bills, I feel very confident that *'something good'* will happen in a Swiss bank. Two female bank employees stand behind the counter and flank a male teller. I assume he is a *'teller in training.'* After explaining what I need, he takes my 300 Swiss Francs, runs them thru a money counting machine, and asks, "How would you like your change?" He enters the number of 10 and 20 Swiss Franc bills that add up to 240 Swiss Francs and hands me the cash. The remaining 60 Swiss Francs are converted to one and five Swiss Franc coins. Swiss currency does not have five or one Swiss Franc bills. Amazing, I am in a bank that not only has money but can also make change!

It's time to reunite with Greta and take a taxi to the train station for our 12:14 departure on the Glacier Express, a six hour scenic train ride to *Zermatt*.

A little bit about the *Glacier Express* from the website: "The Glacier Express route through the Alps takes eight hours from St. Moritz to Zermatt and boasts spectacular panoramic views, bridges, and tunnels. The journey in what has been dubbed the world's slowest express train takes travelers across the Alps in roughly eight hours, passing through 91 tunnels and over 291 bridges."

We will ride the train from Chur to Zermatt in our reserved, first class seats that include a three course lunch.

The train staff is friendly and professional. *'Joe muscles train greeter and conductor'* takes our suitcases and places them in the train car's storage area. He makes it look so easy!

A Taiwanese family — mom, dad, and Carina, their 30-year-old daughter, sit across the aisle from us. Carina's English is very good. She completed her studies in Boston but chose to take her marketing degree back to Taiwan.

Greta and Luca enjoy their meal. The first course is a mixed salad. While eating the second course of creamed chicken, seasonal veggies, and a wild rice medley, our new Taiwan *'besties'* take out their *'we brought our own lunch'* consisting of a green salad, oranges, blueberries, strawberries, and a sandwich.

Quick memo to Joe Biden regarding his falling over backwards (literally sometimes) catering to the progressive far left members of the Democratic Party and their green energy demands and war on fossil fuels — Switzerland runs on clean, efficient electricity that seamlessly moves trains throughout their country. As we ride through the countryside, nary a windmill is seen.

Switzerland uses trains extensively every day to transport passengers and goods around the region. They include:

1. SBB (Schweizerische BundesBahn): The national railway company.
2. High-speed trains: ICE, Railjet, Eurocity, and TGV Lyria connecting Switzerland to Germany, Austria, Italy, and France.
3. Regional and Intercity services: RegioExpress, Regio, InterCity, InterRegio, and S-Bahn operating within the country

The scenic view from the train is very hard to accurately describe. But I'll give it a go.

Dandelions are abundant on the lush green hillsides. Small and large villages set on hillsides and in valleys are perfectly laid out, usually around a small, community church. Snow-capped mountains stretch for miles on either side of the train. Every now and then, we see adventurous hikers walking on snow covered paths. The sun creates a strong glare on the snow covered hills. Avalanche barricades are aptly placed on hillsides to prevent dangerous outcomes for homes and rail lines by out of control snow tumbling down hillsides. Ski lifts take avid skiers thousands of meters up the ski slopes. The melting snow creates impressive waterfalls sending clear and crisp ice cold water tumbling hundreds of feet down hillsides into streams.

Halfway through the journey, the trains stops and waits for another train to pass on this one track section of the route. Good choice. Passengers can exit the train cars and gaze at and enjoy the sheer beauty of the snow covered mountains. There is an unusual, but apparently common occurrence when one trains passes another on the one track section of this route. Passengers get off the train for about five minutes and snap touristy pictures of themselves and the countryside. Everyone has their iPhones out snapping pictures of the surrounding area, group pictures, and selfies. A young German couple asks Luca to *'make a photo'* for them using their iPhone. "My normal rate is five Euros a photo; but today is your lucky day, **FREE**." Once the other train passes and the conductor yells "All aboard," one better get back on the train quickly, or else they'll be left behind, miles from nowhere.

Note to grandsons Hunter, Brady, and Tanner: there are many, many snowboarding opportunities in Switzerland. I suggest that your save your money, plan a trip to this beautiful country, and go exploring while you are young and *'NOT tied down.'* No, the bank of Papa Keoni will not be financing travel to Switzerland!

In the town of Andermatt, the train stops. Rail personnel replace the current engine with a new one for the remainder of the journey. A stronger engine is needed because the air is thinner at this altitude.

While walking up and down our train car aisle, I meet a lady who lives in Willow Grove, Pennsylvania, roughly half a mile from the first house I purchased in May 1974.

Back on the train, and after a full six hours of riding through the Swiss mountains and countryside, we arrive *'safe and sound'* at 18:15 in Zermatt for our three night stay. It's cold and although the hotel is *'close by,'* we take a four minute, 15 Swiss Francs cab ride to our hotel. Believe me, at these prices, we will walk for the rest of our stay! Things are a bit more expensive here than they were in Italy.

Once checked into our new home, the *Hotel Butterfly BS Signature*, we unpack and head out into the cool night. The *'roadway/path'* through Zermatt's tourist area only allows taxi cabs and delivery trucks access. Along the way, we check the menus at various restaurants. Believe me, Zermatt is an **EXPENSIVE** ski resort town just like Aspen, Colorado. We settle for *The Derby* restaurant, order a ginger ale, a glass of wine, and two cups of soup that cost, hold onto your hats, $38.10! **This is beyond outrageous!** We may look for a grocery store for in-room dining for the next two nights.

Back at the hotel, I spend time with the front desk lady reviewing a map of the area and highlighting the important places to visit during our two day stay. It's been a long day of traveling and changing hotels. Time to deposit our weary bodies into bed, recount today's scenery, and dream of upcoming adventures in Zermatt. Nighty, night!!

*****

Friday, April 26 — Day 32
Zermatt, Switzerland

Our bodies say, *'Rest, stay in bed.'* We rise at 08:20 to a partly cloudy, one degree above freezing, 33-degree morning. We are ready to launch day one of our two day attack on Zermatt. Our initial Plan A calls for us to take the 09:15 train up to *Gornergrat.* That ship has sailed. There's no way we can do that! So, we immediately implement Plan B. Luca and Greta shower, get dressed, and head to the breakfast buffet.

Today's mountain assault will take us to a very high elevated, much colder environment. I am prepared. All of my *'keep him warm clothing'* is now in play after 30 plus days of being hauled around Italy. Out comes the long john's, extra heavy mountain man socks, a long sleeve black Footjoy compression shirt, and my Rio Secco rose colored golf vest. Other accessories include an Under Amour black and grey hoodie, a heavy zip up black jacket, gloves, scarf, and a navy blue sock hat! (Griff, my friend, you forgot to send me off with packs of hand warmers bro!) Greta is *'thinking'* long pants, long underwear, a long sleeve rose colored shirt, sweater, coat, heavy white hat, gloves, and scarf. We are properly dressed and ready to tackle the elements for our invasion of Zermatt!

The breakfast buffet has the usual array of hot and cold items plus small, bite size cooked sausages, a collection of exotic cheeses, lunch meats, pancakes, rice, baked beans, jams, jellies, grandma's homemade breakfast cake with apples, and a butter dispensing machine. Two machines produce a variety of coffee drinks.

Zermatt is a *'no cars'* city. Only box style cabs (good for hauling suitcases and skis) and small delivery vehicles are permitted to operate on the main tourist area roadway. Some residents ride bikes. Most ride the trains, buses, or walk. Scooters and motorcycles are banned.

We walk to the ticket office and purchase two round trip tickets on the 10:55 train up to Gornergrat. Don't ask what these two round trip tickets cost. Ok, a total of 210 Swiss Francs!!! (Approximately, $257 but who's counting?) We rationalize the cost by thinking, *'we are on vacation and we only go around once in life'*! The round trip excursion allows us to get *'on and off'* at four mountainside villages. The price **NOW** makes much more sense! **NOT!**

The cogwheel train that takes us up 3,100 meters (or 10,170 feet for those scoring at home) to Gornergrat. A little history about the special train from their website:

"On August 20, 1898, the Gornergrat Railway made history as the first electric cogwheel railway in Switzerland, reaching the Gornergrat summit at an elevation of 3,089 meters for the very first time. The Gornergrat offers a unique panoramic view of the Matterhorn and stands as a true natural wonder. It takes 33 minutes for the train to climb 1,469 meters over a distance of 9.4 kilometers (5.2 miles), which we can all agree, is impressive."

On a clear day at the summit, travelers will witness the breathtaking sight of the Matterhorn, 28 other peaks over 4,000 meters (13,123 feet) high, and the Gorner Glacier.

Luca hopes and prays the views at the top are spectacular and that it is a cloudless sky because I can't tell from the confines of the hotel. The train company does not offer refunds or rain checks if the mountaintops are covered in fog or clouds or any other *'you can't see the mountain peaks'* weather event. It's time to board the train for our 30 minute ride to the summit. Today's 10:55 five-car train up to the summit is 99% Asian tour groups enjoying their holiday.

Travel expert Rick Steves, who I relied heavily on while doing my research, recommends sitting on the right side of the train car going up and down. When we back get home to Henderson, I will surely watch Rick Steves' video episodes of traveling through Switzerland and say, "We were there!"

Today is the third Swiss rail engineering marvel we experience. So far, we've travelled on the *Bernina Express*, the *Panorama Express*, and now, the *Gornergrat* cog wheel train! Sitting on the right side, we marvel at the deep snow banks which are mere inches away from the train. We also see animal footprints in the snow and spectacular views of the snow covered hillsides.

We get off the train at the summit. Greta feels a little dizzy—altitude sickness, maybe? I plop her down in the coffee shop and, after making sure she's okay, I go searching for that *'just right'* picture of the surrounding mountains. Black birds gracefully float through the cool air and recognize just how lucky they are to live here. Unfortunately, the clouds haven't lifted enough to see the Matterhorn; however, we can watch a YouTube video tonight and say, "We were there!" While I am taking pictures from all angles, Greta makes *'new friends'* with a group from the Philippines. On our way back to the train, we *'cross paths'* with yesterday's new friends from Taiwan.

It is time to head back down the mountain. We get off at the second stop on the way down, *Riffelberg*, which is 3,582 meters (8,471 feet) above sea level. We enjoy a light lunch at a small, funky cafe with both inside (our choice) and outside seating. We split a Swiss hot dog and wash it down with a beer and cappuccino. Sheepskin rugs cover chairs sitting outside. I imagine this place is a *'gold mine'* in the summer tourist and winter ski season. And being the only place in *'Dodge,'* it has a captive audience that keeps the drink prices high.

On the ride down, I record a number of videos to remember this day's trip. Greta and I return to Zermatt at 14:30, walk the *'no cars street,'* and window shop. At 16:10, we return to the hotel for afternoon tea.

I use this time to chill, relax, edit pictures, and text some pictures to family and friends. My body is saying **SLOW** down. We spent a lot of time outside today in the cold weather, which is turning Luca's Italian sun tan into cold, weathered, almost frost bitten skin.

It's time for a quick, inexpensive dinner. I pass on McDonalds (yes, there are McDonald's in Switzerland and we can eat there anytime we want at home). I remember passing a local sports bar 200 or so meters up the street. Success. We enter the *Brown Cow* bar and restaurant. There are no seats in the bar area. A women's gymnastics match is playing on the TV. Sports on TV in Italy and Switzerland include team handball, soccer, bicycle racing, rugby, darts, as well as auto and motorcycle racing. There's no baseball, American football, hoops, or hockey. We find a small open table for two in the back corner. Luca orders a large, local Swiss draft beer and a bowl of beef vegetable soup while Greta goes *'American,'* ordering a cheeseburger, fries, and a glass of wine. Our friendly and spirited young waiter quickly brings the drinks and food. The *'dynamic duo'* enjoys the excellent meal and excellent price, only 48 Swiss Francs! We stroll back to the hotel to plan our final day in Zermatt, then retire for the night!

Zermatt

From Wikipedia, here's a brief overview of this magical town. Zermatt, in southern Switzerland's Valais canton, is a mountain resort renowned for skiing, climbing, and hiking. Its main street,

Bahnhofstrasse, is lined with boutique shops, hotels, and restaurants. Skiers from all over the world flock to Zermatt. The town sits at an elevation of 5,315 feet. Over 6,000 residents make Zermatt their year round home.

Zermatt lies at the foot of the Matterhorn. It is almost completely surrounded by the high mountains of the Pennine Alps. The town's touristic development is closely linked to what is most probably the world's most famous mountain. The vacation destination is a car-free zone, has preserved its original character, and offers nearly unlimited excursion possibilities.

Much of the local economy is based on tourism, with about half of the jobs in town in hotels or restaurants. Just under half of all apartments are vacation apartments. Over one-third of the permanent population was born in the town, while another third moved to Zermatt from outside Switzerland.

The town of Zermatt, while dense, is geographically small. There are three main streets which run along the banks of the Matter Vispa, and numerous cross-streets, especially around the train station and the church which forms the center of Zermatt.

Zermatt has a subarctic climate. Summertime is cool, with mild days and cool nights, while winter is cold and snowy, with highs around freezing and annual snowfall averaging 128 inches.

Zermatt is a starting point for hiking into the mountains. Cable cars and chair lifts carry skiers in the winter and hikers in the summer; the highest of them leads to the Klein Matterhorn at 3,883 meters (12,740 feet), a peak on the ridge between Breithorn and Matterhorn that offers extensive views in all directions.

The location of Zermatt at the foot of the Matterhorn and in the middle of an enormous hiking and ski region makes it one of the world's most attractive vacation villages. The ski region encompasses 54 mountain railways and lifts. The region called *Matterhorn*

Glacier Paradise' is Europe's largest and highest lying summer skiing region. Numerous national ski teams train here in the summer.

*****

Saturday, April 27— Day 33
Zermatt, Switzerland

A few times a month when reading the Las Vegas Review-Journal Opinion page, the lead article *'catches my eye and fires up my jets.'* It usually takes me 30 minutes or less to crank out a *'letter to the editor'.* During our 18 year Henderson residence, the *'RJ'* has published over three dozen of my letters. A few days ago, when reading about the $10B Los Angeles to Las Vegas High Speed Rail Line breaking ground, I felt compelled to add my two cents, challenge those responsible for construction, and ask two questions. Question 1: will the project be completed on schedule (4 years)? Question 2: will it be completed on budget? I guess the Review-Journal editorial board likes my comments. Today, when I read the online edition of the RJ, my letter is there! I alert my Vegas friends and leave a message for our house sitter, Cindy to trek (she's an avid walker) up to Walgreens, buy today's edition, and leave the Opinion Section in my man cave. Nice way to start my day 9,237 kilometers or 5,740 miles away from Henderson, Nevada!

After yesterday's cold, high altitude adventure, sleeping in is a great idea. There's only three items on today's agenda: the Matterhorn Paradise gondola ascent to the top and back, stopping at the Apotheke (pharmacy), and doing the laundry.

After breakfast, the first two items on our agenda call for a stop at the Apotheke for some drugs and ride the Matterhorn Paradise gondola up the mountain. On our way out the front door, the front desk staff informs us there is a coin operated washer and dryer in the basement. Later today, we can wash our clothes and avoid dragging dirty laundry to Interlaken.

One of the first things you notice in Switzerland is everything is **SO** clean. There is no graffiti or trash in the streets. All storefront windows and every store we enter are clean. People are polite and helpful. Last night, when I was clearly frustrated looking for a convenience store to buy some water and a Coke Zero, my *'what the hell is going on, every convenience store is closed'* body language surfaces when I learn the stores close at 20:00. A Good Samaritan asked me what I am looking for. "Coke Zero." He said, "Everything closes at 20:00". He directs me to vending machines in the train station.

Let's get back on track with what's happening today. After breakfast, Luca and Greta head to the local Swiss Apotheke. I feel a cold coming on. Using my iPhone, I pull up the prescription medications I take for chest colds and create screen shots. I explain my backpack with all my prescription drugs was stolen in Milan. "I have a police report if you need to see it," I say. "No, that won't be necessary," says the Pharmacist. "What drugs are you looking to purchase?" I show the druggist the picture of my inhaler, the Azithromycin 250mg Tablets-6-Pak, and the Methylprednisolone-4mg Dospak 21S. The druggist asks for my driver's license, enters some information into his computer, prints a copy of the report showing my purchases, and asks me to sign. That was easy! Let's hope these drugs *'do their thing'* quickly.

One chore down, two to go. Next, we head down the main walkway just past the train station and catch the **FREE** city operated Green Bus. The bus takes us to Matterhorn Glacier Paradise. Here, we board a ski lift gondola and head up over 12,000 feet (3,883 meters) to the summit.

From the Matterhorn Glacier Paradise website: "At an altitude of 3,883 meters (12,740 feet), the Klein Matterhorn really does stimulate the senses in this Alpine wonderland, aptly named the Matterhorn Glacier Paradise. This is the peak on which the highest mountain train station in Europe is located. Surrounded by 38, four-thousand foot high peaks, and 14 glaciers located in three countries, the Klein Matterhorn holds all in its sway."

The ticket seller advises us that winds past 8,000 feet are too severe today to ascend to the summit but we can go part way up the mountain. Whatever...you just can't mess with Mother Nature. I wonder how the gondola operators define *'excessive wind gusts.'* Later on, while in the gondola, we find out! We walk up to the gondola loading platform. Every five seconds, a gondola comes by. We jump in and begin the ascent to *Guru* at 6,125 feet. Here, we change cars and begin the ascent to *Aroleid* located at 7,625 feet. Winds cause the gondola ascent system to **STOP** leaving the gondola, with us in it, fully exposed to the raging winds. Our gondola stops at 7,250 feet, is suspended by **ONE** wire, and rocks back and forth. It feels like we are sitting on a two person swing, hanging on by **ONE** wire while swaying back and forth in the 40 plus mph winds! There is no additional charge for this *'experience.'*

We look at each other whimsically and say, "Is this how we go out?" At least the kids have copies of our wills, important personal information, and the phone number of the worldwide cremation company to scrap up what's left of us after wild animals find our bodies and enjoy a surprise lunch! We dangle *'so close and yet so far away'* from the next station.

Finally, the system restarts. Our car comes to a rest in the Aroleid station; however, the *'ride'* is shut down for about 15 minutes while the gondola operators wait for winds to calm down before resuming the journey down the mountain. Remember, the final 2,500 foot climb to the summit is shutdown. Today, we have witnessed and experienced enough **WIND** for a lifetime. We can always Google a YouTube video to *'experience'* the rest of the ascent.

While waiting for the gondolas to restart for the descent, a young couple from Nova Scotia, Canada joins us. After another approximate 10 to 15 minute delay (hey guys, take **ALL** the time you need prior to sending us down from 7,625 feet), we begin our descent. We see a restaurant at the next stop, Guru. We exit the gondola and head to *'the stop'* where many skiers and travelers gather. However (or **BUT-reader's choice**), the pathway is blocked by snow, ice, and pooling water. While I am *'game to give it a go,'* Greta wiggles her right hand gloved index finger *'left and right'* communicating, *'not today, not even gonna try it with this bum right knee, NFW!'* Journey aborted.

I make my way back to Greta. We mosey to the entrance turnstiles and use our round trip cards to gain entrance to the gondolas going down. Greta stops and says, "I dropped one of my priceless, irreplaceable gloves". I scan the area and locate the slightly dirty, tan glove lying on the cement station floor. However, it is impossible to reverse field and go back in the other direction using our one day pass card. The entrance control system **DOES NOT** allow me to *'go back.'* While I prepare to hurtle the turnstile, Greta notices an unlocked *'Do Not Enter'* gate and sends me to retrieve my distraught wife's glove.

The rest of the descent is *'uneventful.'* We marvel at the spectacular views of Zermatt's residential section. Upon exiting the gondola, we go to the bus stop to catch the green line bus back to town. It's really cold and windy, so we hang out in a ski rental store to get warm and avoid frostbite.

The bus gets us back to our morning starting point. Two-thirds of today's to-see list is complete. Greta and I wander up the city's main pathway to find a place for lunch. I remember spotting a café that sits on the second floor above the city's *'best bakery.'* Good choice: *Fuchs Restaurant* is a winner. Greta enjoys an egg and bacon quiche and cappuccino while I enjoy homemade vegetable soup served in a bread bowl and hot tea.

After lunch, we return to the hotel. Greta gets a lesson from a staffer on how to operate the washer and dryer in the hotel basement. *'Damn, all the machines are being used.'* So, she waits for about an hour before she can use the single washer and dryer combo. The machines are small, but the hotel staff provides laundry detergent and adds the nine Swiss Francs per load charge to our hotel bill. I *'chill'* in the lobby, enjoy a cup of hot tea, and write postcards and today's adventures. Greta superbly handles our three loads of wash. Anyway, it's close to 19:15 when the laundry is done. Our clothes are clean and ready to pack. It's now time for our last night's dinner in Zermatt.

Chad and Greta wander up the *'no cars street'* and choose *Walliserkanne*, a large, three story restaurant. While the service is slow (only two waiters on our floor), the meals are excellent. Greta enjoys grilled salmon over risotto and a glass of red wine. I dig into a baked chicken breast, a side of risotto, and a ginger beer. Greta finishes off her meal with a scoop of chocolate ice cream. I pass on dessert. It's past 22:00. We are dining at times *'way past our bedtime.'* We go back to room 104 in our wonderful hotel, ending another fabulous day of new experiences. I turn out the lights as we retire for the evening. In the morning after breakfast, we check out and head to the train station to catch the train to *Interlaken*! Good night from chilly Zermatt!

*****

Sunday, April 28 — Day 34
Zermatt to Interlaken, Switzerland

Sunday, April 28. It's raining and it's a cool, 34 degrees outside. Luca and Greta are up at 07:15, pack, shower, and get ready to roll out and catch the 10:13 train to *Interlaken*. But not before we have our last meal in the hotel. The breakfast room is packed because the hotel is 100% occupied. A group of ten women traveling together sit at a long table just behind us. It has to be a typical *'girls'* weekend trip; all ten women are talking at once!

After we eat, we ask the front desk to call us a cab to take us to the train station, why, it's raining. But we learn the hotel offers **FREE** shuttle service. One of my favorite words is, *'FREE.'* It's always ahead of my other favorite sayings...*2 for 1 and discount'*.

Train RE 332 to *Visp*, Switzerland departs at 10:13. I scan the departure board; however, RE 332 is **NOT** listed! Was the train cancelled? Did we get here too early or too late? Do we have the wrong day? What's up? Over on track five, I see Train RE42 leaving at 10:13. Confused and not sure *'what is what'*, I go to the ticket office which is located halfway down the track five platform on the right. I explain my quandary to Mr. Sunday ticket agent. The reply is priceless, "RE 42 is the name of the rail line. It's also the train you want to get on." "But sir, what about train RE 332?" No reply, whatever. Another unsolved mystery that even Columbo chooses not to solve.

We board the non-stop train to *Spiez*, a 26 minute journey. We don't have first class tickets; however, we are seated in first class. Will we get caught? Who knows, we never see a conductor! Later on, I learn our two month senior *Eurail* passes include **FREE** first class upgrades!

We arrive in Spiez at 12:23. Our next train departs at 13:08. I spot a train on the adjoining platform heading to Interlaken West. It looks like a *'high end'* train. I chat with the conductor and attempt to *'talk our way on.'* A language barrier limits conversation; go figure. Finally, I hear her say, "Get lost you old Americanos. You are not getting on this luxury train for free!" Yes, she actually said that!!!

I hustle back to check the departure board and get the track number for our 13:08 train. It's too early, it's not posted yet. **BUT** (don't you just love a good **BUT**) I see a train departing to Interlaken West at 12:35. It's 12:33. Frantically, I use my iPhone to bring up our rail passes and make reservations on the 12:35. Success, we grab the suitcases and hustle (walk fast = running at 75), to platform four and push the green button to open the train door just as it was about to close. We toss the suitcases on the train, jump on, and grab two seats.

I have no idea if we are on the right train. The departure board lists this train as IC 81. I booked us on IC 375! Time will tell if this 18 minute, non-stop journey takes us to Interlaken West. Will we make it? God only knows!! Suddenly, mid-journey, the train stops. I assume it's to let another train pass or the word got out that Greta and I jumped on this train without the right tickets? We both let out a sigh of relief when the train starts up and pulls into Interlaken West. Success, we made it! A 15 minute walk to the hotel is **NOT** an option, so we take a cab.

We arrive at *Hotel Restaurant Hirschen*, a Bavarian style, four-story building with 14 rooms. Our first challenge is the 11 very solid uneven stone steps that lead up to the entrance followed by *'opening'* a 200 plus year old, extremely heavy, wooden door. It takes me three trips to bring the suitcases and our belongings into the hotel lobby. Greta carefully navigates the steps, one foot at a time, using the railing and her blue cane for balance and stability.

There's no one at the front desk. After a few minutes, we see a note stating, *'we are in the restaurant downstairs.'* I head down, meet Zuzanna, one of the waitresses and let her know we are here to check in. She informs me someone will come up to the reception desk. A few minutes later, we meet a lady dressed from head to toe as a Chinese cook. She looks up our reservation and provides the room key. "Do you need our passports or identification?" I ask. "No, all good, room not ready," she answers.

A 6'4" stud with arms like tree trunks appears. He carries our bags (in one trip!) up the narrow, low ceiling 11 steps to our room. There is no elevator. The Chinese cook lady gives us the WIFI password and two Interlaken pass cards good for **FREE** (favorite word) rides on all local city owned bus lines.

It's a little past 13:30 and lunch time. We head to the restaurant one floor below. Greta has two options to get there – 1) Walk down 11 very solid, but narrow, steep steps with a low ceiling or 2) Go out the front door, use the handrail to walk down the 11 very solid, uneven stone steps, turn right at street level, walk 15 paces, and walk down three more steps to the restaurant. Greta chooses option two.

It's Sunday afternoon. Large and small families enjoy a Sunday family dinner in the restaurant. A party of 16 celebrates someone's birthday. Check out, below, to read about what they are eating.

We take over a table that has a *'reserved'* sign on it. No problem for us — maybe staff knew we are hungry after checking in. We study the menu. You will not believe what is on this menu —- calf's head and horse meat! There is **NO** way I will eat some cow's kid's head or a steak from Mr. Ed! Seriously, calf's head and horse meat! We each order wonton soup and split a salad.

Zuzanna, our waitress, speaks excellent English. She is from Slovakia! I mention my father came from Sklene, Slovakia. Who knows, we could be third cousins on my father's side of family.

Now, let me explain what's going on with the birthday party gathering. Author's Note: (In the 1950's, comedian, and actor George Burns, who was married to Gracie Allen, had a hit TV show called, *"Burns and Allen." In it, G*eorge would spy on Gracie in a variety of ways and then show the audience the hilarious results. You'll understand this paragraph better after I explain what's going on with the birthday gathering.)

The 16 birthday party goers start their meal with salads. Then, the wait staff places large, full length (head to waist) bibs on each guest. Out comes out 16 trays with a variety of meats including steak, chicken, pork, and deer placed on dark, rectangular shaped, **SUPER-HOT** grey stones. Side dishes include pineapple and cantaloupe. Each person uses the super-hot stones to cook their main course meat! The meat is cut into small bites and then placed on hot stones to cook. Depending on how long the meat is left on the stone, the "cooker" can make rare, medium, or well done bit-size delicacies. I had never saw this before but I guess it's common practice at Brazilian steakhouses in many countries and cities, including in Las Vegas. The sound of the sizzling meat, the aroma of it cooking on the stones, and the joyful laughter that fills the air makes me want to join the party!. As I start to get out of my chair, party-pooper Greta says, in a stern voice, **"SIT DOWN…. NOW!"** Well, I tried to *'give it a shot.'* Moreover, I hate to see the bill for this party!

A little girl sits at a table behind me. She doesn't finish her French fries. Before the waiter clears their table, I think hard about asking if I could enjoy the rest of the fries; but too late….the table is cleared.

As we leave the restaurant, I jokingly ask Zuzanna if she would make us a *'doggy bag'* of the leftovers from the birthday party and bring them to our room. Greta and I hate to see good food go to waste. But it's **NOT** going to happen. Everyone cleans their plate!

Slowly, we walk up the steep, narrow, *'no hand rail'* steps to the hotel and settle into our room. For some reason, European hotels are not as tall as they are in the U.S. Walking up and down the steps and stepping into a room requires anyone over 5'11" to **DUCK** or they will hit their head on the overhangs. The room ceiling appears to be no higher than 6' 4". I suspect basketball teams don't stay here. It only takes me *'one smack of the head'* to ensure I duck for the rest of our stay! Also, if you suffer from claustrophobia, this hotel is not the place to stay.

Luca decides to walk around the neighborhood and *'check out'* what's nearby. It's chilly and breezy, so the walk is short. I pass by a few restaurants and an adventure company offering parasailing, helicopter rides, and other *'over the top activities'* for fearless young people. Clearly, we are **NOT** the top demographic in the company's marketing plan. On each corner, I observe numerous directional signs, something we did not see in other European cities we visited. Back at the hotel, I feel a short afternoon nap will partially revive my body. It's time for dinner.

We have *'zero desire'* to head to the main part of town. With a unanimous vote of 2-0, we make the decision to eat at the hotel's restaurant. Now that we understand how ultra-hot stones are used in the meat cooking process, Greta orders a steak, salad, and mashed potatoes. She plans to cook her steak on the hot stone. I order a baked chicken breast with salad, and noodles; however, I can't see myself cooking pieces of chicken breast on the hot stone. So, I select the *'we cook it in the back for you'* option.

Greta chats with the people sitting at the adjoining table, a young couple from South Florida. She overhears the gentleman orders the horse steak. When his meal arrives, the steak looks really good. He is originally from Cuba where horse is an *'accepted'* meat option. We learn the meat is lean and a little on the sweet side; however, he doesn't offer us a small piece to taste. It's probably for the best.

Tipping is **NOT** required in Switzerland; however, if you feel you receive very good service, tipping is acceptable and *'the right thing to do.'* Today, both Zuzanna and our dinner waitress provide excellent service and receive a nice tip from us.

It's time to retire to the room and review our plans for our nine day stay in Interlaken. Good night.

Hotel Restaurant Hirschen

Here's a little history about the hotel from one of the owners, Nicole Forderer. She tells us the building is 350 years old. Think about that, it has been around longer than the American Revolution of 1776! The original wood in the stairwells, the entrance lobby, the entrance and lobby ceilings, and the front door are magnificent pieces of woodwork.

Nicole Forderer and Jacqueline Feuz bought the Hotel Restaurant Hirschen in 2006. Fourteen rooms are available for rent. During the past 17 years, the owners have refurbished and modernized the rooms and building. The 11 stone front steps are challenging because the height of the steps are slightly higher than normal steps. The eleven steps up to our floor, floor one, are steep, narrow, and require slightly ducking down when you hit step three going up and step eight as you walk down to the lobby. And the 12 steps down to the restaurant are very, very, narrow, steep, and lack a handrail for the first five steps. To keep your balance walking downward, one needs to grab onto the walls to prevent falling until you reach step six where a hand rail starts on the right side. And don't forget to slightly duck at step 10 or else you will wind up in NFL concussion protocol. Going up, just reverse the acrobatics.

Each room has low ceilings. When entering your room, you must step up and *'duck'* again if you are over 5'10" tall. Large twin beds are pushed together. Each bed has its own set of sheets, warm blankets, and soft feather pillows. The shower is similar to an old-style English telephone booth measuring 2' by 3'. Turning around will be challenging. The good news is you don't have to worry about bending over if you drop a bar of soap. Soap, shampoo, and conditioner dispensers are attached to the shower wall. Don't take any of our hotel comments the **WRONG** way; we love the hotel, the staff, and the location.

The bus stops for two city operated bus lines, 104 and 105, are a short walk from the hotel. One bus goes to the Interlaken Ost Train Station part of town and the other bus takes you to the Interlaken West Train Station part of town. The Interlaken Bus Company App makes it so easy to use public transportation to travel around town. Trains leaving both stations will take us to towns and sites we plan to visit. We can ride the buses for free with the Interlaken card provided at check-in. We love the hotel's location. It's a quiet residential neighborhood that's close to town but not in either touristy section of town.

Interlaken

Before we start our adventures in this wonderful city, here's something about Interlaken, courtesy of Wikipedia and the Interlaken Bureau of Tourism.

Interlaken is a Swiss town and municipality **in the** canton of Bern. Sometimes known as the Bernese Highlands, it is the highest and southernmost part of the canton. It is one of the canton's five administrative region. It's capital city, Bern, is also the de facto capital of Switzerland. It is an important and well-known tourist destination in the Bernese Oberland **(Highlands)region of the**

Swiss Alps, and the main transport gateway to the mountains and lakes of that region.

Interlaken is the starting point for unforgettable excursions to the *Bernese Oberland*. A full range of adventure sports are available here. Lakes, mountain villages, and the Bernese Alps with their glaciers await you, all accessible year round by rail, road, and mountain railway. Interlaken provides easy access to many small towns and villages within 45 minutes of the Interlaken Train Stations. We chose to stay in Interlaken because it provides easy access to the Lauterbrunnen Valley with its waterfalls, and easy access to the top of the Schilthorn via cable car from Stechelberg. The traffic-free mountain villages of Mürren, Wengen, and Gimmelwald, Rick Steve's favorite place in this region, offer a glimpse at a slower pace of life for hard working, independent people.

You can experience an action-packed day in the village of Grinderwald. The valley of Grinderwald forms part of the Jungfrau Region of the Bernese Oberland between Interlaken and the main crest of the Bernese Alps. The Jungfrau Region leads to Kleine Scheidegg via the Jungfrau railway, the highest railway in Europe.

Interlaken has a year round population of over 6,000 residents. Most of the population speaks German as their first language. Portuguese is the second most common, and Italian is third.

Lake Thun and Lake Brienz are both close to Interlaken. The Aare River flows east to west through the town. Boat trips operate on both lakes, serving various lakeside towns."

*****

Monday, April 29 — Day 35
Interlaken West, Switzerland

It's our first day in Interlaken. Luca is not feeling well. He is leaking *'a little oil.'* On the east coast, we use this phrase to mean one is not feeling well. Our Interlaken daily schedule has two free days built in. So, today Greta and I use one of our free days to relax, allowing me to recover, and let the prescription drugs kick in. After breakfast, (yes it's included in the daily room rate) I spend three hours in the breakfast room catching up on two days of travel happenings. Our fans at home are clamoring for more stories! I am also organizing our daily Interlaken things to do plan. If you recall, the day by day schedule for our trip was in the backpack it was *'borrowed'* and not returned on March 31 while we were in Milan. All of the Switzerland daily things to do are backed up on the iPad.

The hotel owner is working at the front desk today after cleaning up the breakfast room. She says it's **"OK"** to email her some files. She will print them for me. It's so, so much easier for me to organize activities with *'pieces of paper'* in hand, including the daily *'things to do'* on the Interlaken summary page.

Greta and I have lunch at the hotel. The soup of the day and a shared salad *'hit the spot.'*

After a two hour nap, we take the bus to Interlaken West and do some exploring. I download the Interlaken Bus System App. It only takes a few minutes to figure out how to efficiently use the App. It informs me when the bus (104 or 105) is scheduled to arrive at the designated bus stops two blocks from our hotel. It also provides the names and number of stops prior to arriving at our destination. Bus 104 takes passengers to the Interlaken Ost Train Station section of town and Bus 105 takes them to the Interlaken West Train Station area of town.

We jump on Bus 105 and head to the Interlaken West area of town. It's a quick five minute ride. Right across the street from the train station, we discover *Bebbis Bar and Restaurant* and decide to get something to drink. Sitting at the bar, I enjoy hot tea while Greta enjoys a local red wine. After finishing our refreshments, we search nearby sporting goods stores for a new backpack. Our efforts are unsuccessful.

It's time for an early dinner before heading back to our hotel. We decide to eat at Bebbis because it looks like a fun place, and they have a good menu. There is an abundance of indoor and outdoor seating. We ask for an inside table; but learn **ALL** tables are reserved! Right, not one soul is in the restaurant or waiting outside; but, since we are Americans, there are no tables for us to sit at! So, not wanting to start an international incident, we *'belly up'* to the bar and grab two seats.

We learn the restaurant works with local tour groups. This place is a **GOLD MINE** for the owner and who walks up to our table? Son of a gun, it's the restaurant owner! He is **EXTREMELY** (that is putting it mildly) outgoing and entertaining. He owns three restaurants in Switzerland, has a second home in the Orlando, Florida area, and just loves to bullshit with us. By now, the Asian tour group arrives and occupies every indoor and outdoor seat. The owner loves to interact with his customers. He uses country flags to lead cheers. Surprisingly, he walks out to the street, carrying an extremely long Swiss horn, which he plays to entertain his guests and people walking the village streets.

I order the soup of the day: cream of mushroom. The soup is excellent; however, it is impossible to locate good sized mushroom slices in the soup. Whatever, Greta sternly and to the point says, "**DON'T** bring it to the owner's attention!" Greta orders a cheeseburger and fries. For dessert, a scoop of caramel ice cream with chocolate sauce and whipped cream rounds out her meal. We continue talking with the owner. We offer to send our 18 year old twin grandsons, Tanner and Brady, and their adopted brother and brother-in-law-to-be-someday, Zack, to work here. All of them have years of pizza restaurant experience. Thanks to us, should they ever go to Bebbis Bar and Restaurant, they have jobs waiting for them!

Luca likes the tee shirts and light jackets worn by the staff. I offer to buy some gear; however, no such luck: everything is out of stock. The owner had been waiting for a three month old order from God knows where in Southeast Asia. I give him my business card and ask him to ship me an XXL tee shirt and light jacket the next time he is in the USA. The owner agrees. Let's see, if down the road, it arrives in Henderson! Unfortunately, as of this writing, no *'gear'* has shown up. But, when we make it back to Interlaken someday, I will stop by Bebbis Bar and Restaurant to see if there is any *'gear'* for sale.

After dinner, we cross the street to the Interlaken West Train Station and wait for Bus 105 to take us back to the hotel. As we cross the street, I spot a store selling backpacks! From a distance, they *'look just like'* what I was looking for! So, Luca jaywalks back across four lanes of traffic, buys the backpack, and runs back across the four lanes in time to catch the bus.

Today was a great, relaxing *'chill day.'* We accomplished many things. Our bodies received the necessary rest. And, we have a plan to visit the sites and villages we want to see in the greater Interlaken area over the next eight days!

P.S. while waiting for the bus near our hotel, we notice how *'precise'* the structures are. The multi-floor windows and shutters are **PERFECTLY** spaced and built into the houses. Swiss precision engineering!

*****

Tuesday, April 30 — Day 36
Grinderwald and Lauterbunnen, Switzerland

Luca and Greta wake to a sunny day. We hustle, shower, get dressed, and carefully, one step at a time, walk down the 11 very narrow steps with the low overhang at step eight to the breakfast room. Here, I duck down a few inches to avoid taking *'a shot to the forehead.'* It only took one hard knock when we first got to the hotel to learn that lesson.

This morning for breakfast I decide to enjoy a bowl of corn flakes cereal. I add some sugar and milk from the container next to the cereals. Unfortunately, the *'milk'* has a nutty taste of almond milk, something that makes the cereal **NOT** enjoyable. After the cereal misfortune, I grab a plate, spoon on some scrambled eggs, and place a few *'breakfast weenies'* on my plate. "Why not see what they taste like?," I say to myself. I slice some multigrain bread I find on the bread selection table and grab a dish of **REAL** butter. The bread is the best when baked fresh, like it was today. The breakfast weenies taste like polish sausage. Two cups of hot tea and a large glass of multivitamin orange juice (at least that's what the sign says) complete the satisfying meal. Greta enjoys eggs, fruit, cheese, some granola, and yogurt washed down with a glass of orange juice, and a cappuccino.

Our day two plan is a trip to *Grindelwald*. Here's how the village's website describes Grinderwald: "The Eiger village of Grindelwald in the Bernese Oberland lies embedded in a welcoming and green hollow, surrounded by a commanding mountain scape with the Eiger mountain north face. This mountain scape and the numerous lookout points and activities make Grindelwald one of the most popular and cosmopolitan holiday and excursion destinations in Switzerland, and the largest ski resort in the Jungfrau region."

Exiting the hotel, we walk one block to catch Bus 104 to the Interlaken OST Train Station. Once there, we board the 09:34 RE 259 train for the 36 minute ride to our destination. Swiss trains are **ALWAYS ON TIME!**

We exit at Grindelwald station, start our slightly uphill journey to the village, and stop at a local coffee shop for Americano coffees. Greta also orders herself one scoop of coffee ice cream (before lunch, her philosophy is simple — I am on vacation!). While Greta window shops, I use my iPhone to take numerous photos of the village and surrounding mountains, snapping pictures from every angle imaginable. Let's leave it at *'the views are spectacular'*! A variety of souvenir, clothing, winter sports shops, and restaurants line the main walkway through town. The surrounding snow-capped mountains provide an impressive backdrop to this quaint Swiss village.

Lunchtime rolls around. Lo and behold, we spot Beebe's, the same restaurant we ate at last night in Interlaken. I enjoy a bowl of potato and carrot soup. Greta orders a pizza for us to share. The soup is good; however, we were a bit disappointed with the pizza as the crust was a pre-made (versus tossed in house) pizza shell. It's not **CLOSE** the same quality we enjoyed in Milan.

With lunch behind us, we catch the 13:47 RE 252 train destined for *Lauterbunnen* passing through *Zweiluetschinen*. Here, we change to train RE 167 for the nine minute ride to Lauterbunnen.

While riding on the train, we notice that at every road crossing, no matter how many lanes of traffic are travelling in either direction, automatic 'D*o Not Cross'* barrier arms activate and drop down prior to the train crossing to prevent pedestrians and vehicles from crossing the tracks. The control arms appear to be very heavy and leave no gap for anything or anybody to squeak by. Just in case some fool would try to manually lift the restraining arm, the ends are weighed down.

From the Lauterbrunnen Village website: "Lauterbrunnen lies 795 meters above sea level in an impressive trough valley between gigantic rock faces and peaks. Seventy-two waterfalls cascade over the rock faces into the valley. The Staubbach Waterfall – one of the highest free-falling waterfalls in Europe – inspired Goethe to author his poem "Song of the Spirits over the Waters." Lauterbrunnen is the starting point for many excursions. In summer, there are many hiking trails and mountain biking trails to explore. In winter, you can hit the nearby *Mürren-Schilthorn and Kleine Scheidegg-Männlichen* ski slopes. One of the longest ski runs takes you from the *Schilthorn* down to Lauterbrunnen – a descent with a difference in altitude of over 2,000 meters. For cross-country skiers, Lauterbrunnen offers nearly 16 kilometers of trails alongside the icy waterfalls."

Lauterbrunnen is a sleepy village surrounded by numerous snow-capped mountains. Keep in mind, we are having spring-like weather in Switzerland, so melting snow sends water forcefully cascading down several waterfalls, seemingly hundreds of feet into swift flowing streams. So technically, you can ski on the snow, then, when the snow melts overnight, you can watch the water tumble down the waterfalls into streams that lead to water filtration plants which bottle the water for drinking. From the majestic mountainside, down fast flowing waterfalls, and bottled locally, you can have fresh, clean water into your homes and onto your table in a matter of days!

The *'kids from Henderson'* walk up the narrow village road taking in the sites and occasionally window shopping. So far on this trip, we have *'purchased'* at least two dozen or more *'windows.'* (I say sarcastically to myself!)

Greta decides to sit and chill on a rock wall while I march on in search of that magical, *'one of a kind'* photo. A path takes me past the well-manicured, flower covered village cemetery, and to the base of the 297 meter (1,303 feet) *Staubbach Waterfall.* Standing at the base of the waterfall, I watch in awe as the water cascades down with relentless force, creating a fine mist that envelops the tourists, including me. Truly, this is one of the scenic highlights so far on the trip.

I continue my journey down the path that doubles as a roadway for cars and trucks. Along this stretch, green fields replace buildings. Three smaller, yet at least 300 meters (1,000 feet) high, waterfalls grace the mountains on the right. On the left, in the distance, I see more narrow waterfalls. Before heading back to pick up Greta, I observe a herd of light brown and white cattle leisurely, seemingly without a care in the world, munching on the green grass. Clearly, they enjoy living in Lauterbrunnen.

I reunite to Greta, who established temporary Lauterbrunnen residency by sitting on the low stone wall for over an hour. It's time, once again, to chill, relax, and enjoy adult beverages. **IT MUST BE 5:00 O'CLOCK SOMEWHERE!** A nearby hotel has a large outdoor restaurant that beacons us like the mythical Sirens calling out to the pirates to join them. I enjoy, what else, a local draft beer while Greta does the red wine thing.

It's time to walk back to the train station and head for Interlaken. We board RE 156 at 15:02 and arrive at Interlaken OST at 15:24.

Restaurants in Switzerland are very expensive. Plus, we are not looking for a big meal. We decide to visit the local grocery store **CO-OP,** buy snacks and some takeaway items for a picnic dinner in our hotel room. After going up and down most of the aisles, (pushing and shoving are acceptable ways to get around in this store), we grab a half baked chicken, a mixed salad with balsamic vinegar salad dressing packets, two plastic combination fork/spoon utensils, a bag of tortilla chips, cheddar cheese, yogurt, blueberries, raspberries, a soft pretzel, one sugar free Red Bull, two cans of Coke Zero, two bottles of water — one carbonated and one not carbonated — and a half bottle of a 2019 produced red wine.

We struggle at the self-checkout area because the screen instructions are in German. Like I said before, nowhere in Europe do you hear or see "Press one for (name of country) and Press two for English. Baffled, confused, and frustrated, I do my normal *'hit all the buttons and hopefully something good will happen'* trick. This time I miserably fail. Meanwhile, the 15 people behind us are ready to check out and head home to their anxious families. Family members most likely are wondering where is (inset name)? He/she should have been home 35 minutes ago! The 15 men and women behind us band together. They are ready to confront us, gladly pay our bill, pack up our groceries, and escort us to the exit door with a stern, forceful warning, "Never, ever set foot in this store ever again or else." With two outstretched arms, I frantically try to get the self-checkout customer service lady's attention (think of a football head coach trying to get an official's attention to grant a timeout with seconds left in the game). Much to our dismay, she is overseeing 25 checkout stations. Plus, her dinner hour begins soon. She finally sees my frantic waving, gives up her dinner break, comes over, evaluates the chaos, finishes our checkout, processes our payment, and gives me the credit card slip to sign. She expeditiously packs our groceries, emphatically points to the exit doors with her right index finger and shouts out in German, "**OUT** you two stupid old American tourists! **GET OUT OF HERE** and **NEVER EVER** come back again .... **AND** thanks for shopping at the **CO-OP!**"

Exhausted and frustrated, but still alive and breathing, we hastily cross the busy four lane street and patiently wait for Bus 104 to get us out of town fast and back to the hotel. On the bus ride home, a gentleman facing me has a horseshoe shaped left eyebrow piercing and a horseshoe shaped nose ring piercing. Whatever floats your boat! By the way, this is the first piecing we've seen, so far, in our brief stay in Switzerland.

Back at the ranch, I scamper down the steps, break into the breakfast room, gather up two plates, two sets of silverware, two small glasses, and head back upstairs to the room without being noticed. Greta grabs a small bathroom towel to use as our tablecloth and spreads out the food. We are ready to enjoy our Switzerland room picnic! Greta is having trouble removing the cork from the bottle of red wine. The cork is way past dried out! We both struggle with the cork. Wine bottles should be kept on their sides so that the cork is kept moist, thus allowing for easy extraction. We speculate that the bottle has **NOT** been on its side since birth. It also helps if you have a wine bottle opener, too! We try using a knife to break up the stubborn *'I ain't coming out tonight'* cork. Finally, after 18 minutes of trying, we give up!

The half chicken is getting cold. No matter, we woof it down along with the sliced processed cheddar cheese, chips, and fruit.

Before retiring for the night, we plan our Wednesday travel schedule. We will be heading up to the Schilthorn summit, 2,970 meters (9,744 feet above sea level) for lunch at a revolving restaurant made famous by the 1969 James Bond movie *'On Her Majesty's Secret Service'*.

We also consider a day trip to *Iseltwald*, a small village on *Lake Brienz*. Zuzanna, the waitress in the hotel restaurant, recommends a visit to this tiny, fairy-tale village where less than 500 lucky people get to call it home. Until tomorrow....lights out, good night, sweet dreams!

P.S. Note to grandkids — Lauterbrunnen has multiple hostels where you can stay should you want to visit someday.

*****

Wednesday, May 1 — Day 37
Schilthorn Summit, Piz Gloria Restaurant, Mürren, Gimmelwald, Switzerland

Little did we know when waking up that today would be, without a doubt, the **BEST** day on our trip. So, hang onto your hats, here we go!

Luca forgets to turn on his iPhone alarm. It is set for 07:15; but the first thing we know it's 08:10. We quickly arise, shower, dress, and grab a quick breakfast. We are heading to the top of Schilthorn Summit, 2,970 meters up (9,744 feet) for lunch at a revolving restaurant made famous by the 1969 James Bond movie *'On Her Majesty's Secret Service'*.

We have become real Europeans. We learn to plan our day trips by studying the bus and train schedules and riding the correct bus to the correct train station. Unlike at home, there is no hopping in the car and *'just going.'* So, our travel times and days are longer, but most enjoyable, and dictated by the train and bus schedules.

Our goal today is to reach the Schilthorn Summit by 11:30. We have a 12:30 lunch reservation at the *Piz Gloria* restaurant. Today's journey starts with taking Bus 104 to the Interlaken OST station. There, we board train RE 134 at 9:34 to Lauterbrunnen and take Bus 141 to the gondola starting point. Here, we purchase round trip tickets for the gondola that takes us up the mountain to the restaurant. Little did we know we would change gondolas at *Mürren* and *Birg* to get to the top!

After train RE 134 gets rolling, along comes Ms. experienced train conductor. I am struggling with my iPhone and the Eurail App. I can't get the rail passes and today's trip up on the screen. And I **JUST** had it ready minutes ago. After a few minutes of watching me fumble with the iPhone and App, the conductor sternly says, **"I'll BE BACK!"** Here we go again. We are **NOT** stowaways looking for a free ride. All the tickets are on the Eurail App on my iPhone. Right now, it is not cooperating. What to do? Jump off the moving train? Just buy two tickets and *'bite the bullet'* or turn the phone off and back on? Success, I go with choice three, turn the phone off and back on and our Eurail passes and today's tickets *'magically'* appear. The conductor can now verify everything is *'in order'* using her hand held electronic device. We get *'lucky'* as we sense the conductor was *'looking for'* a confrontation today.

Now that we are *'besties'* with the conductor, Greta asks her where the Bus 141 stop is when we exit the train. With her *'newly found'* customer service attitude in play, she provides clear instructions. Luca opens up a discussion about the train conductor whistle sounds being *'different'* in Italy and Switzerland. While the difference remains a mystery, I want to know where the Switzerland conductors purchase their whistles. I am thinking about starting a collection of European train conductor whistles. While I did not get an answer, I use Google to learn where to purchase one. As we exit the train, our new *'bestie'* conductor points us in the right direction to catch Bus 141.

Bus 141 is part of the same transportation company we travel for *'free'* with our Interlaken card. However, there's a sign indicating that *'The Interlaken Card is **NOT** valid to ride for free on Bus 141, see the bus driver to purchase a ticket'*. What — do we have to pay for a ten minute bus ride? Since we are experienced stowaways on trains and buses, we enter and sit in the rear section of the two car bus. Who is going to check for tickets here? Success, we get to the Stechelberg LSMS Gondola Lift Station without incident.

Last night, I purchased discount round trip tickets to Schilthorn Summit, Piz Gloria Restaurant. Our tickets include lunch, a savings of 48 Swiss Francs each and we have reservations! When I mention this to the ticket seller, he gives me the '*RIGHT, what are you talking about special?*' Again, I explain and show him a photo of the deal. He consults with the more senior ticket agent sitting to his right. This agent confirms what I am saying is true. With tickets in hand, we walk over to the gondola starting location.

Obviously, we are rookies at this game. It's our first trip of this magnitude and importance. We enter a large gondola, join 50 to 60 people standing close together, and grab onto part of the gondola car wall for balance. Sitting in the middle of the gondola is a pallet of flat cinderblock bricks neatly stacked and tightly bound. What are these for? Are they planning to put us to work on a construction assignment as part of the trip up the mountain?

A few wires support the gondola as it slowly climbs the mountain. Let's hope the wires are in '*tip top*' shape, perhaps even new.

Just prior to docking at the Mürren/Gimmelwald station, the wind picks up. The car starts to sway and makes **HARD** contact with the rubber siding as it enters the station. Riders let out in unison, **"OH!"** When the docking process is complete, the driver says, "Sorry!" in multiple languages.

When the gondola pulls into the Mürren/Gimmelwald station, riders have three choices: 1) Exit and continue up in a different gondola, 2) Exit and take a gondola to Mürren, a small hillside village, or 3) Exit and take a gondola to Gimmelwald, another small village and one of the top destinations on our trip to Switzerland.

We chose option one and head with a majority the riders to the next gondola and continue our assault up the mountain. Every time we exit and enter a boarding location; we point our bar code ticket toward the card reader that allows us to enter.

Phase two of our gondola journey takes us up the mountain to Birg. The gondola is packed with tourists from the Far East. The winds have thankfully died down making for a smooth, vertical climb. Nothing eventful happens during the docking process. From the Birg website, "The entrance here is an approximately 200 meters long rock walkway that was built into the rock along the vertical abyss. The construction made of steel and glass as well as a floor made of gratings blends seamlessly into the angular rocky landscape." Given the cold weather, the wind, and being two old farts, we pass on the *'thrill walk.'*

Bistro Birg offers indoor and outdoor seating to enjoy great views from 2,677 meters (8,783 feet) up while having a beverage and a snack.

We get sidetracked taking pictures and miss the next car to the summit. The next gondola leaves in 15 minutes. So, it's a good time to catch our breath in the thinning air, rest, and take full advantage of free potty and ultra-clean restrooms.

Our final ascent is *'clean,'* no bumps, and no wind. We have one hour until our lunch reservation. So, we have ample time to walk through, read about, and watch a short film about the making of the 1969 James Bond movie *'On Her Majesty's Secret Service'*. Actors, actresses, cameramen, and stunt personnel went to great lengths and sometimes dangerous situations to make this outstanding film, especially considering that the conditions and equipment available in 1969 for working at 10,000 feet were far more rudimentary compared to what we have today.

It's 12:25 — time for Luca and Greta to make our way up to Piz Gloria, the revolving restaurant, for lunch. It takes 47 minutes for the restaurant to make a complete revolution. The maître' d seats us at a window table. We sit across from one another. The table is ours for up to 90 minutes; plenty of time to enjoy our meal and take in the magical views. Greta and I order local beers and our lunch, starting with a choice of four soups. We both select goulash. It's thick and tasty, with a consistency just like chili. Next, we choose from one of five burger sandwiches: beef, salmon, pork, chicken, or vegan. I order the salmon burger while Greta goes for the chicken. Both sandwiches come with an ample serving of fries. Desert is a coconut chocolate piece of cake.

To say the least, the views are spectacular! Mountains are covered in pure white snow untouched by humans and animals. It's really hard to describe what we are looking out at. The light blue sky is peaking thru the clouds. The scene *'looks like'* a painting.

After completing one and a quarter rotations in the restaurant, we head out onto the viewing platform for one last look at the spectacular views and we take dozens of pictures. Occasionally, we both experience mild dizziness and lightheadedness, common symptoms of exposure to high altitudes.

Switzerland is in the midst of a four-year project to construct state-of-the-art cable car stations. Workers are diligently laying the foundations for these new structures, surrounded by neatly arranged stacks of rebar and other construction materials to ensure both efficiency and safety. Wearing hard hats and sturdy work boots, they secure safety straps as they move gracefully along the scaffolding, almost like ballerinas, to assemble the new stations. Single-wire cable systems continuously transport skid after skid of building materials up the mountain to support the construction of three new gondola stations.

It's time to head down the mountain to visit Mürren and Gimmelwald. Just like on the ascent, we change cars at Birg, continue our descent, and exit the gondola at the Mürren/Gimmelwald station. The ride up to Mürren takes a few minutes. This village is car free and only accessible by cable car or on foot from Gimmelwald. In short, it's undeniably remote. There are a few hotels, restaurants, and homes; all come with breathtaking views of snow covered mountains and cascading waterfalls. After walking around and taking more '*just gotta have*' photos, we return to the gondola station and descend to our next stop, Gimmelwald.

Many years ago, Luca watched a Rick Steves travel video highlighting his many trips to this tiny hillside village accessible only by cable car. The much anticipated visit to this magical place is coming to a crescendo as we descend from Mürren to Gimmelwald. This tiny alpine hamlet has been on my bucket list for years and now, as we slowly descend, my heart races; I am on my way to Gimmelwald!

We exit and set out on foot to explore Rick's favorite Swiss village. We walk up a hill past the village children's playground. Here, mothers and fathers watch their young children having fun while playing in the partly sunny comfortable weather. We come across a fenced-in group of seven chickens and one rooster. Directly across the path, we see a lady weeding a flower bed. We stop and chat. The lady lives in the village and manages the hotel we are standing in front of. She is also babysitting the chickens while the owners are away on holiday. She offers to sell us ice cream cones made by a local creamery. How can these two ice cream aficionados pass up ice cream even before dinner? I select the berry ice cream cone while Greta selects caramel. Each treat costs six Swiss Francs, a little '*spendy;*' however, considering where we are, I'm good with the price!

We sit on the hotel's covered porch enjoying the local '*to die for creamy ice cream.*' It's so peaceful. Temperatures are very pleasant. We listen to the sounds of water falling in the distance from the snow-capped mountains, kids playing in the local playground, chickens doing whatever chickens do, tree branches swaying in the wind, and birds chirping a tune reminiscent of a Swiss melody.

Luca and Greta discover a unique store called 'The Honor Store.' It's located right off the main village walkway and it's an unstaffed retail store that relies on the honor system. Antiques are individually priced. A buyer places money in an envelope and drops it into a mailbox style locked box. Reminds us of the unmanned flower and fruit stands found along upcountry Maui roads. I continue walking through the village taking pictures of the surrounding steep hillsides, homes, and local businesses. Sadly, our brief visit is coming to an end. We have an hour plus journey back to our hotel. Later in the week, we will consider taking a walk from Mürren to Gimmelwald.

The gondola quickly descends to *Stechelberg*. Here, we catch another *'free ride'* on Bus 141 to the Lauterbrunnen Train Station where we catch train RE 176 for the 22-minute ride to Interlaken OST.

Excited and exhausted and not wanting to eat out, we run into the **CO-OP** grocery store for a bottle of wine, drinks, cooked shrimp, lunch meat, pretzels, and a new wine bottle opener we hope works. Knowing our limitations at the self-checkout stations, we get in line behind three people and allow the cashier to scan our items and collect our money. We automatically become *'locals'* when we purchase a .40 Swiss Franc reusable grocery bag!

We dash across the street, wait a few minutes for Bus 104, and arrive back at our hotel. We enjoy another in room picnic dinner and watch episodes four and five of the six part Netflix political intrigue mini-series "*Pine Gap*." After an 11-hour day and 7,552 steps, we *'crash and burn'*. Without a doubt, today was the most exciting and *'best day'* so far on our European journey.

*****

Thursday, May 2 — Day 38
Laundry Day, Shopping in Interlaken, Switzerland

Today ties our longest European holiday trip; 38 consecutive days back in 2013. The *'happenings'* on that trip became the stories in my first book, *"SH?#! Happens Traveling With John and Leslie."* This book made the New York Times Best Seller List for nine minutes, 38 seconds and grossed $20 in on-line sales. I guess I shouldn't have given away 200 autographed copies when it first came out! In any event, the entire project created a $9,500 business loss on Schedule C on our 2013 federal income tax return. At least the loss reduced our taxable income for 2013 and increased our 2013 tax refund!

This day also marks the halfway point of this year's journey. Why such a long trip this year? Good question. Our 2021 and 2022 plans were victims of the Covid pandemic shutdown. Luca and Greta had big plans for 2023, starting with a 21-day Baltic Holland America cruise with Philadelphia friends Pat and Helen, followed by 40 plus days traveling thru Europe. Sadly, these plans came to an abrupt halt when I tore 90% of my left Achilles tendon on January 16, requiring surgery shortly thereafter. Seven weeks later, an accident tore the same tendon forcing another surgery on April 6. Three months in a cast, then three months in a walking boot, nine months in physical therapy, and many months using a knee scooter to get around followed. In December, I started to learn how to walk again. While still in physical therapy, I slowly began walking, taking a few blocks at a time. Eventually I built up enough strength to walk three to four miles up and down hilly streets in Sun City Anthem, the 55 plus community in Henderson where we have lived for the past 17 years. I racked up over 300 miles prepping for the trip prior to our March 26th departure. So, during the months when I had limited mobility and lots of time on my hands, using the 2023 trip plan as a guide, I constructed our 2024 78-day extravaganza. I planned it all, including our train trips, car rentals, hotels, things to do and see at each stop, and airplane tickets. I documented the plan in a series of Excel spreadsheets, Word, and Adobe PDF files. Anyway, that's how this trip came to be.

Let's get back to Day 38, May 2. We woke up at 08:30. Yesterday was an incredibly active day—undoubtedly one of the best, if not the very best, of the trip so far. I mean, who takes three gondolas up almost 10,000 feet just to have a burger and fries for lunch at a revolving restaurant made famous by the 1969 James Bond movie *'On Her Majesty's Secret Service'*? The dining experience at this restaurant makes the roof top revolving restaurant at the Stratosphere Hotel and Casino in Las Vegas look like it's at the top of a mole hill.

The weather forecast today calls for a 50% chance of rain. So, today is an excellent time to relax, chill, recharge the batteries, and do the laundry. After a nourishing breakfast, we pack up the *'dirties'* and head to the Bus 105 stop. The self-service laundry is very close to the Interlaken West Train Station. This also gives Greta a chance to window shop and me to catch up on writing about the last four days. Our four fans are eagerly demanding more and more stories. Hang tight; I'll catch up in a few days!

We board Bus 105, which drops us at the Interlaken West Train Station. I **NEED** to locate a close by potty. Quickly, I head into the train station. One level down, there are bathrooms; but why is there always a **BUT** when there is a pending emergency? I broke Rule One when traveling in Europe, I do **NOT** have any coins on me. And what does everyone need to enter most public potties in Europe???? Coins! Although some train stations offer *'free potty,'* that's not the case at the Interlaken West Station. This relief station requires one Swiss Franc to enter. No paper money, no credit card, just **ONE** stinking Swiss Franc! Forcefully, but to no avail, I bang on the glass door. No one is inside using the facilities. Folks, it is **DANGER TIME!** What can I do? Look for a dark alley, rob someone of one Swiss Franc or **RUN** up the stairs to a convenience store?

I sprint up 12 steps, take two at a time, rush into the store, and grab a bottle of who knows what kind of water. I dart left and right around other customers and head to the cashier. **Why is the checkout clerk training a new employee TODAY**? I thrust a 10 Swiss Francs bill towards her. She senses my *'urgency'* to complete the transaction. I politely ask for change in coins only. Next, I slide down the handrail to the basement floor — tick, tick, tick my bowels are screaming. I drop the correct coin into the slot that unlocks the entry door, scramble to the toilet, lock the door, drop my drawers, and **INSTANTLY** feel relief! The moral of this story is always carry a supply of local currency coins. I will **NOT** break that rule again!

I meet up with Greta and tell her the story. She smacks me **HARD** twice on the back of the head with her right hand and says, "You are a real dumb ass!" No biggie…I earned her wrath.

Following directions on Google GPS, we walk six minutes to the laundromat. As we pass by a USB Bank, I want to change the ATM generated large bills into smaller bills. I hate giving small, local merchants large bills for minor purchases. Anyway, it's lunchtime. The bank is closed. No problem, we can stop on the way back. Not so fast! A large sign behind the locked entrance door reads, "This bank

DOES NOT change money!" Here we go again. Am I back in Italy? Remember in Chur, Switzerland, the USB Bank teller graciously converted large bills into smaller currency without incident. Maybe the sign means they don't change foreign currency? Not willing to wait for an answer, we just move on.

There are numerous washers and dryers in the laundromat. The facility must be mob owned! It's the **ONLY** self-service laundromat in Interlaken. The prices for washing and drying clothes are set very high, thus reflecting supply and demand. However, pray tell, where else can one go locally to wash and dry clothes? It costs 14 Swiss Francs to use each washer and eight Swiss Francs to use each dryer. Are you kidding me? It cost **ONLY** nine Swiss Francs to wash **AND** dry our laundry at the Zermatt hotel! Plus, the washers here are very small. Greta **SQUEEZES** our clothes into two machines. I use our MasterCard to activate both washers. Forty minutes later, Greta loads two dryers. I invest 16 Swiss Francs to get them going. Wouldn't you know , when the drying cycle finishes, the clothes are **NOT** close to being dried. So, another 16 Swiss Francs *'investment'* turns the machines back on.

While sitting and waiting, Greta engages in conversation with a lady from Alabama. You can quickly tell she and her family are huge Alabama *'Roll Tide'* fans. She refers to the recently retired football coach as *'Nick.'* Her husband, and her 22-year old daughter, an international exchange student living in The Hague in Amsterdam, return after doing some touristy things. When I drop an "I was sitting in the end zone at the 2024 Rose Bowl game where Michigan scored the winning touchdown in overtime to beat Alabama", her husband chimes in "I was there too"! Later on, small talk reveals he also attended the NCAA Men's Basketball Final Four (Alabama was one of the four teams playing) and attended the recent Masters Golf Tournament in Augusta Georgia! Putting all this together, it's easy to conclude these folks have *'big bucks.'*

Probably belong to the same country club as Nick Saban and other big Alabama boosters in Tuscaloosa!

After finishing the laundry, we board Bus 105 and head back to the hotel. We drop off the laundry, eat leftovers from last night's picnic dinner, and catch Bus 105 to *Dork/Gsteigwiler*. Why here, you ask? Well, on the 105 bus route map, this *'town'* is at the end of the Bus 105 route! Let's *'give it a shot'* and go on an adventure. Despite Greta's incessant pleas, when we get on, I don't put Dork/Gsteigwiler together as the same *'end of the line stop'* as she does. She's right, I am wrong and like a man, I take the verbal tongue lashing I deservedly earned. We exit the bus in *Wilderswil*, take more *'gotta have pictures'* and wait for the next Bus 105 back to Interlaken West!

While waiting for Bus 105, we see a mother pushing a baby carriage as she jogs. Her child is lying down and enjoying the ride. Her young son and daughter ride bikes. The little boy is **FLYING** down the brick pathway with **NO** intent on stopping at the main road intersection. The mother senses that the little guy *'ain't gonna stop,'* runs towards the boy, and yells, "Stop, stop! Do not go into the street. You could get hit by a car and become a hood ornament!" Hey mom, at least he is wearing a helmet. When she catches up to him, she reads him the riot act, threatens to take away his bike, cell phone, and PlayStation 3. It goes in one ear and out the other. I think he is about two - three years old with nary a fear or concern in the world.

After making an executive decision **NOT** to go to Dork/Gsteigwiler, we flag down Bus 105 and head back to Interlaken West. You have to be really alert while waiting for the bus at this stop because from what we can see, **FEW** people get on and off the bus here. At the station at the end of the bus ride, Luca and Greta get a two-for-one potty trip. We insert one Swiss Franc into the slot that *'opens the potty door'* and we **BOTH** enter the facility when the door swings open.

Luca and Greta decide to do some window shopping and add some steps to our daily tally. We know all about precision Swiss watches. But we wonder how the numerous name brand watch stores located on both sides of the main street stay open and make money. I am **NOT** a *'big name'* watch guy. I prefer a $39 Timex digital time and date display watch with **LARGE** numbers and letters for easy reading. I like to keep things simple. I ask my watch to **ONLY** do three things; display the current time, the day, and date. Clearly, I am **NOT** the target demographic for the name brand watch stores.

Greta enters a high-end Swiss chocolate candy store. After sampling seven pieces, she spends 13 Swiss Francs on six pieces of chocolate candy, none of which are chocolate covered raisins, cherries, or nonpareils — three of my favorites. I miserably fail to negotiate a senior's, AARP, new guest in Interlaken, or nice guy discount with the checkout clerk.

I spot a store selling men's golf shirts which hang on a rack outside the store. I think they **MIGHT** be on sale! I take the elevator to the second floor to see if other colors are available. The clerk upstairs tells me that what you see outside on the rack is all they have. But he states the shirts on display outside are 50% off the price on the tag. Now we're talking. I return to the ground floor and ask the store manager if the shirts are 50% off. She replies, "They are **NOT** on sale, the price is on the tag." I locate Greta and ask for her opinion. She likes the shirt I am holding; but she is not sure about the washing and handling instructions. I tell her about the clerk on the second floor who says the shirt is **ON SALE** at 50% off while the sales manager over there indicates **NO DEAL.** We take the elevator to the second floor to buy the shirt there. Greta, however, expresses her concern over both the garment handling and washing instructions and the *'deal, no deal'* pricing. Her conscience is getting in the way of a deal. I hand the shirt to the clerk.

He confirms the 50% discount. Greta asks him to check the price with the sales manager. He calls downstairs and learns the shirt is **NOT** on sale. We thank him for his time and head out. So far, Luca strikes out every time he tries to make a deal. The Swiss people are tough, hard-nosed, take no prisoners operators. Luca, however, is **NOT** deterred. There's **ALWAYS** a deal to be made somewhere.

Continuing to mosey, we spot ***Dunkin Donuts***, my favorite coffee shop in the USA. We both agree it's a **MUST ENTER** and enjoy a cup of coffee and a small donut. Greta learns that the customer service manager and counter person is from Tunisia. My Dunkin App does not work when I try to pay their extremely high prices. A small coffee is five Swiss Francs and the cappuccino is six Swiss Francs. Whatever — we are on holiday. Greta learns the Tunisian manager/clerk's family history while I retire to a comfortable chair for the next 90 minutes, write this week's happenings, and nurse my coffee.

The weather forecast called for rain this afternoon. Right on schedule, (the Swiss are **SO** precise) it starts to rain. Greta enters a women's clothing store while I head across the street to First Bank EKI of Interlaken. The sign on the building indicates this bank opened in 1852. Luca has nothing to lose so he enters the bank. I am second in line. When it's my turn, I politely ask the teller if she could change his 250 Swiss Francs large bills into smaller denominations and one, two, and five Swiss Francs coins. I hold my breath waiting for her reply — **SUCCESS**. The teller asks for the denominations I want! Whoa, this bank has money and is able to honor a customer's request. My kind of bank!

It's cold and windy. I pull out the umbrella as a steady rain falls. This weather is not in my best interests. For the past three days, my body has been recovering from whatever type of cold I caught. I am still not *'up to snuff'* and hope that I don't have a relapse or get sicker.

We quickly walk to the Interlaken West station to catch Bus 105 home. After a 15 minute wait in the rain, we board the bus. It's standing room only. We can't see out the windows and we miss our bus stop by a few blocks; but (love those **BUTS**), we exit across the street from a locals bar and restaurant. We try it. Our premonitions are spot on. *La Tap Berne* is a *'locals'* Irish themed neighborhood bar. All that's missing are clouds of cigarette smoke hanging over the bar making your clothes smell like cigarette smoke and filling your lungs with secondhand smoke that creates a nasty cough. A few *'old local guys'* sitting at tables and at the bar throw down draft beers. Local *'small talk'* fills the airwaves. American reggae music and American 'Oldies but Goodies' play in the background. The bar/restaurant reminds us of the locals bar in Wurtzburg, Germany where we ate 11 years ago. Three local ladies, one local gentleman, and four dogs occupy the table next to us! Barbara, our waitress from Portugal, tells us New Zealand businessmen own the bar/restaurant. They converted the bar into an Irish themed establishment. Barbara brings Greta a nice red wine, Luca a cold, local draft beer and a bowl of American bar snacks, pretzel sticks, and crackers! We definitely enjoy this place.

There are a number of great choices on the menu. We split a house salad and a rack of ribs. Another beer, another wine, the food is great. We are stuffed and ready to waddle three blocks to the hotel. When Barbara brings the bill, Luca comments "that's **TOO** much." I go thru my entire list of USA senior discounts, to no avail. Barbara is tough. "Maybe next time you come for dinner, we can work something out. We are closed on Mondays." She does relent and brings us Bailey's and coffee liqueur shots *'on the house.'* As I say many times, **FREE** is my favorite word. I pay the bill while Greta makes a visit to the free potty. It's time to head home and crash. Tomorrow, I will learn the fate of my ill-advised time in the cold rain today.

*****

Friday, May 3 — Day 39
Chilling at the Hotel

I am fighting a cold, coupled with an annoying deep cough so, since I am not 100%, I decide to *'chill'* at the hotel and *'take the day off'*. I hate skipping *'must do'* Switzerland activities; but the body says *'No Mas'* so in the long run, it's better to shake this now rather than prolonging the cold and the hacking, annoying cough.

Greta decides to take the bus to town. This is her first solo bus trip into Interlaken OST. Let's hope she doesn't get lost, get on the wrong bus, and winds up in Geneva! She has a plan — stop at the *'Apotheke'* to get some good drugs for me and stop at the CO-OP grocery store for some chicken strips and fruit for our in room picnic lunch. Success. Greta completes her errands and makes it back without incident. She earns a *'way to go Greta'* award for successfully completing her solo trip to and from town without getting lost or winding up in a different country.

Keeping with our *'stay home and chill'* plan today, we dine at the hotel restaurant. I am hungry. I order wonton soup, split a mixed green salad with Greta, and order the panko baked chicken, mashed potatoes, and fresh veggies for my main course. Greta also orders wonton soup and eats her half of the mixed green salad. She also enjoys some of my panko chicken. The chicken platter is superb. I want some gravy to enhance the mashed potatoes and chicken. I walk over to our waiter who is standing at the left end of the bar and ask for hot gravy. The waiter looks at me like I am speaking Chinese! He has a very confused expression on his face and says, "Gravy?" When he pulls out his smart phone to Google *gravy,* I blurt out, *'brown sauce.'* The waiter's body language and face light up. Gravy is referred to as *'brown sauce'* in Switzerland. He dashes back to the kitchen and brings out a gravy serving dish with the **BEST** brown gravy in town! It certainly enhances the chicken and potatoes.

Greta retires to the room to play with her iPhone and read. She may also find a movie or mini-series to watch on the iPad. I head to the hotel lobby and talk for 75 minutes with Roderick, my USA based iCloud manager. Roderick has access to my iCloud account. He downloads my pictures and files them by day on his computer. Now, I can delete the downloaded photos from my iPhone and free up space for **MORE** pictures. We discuss many topics. including hanging out in Vegas and taking a European trip someday when he is cancer free.

*****

Saturday, May 4 — Day 40
Interlaken, Switzerland

Luca is still not 100%, so Greta and Luca forgo heading to *Kleine Scheidegg*, a mountain pass with spectacular views (just ask Rick Steves). Vacationers access this area by taking a cog wheel train out of Lauterbrunnen. We rationalize this decision simply by saying that we have seen plenty of snow covered mountain tops. Why spend money to see more? Once you have seen one snow covered mountain top, you have seen them all. We add his journey to our next Interlaken *'must do'* list in 2026!

Today's weather is outstanding. We wait until 13:15 and catch Bus 105 to Interlaken West. We mosey around town, window shop, and take more pictures. Greta finds a local artist's studio and negotiates a good deal, buying her entire inventory of gifts for special people at home. My gifts to friends and family are sharing 10,382 pictures and videos and telling stories about the 78 day journey. After all, who needs a tee shirt that says *'Papa Keoni went to Europe for 78 days and all I got was a lousy, cheap Gildan 100% cotton, tee shirt'* that shrinks two sizes after washing in cold or hot water.

I want a bowl of soup for lunch. It helps with the cold and fills me up. I look at menus at six restaurants. **NONE** of them serve soup for lunch. I find it hard to believe **NO** restaurant in Interlaken West serves chicken noodle soup. Plus, the large grocery store CO-OP does not sell canned chicken noodle soup. How do we know this?

We asked. I guess Campbell's chicken noodle soup never *'made it'* overseas. Maybe there a *'business opportunity'* for someone to introduce Switzerland to this American staple!

We enter Bebbis Bar and Restaurant, Luca's favorite hangout. Why, they **ALWAYS** serve fresh, hot soup. I order the soup of the day, cream of mushroom. It's the same soup I enjoyed a few days ago. I guess several customers also like mushroom soup, so now it's the "Soup of the Week"! Anyway, it's *'the bomb'* and it hits the spot. Greta goes cheeseburger and fries and asks for it served *'protein style.'* The young waiter with a great smile, who we later learn is from Afghanistan, looks at her like *'what language you speaking Americano lady? Greek?'* She attempts to explain *'protein style'* – it means serving the burger without the bun, along with lettuce, tomato, and special sauce. He smiles and nods like he fully understands; **BUT** (don't we love **BUTS**), when he brings her lunch, the burger is between a bun! Again, Greta does her best to explain *'protein style'* and succeeds when she removes the top and bottom bun and tosses them on the floor! Magic, the bun disappears. Our young Afghani waiter is a very attentive worker. His customer service and smile are outstanding. We can't imagine *'things'* he has seen and experienced. He said he fled Afghanistan three years ago and spent time in Turkey before moving to Interlaken. He has worked at Beebis for the past nine months. Someday, we'd love to sit down with him and listen to his stories. Like MacArthur said, "We shall return (in 2026)."

Without a doubt, today is the best, most beautiful, weather day. The sun is shining. White puffy clouds dot the blue sky. It's very pleasant outside. The views are terrific. We enjoy our very slow, *'75-year young, old people'* stroll thru town.

Before heading home, we take a bus to the Interlaken OST section of town. Here, we stop by our friendly neighborhood grocery store CO-OP and buy fruit, chicken strips, and instant soups (just pour into a cup, add boiling water, wait two minutes, stir, and eat). We also pick up a jar of Nescafé instant decaf coffee that we enjoyed in Chur. To the other customers' delight, we **AVOID** the self-checkout stations.

We enjoy another in room dinner of chicken strips, hot instant soup, chips, fruit, and hot tea with honey and lemon. Greta opens a bottle of red wine to drink with dinner.

After dinner, I spend time catching up and finishing the *'what's happening'* past few days stories that our four favorite fans **DEMAND!**

Tonight, I **WILL** get a good night's sleep with the assistance of half a sleep-aid pill. Until tomorrow — good night!

*****

Sunday, May 5 — Day 41
Thun, Switzerland

Well, the sleeping aid really helped me get a good night's sleep without *'coughing up a storm.'* Since I am feeling better, I suggest a day trip to Thun. Greta agrees. We get up at 09:05. I am still a little groggy from the sleeping pill, though. We shower in record time, get ready, and run downstairs to the breakfast room for some nourishment, coffee, and hot tea. We gather up our day traveling things (extra jacket, phone chargers, throat cough suppressants, and umbrella) and get to the bus stop in time to catch the 10:50 Bus 105 to Interlaken West. The bus is one minute late. That rarely, if ever, happens here. When it arrives, we know why. The bus is packed with riders and travelers. It's Sunday, a getaway day for some. When the bus arrives at Interlaken West, we have four minutes to locate the right platform to catch Train IC 817 at 11:05 to Thun. We make it with three minutes to spare. It's a great way to start the day.

The train only stops at Spiez during the 27-minute ride. Sitting across from us is a 24-year old young lady from Dallas. She's on a three week trip thru Europe with, and visiting, some friends. We are sitting in first class. But, she doesn't have a first class reserved seat. "Don't worry," I say. "If the conductor shows up, I will distract him or her. You then bolt for the next car." Within minutes of stopping at Spiez, here comes the lady conductor. She checks our tickets and approaches the gal from Dallas who doesn't have the upgraded ticket. The young lady explains *'what happened'* (got on wrong train or some other BS story). It works. She gets off with a warning from the conductor, "Next time, have a ticket." When the train pulls into Spiez, she exits. How come a few weeks ago in Monterosso, Italy, two conductors nailed me for 60 Euros or face the prospect of going to jail for a ten minute train ride for not having the correct ticket that day in my Eurail account? If you recall, I filed a complaint with the Italian train company and told Citibank not to pay the 60 Euros charge. Great news, Trenitalia refunded my 60 Euros and emailed me an apology letter.

On the right side of the train, we see Lake Thun. There are many spectacular homes built along the water's edge.

We leave the train in Thun. Well, in reality, we almost forgot to get off. We didn't hear the garbled conductor's announcement over the PA system of the *'Thun'* stop. Just before the train pulls out of the station, I see a sign *'Thun'* on the platform and bolt for the exit with Greta in tow. We barely make it off. All that excitement creates the need for a potty break. Yes, many Swiss train stations, including Thun, charge a fee for using public restrooms, often around 1-2 Swiss Francs. These fees help maintain cleanliness and cover operational costs. While it can seem steep, Swiss public facilities are typically well-maintained and equipped! While I look for the correct coinage, an elderly gentleman looks at us and waves us over to the potty entrance he was standing by; he is paying for our potty break!! Here is what he does: he deposits the 1.50 Swiss Francs, then walks six steps to his left, opens the exit door, and waves us in! Whoa! I just learned a new trick for future Luca and Greta's future potty stops. "Danka, Danka sir," I say. As we enter the water closet, we sure hope there are no security cameras recording our every move.

It's Sunday. Most shops are closed. We discuss taking a ferry boat to Spiez later in the day; but first we want to visit a famous local castle. Using Google Maps, I locate the castle and get directions. We jump on a Bus without buying tickets. We are only going one stop three minutes away. Luck is on our side, especially when we enter and exit the bus from the rear door. The castle's website directions are in German and impossible to understand. I walk in four directions while the GPS keeps showing I am going in the **WRONG** direction! How can I be going in the wrong direction when I start down every street at this circle intersection? Frustrated, pissed off, and ready to toss the phone in the river, I think twice. Greta walks away in frustration with Luca's attitude. Luca sees a couple out for a walk with their baby and asks for directions of the castle. The gentleman turns around and points to a staircase tucked between two buildings and says, "Cross the roadway and take those steps up to the castle." "Danka," I reply.

Greta and I dodge traffic coming at us from all directions as we cross the busy circle interchange. Circles are big traffic movers in Switzerland. Well fans, we make it to the base of the steps and look up: approximately 60 stone steps to the top. Fortunately, there's a handrail and we use it to begin our climb. Slowly but surely, we walk to the top. Exhausted and worn out, we make it. We get to the castle ticket office and castle entrance, which is 200 - 300 meters down the path. I pay the entrance fees and add two handheld audio listening devices that are supposed to translate the Swiss language into English and tell us what we are looking at during the self-guided tour. The audio devices cost me six Swiss Francs; what a waste of money.

Off we go into the twelfth century castle. The tour takes us up four stories. However, based on the number of steps we will be climbing, I suspect the climb to be at least eight stories. Fifteen to twenty well-made steps up to the first level are easy to climb. No issues here. We get to see items from the 12th through 15th centuries which were discovered during excavations of the area surrounding the castle and found in churches. The most phenomenal items displayed are religious alter tapestries dating back to the 16th century. Each tapestry *'tells a religious story.'* Some of the tapestries are booty from winning wars. It's really hard to believe they are still in excellent condition after all these years.

Ascending to the next floor becomes our next challenge as it is a narrow, steep, circular stairwell. The steps get narrower and smaller making the ascent up the **VERY** tight and circular staircase, to say the least, an adventure. Coats of arms, representing the lineage of numerous town mayors who were here for over hundreds of years, are displayed on the third floor. (I bet my friend, Thom Metcalf, a coat of arms aficionado, could spend hours in this room.)

We also saw an exhibition of the Scales of Justice. According to Wikipedia, Lady Justice is often depicted with a set of scales, typically suspended from one hand, upon which she balances the relative substance and value (i.e., the 'weight') of the available evidence and arguments on both sides of any bilateral dispute. The scales can therefore *'tip in favor'* of either side and justice, in terms of the metaphor, can be enacted upon seeing the result.

All in all, we *'hang out'* on the third of four floors for about eleven minutes and move to the top floor. This ascent is the toughest yet. Not only are the steps different sizes (small and smaller), but the stairwell is also a **VERY** tight, circular walkway. People are encouraged to use the very thick rope attached to the wall as a hand rail. Essentially, you pull yourself up and up hoping that around the next bend you will see the top step and landing area. I also think while the ascent is very difficult, the descent is *'going to be a bitch!'* I reach the top step. Greta is a trooper but is eight steps behind. She finally makes it. We find a couple of chairs, sit down, catch our breath, and rest what's left of our bodies. Whose idea was it to climb this medieval version of the Matterhorn today?

On the top floor is a large meeting room. Five rows of chairs provide room for more than 100 people to sit (and/or die after climbing the steep, narrow circular stairways) and listen to the speaker. This floor presents spectacular views of the town below. Our camera phones are on overdrive as we snap picture after picture. We both pass on the final ascent up to one of the lookout posts. We **KNOW** our limits. It's now time for the descent. It's too bad there isn't a rope hanging from one of the windows to allow us to rappel down the side of the building. This would make the descent so much easier and faster. However, since we couldn't find the rope, we slowly but surely begin our downward trek taking one small step at a time down three flights of circular stairwells until we reach floor one. After surviving the treacherous decent and reaching floor one, we are rewarded with a long, well-built staircase with a handrail leading down to the ground floor. We survive to live another day. As we start to walk down to street level, someone points to an elevator close by that we can take to street level without climbing down seven flights of stairs.

Success. We make it and find ourselves in the Old Town section of Thun. There are numerous restaurants situated along the river. We are entitled to a well-deserved lunch. We find an outdoor cafe, sit at a two-seat table, and order a bowl of soup and a seafood salad. The soup is excellent; however, the seafood salad contains '*creatures of the sea,*' a potpourri of poorly cooked crustaceans and squishing sea surprises that we have never seen before. Greta takes one bite and passes on the salad. I remove '*never before seen seafood objects*' and eat what's left. Clearly, my ordering the seafood salad was a poor choice for both of us. We end our stay in Thurn by walking six blocks to the train station and waiting less than five minutes to board the train back to Interlaken OST. Sometimes, our timing is spot on.

We depart the Interlaken OST train and plan to hit up our favorite CO-OP grocery story for some additional nutrition. Unfortunately, it closes at 15:00 on Sunday. So, we catch the next Bus 104 back to headquarters and die. The results of the castle hike are eerily similar to my Monterosso to Vernazza six kilometers up, over, and down the mountain *'death march'* hike on Day 22, our first day in the Cinque Terre. We are both beat. So, I forgo dinner, climb into bed at 16:00 (4:00 p.m. for those keeping score at home) and for the next 14 hours, I am fast asleep. The climb and the sinus cold kicked my ass. Greta staggers down two flights of the 24 steep and narrow steps to the restaurant for dinner.

Lesson learned today – We shouldn't say *'we can do this'* when, in reality, we shouldn't attempt to do it. We will both be paying the price tonight and tomorrow. So be it. Good night.

*****

Monday, May 6 — Day 42
Our 41st Anniversary in Interlaken, Switzerland

Happy 41st Anniversary Greta!! If I had a bag of Uncle Ben's rice, I'd toss it at you like you did 41 years ago, a little past 5:00 P.M. in a 7-11 convenience store in Santa Ana, California. We were married at the Santa Ana courthouse on Friday, May 6, 1983 at 4:55 p.m., five minutes before they were closing for the weekend. After buying rice and cigarettes (yes, I used to smoke) at the 7-11, I stopped by my office to pick up materials for a Monday sales presentation. Next, we grabbed a quick dinner in a Woodbridge restaurant. One of my co-workers, Pete Meade, was at the restaurant. When he heard the great news, he sent a bottle of champagne to our table. With a *'buzz'* affecting my senses and concentration, we stopped at my home so I could grab my softball gear. We drove to Heritage Park in Irvine, CA where I had a 7:30 p.m. co-ed softball game. I played center field for the team. I hoped and prayed, *'Please don't hit the ball at me, I was having trouble seeing and maintaining my balance.'* Our postgame *'wedding celebration dinner'* was held at Lamppost Pizza, complete with pizza and beer (now, dear reader, you understand why I like that combination!). The sheer excitement of the last five hours found both of us crashing and burning on my waterbed. Let's leave it that: it was a wedding day like no other. Ah, the memories!!

Now back to our trip. In Interlaken, we wake at 09:05, eat, gather our souvenirs, and catch Bus 105 to Interlaken West. When we leave the bus, Mother Nature is calling me: *'gotta go'* **NOW!** This time, I am prepared. I have one Swiss Franc in hand and descend one level down to the pay potties. Carrying the backpack, Greta sets out for the post office that's three blocks up the street on the left, directly across from McDonald's. I expect to meet Greta there and head up the street. Along the way, I stop at a souvenir store and find the *'just right Swiss hat'* I've been looking to buy!

When I get to the post office, Greta is **NOWHERE** to be found. Did she run away? Did she mail herself back to Henderson? Was she across the street at McDonald's having a cup of coffee? Did some young Swiss hunk *'sweep her off her feet and promise her eternal fame and fortune?'* Where's Columbo when you need him? I call Greta. While I was navigating the pricey restroom situation, Greta decides to wait comfortably under an awning down the street because the backpack, which contains all the goodies we are mailing home, is too heavy to carry. She says she sent me a text to let me know where she was. I didn't check my texts because I assumed Greta was waiting patiently at the post office. The score is Greta 1, me 0.

Here we go again. I'm sure you've heard that to **'assume'** means making an ass out of you and me. Luca wins the **'ass'** award. I walk back three blocks and find Greta exactly where she says she is sitting. I am expecting another whooping: two shots with her right fist to my gut and two shots to the kidney with her left fist. (OK, she didn't actually do this...I'm melodramatic at times, if you haven't noticed.) Luca catches his breath, grabs the backpack, and starts walking back to the post office with Greta trailing behind.

Today's mission is halfway completed. We are easing our load and shipping our *'just hada buy stuff'* home. I previously set up the mailing labeling on-line using the Switzerland Post Office QR code found in their mailing instructions. This is a significant time improvement over the two-plus hours it took to mail things in Como, Italy 11 years ago. Greta took a few minutes to box everything *'nice and tight'* to avoid any breakage. The young lady post office clerk presses all the right buttons and collects cash (no credit cards allowed) from our bank account when I provide our Wells Fargo debit card. Then, I sign five copies of the mailing order. The clerk gives us our receipt and says, "Arrivederci. Your junk should be delivered in four to eight days. And thanks for using the Swiss Postal System."

As forecast, it's raining. Greta wants a traditional collapsible cane. The cane I bought in Italy was too cumbersome to use as it has a support section for her elbow. We J-walk across the busy street, barely dodging a car and an elderly lady riding an electric bike (slow down *'Sista'*, we are old and walk accordingly). We head to the *'Apotheke'* one block up the street to the left. Greta selects the proper color and design (extremely important features, it's not about stability, it's about *'looking good'*) of a collapsible cane with a cute carrying case. I buy a fresh supply of the *'over the counter'* day and night cold pills and a bottle of cough syrup with codeine to suppress my cough and knock me out at night. (Yes, I didn't need a prescription.)

Next door is the Dunkin coffee shop. Two couples are *'hanging out'* in the **ONLY** two tables, four chairs indoor seating area, so we mosey down the street and stop at *Tchibo*, a coffee shop that also sells dishes, women's under garments and tops, small household appliances, baby clothes, bath towels, and coffee. To say the least, it's a very unusual combination of items under a coffee shop roof. Why? Well, the coffee shop owners are paying rent on the entire floor space so why not maximize revenues by selling some everyday items to a wide customer base? These are savvy business owners, to say the least. We order hot tea, a cappuccino, and a fruit muffin. The muffin is simply *'to die for,'* the best pastry in 44 days. I return to the counter and order a coffee with cream and the last, delicious muffin. It's raining pretty good outside. We are on vacation. So, we play Swiss *'locals,'* nurse the teas and coffees, thoroughly enjoy the two muffins, and sit and relax for the next 90 minutes. My body needs a good days rest **PLUS**... no one is rushing to usher us out.

An hour and a half later, with the rain slowing, it's time to move on and head to Bus 104 for the ride home. Our bus leaves the station in 15 minutes. I make one final stop at the souvenir store and purchase a *'Switzerland'* grey and red baseball cap. We make the bus with moments to spare and arrive back *'at the ranch'* to continue our *'chill day.'* I settle into my favorite chair in the lobby surrounded by the ambiance of the hotel and I dive into some more storytelling about the past few days. Greta chills upstairs icing her sore knee. About an hour in, Greta calls to say the ice pack bag leaked all over the bed comforter on her side of the beds. "Come get it and ask Nicole for a new comforter," she says. I climb up 12 steps in the narrow stairwell to the room, pick up the wet comforter, and head back to the lobby. I explain the situation to Nicole and I ask if she could place it in the hotel dryer in the basement and *'make it good again.'* No problem. Nicole returns about 12 minutes later with a completely dry bed comforter.... "Danka Nicole!"

We're hungry (what's new?) so we make plans to return, one more time, to the Irish pub three blocks up the street. However, it's Monday. The restaurant is closed. Instead, we make the journey downstairs to the ground floor restaurant. Greta orders barley soup and mixed green salad. I also order the soup and a bratwurst platter with a side of mashed potatoes and green salad. Greta's four ounce red wine is **EXACTLY** four ounces, not one drop more. When Zuzanna, our waitress, places the glass on the table I point to it. I tell her it's our wedding anniversary. I place my right index finger two inches higher on the wine glass, hopefully communicating that she could fill it up a little more. "That's how we serve it," she says.

We can't get another two inches of wine on our anniversary! Oh well, I tried.

The soup, salad, brat, and mashed potatoes are outstanding. To celebrate our anniversary, we order two ice cream sundaes with chocolate sauce and two squirts of whipped cream. I generously tip the wait staff, thanking them for the excellent service we experienced during our nine night stay.

Let's take a moment to reminisce about our anniversary dinners. A mere ten years ago, we were driving cross country to attend my mother's 90th birthday celebration in Willow Grove, PA. On our anniversary day, we stop in Harlan, KY. Harlan is special to us. Why, you ask? Harlan is the 'setting' for 'Justified' an American neo-Western crime drama television series that premiered on March, 2010, on the FX network and can now be found on Prime Video. According to Wikipedia, the series revolves around the inhabitants and culture in the Appalachian Mountains area of eastern Kentucky, specifically Harlan County where many of the main characters grew up. The series, comprising 78 episodes, was aired over six seasons and concluded on April 14, 2015. We didn't miss an episode.

Anyway, when we arrive at the only hotel in town at 5:00 p.m., a group of railroad train maintenance workers are enjoying their hot dogs and beer happy hour. With open arms, they greet Greta. One of the workers offers her 'a dog and a beer.' She politely declines. We check in, unload the bags, learn the location of the opening scene of the 'Justified' TV series, and the location of the only restaurant open tonight in this railroad town. Using the map obtained from the front desk clerk, we drive to the **EXACT** location of the opening TV scene and take what seems like an album of pictures. It's truly just like we see on TV. Next, we head to *Piggly Wiggly*, a ten seat local barbecue joint. We immerse ourselves in barbecued ribs covered with homemade BBQ sauce, beans, and potato salad. Extra napkins keep our hands and face from being a walking commercial for this restaurant. We wash it all down with two Cokes. Happy 31st anniversary Greta, a trip and dinner we shall **NEVER** forget!

Now let's get back to our last evening in Interlaken. I decide to take an after dinner walk. The rain has stopped. I am checking out a Booking.Com rental apartment for a friend. Waze GPS gets me to the front door. Sadly, the building exterior and surrounding properties don't look like the pictures on the website.

Greta heads up to the room. Shortly thereafter, I return. It's time to pack up. At 10:00 tomorrow, we board a train to Strasbourg, France.

We have super great memories of our time in Switzerland. Luca unequivocally proclaims we *'shall return'* to visit the three adventures we sadly did not get to see - spending a day in Gimmelwald, hiking from Murren to Gimmelwald and taking the Kleine Schedidegg train up the snow covered mountains.

All we need is another week – but....lights out and good night.

*****

Tuesday, May 7 — Day 43
Interlaken, Switzerland
to Strasbourg, France

After a restless night of coughing, I am up and although groggy, I jump into the shower. I use the rushing hot water to wake me up plus massage my neck and back. Greta is fixing her hair. Today, sadly, we leave Interlaken, Switzerland after nine great days and nights. The bags are packed; we are ready to roll.

Summarizing our last day events - we enjoy our final breakfast and see a 6' 6" man who **MUST** significantly duck his head to enter the breakfast buffet room. The archway between the buffet area and the dining room ceiling is less than 6' high. If he doesn't duck, he will undoubtedly get a nice bruise on his head. By the end of breakfast, I suspect he's going to need a massage to loosen up a stiff neck and back that he got while bending over to avoid the entryway and to eat!

After breakfast, we ask Nicole, the owner, to please call us a cab. It's raining. We don't want to be stupid and wet and attempt to haul our suitcases onto Bus 104 and save the 15 Swiss Francs cab fare to the Interlaken Ost Train Station. We say our goodbyes to the owner, exchange email addresses, and accept Facebook requests. We are really going to miss this place. Nicole is traveling to the USA for five weeks to attend her exchange student son's high school graduation In Michigan. For the balance of her holiday, she plans to explore the West Coast, including a stopover in Las Vegas. Greta will email her suggestions on where to stay and things to do in Vegas. Unfortunately, we will still be on our 78-day adventure when she is scheduled to stay in Vegas.

Our cab arrives. Nicole grabs both of our suitcases and marches down the 12 stone steps (like she's done this a thousand times before), one at a time, in near world record fashion to the awaiting cab. We bid ado. Off we go to the Train Station and our next five day adventure in Strasbourg, France. The cab ride costs 17 Swiss Francs.

Our train departs from platform five at exactly 10:00. Swiss trains are **ALWAYS** on time. After our last, free potty stop, Luca and Greta head down the walkway, walk through the underground tunnel, and up the ramp to platform five. We have First Class seats.

The train departure board shows cars one to four are all First Class and they are the last four cars at the rear of the 15 car train! As quickly as two old farts can, we hustle down the platform, toss our bags onto car three, fall exhausted into two window seats, and begin the two hour journey to Basel SBB. The **SBB** refers to the Swiss Federal Railways to distinguish it from Basel's other main train station, Basel Bad Bf.

Prior to getting on the train, I talk with a rail station ticket agent and learn that our two month *Eurail* passes **INCLUDE** free first class seats. We can sit in the first class car without a seat reservation unless the schedule indicates we must purchase one. We now understand why train conductors have been so nice to us when we sit in the first class car on various trains as we travel to our Swiss adventure destinations. It **ONLY** took me 44 days of traveling throughout Europe on trains to learn we have first class rail passes. Greta shouts out loud enough for everyone within two blocks of the Train Station to hear her rip me a new asshole saying, "A triple dun cuff old Americano man."

Luca has not coughed in over 90 minutes, a good sign. I chugged a capful of the nighttime codeine cough syrup before leaving Interlaken OST. I just hope I don't fall asleep and miss our stop at Basel SBB.

The train conductor is wearing his official SBB black suit, red tie, white shirt, and a red man purse strapped over his left shoulder. He scans our tickets and quickly confirms they are valid. The lady sitting across the aisle in First Class is asked to leave the car because she doesn't have an FC ticket. Nice try lady.

Shortly thereafter, a second conductor comes down the aisle offering coffee and cappuccino drinks. We **ASSUME** the drinks are **FREE** because we are in the First Class car. *'Wrong you idiots'* there's a ten Euros charge! Prior to getting on the train, I did a great job getting rid of the Swiss Francs we had. Neither of us have any Swiss Francs or Euros left! Even though we took a sip of our drinks, do we return them with a *'sorry no can pay'* comment to the conductor? Unfortunately, he does not accept credit cards. So, we scramble to find the cash! We dump the contents of our purses and backpacks and come up with exactly ten Euros in coins. It would have been really embarrassing if we hadn't come up with the money. Chances are very high he would have taken any amount of Euros and Swiss Francs as we had and called it a day while at the same time muttering to himself, "Stupid American tourists!"

The Swiss train arrives on time, of course, at 12:00 in Basel SBB. The Swiss railway prides itself for being on time **ALL** the time. The Basel SBB station is located on the border of France and Switzerland. Once we get off the train, our first order of business is to locate an ATM machine that dispenses Euros.

We exit the train on Platform 9 and **MUST** quickly get to Platform 31 to catch TER 96224 which is scheduled to depart at 12:21. Are you shitting me? That's like .5 mile away!!! The journey takes us up one floor, then down a corridor. We carefully watch for directional signs. In lieu of dragging our suitcases down a long escalator, we take an elevator one floor down, turn left, and follow the signs to Platform 31. This station is **HUGE**, the largest we have seen in Europe and much larger than Penn or Grand Central Stations in New York City. There are many restaurants and take-out food options. Since we just don't know how long it will take us to reach Platform 31, we just *'keep on rolling'*. There's just not enough time to stop for snacks and drinks that we can enjoy on the train to Strasbourg. It's clearly evident we are now in France. How can I tell? The train cars are ancient and dirty. As we do, every time we enter a new country, we change our names to Collette and Jacques!

Our First Class seats are in car one, another 15 car walk almost out of the terminal. Collette is a real trooper. She not only beats me to Car 1, but she also lifts the suitcases and travel bags up onto the train! I dump our *'stuff'* on the floor between cars one and two and assist her up the steps. There are **NO** motion sensors to automatically open the doors into the car. You must turn a white handle that clearly needs a fresh coat of oil based paint,45 degrees to the left and hope the doors open and stay open. Welcome to 1980's French train technology. We already miss the great Swiss engineering. There are luggage racks on the left and right side of the train car entrance. I place our bags in what I hope is a safe place. The French train cars are very old and dirty, but what are our options? We settle into two very comfortable lounge type chairs for the one hour, 18 minute ride to Strasbourg.

Along the way, it is clear that French graffiti artists have been out in full force decorating the concrete walls along the train route.

When we exit the station, I attempt to hire a cab for a ride to the hotel. We are tired, hungry, and quite honestly, are not in the mood to hike however close, or far, it is to our new five day home. The French cab driver in position one at the station (there are 10 to 15 cabs behind him) **REFUSES** to take us to the hotel! He claims it is just a mere 500 meters away. He points in the alleged direction of the hotel, so we attempt the walk. He lied. We get lost following Google Maps directions. Some of the street intersections have no signs or markings on buildings indicating the name of the street. I call the hotel but get nowhere with the front desk. After a few more blocks, we need potty and food. We set our bags down at a corner outdoor cafe and take turns using the facilities. After a few minutes, we flag down a waiter and ask for menus in English. He tells us the kitchen is **CLOSED**. It's 14:30 and the kitchen is closed? **REALLY**, it's closed? So, we gather up our belongings and continue our journey, **HOPEFULLY** in the right direction to our hotel.

Jacques, (that's me), switches to the Waze directions App and gets a bead on the route to our French home. We are in what appears to be the historic, old section of town. The roadway is a collection of 3" x 3" stones. Pedestrians make up most of the traffic. A few *'kamikaze'* bikers have no regard for people walking the pathway and wiz by. Small retail stores selling clothes and tourist souvenirs are located on both sides of the pathway. Small local restaurants occupy both sides of path.

Hunger sets in, especially for Jacques. He is pulling **BOTH** suitcases with their two travel bags attached. We stop at a very small outdoor restaurant, *Au Fond de la Theiere*. We split a cold chicken sandwich on a long baguette, a bowl of homemade vegetable soup, and down a Sprite and Coke Zero. Collette engages in life and family history with a French couple sitting at the table next to us. What's new?

While enjoying lunch, five heavily armed French soldiers wearing their official military issued uniforms and heavy battle gear, walk down the path. Clearly, these are *'no nonsense'* guys. They carry automatic weapons ready to use in a second's notice. Are we visiting a country reminiscent of our experience in Fiji some 40 years ago, during the first anniversary of their military coup? Has the military taken over the weak French liberal government? Colette asks her new friends, "What's up?" They tell her the military can't do anything unless police ask for help. It's more of a show of force. Let me say this, their automatic weapons look **BIG** and ready to use if something *'bad'* happens. We also wonder if they are looking for Luca and Greta. Thank goodness we changed our names to Collette and Jacques.

After finishing our lunch with you guessed it, a *'to die for local desert,'* it's time to resume the march to the hotel. Waze tells us we are less than half a mile away! *'Thanks Waze person,'* we are tired. The French are notorious for not moving or *'giving an inch'* when walking in the opposite direction in your direct path. Walking is definitely a contact sport. We notice that cyclists show no intention of yielding, slowing down, or going around when encountering pedestrians head-on. In the meantime, my crotch almost meets three front bike tires during a ten minute walk. Before we leave, I hope to clothesline one bike rider in our path who fails to yield!! I have no problem sticking my left or right arm out parallel to the ground and give them *'something to remember.'* Don't mess with the Americans.

Finally, success, we reach our destination — *'Hotel & Spa Le Bouclier D'or.'* It's a first rate, top notch hotel. Alexander, the front desk clerk, gives us a map to show us where the hotel is located in relation to top tourist attractions, the closest bank, and the self-service laundromat. Strasbourg is Collette's *'must do'* segment of the journey. Jacques is just *'along for the ride.'* With all the things to see and do locally, it's possible we may cancel our Friday day trip to Stuttgart, Germany.

Collette is tired. Her sore knee is barking. She decides to get ice from the bar and ice down the knee. I will go to the bank to withdraw some Euros (we have 0 cash in our possession) and head to the laundromat with our dirty clothes. The bank is a few hundred meters to the right on the main path and the laundry is 400 meters to the left. (For those not familiar with meters, there are 3.28084 feet in one meter. To convert meters to feet, simply multiply the length by this conversion factor.)

I quickly locate an ATM machine. It dispenses 300 Euros in 6-50 Euros bills. I hate giving a small local merchant a 50 Euros bill for a small purchase. I spy a bank that is open, enter, and ask the lady sitting behind a desk at the bank's entrance if someone can change 4 of the 50 Euro bills for smaller bills and some coins. You are **NOT** going to believe what I hear her say —"Sorry, we don't change money. We have no money in this bank. French banks don't change or have money." Wait a minute! Am I back in Italy where I heard the exact same line? Shocked and caught off guard, I give my best young John McEnroe tirade when he was not happy with a tennis referee's in/out call, *"You've got to be kidding me! This is a bank but you have no money! I guess I will go find an American bank. Our banks have money!"* I stomp out without wisely using a series of inappropriate hand gestures. I'm so, so glad that I didn't lose my cool and make a scene in the bank. Most likely, I could have caused an international incident if I hadn't stopped my *'you got to be kidding me'* rant with the bank lady. Why, you ask? Because as I exit the bank, five very *'bad ass,'* armed French soldiers carrying automatic weapons, ready to use at a second's notice, walk by. And I definitely know that former President Joe Biden, former V-P Kamala Harris, former Secretary of State Antony Blinken, and DoD Spokesperson John Kirby wouldn't spend 30 seconds trying to secure my release from a French jail in exchange for 17 known French bad guys in American jails. Even if the former foursome threw in four tickets to a Las Vegas Raiders Kansas City Chiefs football game in Las Vegas, and a deluxe, 16-seat luxury box behind home plate at game two of the 2025 World Series, there would be no deal.

Without further ado, I set out for the laundromat. It's my lucky day! There is one super large 18 kg washer that costs 10 Euros for the wash plus one Euro for the soap powder. After forty minutes, I split the clean clothes into two piles. Heavy clothes go into one dryer and lighter clothing goes into the second dryer. I spend six Euros for each dryer, buying 32 minutes of drying time. At the end of the drying cycle, some clothes are dry while others are still damp and need an additional 32 minutes of drying time. Jacques spends six Euros for more time on one dryer. All's well that ends well. When the drying cycle ends, the clothes are dry and ready for folding. I set out for our new home, stopping along the way to buy some fresh fruit.

Once the clothes are put away, Collette and Jacques head out for dinner. We find a trendy and lively bar/restaurant nearby. We share a burger, fries, and a small salad. A local draft beer and a glass of white wine finish off the meal. We meander 100 meters up the pathway to the left and settle into another trendy bar/restaurant and order dessert and beverages. Collette enjoys the crème brûlée with a decaf cappuccino while I dig into a bowl of vanilla and chocolate ice cream (one scoop of each) and a Bellini adult drink. Our bodies are *'leaking oil'*. It's been a long day. Time to head home and hit the sack. Until tomorrow, good night from Strasbourg France!

Strasbourg, France

Here is some important information about this city, according to Wikipedia and travel expert Rick Steves.

- Strasbourg is the largest city of the Grand Est region of eastern France and in the historic region of Alsace. It's the official seat of the European Parliament. Strasbourg is a city that often confuses people when it comes to its location. Is it in France? Or is it in Germany? The answer is Strasbourg is located in France. Situated near the border with Germany, the city has a rich history that reflects both French and German influences, making it a unique blend of cultures. Roughly 300 thousand people call Strasbourg home.

- Nestled on the Rhine across the border from Germany, Strasbourg offers you the best chance to experience the urban side of France's Alsace region. Forward thinking leaders created a vibrant *'city feel'* with generous space devoted to pedestrians and bikes, sleek trams, and meandering waterways. With delightful big-city energy and a name that means the "city of streets," Strasbourg is the ultimate crossroads.

- Economically, Strasbourg is an important center of manufacturing and engineering, as well as a hub of road, rail, and river transportation. The port of Strasbourg is the second-largest on the Rhine after Duisburg, Germany, and the second-largest river port in France after Paris.

- Together with Basel (Bank for International Settlements), Geneva (United Nations), The Hague (International Court of Justice) and New York City (United Nations world headquarters), Strasbourg is among the few cities in the world that is not a state capital that hosts international organizations of the first order. The city is the seat of many non-European international institutions such as the Central Commission for Navigation on the Rhine and the International Institute of Human Rights. Strasbourg is immersed in Franco-German culture and although violently disputed throughout history, has been a cultural bridge between France and Germany for centuries, especially through the University of Strasbourg, currently the second-largest in France, and the coexistence of Catholic and Protestant culture. It is also home to the largest Islamic place of worship in France, the *Strasbourg Grand Mosque.*

- While the city dodged serious damage in both world wars, Strasbourg has a dizzying history. It was hit hard during the Franco-Prussian War, becoming part of Germany in 1870. After that, there was a period of harsh Germanization, followed by extreme Frenchification after World War I, a brutal period under Nazi rule during World War II, and then the strong need to purge all that was German after 1945. Now, while probably more definitively French than it›s ever been, the city exudes a bicultural gentleness in its architecture and all-around ambience. Street signs are commonly bilingual, with both French and the Germanic Alsatian dialect.

- After World War II, British Prime Minister Winston Churchill called for a union of European nations, with the goal of winning an enduring peace by weaving the economies of France and Germany together. Given that Strasbourg had changed hands between Germany and France so many times, it seemed logical that it be a capital (along with Brussels) of what would eventually become the European Union. Today, Strasbourg shares the administrative responsibilities of the European Parliament with Brussels and Luxembourg.

- Most visitors come to Strasbourg to see the massive *Notre-Dame Cathedral* for good reason. The delicate Gothic style of the cathedral (begun in 1176 but not finished until 1439) is the work of a succession of about 50 master builders. The cathedral somehow survived the French Revolution, the Franco-Prussian War, and World Wars I and II.

- The history of Strasbourg, the capital city of the political pawn zone between France and Germany, is fascinating to contemplate. With its high-powered and trendy bustle and hybrid culture, it's one of France's most intriguing cities.

*****

Wednesday, May 8 — Day 44
Strasbourg, France

Good morning from Strasbourg, France. For some strange reason, Jacques is up at 07:38 and ready to go. He turns on the tea pot to boil water for tea for us. The TV remote is not working. It appears the batteries are dead. He contacts the front desk. The young lady replies, "I will be right up with new batteries." I better put on a pair of pants and a ball cap. The young lady arrives and switches the batteries. The remote works. While enjoying our tea and a Portugal orange, there's a knock on the door. The front desk lady brings us two croissants and two soft pretzels '*for the inconvenience*' of the TV remote not working. This hotel has class! So, we enjoy the goodies with our tea. Then we shower, dress, and head out for breakfast before today's '*let's see what Strasbourg is all about mission.*'

Before we begin, I want to tell you about our hotel room. For starters, it's the largest room we've stayed in, so far, on our journey. There's a large wooden, two-door closet, a table with an electric pot to boil water, tea cups, two high back sitting chairs with arm rests, a small dresser, a glass chandelier over the foot of the king size bed, end tables with reading lamps, a separate toilet room with a raised toilet, and a bathroom with a large shower and two sinks! The hotel provides two terry cloth robes for lounging. We are definitely '*living large*' at 250 Euros (about $260) a night. This is the first hotel since leaving Milan that **DOES NOT** include breakfast in the overall rate. This breaks a string of 40 days we didn't have to pay for our breakfast. All good things must come to an end.

Turning the shower on to get hot water challenges Collette. She can't get the hot water to stay hot. I do a physical inspection of the water on/off handles and notice a metal button. I turn the handle in the direction of hot water, press the button locking it in place and — drum roll please — we have a steady stream of hot water descending from the overhead, rain style shower head.

Let's get back to what's happening today. We leave the hotel and notice the gentleman who checked us in yesterday is cleaning up the outside patio. Clearly, when you work for this hotel, you are a multi-tasker. The dynamic duo heads up to the main walkway and searches for a coffee shop to enjoy a light breakfast. The first place we pass must be good. All outdoor seats are *'spoken for'* and there's a line waiting to get in. I remember a bagel shop one street down. When we get there, it's closed. It doesn't open until 11:00. **You've got to be kidding me!** A bagel shop, with breakfast items on the menu, doesn't open until 11:00? I can't understand the owner's opening time logic, especially with their great, visible, corner location.

We make an about face, head back up the pathway, and stop at *Artisan Boulanger*, a small takeout pastry, breads, and hot and cold drinks cafe. There is no inside seating, just four, two person tables outside. We order a large piece of white sauce pizza with cheese, onions, and ham, as well as a cappuccino and Coke Zero. The counter lady heats up the pizza, cuts it in half, and places our items on a round serving tray. We enjoy our breakfast outside; however, it's starting to get cold, the wind is kicking up. While we are eating, a group of eight teenage boys appear to be looking for some place to *'chow down.'* A few of the hungrier lads closely examine the cafe's food options. Jacques makes eye contact with the group. Thinking they were French, I chide them about France's upset loss in the Championship League semi-finals last night to Dortmund,

Germany. I stand up and salute the Dortmund victory thrusting my right fist in the air proclaiming *'Dortmund, Germany'*! Lucky for me, they didn't jeer me or flip me off! They just looked at me like a crazy American.

Today's plan is simple — mosey about town and if we see something that *'catches our eye,'* stop and visit. We pass by numerous restaurants and clothing, souvenir, candy, and ice cream shops. Our first stop is at a historic Lutheran Church just minutes from the hotel. We take the *'gotta have'* remembrance photos. I have strict orders from my sister Barbara that every time I visit a church, no matter what the denomination, I am **REQUIRED** (*'do it or else be sent to Hell when you die! That's a pretty strong request if I must say'*.) to light religious candles for our mother and family members. Barbara, I lit two candles today. You owe me $2!

Today must be our *'visit churches'* day. The sound of the church bells ringing leads us to our next stop, the Notre-Dame Cathedral. The delicate Gothic style Cathedral (ground broken in 1015, many additions completed in 1439) is the work of a succession of 50 master builders. Needless to say, the Cathedral, which took 424 years to finish, is **HUGE**. Stain glass windows line the building's exterior walls. Pictures celebrating the lives of the Virgin Mary and large statutes of saints and apostles, hang on both sides of the Cathedral.

One of the unique items is a clock that features a planetary calendar showing the current positions of the sun and moon and a mechanical rooster. Every day at 12:30, the rooster crows and apostle statutes move around the clock. On August 11, 1944 during World War II, the Cathedral was hit by American and British bombs. War damage repairs were completed in the early 1990's. Rather than overdo it with specific details, if you want more information about the history of the Cathedral, Google *'Cathedral of Notre-Dame Strasbourg.'* Yes, Barbara, I went **LARGE** and lit five candles. Your candle lighting bill is up to $7 cash, no credit cards accepted.

Unfortunately, the cathedral suffered a massive fire in April, 2019. A restoration project, which cost an estimated $800 million, repaired the damage of a destructive fire of this medieval landmark, which was thought to be accidental. According to Rebuilding Notre-Dame de Paris, thousands of expert craftspeople including carpenters, stonemasons, and stained glass window artists helped restore the 860-year-old building's spire and rib vaulting. Notre-Dame's organ required the restoration of nearly 8,000 pipes.

Adjacent to the Cathedral is The *L'Oeuvre Notre-Dame Museum*. The museum is home to some of the most important art masterpieces of the German Empire, from the 13th to the 16th centuries, including medieval and Renaissance paintings by *Conrad Witz, Hans Baldung Grien,* and *Sebastien Stoskopff.* Some of the framed paintings were not centered correctly on the walls. Attention Christy Griffin, please grab the next flight to Strasbourg and get over here to straighten the famous works of art.

Incredible sculptures by *Nicolas Berhaert* from Leiden and many of the Cathedral's original statues, wooden beams, stained glass, and other artifacts are on full display. This museum houses the oldest intact figurative stained glass window in France called "the *Wissembourg Christ.*"

It's hard to fathom how the craftsman from the 12th to 16th centuries used crude, rudimentary tools to meticulously create the magnificent sculptures, wood carvings, and other items on display. The same *'crude tools'* were used by builders and laborers during construction of the Cathedral's exterior and interior. It just *'blows my mind'* how they accomplished this! And finally, how did the builders hoist up the heavy materials used during construction? Normally, I am not a *'museum'* guy. I just *'take one for the team.'*

However, I have to admit I thoroughly enjoyed the history on display at the Notre-Dame Museum.

It's time for lunch. We stumble upon *Aus Douze Apotres* where we split a smash burger and fries. We also enjoy a local French beer and honey and lemon hot water.

We discover there's a tour boat company that uses local canals to circle the city. The company's dock is just minutes from the Cathedral. Google Maps gets us to the launch point. While heading there, we notice the wind is blowing and the temperature feels much colder than 63 degrees. We buy tickets, *'que up,'* and board the boat. Thank goodness the boat is fully enclosed with viewing windows on the sides and roof. During the 90-minute canal cruise, we get to see many parts of the city influenced by German and French architecture. The tour guide discusses the history of the buildings on both sides of the canal. This tour was well worth *'the price of admission'* and allows us to see many of the areas and buildings in Strasbourg.

We decide it is time to head back towards the hotel, chill for a while, and then go out for dinner. Jacques suggests heading up the touristy pathway. Here, I find a crowded *'locals'* bar where patrons enjoy the late afternoon weather and adult beverages. The host grabs two menus, leads us to the rear of the crowded bar/ restaurant, and deposits us at a table for two. After ordering drinks, we learn about some of the local items on the menu. However, none sounds interesting so we order American: burgers, fries, and a salad to share. Collette wants dessert. We all know what that means — gelato or ice cream. A short walk up the path brings us to a fancy corner bar and restaurant. We grab two seats at the bar, order ice cream, and Americano decaf coffees. Remembering it's our first day in Strasbourg and not wanting to *'overdo it,'* Jacques and Collette slowly walk a quarter mile back to the hotel and retire for the night.

P.S. Happy or disappointed, pick one: Sophia/Greta/Collette has not been up to her *'Lucille Ball'* act like she was on our 38-day European trip 11 years ago. She is either mature beyond belief, battling an injured right knee navigating the uneven Pompeii stone streets, and a sore head from her fall in Amalfi, so she lets Giovanni/ Marcello/Luigi/Antonio/Luca/Jacques handle everything and just *'goes along for the ride.'*

Several of our five valued fans and readers have reached out to me wondering *'what's wrong'* with Sophia/Greta/Collette. She is clearly not living up to her *'reputation'* and past all-star performances. Tell you what. I'll have a chat with her tomorrow and plead with her to *'please get back on your game'* if, for no other reason, than her fans are demanding and clamoring for tantalizing tales. After all, the fans really want much more *'entertainment'* from Sophia/ Greta/Collette.

*****

Thursday, May 9 — Day 45
Alsace, Colmar, Medieval Villages, and Castle Tour

After a good nine hours of sleep, Jacques is up at 06:30. While Collette is still asleep, I catch up on the news and sports scores from America, use the electric pot to boil water for a cup of tea and a cup of instant soup, then enjoy half of a delicious and juicy orange from Portugal.

Using the *Viator App*, I purchase a 10+ hour tour for today to take us into the surrounding countryside. Not knowing exactly how to get to the tour van meeting site, and having no desire for an early morning hike, I ask the front desk to call us a cab. It arrives in front of the hotel at exactly 08:15 and takes us to the meeting place for our first organized excursion on this trip. We have about thirty minutes to kill before we begin our adventure; however, we cannot locate a local coffee shop, Starbucks, or Dunkin. I spot Boura, a coffee and snacks *'entrepreneur.'* I buy each of us a cup of coffee. We share a small box of biscuit cookies. Boura and I strike up a conversation and become *'besties'* for the next 15 minutes.

Four motorcycle police officers with lights on and sirens wailing pull up and stop in the middle of an adjoining street. Are we getting a police escort? Is some top European, French, Asian, or American dignitary holding up traffic while being escorted thru the streets of Strasbourg? There is a European Union headquarters in Strasbourg. It turns out to be a false alarm – there's nothing to see here folks. The police pull over a tour bus to check the driver's license and bus registration papers. Rather disappointing, but I wonder why it takes four motorcycle cops to pull over a tour bus!

Our transportation today is a 20-person, mini-van bus. Our tour will take us over 70-kilometers (about 45 miles) into the countryside wine region. We start out looking at flat, large fields on both sides of the four lane (two in each direction) superhighway. It appears landowners are growing some kind of grassy vegetation.

Our first stop is the *Haut Kœnigsbourg Castle*. We enjoy a 90-minute self-guided walking tour. Collette is a real team player today. The **WALK** through the castle involves many steep climbs up narrow staircases and spending time in small rooms full of tourists. Of course, what goes up must come down. So, she carefully navigates the steep, narrow staircases back to ground level. Good news, her knee survives the tour. After that, our van driver takes us thru *Kintzheim, Bergheim, Ribeauville*, and *Hunawihr*. Acres and acres of vineyards on both sides of the country roads surround these small towns. Our next stop is *Rinqueeihr*. We have two hours for roaming and enjoying lunch. The bus driver walks us to a small winery tasting store where we sample four wines. I purchase one bottle of champagne.

We enjoy a fabulous lunch in *Rinqueeihr*. I feast on a sausage and sauerkraut crepe and a cold one while Collette enjoys a ham and cheese crepe and wine. I have a very, very difficult choice to make for desert — lemon meringue pie or a topless blueberry pie. I go with lemon meringue pie. *'It's the bomb'*! I share some pie with Collette. Somehow, and we don't know how, some of the pie gets in her hair. I use a knife to cut her hair and remove the pie. The *'cut'* creates a small, but cute bald spot. She hopes the hair will quickly grow back. Time will tell. By the time we get to Iceland next month, we hope it will *'all be better.'*

While out and about in the village, I purchase some postcards and ask the shopkeeper the location of the village's post office. His reply is, "It's closed today, Thursday." Why?? Let's just leave it as an unsolved mystery that even Columbo, on his best day, could not solve even with his iconic, "One more question..." I guess I have to ask France's President Emmanuel Jean-Michel Frédéric Macron why the post office is closed the next time I see him.

When the two hours is up, it's time to get back on the van and drive through *Sigolsheim* and *Kientzheim*, two more small villages. Mile after mile of vineyards, as far as the eye can see, are planted on both sides of the roadway. Some village residents have vineyards in the back yards. I guess the owners create their own **SPECIAL** wine. Moving on, our next stop is *Kaysersberg.* Here we have another two plus hours of free time. The van driver picks us up and our tour continues. I wonder what he does while we're visiting the vineyards and villages. Perhaps he fills the tank, grabs something to eat, and maybe a few winks. Curious as I am, Greta says, "Leave it be!" Next, we drive through *Ammerschwihr*, another small village. And what do we see...additional acres and acres of vineyards.

Our last stop is *Colmar.* The tour operator arranges for a 30-minute tram car ride through the narrow streets of this tourist city. For a moment, while riding in the tram car, we think we are at Disneyland in Anaheim, CA, or Universal Studios in Hollywood. Jacques and Collette feel like *'old tourists'* riding in this car. Guess what....we are! People along the streets stare at us, thinking, *'who are these old Americanos and what are they doing here in Colmar?'*

We have 105 minutes to meander through the village, explore, do a little shopping, and just admire this quaint town. At 17:00, it's still warm outside. We are beat, especially Collette. She *'took one'* for the uniform-less team today. She refuses to wear matching *'his and hers'* team jerseys with our names embroidered on the back above the numbers. Her knee is barking from a long day walking around. We *'retire'* to *Patisserie Dv Mvsee*, an outdoor café, where we relax and chill at a small table. A large umbrella provides adequate shade from the sun. For the next 75 minutes, we nurse drinks until it's time to head back to Strasbourg.

Before heading back to the van, Jacques needs to make a potty stop. There is a father and his young daughter in line in front of me. When it's their turn *'in the barrel,'* the father says to the daughter, "Do you need my help?" She looks at her dad and rolls her eyes, clearly communicating to him, *'Dad, I am a **BIG GIRL** and I don't need your help!'* The dad licks his wounds while Jacques says to him, "She's a **BIG GIRL** now dad!"

Let's take a moment or three to highlight what we saw and learned today.

- The grapes grown in this region are used primarily for white whites and secondarily for a red Pinot Noir.

- The climate in these villages and towns is well suited, even perfect, for growing grapes. The vineyards, planted on terraced hillsides, appear to be located much higher up than what we saw in Italy.

- Chirping birds sound like they are speaking French.

- The small villages that we pass thru are accessed by two narrow lane roads. Traffic significantly backs up just like rush hour in any major city in the USA or bumper to bumper stop and go traffic on Las Vegas Boulevard (aka the Strip) on any given weekend night.

- Houses are built very, very close to the narrow main street through the small villages. It seems like you can just reach out the van window, touch the houses, and people walking on the very narrow sidewalks. My gut tells me the houses were there when horse and buggy was the main transportation option.

- Some of the houses we drive past date back to the 1600's. Some have been restored and renovated. The older homes are identified by the old style French and German architecture, wooden slatted shutters, wrought iron railings, and small balconies. It's evident that many older homes could use some work, at least on the tired looking, faded shutters. Germany controlled this region for years, until the early 1900's, when it was returned to France after World War 1.

- Newer homes have no shutters. They have floor to ceiling roll down metal window coverings and larger, more traditional balconies.

- The roofs on all homes are very steep. They are designed to keep snow from building up.

- Very few homes have satellite TV dishes. Most sport 1960's outdoor TV antennas mounted on their roofs.

- People of all ages ride bikes on the village roadways. Most are decked out in their *'look at me'* bike riding clothes clinging tightly to their bodies to the point of where it appears to almost cut off circulation. It's time for a **HUGE** shout-out to Danielle Mollett Cladis, my former physical therapist friend with two last names. She put me *'back together'* after knee surgery and a knee replacement. Danielle is a huge bike riding enthusiast who proudly wears *'all the cool gear'* when she hits the streets and trails in Colorado.

Below are some things we saw or experienced for the first time on the trip:

- I saw two outdoor basketball courts, for the first time in 45 days.

- A big European shout-out to my Maui friend and fellow basketball referee, Nathan Kurisu. On the tour today, I saw my first auto parts store. There was a sign outside *'Help Wanted Inquire Within'* in French, of course. Nathan, this is a *'once in a lifetime opportunity'* to *'get off the rock.'* This part of France has your name *'all over it.'* All you have to do is learn the metric system and the French language.

- We stopped at the Sigolsheim National Cemetery where French soldiers killed in the Battle of Colmar Pocket from December 5, 1944 to February 9, 1945 during World War II are buried in what's called the *'Hill of Blood'.*

- As noted above, many older homes need some **'TLC.'** Clearly, the area could use a general contractor like Thom Metcalf. Thom would be *'a natural'* for this work. He has extensive home construction background, is semi-fluid in French, and enjoys a glass or three of good French wine.

On our one hour ride back to Strasbourg, we see miles and miles of fields growing some kind of grain. Also, on the ride back, there is a major backup on the freeway. Traffic has come to a complete stop. Our bus driver, however, has a *'back-up'* plan. Clearly, today is **NOT** his first day managing this tour. Instead of getting on the freeway, he takes the *'back roads'* and avoids the mess.

Today was our greatest day at sea level. Without a doubt, the tour gave us more than our money's worth of sightseeing and adventures.

Needless to say, we are *'way tired'* after this fantastic 12-hour excursion. Tonight, we agree on the same thing — postpone going down to the river, sitting on a bench, and watch the *'submarine races.'* Maybe we won't be so tired Friday night. We hate to back down and be quitters, but we both agree to cancel our Friday trip to Stuttgart, Germany. I was able to get a refund for the round trip, first class train tickets.

We arrive back in Strasbourg at 19:45. Not seeing any cabs, we start to walk home and use the top of the Notre Dame Cathedral as a landmark. Along the way, Collette ducks into a restaurant for a potty break while I distract the staff from chasing us out for not buying anything. We slowly *'march on,'* — left, right, left, right. With the Cathedral now in clear site, I use Google Maps to plot the rest of the journey home. It's less than a 10 minute walk. When we reach the river, I know **EXACTLY** where we are and how to get home without the aid of Google Maps. A right turn takes us over the river and up three blocks. We see the church located 100 meters from the hotel entrance.

Before retiring for the night, we stop and eat at a 1960's American themed diner on the main pathway. Jacques orders a veggie burger that includes a small salad and *'short'* glass of *Kronenbourg 1664* French beer while Collette chooses the onion soup, a small dinner salad, and red wine. I *'borrow'* my fourth beer glass of the trip and third today – the glass just happens to fall into my backpack. Quickly, I pay the bill. We **BOLT** for the exit and head down the street before anyone notices the missing beer glass.

Tired and worn out from today's tour, we ride the elevator one floor up, unlock the door, and collapse on the bed. But before I get too comfy, I make my way down to the bar with Collette's plastic zip lock quart size bag. The bartender gladly fills the bag with ice. Back at the room, Collette ice's her barking *'out loud'* knee. After I deliver the ice, I go back down to the lobby and chronicle today's journey while it's still fresh in my *'ever forgetful aging mind.'* Remember, I am a 75-year young senior. What a day — a day we surely will remember — at least until Friday afternoon.

It is time to retire for the night. When I reach our room, Collette is *'out like a light.'* Quickly, I join her in *'nightly, night land.'*

P.S. Here are some questions to ponder: Who picks the acres and acres of grapes at harvest time? How are the grapes picked, by hand or by machine? We asked Columbo and Sergeant Joe Friday to get on this and get us the answer!

*****

Friday, May 10 — Day 46
Kehl, Germany

We sleep in till past 09:00 allowing our bodies to recover from yesterday's 12-hour castle and multiple villages' tour. Plus, on Thursday, we added 12,000 steps to our steps count. Without a doubt, the tour *'exceeded'* our expectations. The 200 steps up and down during the castle self-tour, including multiple circular staircases, took a toll on Collette's sore knee. We made a unanimous decision last night to cancel today's trip to Stuttgart, Germany.

Jacques consults with the helpful front desk person to learn if it's possible to take a trolley car to Germany, just a few miles across the Rhine River. Yesterday, the clerk told me how to get to the *'post office.'* However, that turned out to be a false alarm. His *'post office'* recommendation was actually a store that sells stamps, packing materials, and other non-shipping items. Today, I tell the front desk clerk I need to mail a box of items back home. **NOW**, he tells me the Main Post Office is near the Strasbourg Central Train Station. So, I put this on my Saturday A.M. *"to do"* list.

Yesterday, Colette and Jacques purchased a bottle of champagne. This morning, we ask the bar for a bucket of ice to chill our *'adult beverage'* for tonight's in room happy hour. Bingo, the bartender *'comes through'*. We place the champagne in the ice bucket.

Although we cancelled today's trip to Stuttgart, our front desk host lets us know we can take a 15-minute trolley car ride across the Rhine River and get off in Kehl, Germany. Bingo, we agree this will be today's field trip adventure.

Collette, with cane in hand, and I set out to find a place to eat breakfast. The establishment just up the street is again standing room only. There is a waiting line for outside only seating. We venture down the street to yesterday's breakfast stop; however, no tables are *'open.'* So, we turn left, head down the alley, and locate an outdoor table shaded by a large tree at a local café. While it's only 10:15, the sun is out, the sky is blue, and it's warm. The initial service is **SLOW**. Do they have a staffing shortage? I put them on a two-minute countdown clock to come to our table, take our order, or watch us leave. With 37 seconds left on the clock, a smiling waitress shows up, takes our order; granola with yogurt, one baguette with real butter, one croissant with jelly, one cappuccino, and one large Americana coffee. The food is great! So is the price: 15 Euros.

Earlier, we agreed on a plan to head to Germany for lunch. But first, we need to finish our *'local chores.'* Collette looks for a pharmacy to restock my cough medicine and nose spray. I head to the *'post office'* and purchase eight post card stamps. As mentioned above, this location is **NOT** a *'full service post office.'* It's a souvenir store that sells stamps, shipping boxes, envelopes, and all kinds of souvenirs. The store owner tells me I must go to the Main Post Office by the Strasbourg Central Train Station to mail a box to the USA. That post office is open on Saturday from 9:00 to 12:00.

We rendezvous at the hotel and start our journey to Germany. After one block, Colette says "no mas, my knee is barking, I gotta take a rain check and head back to the hotel to ice and rest the knee." So, I head off to board the Line D trolley car to Kehl, Germany. I am out of Euros so I first head to a bank across the street from the trolley car stop and withdraw 300 Euros. I know the answer to my question to the bank receptionist; but ask anyway, "Can you break 50 Euro bills into smaller bills and coins please?" "No," she replies. "Banks in France don't have money. Try one of the locations that convert currencies." I badly want to say to her, *"Right, I already paid a USA dollar to Euros conversion fee with the withdrawal. Now, you want me to pay another fee to have those 'loan sharks' convert my large bills into smaller bills"!* Wisely, I keep my *'appropriate off color'* response to myself. Don't need the local police to show up and question my *'people skills.'*

I walk across the trolley tracks to board the D-Line trolley to Germany, decide to *'play it straight,'* and purchase a one-day all-you-can ride ticket for 4.50 Euros. The ticket purchase touch screen is, of course, in French with no press two for English option. Twice, I try to complete the transaction; but I cannot comply with the on screen French instructions. Was either transaction completed and, if so, where are my tickets? The trolley is fast approaching. I say to myself, *"Screw it. I will just get on the trolley, sit in the last car, and hide, hoping to get to Germany without detection."* I enter the trolley and nonchalantly sit in the back car, looking like *'I belong'* and play with my iPhone. (FYI, when we return home in June, I check my MasterCard statement and see I was charged for two tickets!) Later that day when buying a return ticket home, I discover a covered slot on the ticketing machine where tickets are dispensed! How did I miss the slot prior to boarding? A few strangers will soon learn it's their lucky day and find two free all day trolley tickets. So far, so good, no trolley police or conductor asks for my ticket. Success! I make it to the end of the line; however, it's in France on the Rhine River, **NOT** in Germany. Everyone except me gets off. A lady passenger motions to me to get off as this is the *'end of the line!'* Now, I must walk about 3/4 mile over a bridge that crosses the Rhine River to get to Kehl. I follow the lady's lead; but I observe the trolley going over the bridge into Germany! (When I returned later that day, I learned I can catch a D4 trolley in Germany and return to France.) What is **UP**? Did someone just pull a *'fast one'* on me? It's obvious my lack of knowledge of the French language and unfamiliarity with the trolley system play a huge role in my misunderstanding.

When Gustav (formerly Jacques but just for the time in Germany) reaches Kehl, Germany, he sees a man driving a Porsche; however, the driver's seat is on the right side of the car. All cars in Europe, except England, have the driver sitting in the front left seat. Strange I thought.

As my mind wanders, I **DAYDREAM** that once I cross the street into Kehl, the German police, with guns drawn, will stop me, and command me to *'get up against the wall, hands up, and spread your legs.'* It appears there is some confusion over a photocopy of my passport. In no uncertain terms, the police demand I **MUST PAY** 10,000 Euros or go to the salt mines for 15 years of hard labor. Before I give them my decision, they allow me to flip a coin. I guess I am heading to learn mining. Boy, **I am glad that dream ended!**

There are some old-timers in Germany who think they won WWII. So, Gustav, who bested the police and snuck into Germany, is on high alert for retired, old fart Gestapo dudes. Just like in old WWII movies, I envision they are wearing Columbo style tan trench coats tied loosely at the waist, collars pulled up to cover their necks, and sporting a 1940's fedora top hat. They chain smoke unfiltered cigarettes, most likely Camels or Lucky Strikes, or a home version of *'roll your own.'* They hold the *'cigs'* in their right hand, between the index and middle fingers, and have the day's local newspaper rolled up under their left arm. I *'trust'* you get that picture loud and clear. Anyway, I have my *'antlers up'* and occasionally glance over my shoulders, checking my surroundings.

It's warm in the sun. I stop for a sugar free Red Bull energy drink, water, and an electric European outlet adapter plug. I didn't check both ends of the adapter. Sadly, when I get back to the hotel, I discover the plug only works with a USB cable versus the more modern Apple product cords. It's a five Euros dummkopf by me. Around the corner, I stop at *Landbackerei*, a German bakery and buy a soft pretzel. The pastries, cakes, and breads in the display cases look **SO, SO GOOD** — fat free and of course, sugar free.

After finishing the pretzel and Red Bull, I see a lady walking down the street wearing a tattoo decorated arm sleeve. This is something I have never seen. Obviously, it's less costly than having both arms tattooed from wrist to armpit. Plus, if you don't like it, it comes off very, very easily and cheaper than removing the *'real thing.'*

It's hard not to notice, but I also see four tobacco stores in a two block area. The Germans must love to smoke.

In the distance, I spot a large half mile long street fair. As the day progresses, it seems like all western Germany residents are here! Below are the major things I see:

- multiple nationality food choices: pastries, gelato, beer, wine, liquor, sodas, juices, candy, fresh fruits,

- four musical groups providing live entertainment,

- women's and men's clothing and tee shirt stores,

- children's face painting,

- a small merry-go-round,

- women's cosmetics and fragrances,

- a TJ Maxx type store, and

- two Apotheke (pharmacies in German).

It's a **PERFECT** weather day for the event organizers. The sky is cloudless blue. The sun is out on a warm 75-degree day. Shorts and tee shirts are the order of the day. Long tables and chairs are strategically set up for people to sit down and enjoy multiple hot food choices. After walking the entire half mile long fair, I have my heart set on a grilled sausage sandwich and a draft beer. I choose a Merguez (lamb) sausage on a foot long baguette; but I decline the hot sauce in lieu of brown Dijon mustard. The sandwich consists of **THREE** sausages the size of American all beef hot dogs. I accept the challenge and slowly finish the meal. I wash it down with a local draft German beer. It's now time to get up and start walking off this *'belly bomb'* meal. I take a minute to stop at an Apotheke to pick up more cough medicine and nose spray.

I see a sign pointing to the center of town, so I stroll down a side street and discover a two story indoor mall. It's air conditioned, so I decide to take advantage of the comfortable settings and walk the mall. Potty is the *'cheapest this side of free,'* a mere .30 Euros. I hand the potty operator a .50 Euro coin and motion to *'keep the change.'* Nothing in the mall *'catches my eye'* so I head back to the fair. Along the way, I spot a small corner store selling a quart size container of fresh blueberries for one Euro! I can't pass up this bargain! On my final trip down *'street fair lane,'* I purchase a basket of super red, freshly picked strawberries to share with my beloved Collette.

It's time to return to Strasbourg. I walk to the starting point of the Line D trolley. Folks, you better **FASTEN YOUR SEAT BELTS** because the next 90 minutes or so is one of those *'I can't believe this is happening'* moments.

Gustav sees that the trolley will be departing in four minutes. I couldn't locate a conductor, so I ask a young lady in the rear car if this trolley is going to (now hold on tight) Stuttgart! (Versus Strasbourg, my intended destination). The young lady looks perplexed and indicates I need to go to the Strasbourg Central Train Station to get there. Still not aware of my senior *'Joe Biden moment,'* I *'think'* this trolley **HAS** to be going where I want to go. It's the Line D trolley! When I reach the front car, I knock on the engineer's window and ask if this trolley is going to Strasbourg. "Yes," he replies.

Next, instead of just jumping in the rear car, I ask, "Where can I purchase a ticket?" The engineer points to a ticket machine 25 meters straight ahead and to the left. I quickly head to the machine to purchase a ticket. I unsuccessfully wrestled with this type of ticket machine on my outbound trip to Germany. This time, all the instructions are in German! I insert coins but can't figure out where to get my ticket. A few open right hand smacks on the touch screen yields no results, even though the screen *'seems'* to indicate *'successful transaction.'* At the last moment, I notice a slot where the ticket is dispensed. Now, with ticket in hand, I scurry back to the trolley; however, to my utter dismay, disbelief, frustration, and **WHAT THE HELL IS GOING ON**, the trolley is **PULLING OUT** of the station! I scream and frantically wave my hands back and forth over my head like a D1 men's basketball coach near the end of a tie game trying to signal the closest referee for a timeout.

Gustav's frantic efforts **UTTERLY** fail. **I am way more pissed off than you can imagine.** So, what do I do? I decide to *'chase down'* the trolley hoping it stops at the next red light to take on passengers. **Seriously, what am I DOING, CHASING a moving trolley?** This plan fails miserably. The trolley just keeps going and creates more and more distance between us. *Picture this: close your eyes and imagine me frantically running as fast as I can with the repaired left Achilles, panting, nearly out of breath, shirt flapping in the slight breeze, and baseball cap askew trying in vain to catch up to the fast moving trolley.* Needless to say, it's **NOT** even close...I do not catch up. I see the next station a quarter mile up the road and head in that direction where I hope to catch the next "D" trolley. After a few minutes, another "D" trolley arrives. I get on, confident **THIS** trolley will take me back to where I began today's journey.

Now the **REAL FUN** begins. I know what the stop I need to get off '*looks like;*' however, I don't know the name. Collette has the trolley line map that shows each trolley line and each station's name. I am now in France, **BUT** I have a severe '*senior moment*' crisis. **Unfortunately, I can't quite remember what the stop I need to get off at looks like!** In my first 75 years on earth, **I have never, ever had this problem!** When I look out the window, I see the trolley passing the location where we started yesterday's 12-hour tour. So, I panic, exit the trolley, and **THINK** I need to head in the **OTHER** direction to get home. But my confidence level is extremely low. A local couple sees me struggling with a Strasbourg map and asks me where I am trying to go. Jacques points to the area where the hotel is. The gentleman politely says, "You need to get back **ON** the trolley and continue the journey a few more stops." I call out three '*Merci's*' but skip the cheek kissing and hugging. I am still '*not with the program.*' This is very unusual for me. Normally, once I go somewhere, I embed the landmarks and directions in my mind forever. But today it is clearly different. **Today's journey might not end well.**

Back on the Line D trolley, I look out the right side window and see a restaurant we walked by last night; but it doesn't '*register*' that the restaurant is '*mere steps away*' from where I need to get off! So, overcome by a '*senior moment,*' I fail to get off where I was supposed to. Continuing on, the trolley passes buildings and stores I have never seen before! Then, the trolley goes underground into the '*central train station.*' What the hell!?! The panic level rises to **DEFCOM 5 — MAJOR CRISIS EMINENT**. The trolley continues in a northwest direction of Strasbourg, further and further in the **WRONG** direction from the hotel. Thankfully, Collette skips this trip or else I would be constantly hearing, "Do you know where we are old man?"

Finally, my gut says, *"You are going in the wrong direction! Get off this trolley **NOW** and head back in the other direction."* I watch many Muslim women who are wearing their traditional head to toe religious inspired outfits, get off the trolley. Some are pushing baby strollers and others dragging two to three *'little ones'* by hand. Clearly, I am in the wrong section of the city.

The journey back takes me again under the *'central train station.'* A few stops later, something outside *'looks familiar.'* I quickly exit the trolley and activate the Google Maps App. I plug in the hotel's address and follow the step by step directions. However, the directions just don't *'feel' right.'* I think I should be heading to the right while the App takes me left. So, what's right? Is it the Google Maps App or the 75-year old having *'senior moments'* unlike any I've had before in my past? It takes all the courage I can muster to follow the Google Maps App directions. Son of a gun! Google Maps is right. I am wrong.

The walk home is easy. The sun is out. The sky is cloudless blue. To say the least, I am overdressed. It's warm. People riding bikes in crowded pedestrian walkways are a constant nuisance. Near misses are common between pedestrians and bikers. In fact, I miss getting clipped from behind on my surgically repaired Achilles left leg by mere inches. I pause and consider sticking out my left arm and giving a bike rider a *'shot to the chest'* but I think otherwise. A fight between a 75-year old man and someone half my age doesn't bode well for me. Marty, my man, where are you? JT needs you bro! (For those of you who don't know who Marty is, he was a member of the Saturday golf group and our Monday Night Football TV get togethers who passed a few years ago. He was a man's man, a really an unforgettable guy...that's why I'm remembering him in this book. RIP, buddy!)

Well, after over a three-hour *'journey,'* I arrive back at the hotel hot, tired, and thirsty. I spend 31 minutes telling Collette about my *'journey to and from Germany'*. Can you imagine if she was on this journey with me today? All I would have rightly heard is, "Are you sure you know where we are going?" over and over and over for three plus hours.

After finishing my story, she laughingly wants to celebrate by cracking open the chilled bottle of champagne that was sitting in the ice bucket I obtained earlier in the day. Collette goes into the bathroom and tries to *'pop open'* the bottle of champagne. She gets it started but calls me to *'finish the job.'* Just as I rise from my chair, and Collette exits the bathroom, we hear a loud *'pop'* coming from the bathroom. What was that? Apparently Collette loosened the champagne cork *'just enough'* and the built up pressure caused the cork to fly out of the bottle and shoot straight up at a high rate of speed. Collette races back to the bathroom hoping that the cork did not hit a fire sprinkler head or place a hole in the ceiling. Folks... Collette is **BACK** in the game. Good going dear. Needless to say, we dodged a huge bullet as nothing was damaged!

It is 18:52, time for dinner. Neither of us is very hungry. We mosey up the path with the river on our left and find a seat at a restaurant whose name will remain anonymous. (I forgot to write it down.) Collette orders a flat, crepe style pizza with ham, onions, and cheese (no sauce). We split the pizza, down a beer and wine, and chat it up with a husband and wife from Quebec, who are visiting their son. He's a political science major studying in Paris. Good *'back and forth'* conversation ensues. It's time to head back to the hotel. Before reaching *'home,'* Collette stops for one scoop of gelato. She hits the sack at 22:10 while I finish today's story and retire at 23:52. Until tomorrow, good night now!

P.S.: The weather has been fantastic 90% of the time. Most days, the temperatures are 10 to 15 degrees above normal. When planning the trip, I studied the historical average daily temperatures for the cities we planned to visit. We pack clothes we thought would be appropriate. Most of our wardrobe is for cooler daytime and nighttime temperatures. Consequently, we are forced to wear our limited supply of warm weather clothes for two to three days in a row. When we walk down the street, we wonder why the crowd opens up and separates like the *'parting of the Red Sea.'* Are we *'giving off'* unplanned body odors?

*****

Saturday, May 11 — Day 47
Searching For The Post Office and Laundry Day

Today is our last full day in Strasbourg. There are no *'must do'* things on the agenda today except I need to go to the post office to mail five beer glasses and assorted souvenirs home. According to two people, the post office is near the central train station. So, I walk to the Line D trolley stop and without a ticket jump on the rear section of the trolley heading to the train station. Arriving at the train station, I ride the escalator up one floor and ask three policemen if I should turn left or right at street level to get to the post office.

I have a communication problem with the first officer. Clearly, he doesn't understand my question. My French, after all, is weak to non-existent. Jacques then takes out eight post cards and shows them to the officer. Now, he has an *'ah ha'* moment and realizes I am looking for the post office! Another officer chimes in and says to go up the left escalator and look for the yellow post office sign. This sounds simple and logical. So, upon reaching street level, I scan the extensive outdoor area and neighboring buildings. **NOTHING!** As far as I can see, there is **NO** post office sign. So, I politely ask two locals walking by. However, they are clueless and have no idea where it might be.

Undeterred, I spot a nearby five star hotel and enter. I visit with a well-dressed concierge wearing his official uniform and ask him to help me locate the post office. He replies that the post office on this street **CLOSED**. He looks at the address I have for the post office and tells me it's a 25-minute walk!!! **I have no interest nor do I intend to walk there.** I am tired, hungry, and quite honestly, fed up with the French postal system and *'all the help'* received from the hotel and stamps store personnel. The concierge instructs me to take a Line C trolley, go four stops, get off, activate Google maps on the iPhone, and follow the directions. I give him a huge **"Merci;"** but, stop short of the *'kiss, kiss, hug, hug'* departure ritual.

My next challenge is to locate the Line C trolley in the train station. I remember trolley lines are two flights down in the station. Jacques proceeds down one flight but fails to see any indication where the Line C trolley boards passengers. All I see are references to uptown and downtown Lines A and D. I target two locals and ask where to catch a Line C trolley. But my inquiry is for naught as both people are *'clueless'* about the Line C trolley location. I deduce that the signs I am looking at **ONLY** reference Lines A and D trolleys. So, being an experienced traveler and navigator, I know I will overcome this minor setback.

I go back up to the main concourse and search for signage that hopefully will direct me to the Line C trolley. Luck is back on my side. I carefully follow signs that require a **LONG** walk across the train station to the Line C starting point. Alas, success. I spot the Line C trolley in a *'holding position.'* Being totally fed up with the trolley ticket machines, I just board, cross my fingers, legs, arms, and *'act like I belong.'* I already tried three times to purchase a trolley day pass today but failed miserably. There will **NOT** be a fourth attempt. So, I ask myself, 'Can I make four stops without incident?" Success, playing *'Strasbourg Jacques Cool Local,'* I ride again for free.

I follow the hotel person's directions to a *'tee.'* I exit at the fourth stop and activate Google Maps for the alleged two minute walk. Bingo, Google Maps takes me right to the **SPECIFIC** address; but (and here comes another **HUGE BUT**) I **DO NOT** see a sign for the post office even though Google Maps points out that *'you have reached your destination!'* There's a large five story building, two blocks long by two blocks wide at the address where the post office should be! Plus, based on the securely locked 10 foot iron doors, and doorbell like buttons to reach people inside, it is way past **CLEAR** this is a residential apartment, condo, and office building. But *'Bulldog'* (the nickname my market research client Jeff Perry gave me years ago) is way too invested in this mission to admit defeat. I take a **LONG** lap around the building; zero, zip, nada, nothing. Without a doubt, the post office is **NOT** here.

Looking around, I spot a large directional sign hanging on a pole pointing down the street to the central post office! **Are you shitting me??** Prior to heading in that direction again, (because I've already been there), I point to the sign and ask two policemen standing on the corner, "Where is the post office?" One officer gives me the *'double shoulder shrug and the double left right head movement.'* Obviously, we either have a language barrier or he is clueless. (I bet it's the latter.) I am exasperated. The second officer points *'up the street and turn left.'* In my head I was silently thinking because I did not want to upset the officers, **SO** I mutter to myself, *'Mister police officer, I've been there. I have walked down that street but...here we go again!'* So, there is a one in a million chance I did not see it. It **MUST** be there. But not so fast.....I am a bulldog who never gives up.

I see a man standing outside his tobacco store and ask him for the location of the post office. The owner's English is suspect; however, his friend is walking down the street towards us. They do the local customary greeting, *'kiss, kiss, hug, hug,'* and high five each other. His friend speaks English and once he understands my question, rattles off directions, "500 meters down the street that way, turn left and then right"... yada, yada, yada. Despite not wearing my fitness ankle monitor meters calculator, nevertheless, I set out on what I **TRULY** believe will be the **CONCLUSION** of this *'I can't believe this is really happening journey.'* I head down the tree lined street and stop when I guess I have walked 500 meters. **BEFORE** making that all important left turn, I spot a cab driver. I know from experience good cab drivers are *'all knowing'* on how to get anywhere. The cabbie understands English, a real plus, and confidently says, "Cross the street, turn right and keep walking. You will see it on the left." Son of a bitch, he is the **FIRST** and might be the **ONLY** person in Strasbourg that knows exactly where the post office is!!

Jacques is energized and confident! I can clearly see the end of this *'#*%+#! journey.'* When I enter the post office, I realize there is a **HUGE** language barrier; **NO ONE** speaks English. And unlike in Switzerland, there is no ticket dispensing machine to take a number and wait for customer service. A counter on the right leads me to believe it's for shipping packages overseas. So, I grab a shipping box off the shelf; but it's too small. So, I grab the next size box. I pack my treasures, use newspaper and pieces of the small box (since I used it, I decided to tear it into little packing pieces) to reinforce the shipment. I think I am halfway home. All I need is the shipping label and customs forms. **However, *'shit is about to happen in spades.'***

All of a sudden, an overweight 50+ year old female post office worker, (let's call her **Nicolette),** descends on me, and belts out in her mixed French/English for all to hear in what I can only interpret to be, *"What the fuck are you doing?? You can't tear up a box and use it as packing material. Plus, you have to pay for the box you rendered useless!"* I try to calm her down, *"My bad,"* I say. *"I will gladly pay* *for the box I destroyed. Let's just chill, not call the postal cops, and avoid an international incident.*" She asks me where I am sending the box. I say, "USA." "You are using the **WRONG** box!!" Are there signs **ANYWHERE** in the post office clearly telling customers which shipping box to use? Or maybe **EVERYONE** but me knows which box to use. (There probably are, I just can't read French!) Nicollette grabs the correct box from the shelf. Son of a bitch, it's the **SAME** size as the second box I selected, it's just a *'slightly different color.'* She says, *"Use this one and fill out these two forms, pressing hard as the third copy is yours."*

The forms, which are all in French of course, are the address mailing label, and the customs declaration form. The forms have tiny, hard to read lines with boxes to insert the address and other information. Screw the tiny boxes; I print the hotel address as the shipping address and my Henderson address as the recipient address and declare five souvenirs (stolen beer glasses) worth at best four Euros each. I do not declare my package as beer glasses because the postal clerk may reject the shipment or up-charge me for shipping *'dangerous'* items. So, I just list as *'miscellaneous souvenirs'* worth 20 Euros. I take the box and completed forms to my new *'not so bestie'* friend postal lady **Nicollette.** She takes 10 minutes to do what she has to do to ship the box and charge me for who knows how much for postage, the shipping box, and the destroyed box. No sense asking for the breakdown. She just might charge me for another box or two. Finally, without any further incident, we complete the transaction. I pay 82.30 Euros and take the receipt, a copy of the customs declaration form, and the mailing label. Thankfully, we skip the *'kiss, kiss, hug, hug, high five'* goodbyes. Lastly, I hand her eight stamped postcards that have at best a 50/50 chance of ever arriving at their destination before Christmas 2025! **You can't make this shit up. It really happened, blow by blow, yes it**

REALLY HAPPENED. I guess God is getting even with me for all the bad stuff I have done in my 75 plus years on earth.

In lieu of getting on and off two trolleys, I decide to use the Google Maps App to walk to the hotel. Much to my dismay, the app tells me it is just a **MERE** 15 minute flat walk to the hotel! I start home and follow the step by step commands. Hungry, thirsty, and worn out, I see what appears to be a high end corner restaurant called *Cafe Briglie*. Surely, they have something nourishing to eat. Not wanting to sit outside with the large contingent of local people who are *'smoking up a storm and all talking at once,'* I head inside for peace, quiet, and solitude.

A waitress drops off the All French language menu and shortly returns. I ask for an omelet, tea, and a croissant. She replies, **"We (Cafe Broglie) are out of food!!!! And we do not cook eggs after 11:00. We only have pie or soft pretzels to eat!"** Seriously lady, are you kidding me? It's 11:41 in the morning. The restaurant has no food, no croissants, squat, zero, no food, except pie and pretzels!?! Plus, the kitchen refuses to cook scrambled eggs since it is 41-minutes past their self-imposed 11:00 deadline. Perplexed, stunned, and confused, Jacques cannot grasp this very large cafe on a busy corner, with inside and outside seating near a major tourist location, it is out of food!!!! The best and only good thing that happens is the waitress brings me a pot of hot water, enough for two cups of tea, freshly sliced lemons, honey, and a cookie the size of a quarter. This will definitely **NOT** *'take the edge off'*! (For the record, the wrapper has to cost more than the cookie.)

Now here's the really **BAD NEWS**. Google Maps shows me it's just a 12 minute walk back to the hotel from the restaurant. This is way past nuts! This morning, I spent over three hours looking for and finding the post office that turns out to be **JUST** a short 15 minutes away from the hotel! Just like almost every city in Europe... nobody knows where the post office is located!

Let's recap for the '*doubting Thomas's*' who may be out there:

- The owner of a souvenir store that sells stamps and mailing envelopes, and sold me eight postcard stamps, directs me to the Main Strasbourg Post Office located near the central train station to mail a package to the United States.

- Jacques also looks up the address for the '*Main Strasbourg Post Office*' on France's Post Office Website.

- Jacques took the Line D trolley to the central train station, got off, goes one floor up, and asks three policemen whether I should take the left or right stairs up to street level where I might find the post office. One of the police officers does not understand what I am saying. When I show him postcards to mail, he understands my inquiry and directs me up the steps straight in front of me.

- Arriving at the large park-like square, I unsuccessfully scour the area looking for the Yellow Post Office sign. Asking two locals yields the *left to right head movement signifying 'I do not know where the post office is.'* Spying a five star hotel a block away, I enter it and ask the concierge to direct me to the main post office.

- I learn the post office where everyone told me to go closed and moved to a location that requires a twenty-five minute walk! However, the clerk suggests I take the C trolley, get off at the fourth stop, and walk about two blocks. I use Google Maps App for exact directions. The App indicates I arrived at the post office's alleged address. It isn't there. Instead, in its place is a large five story structure that is two blocks long in each direction and contains offices, condos, and apartments. I take a quarter mile lap around the building... **NOTHING.** I then see a large sign hanging on a street post pointing left to the location of the post office. Spotting two police officers, one confirms the direction while the other officer has no clue.

- Totally frustrated, **BUT** being the bulldog I am, I will not give up my quest to find the post office and mail five invaluable beer glasses collected on this trip. In lieu of collecting one liter and up glasses like in 2013, on this trip, I focus on smaller beer glasses with cool designs. My next move is to ask the owner of a nearby tobacco store for directions to the post office. We have a language barrier. But along comes his friend, and after the *'kiss, kiss'* greeting followed by hugs and high fives, his friend directs me to walk straight ahead 500 meters, turn left, take the first right, and keeping walking until I come to the post office. So, off I go. Not sure if I have walked 500 meters, I ask a cab driver for assistance. I **AM** at the 500 meter spot. "Just cross the street, turn right, and you will find it." Son of a bitch and holy shit, there it is, the post office. After an **ENGAGING** encounter with a French postal clerk, the box is on its way to Henderson.

- The Google Maps directions are perfect. I make it back to the hotel, *'beaten but not down for the count.'*

- When I return to the hotel, I update Collette on the morning's *'shit happens'* ordeal.

It's time to head up the street to the laundromat. Clean clothes pack easier than *'soiled'* clothing. Jacques and Collette make this *'a group of two'* event. The laundromat is crowded. Lucky for us, we only have to wait two minutes to gain access to the one extra-large washer. Collette stuffs all the clothes in while I buy the soap powder and pay 10 Euros to start the 40-minute wash cycle. Collette wants to eat lunch at the small cafe where we ate on Tuesday's arrival. So, we head there. I order hot vegetable barley and potato soup and hot tea. Collette goes cappuccino and rhubarb pie with whipped cream.

So much for a nutritious nourishing meal! Her reply is consistent with other statements she made, "I am on vacation!"

The soup is *'to die for.'* I am energized and order mixed berries with whipped cream pie for dessert. The owners are very nice people. We enjoy our meal and head back to the laundromat. The washer shut off because the clothes are done and clean. I activate two dryers for 36 minutes each, on medium heat. While Collette babysits the dryers, I locate a good size grocery store and load up on some bottled water and snacks for tomorrow's seven hour train ride to Amsterdam thru Paris.

The clothes are dry. We fold and place them in our traveling laundry bags. Back at the ranch, I need to double check tomorrow's train trip to ensure we have the requisite first class tickets and the hotel name and address. We chill in the hotel lobby, sitting in very comfortable chairs. Sure, beats sitting up in bed and trying to read or write.

The clock says it's 17:00, time to grab a light dinner before packing up and getting a good night's rest. We walk up the main pathway and select an American diner style restaurant selling *'the best hamburgers'* in town. Collette wants the California burger while I order a mixed salad topped with diced chicken strips. The food is very good; however, the chef *'over sauces'* the burger. All in all, our meals *'hit the spot.'* The restaurant lived up to its branding.

We head back to the hotel. But first, Collette needs a small cup of gelato, topped with whipped cream, to complete her dining for the day.

That's it fans. Our enjoyable four days and five nights in Strasbourg comes to an end on Sunday morning. After checking out, we will take a cab to the Strasbourg Central Train Station where we will catch the 10:47 train to Paris then onto Amsterdam. Merci! Good night!

*****

Sunday, May 12 — Day 48
Strasbourg, France to Amsterdam, Netherlands

It's Sunday morning in Strasbourg. We woke up after a great night's sleep. Jacques didn't wake up coughing once! We dine on our last cup of instant soup, tea, instant coffee, plums, and the remaining blueberries and strawberries. The tangelo oranges didn't taste good; so, we sent them flying into the trash can. Just a two pointer for Collette; but she swished it. On the second orange toss, she calls *'bank'* and uses the wall to bank it into the trash can; another two pointer.

It's time to shower, dress, and check out. I learn a little about the hotel's history from Mehdi, this morning's front desk person. The building was built in 1552. There is a stone hanging in the lobby with that date carved in Roman numerals. The French used the building for various factory jobs. During the French Revolution, the building was stripped of everything *'that could move.'* Overtime, it was converted to condos and apartments. The current owner acquired the structure 15 years ago. It took three years to convert to the current 16-room, five-story hotel. Within the last 10 years, ownership added a spa in the basement.

A huge shout out to all the hotel staff, including Yann, the bartender, who supplied ice for Collette's daily knee icing; Alexander, the multi-tasking front desk person who checked us in and gave us a fifteen minute *'what to do and where it is'* dissertation on a large colored Strasbourg map; and Mehdi, another front desk person who taught me how the various color coded trolley car lines operate and which directions they travel. Merci, Danka, and thanks much to these fine gentlemen, and the entire hotel staff, for excellent customer service and professionalism. Without a doubt, we unequivocally recommend staying at this hotel. We definitely will stay at *'Hotel & Spa Le Bouclier D'or'* on our next trip to Strasbourg.

Our room was large, in fact it was the largest so far on our 40-plus day journey. Mehdi mentions our room was one of the smaller rooms in the hotel! We had so much room we could *'dump our stuff'* on chairs, tables, in the large closet, and in the large double sink bathroom. Of course, in doing this, we had trouble remembering where we put things. Oh well, it was a nice problem to have, a daily treasure hunt!

Prior to leaving the room, I knock over a glass on my bedside end table. It shatters into many pieces. We clean it up the best we can and take the trash bag with the broken glass down to the lobby. We didn't want members of the cleaning staff to unexpectedly encounter broken shards of glass and possibly cut themselves. It was an accident so we hope they don't charge us for this minor mishap. When I check out, I advise the front desk staff to alert the cleaning people about the accident. I also report that one of the lightbulbs in the chandelier is out.

We bid *'au revoir'* and settle into our 09:45 cab to the central train station. Our high speed train to Amsterdam thru Paris leaves at 10:47. Today's journey will take eight hours. I am not sure if the cab driver *'long hauled'* us; but I thought we drove thru two neighborhoods outside the city limits with signs indicating that Paris is close by. Who's going to argue over a 20 Euros cab ride when we are leaving for Amsterdam?

The calendar reads May 12. We return to Henderson in 31 days! It seems like we just started our holiday! Jacques and Collette enjoy our *'carefree'* lifestyle traveling by train to various cities, living out of suitcases, creating daily adventures, visiting *'must see'* places, finding self-service laundromats to wash and dry our clothes, and eating out almost every meal, except for a few shared in-room dinner picnics.

European bathrooms have two toilet flushing buttons: a small one for #1 and large one for #2. Water pressure is tremendous at every stop along the way. Without a doubt, every hotel has an abundance of water.

Here's another tidbit of meaningless information to share — many Europeans smoke. Ash trays are found on every dining table. However, we never see cigarette butts in the street or on the sidewalks. All smokers use the ash trays on the citywide trash cans that are found on the sidewalks. The streets and walkways are crowded with people, yet we don't see any litter. Everyone is conscious about not littering and maintaining a clean environment.

After arriving one hour early for our train, we stop at *Maison Pradier Cafe* for breakfast. It opened in 1859! Tables and chairs are set up in the train station corridor. We select a freshly made tuna sandwich on a baguette, two Danish pastries with raisins, a large Americano coffee with cold milk, a cappuccino, a bottle of Evian non-carbonated water, and a Schweppes orange flavored non-carbonated drink.

Getting on a train in Strasbourg is not like boarding in any other city. Our train departs on Platform #3. We approach the train on a walkway shared with Platform #2. To our dismay, metal crowd control barriers are chained together blocking our access to our train loading on Platform #3! Is there some kind of protest going on that requires police to set up barriers? What do we have to do to get to the Platform 3 side of the barriers? Do we walk back to the main corridor, look for a secret walkway to the platform that may require a password and hand gesture to get to our train, or leap over the barriers? Or do we just use all the strength we have, which at 75 is not much, and bust thru the barriers to get on our train to Paris?

Alas, I spot an opening controlled by two conductors who use hand held scanners to check tickets. I use the Eurail App to show our rail passes; but this is **NOT** what she wants to scan. "Where are your tickets mister Americano?" Wait. Every other European train ride did not have this setup prior to boarding. I give her an earful then I grab the iPad, fire it up, and display the first class tickets to Paris. She lets us through.

Our seats are in car three, seats 55 and 56. We hustle to what we **THINK** is our car. I jump on. Collette passes my suitcase and bag up to me. I store them on the train luggage racks. A fellow traveler assists Collette with her luggage. He lifts her suitcase and bag up the three steep steps to me. *'Merci kind sir, you earn a good deed pin for the day.'* We *'shuffle'* to our seats. The seat numbers are **NOT** displayed on the walls of the train. Where are they?? A passenger sees our dilemma and points to the illuminated numbers on top of the seats! I guess everyone but us knows that. We say *"Merci"* but decide against filling our brains with meaningless train seat location information that, most likely we will never use again. When we arrive at our assigned seats, two *'seat stealers'* are sitting in our seats. *"These are our seats pal. Out!"* bellows Jacques in a very confident *'take no prisoners'* tone. The suspected seat stealer says, *"These are, in fact **OUR** seats, so get lost and get off the train before I call security."* *"Is this car three?"* I ask? "No, this is car two!," he says. *"Merci, so sorry, we are just two dumb old Americanos in the wrong car.....close but no cigar,"* I mutter as we make our way out of car two and into car three. Finally, just a few minutes before the train pulls out, we find and settle into our luxurious first class reclining seats with foot rests and pull out airplane style tables. (We left our luggage in car two and plan to retrieve it when we exit the train.) I have time to update our stories while Collette reads a *'can't put down book'* or plays with her iPhone. The ride to Paris is super smooth and fast. Our train is flying by the French countryside.

We have an uneventful train ride to Paris. The French countryside is just absolutely gorgeous, just like you see in the movies. The train is on time and pulls into the *Paris Est* station. We see a lot of graffiti even what looks like a *'one of a kind'* original painting by renowned artist Thom Metcalf which, in my interpretation of the French language says, *'Thom and Marie were here many times. We love Paris!'* I theorize that Thom brilliantly accented the mural with a very detailed and colorful depiction of golfers teeing off on a 205 meter, par 3 golf hole over water, with heavily bunkered sand traps and a severe sloping left to right green.

After getting off the train at Paris Est, we successfully navigate through the two-story station and locate the potty. It's in the building basement. Thank goodness for elevators. Using the steps to walk down two floors dragging our suitcases, carrying bags, and backpack may work for me; however, it is *'out of the question'* for Collette and her bum knee. The toilet costs one Euro each. Collette goes first and unsuccessfully tries to open the handicap entrance for me to sneak in so we can get a 2 for 1 potty deal. While the ploy doesn't work, I give Collette a huge *'shout out"* for giving it the old *'college try.'* She fondly remembers the free potty we received last Sunday in Thun, Switzerland when an older man paid the entry fee and subsequently opened the exit door for both of us to sneak in.

It's my turn in the potty barrel. I insert a one Euro coin and push the turnstile with my rolling suitcase. Unfortunately, this *'suitcase on turnstile movement'* locks the entrance. I am on the wrong side looking in. There is no way in hell I will spend another Euro to enter. So, I revert to my youth. What would a kid do? Easy, I drop down on all fours and crawl under the locked turnstile! Thank goodness no one yells for train station security or Paris police to deal with *'A guy sneaking into the potty. Arrest his Americano ass!'* I am ready for an argument so bring on the police and security guards. Luckily, there are no security cameras at the entrance plus, I have just taught 23 people in line behind me what to do if you really *'gotta go'* and are one Euro coin light in the pocket.

We have to get to the *Paris Nord Train Station* to catch the second leg of today's trip. We take the first cab in line and tell the cab driver to, "Please take us to the Paris Nord Train Station." He's not 100% understanding me. He asks to see the station name printed on our tickets. Now he's 99.9% sure where to take us. Traffic is a bitch today in Paris. He expertly navigates thru traffic and gets us to our destination in record heavy traffic time. The fare is 10 Euros including a tip.

We have 90-minutes to kill. A light, *'shared lunch'* sounds like a good idea. The traveling dynamic duo enters a nice restaurant across the street from the train station. We grab two seats at the bar, order a 1664 French draft beer, a white French wine, and share an order of fish and chips. The quantity and quality of the food fills us up. After paying the bill and substituting *'fist bumps'* over the more traditional French *'kiss, kiss, hug, hug'* departure actions, we cross the street. Cars and buses are backed up and *'frozen in time.'* We enter the train station. The departure board lists our train; however, the track number is not assigned. We find a place to sit and enjoy a cup of Americano coffee and a *'to die for'* blueberry muffin. At least I had some time to *'scarf down'* most of the muffin.

In multiple languages, the train lady announces our train departs on Track 9. The platform boarding area is packed with travelers who like us, are heading to Paris. The mass of humanity presses forward to get on the train to find a seat. The 16-car train has three engines that will take us from Point A to Point B. Our first class seats are in Car 3 which just happens to be about 1.5 kilometers down the platform that heads to who knows where. The departure clock is ticking...tick, tick, tick. The anxious conductors blow their whistles indicating *'get on the train, we are pulling out of the station to stay on schedule'* or we could lose our jobs and all of our train company provided entitlements (benefits) like one month paid holiday every year after three months of service.

There are only three passengers **BEHIND** us on the platform. It seems **EVERY** other passenger is on the train. A familial group—mother, father, and daughter—sneak past Collette on the right to board **BEFORE** us. **We gotta hustle.** The conductor is screaming simultaneously in both French and English, "Get the hell on the train you old farts, we are pulling out **NOW**!" It always takes us extra time to board any train with our suitcases, carry bags, back pack, and old tired bodies, especially Collette with her bum knee. We *'shuffle sideways'* from the front of the car to the back, rub butts with people standing in the aisle, and finally arrive at our reserved seats. I toss most of our luggage into the baggage storage racks above seats #71/73. We are sitting on the right side of the train facing each other. We settle in for the 3:22 high speed, limited stops ride to Amsterdam. The expected arrival time is 17:44. I settle in to finish describing some daily adventures while Collette makes a quick phone call, then plays with her iPhone and finishes reading a book.

While on the train, we cross into the Netherlands. Jacques and Collette are now Dirk and Tess. Welcome to Holland you two Americano European travelers.

Arriving at the *Central Amsterdam Train Station*, we head to the left side of the building to catch a cab to the hotel. But first, we enter an Apotheke (pharmacy) and stock up on vitamins and arthritis relief cream for Tess and cough medicine for Dirk. Our ride to the hotel in the electric, four door black Kia sedan, is a quick five minutes and costs 30 Euros. Did the Turkish taxi driver *'long haul'* us? Are taxis just as expensive here as in the Amalfi Coast of Italy, or did our new driver double or triple the fare? He mentions today's been a **SLOW** day. He has been sitting in line at the train station for 2 1/2 hours. This leads me to believe he **PADS** our fare. After all, it was **NOT** that long of a ride like I said above, five minutes max.

As we enter the hotel, we stop for a moment in amazement; at first glance, we think we are checking into the former *Mirage Hotel and Casino* in Las Vegas. This hotel, like the Mirage, has a large indoor arboretum as you walk in. A large restaurant, with inside and outside seating, takes up a significant portion of the riverfront side of the ground floor. Our stay includes breakfast from 07:30 to 10:30 every morning in the large restaurant.

The hotel has nine floors. We are staying on the fifth floor. Our room and bathroom are spacious. The balcony overlooks a waterway. We can see riverboat cruisers, tall office buildings, and hotels. The weather is a picture postcard perfect 76 degrees. A gentle breeze fans numerous country flags hanging from flag polls on the outside sidewalk. Automobiles, motorcycles, scooters, bike riders, and pedestrians can access the other side of the river via a two lane bridge and a pedestrian walkway. The bridge is not very tall, but it is high enough for barges, tugboats, river cruises, sight-seeing, and pleasure boats to pass under.

Tess needs a 'T.O.,' a timeout to ice her knee after today's long train journey. Dirk heads to the front desk and asks for a bucket of ice. Ester, the front desk lady, asks for the room number. I sure hope she won't charge us for the ice. If they do, that ice bucket is coming back to Henderson with us just like the Brussels ice bucket that's featured prominently in our home's living room. Read our first book (*SH?#! Happens*) to learn about that memorable evening in Brussels.

Tess finishes icing her knee. It's 20:00. The sun sets at 21:26. There's a bar on the eighth floor with a magnificent view of the surrounding area. We ride the elevator up three floors, enjoy an adult beverage, and watch two river cruise boats, a barge, three small personal boats, and a petroleum barge pass by. Tess asks the young Polish bartender stud, who has a physique like a tight end, a weak side linebacker, a small power forward, or a Mike Trout or Bryce Harper, about the meaning of his tattoos which cover his arms. He joyfully explains their meanings. For a moment, he thought *'I got me a cougar'*! Not today friend, she is spoken for.

It's way past time for dinner. We take the elevator to the lobby level, sit down at an inside window table for two, order some type of hot chicken based soup, four bite size vegetarian spring rolls, one bite size beef filled croquet, a cup of tea, and a cup of hot water with lemon. Our waitress is **NOT** a *'happy camper.'* She seems *'put out and annoyed'* answering our *'please translate the menu questions.'* Four people sit down at a table to our right. *'Something'* is a miss. While we patiently wait, the table next to us is served their four platters of food before we get ours. What is up? Just as we are about to call over our *'waitress,'* another, much more friendly, bubbly, and customer service oriented young waitress shows up with two spring rolls and four beef croquettes. *'Time out young lady, we ordered four spring rolls, one beef croquet, and the soup.'* The young lady is about to take the order back; however, we say, "No biggie. Just leave what you brought us. *"No blood, no foul."* As we munch on the appetizers, the young, pleasant waitress shows up again with two spring rolls and says, *"These are on the house. Sorry for the mistake."* Whoa, she turns a *'not so good'* situation into a **GREAT** experience...kudos to her!

We still haven't received the soup. The table of four next to us is finished with their meal! But, just as we are about to flag down the pleasant waitress, she serves us the soup! I ask her if I can take the ½ empty filtered water bottle to the room. She indicates normally **"NO"** but today is our lucky day. Not only can we take the water bottle to our room, but she also tops it off with cold, filtered water. Outstanding!

While signing the dinner charges to our room account, we converse with Noha, our young, customer service oriented waitress. She is a 19-year-old college student majoring in hospitality services and management. She recently completed her six month apprenticeship at the restaurant and is working here for an additional three months. Dirk refers to her name 'Noha' and 'Noah's Ark' but the young lady looks confused. Tess handles the situation perfectly. She explains the reference is from the Bible. Noha tells us she is Muslim and mentions the Koran. Anyway, we leave it 'at that,' sign the bill, and thank her for her great customer service. I tell her I have two 18-year-old grandsons, Tanner and Brady, who should someday get to meet her.

We return to the room; however, their electronically coded room key fails to open the door. I head back down to the front desk. Possibly leaving the other keycard in the slot that activates the room's electricity creates this problem. Ester, the front desk clerk, says this situation unfortunately happens sometimes especially if people place the keycard close to their cellphone. It de-magnetizes the key card. She updates the keycard. Back at our fifth floor room, I try the door. Problem solved; case closed. The door opens, it's magic! Time for bed and pleasant thoughts about tomorrow's first day in Amsterdam! Nite, Nite!

*****

Monday, May 13 — Day 49
Amsterdam, Netherlands

It's our first morning in Amsterdam. We get a late start today after hitting the sack around 01:00. I sleep in until 08:00, and wake Tess at 09:07. I have already fixed myself a cup of tea with honey, and I fix Tess a cup of coffee with cream. *'Shake a leg, time to roll.'* We quickly shower, I shave and fix the hair.....let's get the day started. Time to roll out!

The breakfast buffet is calling us....*"**TESS, DIRK**, get your butt-skis up and come down to the restaurant and to enjoy our amazing — it's included in the nightly room charge — breakfast buffet!"*

I arrive first, do the complete *'check it out, walk around the expansive buffet'* to consider my meal choices. I set hot tea, orange juice, scrambled eggs, one pancake, one fully cooked, small sausage, (a first on this trip), extra greasy bacon, sautéed mushrooms, a small mixed fruit bowl, and a slice of brown bread and butter.

The tea making process is unique, another trip first. Here's how it works: There are three types of crushed fresh tea leaves to choose from, and a box of empty tea bags with an opening at the top to place under the *'tea dispensing container.'* Then, I move the leaver left and right and the tea leaves fall into the *'make your own tea bag.'* I got *'just a little excited'* moving the tea dispensing leaver left and right and back again to create my first *'just right'* personal tea bag. Unfortunately, there are enough tea leaves in my bag to make a half gallon of tea! At least I didn't leave crushed teas leaves all over the counter like previous tea drinkers here did. Oh well. I make it a point to do **ABSOLUTELY** better Tuesday morning when putting that *'just right'* amount of tea in my personal tea bag.

One of the first things we noticed last night while sitting at the rooftop bar and looking out the window was how different the blue sky and clouds *'look'* compared to back home. The *'blue'* is clear, light blue. It almost looks like someone painted the sky. The white clouds are pure, clean, *'ivory snow'* white. They are not big and fluffy; they look painted on!

We finish our nourishing breakfast and return to our fifth floor room. We cannot find the typical hotel door hanger that says, *'make up room or stay out for now.'* Alas, leave it to the ingenious Amsterdam engineers. We notice two buttons at eye level to the left of the inside door handle. By pressing either button, a message *'please clean the room or come back later'* displays on an iPad sized screen outside the room next to the room number.....ingenious.

Tess spends time with the hotel concierge getting *'a feel'* for the city and the places she wants to visit. I just *'hang out'* in the lobby. Why, you ask? This is Tess's portion of the journey to plan and implement. With her plan ready to execute, we head out the front revolving door, turn right, and walk to the bus stop just a block away. Bus 43 is the city bus line that will take us to the *Amsterdam Central Train Station* area to begin today's sightseeing adventures. The Google Maps App is screwing with us. Our first adventure calls for us to walk to the *'red light district.'* The App is clearly taking us the *'long way'* to get there. The App directs us to take the path that's to the right next to the water. However, the main part of Amsterdam is on the left! We give up on the Google Maps App, cross the street, and head towards the main part of the city.

Crossing the streets, even at traffic signals, is a *'challenge.'* Major road construction has all but eliminated cross walks and sidewalks.

We decide to give Google Maps another try. The directions take us down a main thoroughfare. We pass many souvenir shops, retail establishments and restaurants. Many of the restaurants sell American ribs, hamburgers, and fries. Tess and I wonder if we are in Amsterdam or New York City. The 15th and 16th century buildings architecture confirms this ain't NYC.

It's another unseasonably warm, 73-degree, sunny day. Normally, it is cooler and rainy this time of year. A mild breeze keeps the temperature comfortable. Tess's knee is barking. We call a *'full timeout'* and settle into a small café. After sitting for what seems like an eternity, I flag down a waiter and order two Coke Zeros, one with ice and one without. Another eternity passes before the drinks arrive. Needless to say, we made a big mistake picking this place. After finishing our drinks, we head down the street and pass a convenience store selling cans and bottles of Coke Zero! Next time, we know where to stop. Extra-long waits are very common in European restaurants. Is there a staffing shortage or is it simply people choosing not to work?

Before crossing the street to continue our journey, I spot a *'Hop On-Hop Off'* bus ticket office. We enter, speak with the ticket selling clerk and learn we can purchase a 24-hour bus tour and canal cruise for 34 Euros each. It's something to consider for later this week. Our jaunt to the *'red light district'* takes us down a narrow pathway/alley that is **NOT** the cleanest part of the city. Tess spots a bakery selling Scandinavian cookies that she likes. Of course, you all know she enters the bakery *and* buys an oversized fat free, sugar free (**NOT**) cookie. The cookie just came out of the oven. It's warm and smells great. Eve (another nickname for Leslie, my wife's real name) shares the *'forbidden cookie'* with Adam, aka John.

The stores and bars along this route *'leave a lot to be desired.'* Smoking marijuana is legal in Amsterdam. We walk past a few drug related paraphernalia stores. We are **NOT** into that lifestyle.

Bars look like something out of the 1930's, dark interiors, heavy red plastic seat bar stools, and that lingering combination smell of beer and cigarette smoke. A sex shop's two front windows display *'things'* in various sizes, shapes, and colors to protect, enhance and stimulate the sexual experience. Unfortunately, our journey down the alley fails to take us to the *'red light'* district. Little did we know we are *'just'* one block from our intended destination. Tess's knee is barking, again! Time to implement Plan B.

Plan B calls for purchasing the 24-hour *'Hop On-Hop Off'* bus and canal cruise tickets. Slowly, we walk back to the ticket office. Along the way, we come across a four story **TK MAXX** department store. (In the states, the store goes by **TJ MAXX**.) Tess takes about an hour to shop on all four floors before making her purchases. I need just 15 short minutes to **BUY** what I need.

Dirk and Tess resume their trek to the bus office and purchase the bus tour and canal cruise tickets. Our plan starts with taking the canal cruise to stop number four, get off, take the 1:25 minute bus ride, then get back on the canal cruise to finish the journey.

The next canal cruise boat leaves in 10 minutes. Sadly, as we reach the pier, the boat pulls away from the dock. Plan B is now on hold. The next boat leaves at 14:45. We consider sprinting thru the train station to catch the tour bus; however, given Tess's barking knee, we settle into a bar adjacent to the dock and enjoy cold, refreshing beverages while waiting for the next boat.

Its 14:45, time for canal cruising. We carefully, and slowly, descend down three steep steps to get on the boat, grab free ear buds to listen to the cruise dialog, and take a seat. The boat is not crowded, maybe 20 people at best. Peter, our driver, provides a brief history of the Amsterdam area. He tells us most of the canals were built in the 17th century. Off we go on what we expect to be a two hour cruise thru various Amsterdam canals. It almost sounds like the opening to the TV show *Gilligan's Island*. Later today on the boat ride, *'expected'* could be a controversial word, so don't stop reading now. The multi-language audio system gives everyone an overview and the history of both sides of the canals.

Many house boats permanently park on the canal banks. They remind us of single-wide and double-wide mobile homes. We learn residents and vacationers reside in over 2,500 house boats. Each home is connected to water, sewer, and electric service. Single family homes, condo buildings, and apartments fronting the canals cannot exceed five stories. Every building is constructed on piers whose pillars are driven 50 to 60 feet into *'bog like'* wet ground. As long as the piers remain under water, they continue to support the structures. However, should piers come in contact with the air, they run the risk of deteriorating. Buildings built in the 16th century by good builders survive today, while those built by inferior builders wind up collapsing and must be rebuilt. Tess and I notice upgraded exteriors on some residential buildings represent the original 16th and 17th century architecture. Our boat driver Peter points out hoists built into the roofline of four and five story structures. Contractors use hoists to haul heavy equipment during construction, and residents use hoists to deliver heavy personal items to a home's upper floors.

Someone on the ride asks Peter, our captain and driver, how far Amsterdam is from Russia. Somehow United States/Russia relations and politics enter the conversation. Peter, clearly an ultra-left liberal, cringes at the thought the world will come to an end if Trump is reelected president and threatens Putin. I am *'more than ready'* to pounce on Peter and his *'crazy'* views. However, Tess knows well enough to put the clampers on me **ASAP** before I create an international incident. She holds up the cane in her right hand and threatens me with severe physical harm. Tess forcibly restrains me by pushing me so close to the edge of the seats perpendicular to the boat exterior that I am trapped and have trouble breathing. Tess's threatening words were simple and to the point, "Don't say a word or else!" Dirk *'gets the message;'* however, I secretly think *'something bad'* will happen to Peter today.

Let's learn about the residential area along the canals. To say the least, parking is a premium within the city limits. Some car owners park their vehicles on the outskirts of town, use the excellent public transportation system to get home, and get to their car when needed. Others spend 300,000 to 400,000 Euros and build garages. Having a car within the city limits costs 700 Euros per year to park the vehicle in your neighborhood if you are *'lucky enough to find a spot'*. All parking is *'first come first serve.'* This situation is very similar to the car parking situation in Boston.

Its *'crazy/nuts' to* own a car and try to park it anywhere in the city, especially on weekends when people drive into the central city area. Captain Peter calls their decision *'questionable and somewhat confusing.'* He is a big proponent of bike riding. He owns three bikes: one for riding in the city, one for long distance riding outside the city, and one as a backup. He's a huge proponent of using public transportation options including busses, tram/trolley cars, subways, and trains. However, he cautions tourists that bike riding in Amsterdam can be *'dangerous to your health.'* While the *'locals'* know the rules of the road, tourists who rent bikes can easily become injured in bike accidents (contacting walkers, other bikers, cars, busses, or trolleys) by *'trying to live like an Amsterdam local.'* Duly noted. Locals ride bikes without helmets, have no fear, ignore speed limits, and have no regard for pedestrians. We observe helmet-less people nonchalantly riding sidesaddle as rear bike passengers without a care in the world. *'Hey folks, we do this every day.....what's the big deal?'* Bikers easily cut *'in and out'* of car and bus traffic. For the most part, they ride in designated bike lanes parallel to the street and pedestrian sidewalks. Pedestrians who attempt to cross a street whether there is a traffic signal (walk/don't walk) or not at a clearly marked crossing lane, need to look **BOTH WAYS** a minimum of three times or risk being *'run over'* by a speeding, manually leg powered bike, an electric bike, or a scooter. I kid you not. Bike riders **DOMINATE** the roadways and bike path lanes and use that dominance to sometimes wreak havoc on tourists walking down the street minding their own business. As a side note, for those considering a move to Amsterdam, if you don't like to ride a bike and wear a back pack, this city is definitely not for you.

Captain Peter tells us city workers pull over 10,000 bikes out of the four to nine foot deep canals every year. Why do people toss bikes into the canal? According to Peter, it's a *'mystery.'* It's just like why some golfers toss a club or three into a pond after hitting a bad shot.

Peter informs us there are easily more than 831,000 bikes in Amsterdam. That's roughly 1.33 bikes per person. And there are only around 200,000 cars in Amsterdam. Bike usage in the city has grown by almost 40% in the last 20 years! On average, only 19% of citizens use private cars on a daily basis.

At the central train station, more than 10,000 bikers can park their ride in an indoor bike garage. Also, on every street in Amsterdam, especially in residential areas and near public transportation facilities, bike riders park and lock bikes *'bumper to bumper.'*

The two hour canal trip is almost over. Tess and I are more than pleased with our decision to take part in this activity. We get to learn about and see things not visible from the main streets.

It's starting to rain. Peter pulls the boat over to the left side of the canal and shuts it down. He gets up, closes, and locks the glass top sliding roofs.

Now here comes something clear out of *'left field'* that no one *'ever, ever, ever expected this to happen.'* Peter cannot, no matter how many times he tries, **RESTART** the boat engine! The boat is now aimlessly drifting in the canal. With no power, Peter cannot control the boat! Are we doomed? Is this a Titanic replay? Are we goners?

Some people on the boat pull out their cell phones and text or call their family and friends. The boat had no life vests or escape vessels to jump into! Peter sends corporate a *'mayday'* distress signal. We wonder if the tour boat company has an AAA boat assistance plan. Unfortunately, it doesn't look that way. If anything does happen, Peter, as captain, **MUST** go down the boat! It's in his job description, employment contract, and navigation law. Remember what Peter said about Trump earlier on this cruise? I'd bet 100 Euros Peter blames Trump for this unfortunate situation.

About ten minutes into our impending tragic ending, a *'Happy Hour'* open bar floating canal cruiser pulls up along our boat's right side. A young boat captain named Deunis and his 20-year old college student assistant, Marije, assess our situation and offer to take the stranded passengers back to the trip's starting point, less than 10 minutes and three canals away.

The *'booze cruise'* boat pulls right next to our stranded vessel. With Peter on one side and Deunis on his boat, they assist and transfer each stranded passenger onto the new boat. They work extra slowly and gingerly assist Tess with her bad knee. Everyone thanks Deunis and Marije for rescuing us. By the way, its navigation law if you come across a boat in distress, you **MUST** stop and render aid or risk a steep fine. With everyone safely on board, our new heroes start the short trip to *'take us home.'* Unfortunately, Captain Peter must remain with the stranded boat until help arrives. Our group bids Captain Peter "adieu," and we head back to our original starting point. Hopefully, assistance shows up in a day or two.

The rain has stopped. Tess and Luca grab a table at *Loetje*, the top rated steak restaurant located next to where we started the canal cruise. Tess orders the eight ounce tenderloin steak medium in au jus sauce and adds sautéed mushrooms and onions as her side dishes. I also order the eight ounce tenderloin steak medium, and upgrade my order to include sautéed chicken livers, onions, and bacon for only four more Euros. We start dinner by splitting a side salad — gotta have some greens every day. Tess enjoys a glass of Cabernet Sauvignon while Dirk orders a Pinot Noir and a short draft beer.

The steaks are perfectly cooked and melt in our mouths. Most diners have heard about the outstanding steaks. Cooks are cranking out steaks like *'there's no tomorrow.'* While I settle up with the waitress, Tess asks her if the steaks are frozen or fresh cut. The confused and busy waitress says, "What are you asking about Americano tourist lady? Do I look like the person who buys and stores the food we serve? I cannot answer your question. By the way, we have customers waiting for tables so hit the road and consider not coming back. And thanks for dining with us tonight!"

It's time to catch Bus 43 back to the hotel. But first, I make a pit stop. Tess engages in conversation with two elderly women who are sitting at the adjoining table on her left. Tess learns they are highly educated, retired college professors who taught anthropology and genetics — subjects way above our pay grades! I return and like a third base coach, signal Tess, *'it is time to go.'* We begin the 10 minute walk to the bus stop.

Tess wants to play **NAVIGATOR** and lead the way to Bus 43. Instead of cutting thru the train station, she leads me on a **LONG** journey around the perimeter of the station. Initially, I think she is trying to add more steps to today's adventures. This route takes us under the train tracks on a street that looks like nobody has walked on it in years. It's evident the city works department hasn't picked up many years accumulation of trash. When we get thru the tunnel, we come upon a road construction zone fenced off and locked. I spot a Bus 43 heading our way. I try to flag it down. No luck. Dirk seriously considers chasing after the bus after it briefly stops for a red light; however, Tess uses her cane to whack me hard, once on each leg ending **ANY** chance of my *I'm gonna catch up* *to this bus'* sprint. Now, we must walk up the no sidewalk road **AGAINST** traffic to get to the Bus 43 stop. We can see the next Bus 43 directly across from our current location. **GREAT** navigation (**NOT**) tonight Tess! Luckily, we don't get robbed, picked up by the police for walking the wrong way in the street, or for just being *'stupid Americano old tourists.'*

Back at the hotel, why not end the evening with dessert? I select lemon meringue pie and hot tea. Tess orders one scoop of hazel nut ice cream and a decaf Americano coffee. The *'kids'* walked 9,364 steps today — a very good workout.

Originally, we thought *'Shit Happens'* stuff was going by the wayside. Today, however, the canal boat trip got things *'back to normal.'* Bedtime..... and until Tuesday, and our trip to a museum, good night now!

Amsterdam Facts

Below, courtesy of Wikipedia and Britannica.com, is important information about Amsterdam.

- Amsterdam is the capital city and most populous city of the Kingdom of the Netherlands. Its status as the Dutch capital is mandated by the Constitution of the Netherlands. It is however not the seat of the Dutch government, which is The Hague. It has a population of 921,402 within the city proper, 1,457,018 in the urban area, and 2,480,394 in the metropolitan area. Located in the Dutch province of North Holland, Amsterdam is colloquially referred to as the "Venice of the North", for its large number of canals.

- Amsterdam was founded at the mouth of the Amstel River, which was dammed to control flooding. Originally a small fishing village in the 12th century, Amsterdam became a major world port during the Dutch Golden Age of the 17th century, when the Netherlands was an economic powerhouse. Amsterdam was the leading center for finance and trade, as well as a hub of secular art production.

- In the 19th and 20th centuries, the city expanded and new neighborhoods and suburbs were built. The city has a long tradition of openness, liberalism, and tolerance. Cycling is an important part to the city's modern character. There are numerous biking paths and lanes spread throughout Amsterdam.

- Amsterdam's main attractions include its historic canals, the Rijksmuseum, the state museum with Dutch Golden Age art, the Van Gogh Museum, Stedelijk Museum with modern art, the Anne Frank House, the red-light district, and cannabis coffee shops. The city is known for its nightlife and festival activity. Its artistic heritage, canals, and narrow canal houses with gabled façades, well-preserved legacies of the city's 17th-century Golden Age, attract millions of visitors annually.

- The Amsterdam Stock Exchange, founded in 1602, is considered the oldest "modern" securities market stock exchange in the world. As the commercial capital of the Netherlands and one of the top financial centers in Europe, Amsterdam is considered an alpha world city. The city is the cultural capital of the Netherlands. Many large Dutch institutions have their headquarters in the city. Many of the world's largest companies are based here or have established their European headquarters in the city, such as technology companies like Uber, Netflix, Booking.Com, and Tesla. In 2022, Amsterdam was ranked the ninth-best city to live in by the Economist Intelligence Unit. The city was ranked 4th place globally as top tech hub in 2019. The Port of Amsterdam is the fifth largest in Europe. The KLM hub and Amsterdam›s main airport, Schiphol, is the busiest airport in the Netherlands, third in Europe, and 11th in the world. The Dutch capital is one of the most multicultural cities in the world. About 180 nationalities are represented here.

- Amsterdam's notable residents throughout its history include painters Rembrandt and Vincent van Gogh, 17th-century philosophers Baruch Spinoza, John Locke, René Descartes, and the Holocaust victim and diarist Anne Frank.

- To the scores of tourists who visit each year, Amsterdam is known for its historical attractions, for its collections of great art, and for the distinctive color and flavor of its old sections, which have been so well preserved. However, visitors to the city also see a crowded metropolis beset by environmental pollution, traffic congestion, and housing shortages. It is easy to describe Amsterdam, which is more than 700 years old, as a living museum of a bygone age and to praise the eternal beauty of the centuries-old canals, the ancient patrician houses, and the atmosphere of freedom and tolerance; but the modern city is still working out solutions to the pressing urban problems that confront it.

- The inner city is divided by its network of canals into some 90 "islands." There are approximately 1,300 bridges and viaducts. Although the city has a modern metro system, about one-fifth of the workforce still relies on the time-honored tradition of riding bicycles for transportation. The city continues to be famous for its countless Chinese and Indonesian restaurants and the hundreds of houseboats that line its canals. Since the mid-1960s Amsterdam has also been known for a permissive atmosphere. Marijuana usage is legal. The city attracts many people seeking an alternative lifestyle.

- Like most modern cities, Amsterdam is a service center, with only about one-tenth of its workforce employed in manufacturing. The most vibrant and expanding part of the dominant service sector is its business services component, including consulting, information and medical technology, and telecommunications. The consistent lifeblood of the city for the past seven centuries has been international trade and transport, which together account for about one-fifth of employment. The banking and insurance sectors are a mainstay of the Amsterdam economy, together accounting for about one-eighth of all jobs. About one-sixth of jobholders are employed in health, cultural, and social services. Another important part of the city's economy, tourism, accounts for about one-tenth of all jobs. However, despite this thriving service sector, at the turn of the 21st century, the city had many job seekers who lacked marketable skills. About one-eighth of the workforce was unemployed.

- Amsterdam-Rhine Canal Dutch waterway connects the port of Amsterdam with the Rhine River. From Amsterdam, the canal passes to the southeast through Utrecht on its way to the Waal River near Tiel. Inaugurated in 1952, the canal has a total length of 72 kilometers (45 miles) and contains four locks. It was enlarged in the 1970s and reopened in 1981. It is the most heavily used canal in Western Europe and can handle up to four 3,000-ton lighters (unpowered barges) tied together and push-towed by a tug. The canal's minimum depth is 5.5 meters (18 feet).

- The Netherlands has thousands of kilometers of man-made dikes that protect the country from water, climate, and altitude. These dikes are a key part of Dutch history and contemporary life and have been in development for 700 years. Without the dikes, much of the Netherlands would be underwater, as roughly half of the land and people are below sea level.

*****

Tuesday, May 14 — Day 50
Amsterdam, Netherlands

Whoa...Day 50 has a nice ring to it! We have spent 50 days visiting outstanding places in Europe. Dirk and Tess made their way north from the beautiful hillside Amalfi Coast in southern Italy thru Florence, Tuscany, Cinque Terre, and into Switzerland. Over the course of two days, we rode the scenic Bernina and Glacier Express trains from Tirano to Zermatt, a trip that took two days and 10 hours. Zermatt and Interlaken Switzerland gave us 13 days of magnificent snow covered mountain scenery, stopping at remote, small mountain villages, and lasting memories of riding over 10,000 feet up to mountain tops. A five night stay in Strasbourg France predates Sunday's arrival in Amsterdam.

Day 50 starts at 07:00. Tess is up first. She pulls the curtains back to a cloudless, light blue, sunny sky. A slight breeze moves the many national flags hanging from flag poles along the canal sidewalk below our balcony.

Another city and another hotel buffet where breakfast is *'included in the nightly room charge.'* The restaurant is packed with travelers. Tess and I fill our large, grey, stoneware plates with a variety of healthy options including eggs, bacon, sausages, pancakes, donuts, hash browns, and fresh fruit washed down by fresh squeezed orange juice, coffee, and tea. I do a much better job this morning creating my personal tea bag. I fill it with *'just the right amount'* of crushed tea leaves to make at least a quart of tea versus the ½ gallon size tea bag created yesterday.

Let's focus a minute on the staff. They obviously all have great Dutch names. Hotel employees wear light grey, professional looking uniforms that include white shirts or blouses, and clean, white tennis shoes. They all multi-task, never say no, and have one goal in mind, *'enhance and maximize the guest experience.'* They always have friendly smiles on their faces, address you with a good morning, good afternoon, good evening, and never say no to any request including printing 52 pages of the many important documents needed for our upcoming 14-day Norway/Iceland cruise. It might cost us a few Euros for paper and ink cartridge use. Viking Cruise Lines emails us many pages of *'you just carry with you'* information. Dirk plans to carefully review the hotel bill when we check out. Good news.....there was no charge for printing the 52 pages.

Today's main activity is a visit to the *Rijks Museum*. From their website, "The Rijksmuseum is the national museum of the Netherlands. It tells the story of 800 years of Dutch history, from 1200 to now. At the Rijksmuseum, art and history take on new meaning for a broad-based, contemporary national and international audience.

As a national institute, the Rijksmuseum offers a representative overview of Dutch art and history from the Middle Ages onwards, and of major aspects of European and Asian art. The Rijksmuseum keeps, manages, conserves, restores, researches, prepares, collects, publishes, and presents artistic and historical objects, both on its own premises and elsewhere."

Tess is in **NO** mood to use public transportation options or walk to get there. So, she asks the front desk to call us a cab. The cab arrives promptly at 09:00. 'Ale,' our Turkish taxi driver, greets us. He is driving a black, Mercedes Benz passenger van with leather seats. We are definitely *'styling and living large.'*

The drive takes about 20 to 25 minutes thru heavy morning traffic. Along the way, we pass the *Heineken Museum*. Sorry Ed and other beer drinking Las Vegas golfers back home, there are no bottles of Bud or Bud Light in Amsterdam.

When we arrive at the museum, I have a coughing fit. I ask Tess for the new water bottle. She can't find it. Did she leave it in the cab? No sports fans, she left it on the hotel check-in counter! Really Tess! She calls the hotel and asks if they found the bottle. They reply, "Yes." "Great, can you please place it in Room 534?" "No problem." Today's first crisis is averted.

Tess decides to enter the museum while I roam the neighborhood looking to buy a bottle of water. Mission accomplished. I find a store two blocks away and buy water. With my cough now under control, I walk back to the museum, show my ticket, and enter. The ticket checker sees my backpack and says, "Step over there to have your backpack checked by my colleague." My bag passes the security check. They direct me to a storage area to check and store the backpack. Shortly thereafter, I catch up with Tess.

Let's be honest. Dirk is **NOT** a museum guy. I look for ways to avoid these tourist attractions. However, by the end of the 2 1/2 hour visit, I admit I am impressed with the famous paintings and historical artifacts on display. As I walk through the halls, I take many pictures including the descriptions of each painting and artifact. A **HUGE** *'shout out'* to Tess for bringing me *'screaming and kicking'* to the museum.

Tess and I notice many elementary, middle, and high school boys and girls touring the museum on what we suspect are class trips. The younger children seem very interested, while the older kids spend more time chatting with classmates.

Here's some historical background about the museum courtesy of Wikipedia. "Many of the paintings date back to 14th and 15th centuries. Over 8,000 objects are currently on display in the museum. The collection contains more than 2,000 paintings from the Dutch Golden Age by notable painters such as *Jacob van Ruisdael, Frans Hals, Johannes Vermeer, Jan Steen, Rembrandt*, and Rembrandt's pupils. The intricate and pain staking details created with a paint brush depicts excellent hand control and eye focus necessary to create these priceless masterpieces.

The same skills are clearly seen in wood, stone and marble sculptures, the highly decorated glassware, plates, bowls, cups, and the creation of artifacts using silver and gold. Expert wood carvers created very precise and detailed decorative pieces of furniture. Tapestries dating back hundreds of years tell important stories or depict an important scene in time. The intricacy of shaping designs on metal locks, keys, and jewelry boxes using crude tools shows the precision of resolute craftsmen. The Rijks

Museum has more than one million artifacts on display, including priceless paintings."

It's time for lunch. We dine in the museum's restaurant and enjoy a bowl of soup. After lunch, Tess wants to walk through one more section of the museum. I call a *'timeout'* and settle into a seat in the entrance lobby.

It's around 14:30. Tess finishes visiting the final section of the museum. We head out, board the *'Hop On-Hop Off'* bus, and ride to the last stop at the central train station. It's warm, sunny, and pleasant at 79-degrees. Tess needs a *'time out.'* She decides to take Bus 43 back to the hotel to ice the knee and rest. She grants me a three hour *'free pass'* to roam thru Amsterdam.

After walking Tess to the bus stop, I get back on the *'Hop On-Hop Off'* bus and complete the 10-stop circle tour, exiting back at the museum. I decide to complete yesterday's shorted trip to the red light district. After a short beer at a local pub, I use Google Maps to plot the journey. I walk down the street to the D52 subway and I use my four day transportation card to enter the subway station. The map instructs me to go two stops, exit at Rokin, and continue my journey on foot. For some unknown reason, the subway **DOES NOT** stop where I plan to exit! Instead, the subway ride ends at the central train station. This leaves me with a 15-minute walk to my intended destination. After a few wrong turns, I finally arrive at the red light district.

I see multiple *'window display'* locations where ladies seductively sit to attract customers. Just four or five windows have *'ladies'* on display. All are severely overweight and very unappealing. Although I can now say *'I was there,'* the trip is a waste of time. Later, I learn the real *'action'* starts later at night. According to the gentleman who cut my hair later in the week, *'action'* costs 150 to 200 Euros. I saunter the narrow streets and settle into a local bar offering 3.50 Euros *'happy hour'* draft beers. After catching up on Las Vegas, national news, and sports on my iPhone, I plan to enjoy a burger at a cafe near the train station.

Tess calls. Her American/European electric outlet converter is not working. She asks me to pick one up on the way back to the hotel. I head back to the main street and locate the converter in a souvenir store. The clerk says the price is 20 Euros. "Outrageous!!" I think to myself. I could walk four more blocks to **TK MAXX** to buy one for nine Euros; however, time is of the essence so I pay the clerk and tell him, "Sir, the price is *'outrageous and criminal'* and....have a nice night!"

On my way to LA Burger for dinner, it starts to rain. I order a cheeseburger with all the fixings and I wash it down with a large Coke Zero. The burger is very messy and outstanding, the way a great burger should be. The rain has stopped. It is time to head back through the central train station to catch Bus 43. Tonight, I take the efficient route thru the station and reach the bus stop 10 minutes before the next bus departs. Getting off the bus, it's raining again, so I pop out my umbrella. It's been another great day. In the morning, we have an 08:00 pick up for our 10 hour trip to see windmills, the world's longest canal, and the Venice of Holland canals in *Giethoorn*. Lights out, alarms set, until tomorrow —good night!

P.S. I ask a small merchant why banks in Amsterdam and other European countries don't have cash so customers can change large bills into smaller bills and coins. The merchant, who can get paper and coin money at a bank, informs me Amsterdam banks want customers to go **CASHLESS** by 2026. Banks want customers to use credit and debit cards on which the banks make a small fee. The banking system is considering fines on customers who use cash. Banks in France and Italy appear to be heading in the same direction. Stay tuned. Time will tell.

P.S.S. When we board a bus, trolley, subway, or train, we use our bar coded public transportation transit pass to get on. We wonder why we have to use our transit pass when **EXITING** a bus, trolley, subway, or train. So, I ask a local young lady about this. She explains local residents have monthly transit accounts that calculate each fare based on where a person enters and exits. So, if you get on a bus at Stop A and exit at Stop D, your fare is the price of riding from Stops A to D. If you enter at Stop A and exit at Stop F, you fare is the price from riding from Stops A to F. This method of payment does not apply to us as we have prepaid five day public transportation passes. But we still need to use them when getting on and off local transportation.

*****

Wednesday, May 15 — Day 51
Giethoorn and Zaanse Schans Windmills Day Trip

The alarm wakes us from a deep sleep at the ripe old time of 06:15! I am not 100% awake despite an extra hot shower loosening up my tight muscles and steaming up the patio access sliding glass door windows like two or more people have *'gone at it hot and heavy'* before breakfast....wishful thinking Dirk.

I arrive at the breakfast buffet at 06:59. One of my favorite sayings is, *'we're number 1'*. Well, today sports fans, I win a gold medal for being the **FIRST** guest to grace the breakfast room and get first crack at everything. First, I head to the tea bar to create my custom tea bag; however, the tea bag falls off the gismo on the tea dispenser that fastens to the tea bag causing tea leaves to miss the bag and make a mess on the counter. No worries, after I finish creating my tea bag, I use my right hand to sweep the excess tea leaves into my left hand and deposit them into the trash can. No harm, no foul, it's all good in tea bag making land.

I load up on my typical American breakfast of eggs, bacon, bread, and butter, two pancakes with syrup, and a bowl of fresh fruit. *'Gotta keep the train running.'* Two cups of tea, an Americano coffee with cream, and a glass of OJ finish it off. Tess eats much of the same just smaller portions and enjoys a cappuccino.

Today, Tess schedules a full day field trip with a local tour group. The tour guide is scheduled to pick us up at the hotel at 08:00 sharp; but, this morning, the driver texts us he will arrive at 07:55. Hold on Jack, we are **NOT** ready. Drive slowly, stop for coffee, or go around the block a few times. Eight o'clock means 08:00, not 07:55, especially for old, slow moving people. Things are always on time in most European cities unlike showing up *'fashionably late'* in Las Vegas or the hang loose, *'hey brah chill'* Hawaiian *'tomorrow is another day'* mindset. After all, if you miss it today, there's always tomorrow *'cuz.'*

We hustle upstairs, do the potty thing, gather up our gear, including our new water bottle, and head to the lobby. For some strange reason, Tess stops by the front desk for who knows what. I call out to Tess, "Our driver is here, *'Mach schnell,'* hustle, and get in the van." Off we go, stopping to pick up three sets of other couples traveling together. Joining us today are Sylvan and Mylana from Switzerland; Abbey, who is studying in Florence for one month and her mother Anna from Idaho; and Kensey and Tiffany from Illinois.

Dirk is very close to needing a haircut. I delay the decision whether to get an Amsterdam *'shave up the sides bowl cut'* or wait until we get to Stockholm for a *'stylish Swedish men's clipping.'* The jury is still out debating the pluses and minuses of this all important decision.

Our first stop is *Zaanse Schans*, a picturesque small village on the outskirts of town that offers a delightful *'step back in time.'* The iconic windmills, standing tall and proud, are the real stars of the village. We learn there are green wooden houses dating back to 1734 and various shops. We get to meander around, stop in shops, and grab two famous local hot chocolates. Next, we visit the *Henri Willig* cheese company. Here, we learn how they make various cheeses and whey protein powder. It's a slow process taking four to six weeks to age the mildest, creamy cheese and four to 23 months to age hard cheese.

At our next stop in this village, we watch a local craftsman make wooden clog shoes. Their store displays hundreds of colors and sizes of the man-made wooden shoes designed for all occasions. I try on a pair; however, the clogs don't match my outfit. So, I pass on purchasing a pair. Tess takes some time to watch craftsmen cut and polish diamonds while I make an investment at the souvenir stand for those *'gotta have items'* to take home.

Our next stop is the *Afsluitdijk* Dyke. We're told construction of the 33 kilometer (20 miles) long dyke started in 1927 and was completed in 1932. It was built to protect land in the Netherlands from the sea. It dams off the *Zuiderzee*, a salt water inlet of the North Sea and turns it into a fresh water lake of the *Ijsselmeer*. Considering when it was built, it is an engineering marvel constructed with Dutch ingenuity and workmanship.

Next stop is *Giethoorn*, typically referred to as *'Venice of the North.'* Cars aren't permitted on the narrow roads so transportation is traditionally on foot, by bike, or by boat. We share a table with the couple from Switzerland at *Café Restaurant De Rietstulp* for lunch. Tess and I split a salad and an order of fish and chips. After lunch, our group boards a small motor boat. Our fearless tour guide takes us on an hour long tour up and down the numerous canals. We get to see *'up close and personal'* the beautiful (and expensive) houses and beautifully manicured landscaping. We pass under the many picturesque pedestrian bridges in this idyllic village where 2,500 people call home. Before heading back to Amsterdam, we enjoy 45 minutes of *'free time'* to explore and, you guessed it, enjoy ice cream!

After a fun-filled day of exploring the countryside outside of Amsterdam, our tour leader drops us off at the hotel. We are beat and need rest. So rather than head to town or grab something to eat at the hotel, we head to our room and enjoy cups of instant chicken broth soup and crackers. Tomorrow sets up to be a *'chill'* and laundry day. Good night from Amsterdam!

Below are some things we learned today from our tour leader:

- The Netherlands plans to eliminate paper money and coins and convert to digital payment methods.

- To enter a public restroom, you **MUST** use a credit card. Also, there are no 2/1 *'family deals'*.

- The Dutch people love to make fun of Germans who wear helmets when cycling because they look foolish compared to the Dutch, who ride helmetless.

- Cycling creates strong legs and is a great cardio workout.

- Poor weather does not limit cycling. There are more bikes per household than people.

- Stolen bikes foster a black market for pre-owned bike sales.

- Don't expect to see Budweiser or Bud Light in any bars in the Netherlands.

- Windmills on land and in the ocean create hydro-electric power.

- Tulips are brought from Türkiye and are the national flower of the Netherlands.

- Forty percent of the country operates on renewable energy sources including 18% created by wind farms, 12% from solar, and 10% from biomass.

*****

Thursday, May 16 — Day 52
Laundry, Window Shopping, and Hair Cut Day

Day 52 has a nice ring to it! Tess and Dirk both *'died'* last night. Eight plus hours of uninterrupted sleep recharge our worn out bodies. Your body knows exactly what you need after a fun filled ten-hour adventure yesterday. We were so tired last night when we returned to the hotel. We skipped eating at the hotel restaurant and headed to our room for an in-room *'dining experience'* of cups of chicken broth soup and crackers. This morning, I open the balcony curtains and see a massive, 12-story Norwegian cruise ship docked across the river from their room!

This morning, I decide to skip the traditional American morning breakfast and work my way all the way down to the far left side of the buffet where I fill my plate with freshly made tuna fish salad, cucumbers, and tomatoes. Yes, I *'cheat'* and grab a few pieces of bacon. Sometimes, old habits are just hard to break. A bowl of freshly cut mixed fruit and pieces of the *'to die for'* ultra-fresh multigrain bread fill my plate. Today's adventure at the tea bag making machine makes for another great *'story.'* My attempt at filling the tea bag with just **ONE** serving of crushed teas leaves *'utterly'* fails. Instead, I create the largest tea bag known to mankind. There are enough fresh crushed tea leaves in the tea bag to make a cup of tea for everyone in the breakfast room! At least I didn't spill tea leaves all over the spotless counter top. It could have been a lot worse.

Dirk thoroughly enjoys his lunch/breakfast meal. The tuna salad includes pieces of yellow corn and red onion. I create mini tuna sandwiches using slices of the multi-grain bread. The juice bar offers fresh apple along with orange and strawberry juices. I try apple juice. It's the bomb. The juice tastes like fresh apple cider, the kind you get at Halloween. A second glass of apple juice, two cups of tea, and a bowl of fresh fruit complete another outstanding breakfast.

Where's Tess?? It's 10:00. The breakfast buffet is closing. Did she run away with one of the stud hunks working at the hotel? You know, tall, blond, blue eyes, and built like a tight end, power forward, slugging outfielder, or first baseman. I guess this means she will be making a trip to the second floor bakery for a special sweet treat or three. Finally at two minutes past closing time, she makes her grand appearance. Since everyone but me has left the room, there's no *standing ovation* today. Hopefully, she'll get one tomorrow, our final morning in Amsterdam. Even though the buffet was *'officially closed'*, the staff had not completed removing the food items so Tess was able to make herself a nutritious breakfast plate.

It's laundry day so I set out to wash and dry our clothes. After today, we have only one more laundry stop in Stockholm. There is a *'do it yourself'* laundry on the Viking Mars cruise ship, however. I grab the two bags of dirty clothes and head to the bus stop. While waiting for the bus, I observe a lady parking her electric vehicle in a spot next to a public charging station where she pays a fee to charge her car.

I plan to take Bus 43 to the central train station and switch to the M52 subway, exiting at *Rokin*. The trip will end with a five minute walk to the laundromat. I just missed Bus 43. So, I sit at the bus stop patiently waiting 30 minutes for the next bus. Waiting is not one of my strengths; but, what's the alternative? I could walk across the bridge and take Tram 12 to the central station. However, with luck, as soon as I start walking, Bus 43 will arrive and pass me. So, I make an executive decision to stay put.

Bus 43 arrives and takes me to the train station. I diligently follow the signs to subway M52. I think it is just around the corridor to the left; but the M52 directional sign *'disappeared'*. For only God knows why, I keep walking straight. At the next left hand corridor, the M52 directional sign reappears and points back in the direction I just came from! What is up with the signage? One sign points to turn left go and 50 meters. The next sign points in the direction I just came from. So, I retrace my steps and make a right turn down the corridor to the M52 subway entrance. I enter the subway station and use the escalator to go down one flight. I look for the platform for the M52 train heading to *Zuid*. Before I make my next move, (there are signs pointing in four directions to public transportation options) I ask a subway worker which set of steps I should head down to take the M52 subway towards *Zuid*. The worker points to the right and says, "That way, down one more level." I take the escalator down one level and reach the platform just as the subway pulls into the station. This will be a short, three stop ride to Rokin. The other day, Dirk missed this stop. (See Day 50)

Here's what happened. The other day, the subway **DID** stop at Rokin; but I misread the digital sign in the subway. I thought the digital sign displayed **NEXT** stop Rokin when in fact the sign displayed **THIS** stop Rokin.....just some poor reading skills by me resulting in a long walk that afternoon.

Today I have greatly improved my reading skills and exit at the correct stop. At street level, I activate Google Maps to lead me to the *'promised land.'* But wait fans! Google Maps App displays a 12-minute walk!!! The original directions on Google Maps indicated a five minute walk from the subway station. Someone is messing with me. Rather than toss the phone in the canal, I follow the directions and on the third try, I finally get going in the right direction. Thank goodness for the moving light blue arrow on the Google Maps App screen indicating which direction to walk. Without this, I could wind up in Belgium! It takes 40 minutes to complete the five minute walk Google Maps originally plotted! What's up with that? The *'new'* directions take me well over a mile out of my way. I cross four canal bridges. **FINALLY**, a quick left gets me 150 feet from the destination. He **SCORES!** I *'put one in the back of the net'* and do the typical hockey score *'triple right punch'* with my right gloved hand, my stick in my left hand, and skating only on my right skate. If there was a *'people washing their clothes bench,'* I would skate by and *'high five'* everyone.

I locate two washers and, with the aid of the laundromat lady, buy the soap, place it in the proper slot on the washers, put the cash into the slot machine (no frequent player loyalty points, sorry), and activate both machines. Stupid Dirk originally tries to use his Wells Fargo ATM card to start the washers!!! What a dunce! This establishment is *'old school,'* *'cash only,'* no credit cards accepted. The laundromat lady plays *'banker.'* I need her to break big bills. Once the washers have completed their all-important job, I take a one credit course from the laundromat lady on how to operate the dryers. I fire up two dryers on the permanent press cycle for 30 minutes. I *'guess'* the **HOT** cycle would be **TOO** hot. I can always add **MORE** time; but I can't un-dry over dried clothes that have shrunk. With the dryers *'doing their thing,'* I walk outside looking for something to drink.

Across the street from the laundromat, I spy a large sign *'Coffee Shop.'* A cup of Java sounds good on a cool, damp, cloudy day. Something seems **OFF** when I enter and look at the menu displayed on an iPad on the counter. Confused, I ask for an Americano coffee with cold milk. The clerk looks at me inquisitively and says, "Hey old Americano man, this is **NOT** a coffee shop. We sell marijuana and hashish!" Hold on Mr. *'HIGH'* clerk, the sign out front clearly, in plain old US English says, *'Coffee Shop'*! *"I guess we forgot to take it down six years ago when we took over the store."* Whatever, with tail between my legs, I walk out. I am afraid to look back at the clerk who may be extending the not so nice and unkind *'fickle finger of fate'* gesture at me. Still looking for liquid refreshments, I stop at a *'100's of kinds loose candy bins store'* and buy a Sugar Free Red Bull and a bottle of water.

Back at the laundromat, I talk with Simone. She and her husband purchased the laundromat eight years ago. They offer *'do it yourself wash and dry'* and *'drop off and pick up, we wash and dry for you service.'* Simone updates me on the neighborhood. It's relatively safe. Stores include sex shops, pot and drug shops, bars, restaurants, and on the corner out the door left, a former church converted into a gathering place for gay couples to hang out. "We've got a little bit of everything, and we are safe," she concludes. Once the clothes are dry, neatly folded and place in the laundry bags, it's time to head home. Instead of the long walk back to the M52 subway, Simone walks me to the front door, tells me to turn left, walk towards a large circle, and take either the #2 or #12 trolley for a less than ten minute ride to the central train station.

But hold on traveling friends, I don't know what I did or how I did it — **BUT** I get on the **WRONG** trolley. How did I know? After riding for *'way too long'* and heading to god knows where in southwest Amsterdam, I asked a lady passenger if this trolley stops at the central train station. She said, "**NO**, you need to (and pointing to the right across a park), go over *'there'* and catch a trolley to take you where you want to go." I quickly jump off the trolley and take a few steps in the direction I was told to head. However, I look up and see Bus 8 right behind the trolley. The display board indicates it is heading to the central train station! Just how lucky am I? I jump on and ask the bus driver, who thinks he is Dusty Baker playing with a toothpick in his mouth, if this bus is heading to the central train station. He clearly has *'an attitude.'* Did he get out of bed on the wrong side today? Did the wife or significant other ask him to leave? Are any of his kids in trouble with the law? His answer is "**YES**, now sit down and shut up old Americano man."

But yes there is **MORE** to this story. Bus 8 is taking the **LONG WAY** to the central train station. For a moment, I thought the bus must be heading to another city! Looking out the window, **NOTHING** looks familiar. Is this bus really going to the train station in Amsterdam or Brussels? Traffic is heavy. The bus driver is clearly frustrated and honks the horn four to five times indicating, *'let's move it buddy... get out of my way!'*

I have no fucking idea if I am still in Amsterdam or Brussels. It's getting late and even worse, if I thought the walk to the laundry was long, this is starting to become an overnight trip! I don't have my passport with me!! Despair sets in. The bus stops at a red light. Across the street and in front of the bus, I see railroad tracks! And, if the bus turns **RIGHT**, the train station **MUST** be close by! **SUCCESS**, the bus turns right. The central train station is about a kilometer up the street on the left.

How did all this happen? What went wrong? When I arrive at the train station, I figure out how I screwed up. I got on the #7 tram versus the #2 or #12 that goes directly to where I wanted to go. How do I know this? I saw two of the numbered trollies stop outside the train station. The #7 tram took me on a *'wild goose chase'* way, way southwest, and Bus 8 took the long perimeter route around town to the train station. Dirk is a dumb ass shit. But at least it makes for a good story!

Hungry and pissed off for wasting time, I stop for a hot dog and Coke Zero in a 7-11 type convenience store in the train station. It has just not been my day despite getting the laundry done in record time. I grab a Cherry Coke Zero, not the regular Coke Zero! Really, can't you read?? My hotdog is set in a roll that wraps totally around the dog. Can I get a bigger hotdog in this bread dominated roll? Ultimately, I get on Bus 43 heading to the hotel. The day is **NOT** a total loss. After all, I did the laundry and got to see a part of city I had never seen! Believe me however, after a while, all the streets, corners, buildings, shops, and restaurants look alike.

Finally, I arrive back at the hotel with clean clothes. I stop by the front desk and ask for directions to the nearest post office. We have a box of 'stuff' to mail home. I hear, "We can do it here at the hotel with no mark up and put it on your bill!!!" The front desk clerk gives me boxes and packing material. Tess does her 'magic,' packs the 'just gotta have stuff,' drops it off at the front desk, learns the box weighs 2.7 kilograms, and will cost 45 Euros to ship home. What a **GREAT** deal....no customs paperwork to fill out, the hotel staff does it all!!!

Tess wants to go to the 9th Street shopping area. It's on her 'must visit' list. Bus 43 and Tram 17 get us there. We walk around the narrow streets window shopping. The sun is out. There's a slight breeze on this pleasant 65-degree afternoon. We stop at a convenience store and buy four very sweet tangelos for one Euro.

Tess moseys in and out of stores while I find a bench to sit on. I watch as a 'Dockr' (like Amazon) driver pulls up on his delivery bike and drops off a package at a shoe store. After three blocks, Tess's tour is **OVER!** Her knee is barking. Dirk stops at a men's hair styling salon. He learns haircuts **START** at 40 Euros! What do they do, weigh the hair cut off to determine the price or does the person cutting hair start a stop watch to time how long it takes to cut someone's hair? I pass on the haircut....way too much money. As I turn to leave, I receive a snarly "have a nice day" from the male hair stylist. With that attitude, I am thankful I didn't allow the stylist to get near my 60-days growth with clippers and scissors. On the flip side, I could have *'walked out'* with a Netherlands movie actor look!

The dynamic duo spots a local bar with outside seating under a large tree along the canal. We sit down at the last open table, shoving past three old people to secure the seats. After all, possession is 9/10ths of the law. We order adult beverages and a small bowl of nuts. It's 65 degrees out, perfect 17:00 happy hour weather. We relax, unwind, and watch the boats, bikers, and pedestrians go by.

After having enough *'happy,'* we retrace our steps and catch a tram back to the central train station. It's our last walk through the station to catch Bus 43. Tess is in charge of guiding us to the designated Bus 43 stop. At the "T" intersection, she starts left. Sorry Tess fans who are silently cheering her on, that's the **WRONG** way! I quickly get us back on track by turning right. Tess had a 50/50 chance of getting it right; but *'came up short'*. Towards the end of the corridor, I spot a barber shop. Three hair stylists are sitting and waiting for customers. The cost is 40 Euros, a flat charge, no *'starting at'* pricing. Simon, the young man on the far right is *'next up.'* Dirk has a good feeling. The young barber offers me coffee or water. Sitting in the chair, we discuss the *'plan of attack'* on my flowing *'silver fox locks.'* Short but not too short is the order of the day. You can always take more off but can't put it back on. The barber gives me a choice of clippers or scissors. Knowing how clippers can do serious damage should Simon's hand twitches or slips, I select scissors. During the hair cutting process, Simon and I discuss the places Tess and I have visited and what it's like living in America versus Europe. We discuss *'ongoing'* and *'put to bed'* international world problems. Simon, the young barber from Sicily, and I could be nominated for *'important international problem solving'* posts at the United Nations or the European Union.

I am very impressed with his hair cutting, poise, confidence, and customer service skills. Simon tells me he comes from a family of barbers and has been cutting hair since he was 12 years old! He moved to Amsterdam about 18 months ago seeking *adventure and opportunity*. I just know Simon will succeed if he continues to focus his efforts in the right direction. I thank him for the great haircut and leave a nice tip. It's time to catch the bus to the hotel.

Bus 43 drops us off at the usual stop near the hotel. After sorting the laundry in our room, we head down to the restaurant for our last dinner in Amsterdam. Our five night stay ends Friday morning. It's then off to Stockholm via plane for six nights. The restaurant is busy. Staffing seems light. Even the restaurant manager and his assistant are busy serving customers. We order adult beverages —Tess a red wine and Dirk a Prosecco. Tess orders a shrimp sauté while I go grilled salmon. Both add a bowl of fried rice. The food is perfectly cooked and very satisfying. Our last supper ends with ice cream and sorbet topped with whipped cream. Tess orders a decaf Americano with milk. The waitress says *'normal milk'* versus what Americans call *'regular or whole milk.'* I tease the young waitress, Ayla, a soon to be high school graduate. I try, in vain, to tell her I am a *'famous person in America'* and ask her to change the bill — 77 Euros — to 0 Euros because I charge 77 Euros for my autograph on the dinner bill. She runs it *'up the flag pole'* but returns and says, "Sorry no can do, maybe next time." Ayla is confident, competent, and professional. She *'didn't fall'* for my BS story. She plans to take a year off from studies to work and travel. After that, she plans to *'find some study.'*

We bid ado to the restaurant staff without the *'kiss, kiss, and hug, hug,'* and head upstairs to pack. After getting off the elevator at the 5th floor, we make one final stop. We park ourselves on two chairs to watch the magnificent 19:31 sunset. It is time to pack up and get a good night's sleep before Friday's flight to Stockholm, Sweden via Finland. Until Friday morning.....that's all folks!

P.S. When Tess asks the front desk clerk a question she cannot answer, the clerk says she will *"consult with my colleagues in the back."*

P.S.S. Prior to leaving Henderson, packing decisions on what to wear were hard. We used historical weather information to determine our traveling wardrobe. So far, we have experienced many days with about normal warm weather, only a few days of rain, and only cold weather when visiting Switzerland mountain tops. I have unworn heavy clothes in my suitcase I hope to wear in Norway on cruise excursions and in Iceland.

*****

Friday, May 17 — Day 53
Amsterdam, Netherlands
to Stockholm, Sweden

It's a sad day today. Dirk and Tess depart Amsterdam at noon on a flight to Stockholm with a stopover in Helsinki. We have never set foot in Finland and even through it's a short two hour layover, by just placing our feet on the ground at the airport, I say we **ADD** Finland to the list of European countries visited. Tess indicates she may put an asterisk on the stopover since we didn't stay overnight. It's just like the asterisk MLB put on Roger Maris's record setting 61st home run breaking Babe Ruth's 60 home run record. The season was longer in 1961 than in 1927 when Ruth hit 60. Anyway....

It's a completely overcast, cool morning. Rain is forecast. I receive a FaceTime call from grandsons Tanner and Brady. It's 22:00 in California on May 16th, 07:00 in Amsterdam on May 17. They are hanging out in their backyard chilling as a fire blazes in the outdoor fireplace. They look so much older than the last time I saw them. Brady has a full head of hair combed *'Trump style'* while Tanner bounces around wearing a 20-gallon tan cowboy hat. They look happy. Now that school is out for the summer, their father has them working full time, plus overtime, at the Woodcrest pizza location. I am so thankful they call me "Papa Keoni." They are poised and ready to show up in Nevada for a few days later this summer to kick my ass playing golf. They will also get to hang out with some of my golfing friends: Griff, Thom, Mike, Ted, Ben, Dale, Girard, Tommy, and Doug. Remember, I tore my Achilles twice in early 2023. So, it's been a **LONG** time since I swung a club. It should be *'very interesting but dumb'* (an old Laugh-In TV show reference) to say the least.

My last breakfast mirrors every other day. I go *'American'* with eggs, bacon, bread, sausage, and two small pancakes. (It's like the Denny's Grand Slam special for $8.99.) I give up trying to create the *'just perfect'* tea bag. There's enough tea in my bag for at least a quart of fresh iced tea *'for the road.'* Still half asleep, Tess finally shows up and nibbles on fruit, eggs, bacon, and mushrooms while enjoying her daily cappuccino.

Our Uber will arrive at 09:25-ish. There's a five minute window on either side of the expected 09:25 arrival time. But first, we head to the room to finish packing those last minute items, then head to the lobby to check out, and await our chariot. It's been an amazing 4 1/2 days, five nights stay. The hotel is outstanding. The staff are well trained customer service professionals always with a smile on their face and always ready to do whatever is necessary to make your stay enjoyable. Everyone multi-tasks. Managers move personnel into different jobs as needed just like an NFL offensive or defensive football coordinator moves players to different positions based on what's happening right now in the game.

I check out with front desk person, Tess (not my Tess, mind you). She's a young, blue eyed, blonde college student majoring in hospitality. The other day, she took care of mailing my box of *'just had to have'* junk souvenirs. (Clearly, every hotel staff member is *'well aware of'* the **VIP** guests in room 534 from Las Vegas!) We are not sure if that's good or bad, so let's just go with *'popular and charming.'*

Tess offers to print the bill; but, Dirk says, "No, just email it. I know it's big and I don't want it to ruin my day. Thanks, Merci, Danka."

Mr. Uber is right on time. He loads our bags and heads to the airport. For whatever reason, he drops us off 400 meters from the terminal. It looks like a security thing. No vehicles are permitted directly adjacent to the terminals.

Amsterdam International Airport is huge. Seventy-two airlines, including KLM, Delta, JetBlue, Air Europe, British Airways, Air Canada, transavia (with a small "t" decal on the back fin of the plane), and Finnair. Our airline, Finnair, is relatively small compared to the *'big boys,'* so we guess that's why our gate is at the end of Terminal D, Gate 87 of 89. Transavia airlines is a catchy name that grabs my attention. Originally, Dirk guesses it is an eastern European country airline from Slovakia, Albania, or Belarus. However, it's a Dutch low cost airline and is part of the Air France KLM Group. It appears that transavia air flies the discontinued Boeing 727-200 planes that were used in the late 1960's to 1990's by such famous, but now defunct, airlines Aloha and Air Cal.

We enter Terminal 1. Now fans, the *real fun, or fiasco,* begins. KLM is a major airline and dominates the Terminal One baggage check area. Their baggage check-in bins open up like a small elevator door. Passengers deposit their bags into the bins and watch the doors close and take the checked bags to who knows where.

We don't see any signs for Finnair baggage check-in. I ask a flight attendant to direct us to the Finnair check-in area. She points straight ahead and mumbles something about "3". After using the free potty, I set up an account on the Finnair App. We walk into the Delta Airlines baggage check-in area from the **WRONG** direction causing a minor traffic jam for passengers who have checked their bags and are attempting to get to their gates through the Tess/Dirk roadblock. A Delta baggage assistant sends us on a cross country walk from Terminal 1 to Terminal 3 where the Finnair baggage check-in is allegedly located. So off we go.

At the entrance to Terminal 3, something does not *'feel'* right. I ask a customer service agent where the Finnair baggage check-in area is. **Hang on folks .....It's all the way back to the far end of Terminal 1 where we first entered the airport!** We retrace our steps and go on a cross county walk back to our starting point. However, we cannot locate a sign directing us to Finnair baggage check-in. Don't ask me why or how, but *'something'* clicks in my head that it is in Row 4. I break thru the queued up line barriers and crash the line asking for help! It's not the Finnair baggage check-in location. It's a different airline check-in counter! I *'lose it'* on the poor, most likely underpaid and overworked, check-in agent. I *'unload'* my double barrel shotgun, blasting out, *"What the hell is going on here? We need some helpa! Where is the Finnair baggage check-in counter???"* The young agent doesn't shoot back with "You stupid old Americano people," he just points to the end of the counter to the right. We refuse to go around the people in line like we should. Instead, we just *'barge'* through whatever airline check-in line this is and pass confused passengers who are wondering, *"Who the hell are these two old Americano idiots barging through our line with no respect for us? What the hell is going on? Security, we need security here* ***RIGHT NOW.****" (They didn't really say that... It's just what pops into my head as something they might say!)*

Crisis averted. Security lets us off with a stern warning, *"Never come back to this airport ever again or else and ...* ***PLEASE*** *enjoy your flight to Stockholm thru Helsinki today!"* There are only two customers in line at Finnair. Two young agents man the check-in point. Must be a **BIG** airline we are flying on today. The young man and his mate work for a third party luggage check in service *'Vggby.'* I attempt to check in two bags on the Finnair App; but couldn't get the App to take my credit card. The young lad says everything looks *'ok'* as the baggage identification tags print. (Later, we learn we are entitled to two free checked bags each through the American Airlines Business Class Frequent Flyer Miles redemption for today's trip.)

We head to the passenger security area and then onto our gate. Along the way, we are **STOPPED** by the *'carry-on bags screeners.'* They want me to place my carry-on suitcase (with the remaining souvenirs and confiscated beer glasses) into a *'box'* to make sure the carry-on bag is the allowable size. My bag **FAILS** the test. Needless to say, I am **NOT** a *'happy camper.'* Despite all my pleadings and threats, the carry-on baggage screener will **NOT** permit us to head to security and our gate. We **MUST** go back to Finnair and check the suitcase. Further complaining and arguing will get us nowhere except a trip to the airport police station and most likely delay today's trip to Stockholm. I mumble a few *'choice comments'* and return to Finnair to check the bag.

Everything we trust is now in order. We enter the priority security line (like the TSA priority service in the USA) based on today's flight in business class I booked using American Airlines' Frequent Flyer Miles. Every passenger goes thru the X-ray machine with legs spread, arms down, and hands facing front. Tess and I pass with flying colors. No pat downs or magic wand body scans to check out our knee and hip replacements that traditionally set off *'bells, whistles, and alarms'* when traveling through United States airports. (Memo to former transportation secretary Mayor Pete: *'Hey Mayor Pete, how can Netherlands personnel effectively and efficiently pass travelers through airport security when in the USA, passengers **ALWAYS** get the third degree pat down and wand scan with hands over their head and spread eagle up against the wall should they have replacement body parts? Just saying....'*)

Our two carry-on bags and backpack, however, get the *'third degree checking'* by a young, friendly security person. He meticulously goes through our belongings and uses a TV monitor to guide his search. A bottle of cough syrup and a wine cork remover trigger the additional inspection. It's all good. We are now on our way to Gate 85. Our priority status also gains us access to the Finnair priority boarding lounge. We have hit the jackpot today, just like golfing friends Girard, Mike, Dan, Dave, and Ed who score a *Straight Royal Flush* or *Four of a Kind* on a video poker machine.

We locate the priority lounge at Room 26 and enter using the bar code data on our boarding passes. We are *'styling and living large'* today! We enjoy a bowl of creamy tomato soup and non-alcoholic drinks. Time to head to the boarding gate. Gate 84 is **NOT** just a stone's throw away. It's more like a two mile hike across town. Yes fans, the walk is **LONG**. We can't help but notice how clean everything in the airport is. Plus, the various service agents we came in contact with are professional and clearly understand great customer service! It's a far cry from what we experience in American airports. *(Hey Mayor Pete, instead of worrying about racist transit routes and work crews in inner cities lacking DEI, why not take your bike, fly to Amsterdam on taxpayers' nickel, and see how a well-functioning airport and city transit system works. God forbid you learn something and implement it throughout the United States.)*

We board the plane. Our seats are in Row 1, seats A and C. Yes fans, we are sitting in the **FRONT ROW**. There is no screaming like Bob Uecker in a 1980's Miller Lite beer commercial filmed in Dodger Stadium, *"He missed the tag!"* A flight attendant serves us complimentary champagne and orange juice, perfect mimosas. Catch this, on a two hour flight, the 12 business class passengers (middle seat open for more room) receive a hot lunch of chicken, sweet potatoes, and broccoli. The flight attendant also serves us warm rolls. Finn chooses a brown roll. The attendant says, *"It's goot with dabutter!"* The hot meal comes on a tray that includes real silverware, glasses, dishes, and cups...no plastic. It's amazing food service for a mere two hour flight. The ordinary people sitting in the rear of the plane are crammed into three seats on each side of the middle aisle and get a cold drink and a bag of airline peanuts.

When we land in Helsinki, there's a one hour time zone change. In effect, we lose an hour. However, when we get to Stockholm, we get the hour back. Since Tess and I are only in Finland for that one hour layover, we keep our Dutch names until we get to Sweden. Sorry fans, it is what it is...our call.

As soon as the Finnair plane wheels touch down on the runway in Stockholm, we travelers become Bjorn and Elsa. Arriving in Stockholm, we are very disappointed that Annika Sorenstam did not meet us at the airport. We facetiously receive a text from her saying, *"Sorry, tied up with my son who is playing in a junior golf tournament today, Saturday, and Sunday. Maybe we can catch up later during your stay."* Elsa and I are also bummed there is **NO** ABBA music playing in the baggage claim area!

The bags show up quickly. Our plane was the only one that recently landed. Elsa and I saddle up and follow the signs to the taxi stand. A taxi area city employee acts as a greeter and **NOTHING ELSE**. When we ask, he will **NOT** recommend which of the four waiting cab services is the best. I approach the Yellow Ford Escape taxi driver and show him the hotel address. Immediately, Bjorn **SENSES** this driver not only doesn't speak English but also has **NO CLUE** where the hotel is. Rather than debate, I walk over to the next cab — a large, black Mercedes four door sedan. The driver knows where the hotel is (or he *'conveniences'* me he knows, after all he has a GPS system in the car) and places our bags in the trunk. Mike, our cab driver, speaks very good English. The electric car is loaded with all the *'bells and whistles,'* including an iPad size display screen connected to front and rear cameras for the driver to monitor *'what's happening'* both in front of and behind the car. It also has a full size map showing the route and the surrounding area.

Along the way, we pass a man on roller skates apparently training for cross country skiing. He is sweating profusely and uses two ski polls to feverishly push himself down the street.

It's a long ride from the airport to the hotel, especially with Friday night rush hour traffic. Elsa and I strike up a conversation with Mike. He is professionally groomed and is wearing a white shirt, black tie, black shoes, black pants, and a stylish black cap. The Mercedes e-car is a *'sweet,'* quiet ride.

Mike turns out to be a very intelligent entrepreneur. He was born in the Belgium Congo, raised in Kenya until 15 years of age, when he moved to Sweden with his mother and siblings. His mother was transferred to Sweden by her employer, the United Nations. He speaks a number of languages including English, Swedish, Kenyan, Swahili, and French. He is an independent contractor working under the umbrella of a 150-year-old, trusted customer taxi service in Stockholm. When asked about visiting Kenya, he said Nairobi is considered the *'New York City of Kenya.'* Many people who visit go on safaris. Just talking and listening to him, we can tell he is an industrious worker and very smart. And one bonus — Mike tells us potty is **FREE** in Stockholm. Thus, it's not necessary to carry a pocket full of coins.

The Friday night traffic is backed up. As Mike approaches the hotel, there is a tremendous amount of road and building construction going on. The two *'normal'* access roads to the hotel are blocked. On his third try, Mike finds a route through the construction and gets us to our hotel. This journey **MUST** cost over $125 for the approximately 45 minute drive. Mike sprinkles some *'magic'* on the bill getting it down to $80 in Swedish currency. (Don't even *'go there'* to try to understand their currency and compare it to United States currency.) It's called *'Swedish Krona'* (SEK). Let's just say one of their dollars, whatever they call them, is equivalent to roughly $.10. I give him my last 20 Euros (about $21 US dollars) as a tip for his excellent service and information.

Check-in goes smoothly at *Hotel Nacka*. Our room is one floor up, Room 111. After unpacking and unwinding, we head down to the bar restaurant and enjoy a homemade pizza, a small Caesar salad, a Brooklyn lager draft beer, and a fancy red wine. The restaurant's sales system is **NOT** integrated with the hotel's guest billing system. (There's a job here for some software savvy individuals.) I need to run up to the room to grab my wallet. You won't believe this but, when I step off the elevator on floor one, I **CAN'T** remember our room number! This is **NOT** an embellishment.... it's **REAL**. I *'think'* it's an even numbered room, so I try my key card on every even numbered room door. No luck. Because of the multiple tries on the wrong room doors, I think my key card might be deactivated. Sheepishly, I return to the front desk, tell the young lady my key card is not working, **AND** admit I can't remember my room number! She gives *'Bjorn, the stupid old Americano look'* and issues me a new key. My return to floor one, and room 111, is successful. I grab my wallet, return to the restaurant, and pay the tab. I hang around the restaurant to work on today's story while Elsa heads to the room. I later learn when Elsa enters the elevator, she presses the *'5'* button thinking she is still in Amsterdam and heading to room 534!

Tired, exhausted, and just worn out, I join Elsa upstairs, finish today's *'Happenings'* story, and retire in our soft, individual, adult size cradle bed hoping for a good night's sleep in anticipation of tomorrow's first day assault on Stockholm.

Roger, over and out!

*****

Stockholm Facts

According to *Wikipedia and Visit Sweden*, Stockholm is the capital and most populous city of the Kingdom of Sweden as well as the largest urban area in the Nordic countries. Approximately 1 million people live in the municipality with 1.6 million in the urban area, and 2.4 million in the metropolitan area. The city stretches across 14 islands where Lake Mälaren flows into the Baltic Sea. Outside the city to the east, and along the coast, is the island chain of the Stockholm archipelago. The city serves as the county seat of Stockholm County.

Stockholm, one of the most beautiful capitals in the world, is built on 14 islands connected by 57 bridges. The beautiful buildings, the greenery, the fresh air, and the proximity to the water are distinctive traits of this city. The geographical city center is situated on the water, in *Riddarfjärden Bay*. More than 30% of the city area is made up of waterways and another 30% is made up of parks and green spaces.

Stockholm, the largest city in Scandinavia, effortlessly intertwines a rich history and stunning nature with the cultural sophistication, modern architecture, and dynamic attitudes of a thriving metropolis. This unique blend is enhanced by the omnipresence of water, adding an extra layer of charm.

The weather in Stockholm changes according to four distinct seasons. Summers are warm – sometimes quite hot – and it rarely gets dark during summer nights. The winters may be mild and rainy but can also be cold and snowy. The colors of autumn are spectacular in the city parks, and spring is welcomed by locals, wrapped in blankets, and sipping a drink, at outdoor restaurants and cafés.

Due to the city's high northerly latitude, the length of the day varies widely from more than 18 hours around midsummer to around six hours in late December. The nights from late May until mid-July are not completely dark even when cloudy. Stockholm has

SH?#! Happens AGAIN! - Traveling With John and Leslie

the warmest month of July of the Nordic capitals. Stockholm has an annual average snow cover between 75 and 100 days. Winters generally bring cloudy weather with the most precipitation falling in December and January (as either rain or snow). The average winter temperatures range from −3 to −1 °C (27 to 30 °F) and occasionally drop below −20 °C (−4 °F) in the outskirts of the city. Spring and autumn are generally cool to mild.

More than just a picturesque city, Stockholm prides itself on being an advocate of tolerance and inclusivity. Hosting the renowned *Stockholm Pride* festival, the largest in the Nordic region, the city welcomes tens of thousands of LGBTQ visitors from around the world every summer.

This visionary city also stands as the epicenter of a thriving tech-innovation community and a growing array of start-ups, rivalling even the density found in Silicon Valley. Stockholm's influence extends globally, with industry giants such as *Spotify*, the pioneering music streaming service, and *Mojang Studios*, the creators of the gaming phenomenon *Minecraft*.

Navigating the city is a breeze, whether you choose to walk, bike, or use public transport. Each district in the city has its own unique personality. For example, *Södermalm* is known for its creative atmosphere, *Östermalm* for its elegance, and *Norrmalm* for its vibrant energy. In between, you find the Old Town (*Gamla Stan*), contributing to the diverse appeal of Stockholm.

Stockholm is the cultural, media, political, and economic center of Sweden. The Stockholm region alone accounts for over a third of the country's GDP, and is among the top 10 regions in Europe by GDP per capita. Considered a global city, it is the largest in Scandinavia and the main center for corporate headquarters in the Nordic region. The city is home to some of Europe's top ranking universities, such as the *Karolinska Institute* (medicine), *KTH Royal Institute of Technology*, *Stockholm School of Economics,* and

Stockholm University. It hosts the annual *Nobel Prize* ceremonies and banquet at the *Stockholm Concert Hall* and *Stockholm City Hall.* One of the city's most prized museums, the *Vasa Museum,* is the most visited museum in Scandinavia. The Stockholm metro, opened in 1950, is well known for the decor of its stations.

Stockholm is Sweden's primary financial center, one of the largest in Scandinavia, and hosts several of Sweden's largest companies. Furthermore, the headquarters of most of Sweden's largest banks are in Stockholm. Stockholm is one of Europe's major tech centers; the city has sometimes been called Europe's innovation hub.

Stockholm is the seat of the Swedish government and most of its agencies, including the highest courts in the judiciary, and the official residences of the Swedish monarch and the Prime Minister. The government has its seat in the *Rosenbad Building.* The *Riksdag* (Swedish parliament) is seated in the Parliament House, and the Prime Minister's residence is adjacent at the*Sager House.* Stockholm Palace is the official residence and principal workplace of the Swedish monarch, while *Drottningholm Palace* in neighboring *Ekerö* serves as the Royal Family's private residence.

With one-third lush greenery and one-third shimmering waters, Stockholm integrates nature into its urban tapestry, offering abundant ways to enjoy the outdoors.

In the heart of the city, one can take various boat trips, from kayaking journeys to paddleboard adventures. Guided boat tours are another great option allowing you to explore the city from a unique perspective.

Venturing to the expansive Stockholm archipelago, Sweden's largest, unveils a captivating world. Hop on a ferry to charming *Vaxholm,* adorned with traditional wooden houses. Here, the village exudes a welcoming atmosphere, inviting you to explore shops, restaurants, and cafés.

Stockholm boasts multiple references to the legendary pop group, with the *ABBA Museum* being a must-see for music enthusiasts. The permanent exhibition highlights stage outfits, instruments, gold records, awards, and captivating items. However, it goes beyond a static display, inviting visitors on an interactive journey where they can sing, dance, mix music, and become the fifth member of ABBA.

Stockholm's vibrant concert scene caters to all genres. Discover up-and-coming acts at *Debaser*, while major artists grace venues like *Strawberry Arena*.

*****

Saturday, May 18 — Day 54
Getting a Feel For Stockholm, Sweden and Touring the Royal Palace

Boy the sun comes up early here. It's 06:00. I open the curtain to a cloudless, blue, sunny sky. Bjorn learns the sun rises at 04:05 and set last night at 21:22. Do the math that's only 6:13 hours of dark and 17:47 hours of daylight! We are **REALLY** far up north! In winter, the opposite occurs.

Getting up at 06:00 is way, way too early for me. I hop back into my adult cradle and grab three more needed hours of shut eye. At a little past 09:15, we begin the process of getting ready for the day. My sinuses and ears are continuing to clear from the airplane pressure. Bjorn, as usual, finishes getting ready first. I head to the breakfast room. Here, I am **OVERWHELMED** by dozens of *'Swiftie'* fans. They are staying at the hotel prior to attending the Taylor Swift Stockholm concerts on May 18 and 19. I circle the room looking for two seats. I find two at a six seat bar height communal table and I join two young ladies who are visiting from Spain. They plan to attend Sunday night's concert. They can't be more than 18 to 19 years old! One speaks perfect English. She mentions their tickets cost **ONLY** 200 Euros, (about $210 US) much cheaper than Taylor Swift concert tickets in the USA that cost

$1,000 to $2,000!!! Bjorn is **TEMPTED** to stand up and scream *'Good morning Swifties;'* but, Elsa, who just joins me, threatens pain and a severe, life threatening injury, and issues a stern warning, *"Read my lips!* **DON'T** *even think about it!"*

The breakfast buffet is the largest, and most complete so far, on the trip. On Day 54, in addition to the traditional breakfast items, there's a large spread of cheese, fresh lunch meats, sautéed fresh tomatoes, a Swedish pancake with fruit and real whipped cream, lox, Swedish meatballs, and Swedish cookies. Elsa goes **CRAZY** enjoying the Swedish meatballs and cookies and reminiscing about her grandmother. I just *'dig in'* and go *'local'* dishing up a blueberry, raspberry fruit Swedish pancake topped with extra, of course, freshly made whipped cream, a pastrami open face sandwich, bacon, coffee, and tomato juice.

It's time to make our plan for day one. We are in *Nacka*, a city on the outskirts of downtown Stockholm. The hotel provides directions on how to use public transportation to get to the city.

Elsa and I download the **'SL'** Stockholm Transportation System App and purchase seven day passes for roughly $45 American or 494 Swedish Krona (SEK). Time to head to the room, pack our day travel *'essentials,'* including an umbrella, a light jacket, phone chargers, and tissues, and head to the tram.

Breaking news.....Fox News just reported that The State Department urged Americans abroad to exercise increased caution, citing the potential for *'terrorist attacks'* and other violent actions. The US State Department's alert cites the potential for terrorist attacks, demonstrations, and violent actions against American citizens. Joe Biden, Kamala Harris, Antony Blinken, Jake Sullivan, and John Kirby, *'stuff it;'* we are not packing up and leaving....**NFW!**

Elsa and I have two options to get to the Stockholm Central Train Station area by public transportation. One - walk 500 meters down the hill to Bus 401 or two - walk 100 meters down a dirt, uneven hill. Not looking for any day one injuries, we take the longer, safer route. Bus 401, the bus we need to get to downtown Stockholm, is full. Elsa gets a seat; but I have to stand. I find a spot where bus riders park their baby carriages. Apparently I **MUST** really look *'old and worn out'* **as two ladies stand and offer me their seats! I politely decline since I am securely** *'locked in'* the baby carriage storage spot.

I want to give a big *'shout out'* to the people riding the bus for their courtesy and offering me a seat. However, Elsa has *'THAT LOOK'* meaning, *'DON'T GO THERE OR ELSE ......,'* so I *'back off.'* **But there could be a** *'NEXT TIME'* on a bus or subway!

A short Bus 401 ride gets us to the central train station. After exiting the bus, we walk up two flights of stairs, cross the street, and enter the subway for a short T13 subway ride. We head to Track 2 and descend two flights of steps deep underground for the three minute ride to the train station. The subway station is brightly lit. All you have to do is just follow the directions on the Stockholm Public Transportation App and it gets us to where we want to go..

Many people in Stockholm speak English. And many people ride bikes, but not nearly to the degree as in Amsterdam.

Upon arriving at the central train station, potty is one Swedish Krona each (about $1). Hey cab driver Mike, it's **NOT** free! Having no Swedish Krona, I use a credit card to pay for both of us to enter.

Our next move is to get our bearings. Elsa and I head outside into a large courtyard. We settle into a sidewalk cafe and enjoy coffee and a Swedish crème-filled cake topped with meringue. The bomb! A local cultural band plays music and a local dance troop, wearing historical Swedish clothing and shoes, puts on a very precise and well-choreographed traditional Swedish dance routine.

When the performances finish, today's Plan A calls for purchasing a one day *'Hop On Hop Off'* bus and boat ride ticket. However, it's past 13:00. Plus, we can't locate the tour bus stop or where to purchase tickets. Later during our stay, we plan to get up early, buy the tickets, and take full advantage of the one day tour bus and boat ride. So, we switch over to Plan B and slowly walk a little over a mile to the *Royal Palace*. Along the way, we pass by some All American establishments like *McDonald's, Under Armour, Office Depot, Subway, 7-11, Starbucks, Pizza Hut,* and *Burger King*.

During our walk to the Royal Palace, we see locals enjoying an outdoor lunch and listing to a live band and singers playing American and Swedish music. We also see many people *'out and about'* enjoying the bright, blue sky, sunny day. A Hare Krishnas music and dance troop, dressed in their traditional gear, dance thru the narrow streets, and entertain us and others who are enjoying the day. They invite Bjorn to participate; however, I decline. **BUT**, after the palace tour..... **WHO KNOWS!**...maybe I'll partake.

It's 14:30. The palace tour is available for another 2 1/2 hours. Elsa purchases two tickets. We enter a large courtyard and begin the two hour walking tour of the three story, plus basement, Palace. As I stated in a previous city story, I am not much of a *'museum guy.'* However, I am pleased to report I enjoyed our 2 plus hour self-walking tour. We see paintings, tapestries, and ornate rooms used for functions such as sleeping, elegant dinners, meeting guests and dignitaries, and hosting official Swedish national and inter-national business meetings. All rooms are decorated *'as they were'* hundreds of years ago. (Elsa and I are very disappointed we couldn't find **OUR** official paintings hanging in the Palace among all the other Swedish royalty!) Security informs us Palace personnel plan to hang our pictures once we leave Stockholm. Right now, we remain traveling *'incognito.'*

(There's a potential business opportunity waiting for us when we return to Henderson. We give serious thought about opening our house for tours and making some *'walking around money.'* After all, our home is a *'model.'* Plus, Bjorn built a *'Man Cave'* where he displays autographed baseball jerseys and baseballs, and other sports memorabilia items. You never know...)

It's nearing 17:00 when we complete the Palace tour. It is time to work our way back to the central train station. We follow the transportation app's directions to the closest public transportation option. I spot a 'Hop On Hop Off' bus across the river. We see an opportunity to purchase combination bus and boat tour tickets for Sunday. I *'huff it'* as fast as I can with the repaired left leg Achilles tendon and arrive *'just before'* the bus pulls out. I am very surprised when I turn around and see Elsa hustling to catch up to me. With tickets in hand and the bus rolling, we climb aboard for the one hour ride and exit at the central train station. The bus is air conditioned. This is welcome relief for our bodies. Seated in front of me are a lady and a co-worker who, I learn, work for United Airlines. They are in Stockholm for 30 days to conduct customer service training for airline employees. Not a *'bad gig'* if you ask me!

The bus ride is comfortable and gives us a chance to see many of the city highlights and places to visit during our stay. The building architecture reminds us of buildings in Paris. The bus audio dialogue mentions the *'French influence'* on many of the six to seven story residential and office buildings. We also see many fully grown, mature trees that shade the sidewalks and numerous parks where locals are out enjoying the unseasonably warm weather. Elsa points out areas where the grass needs to be cut and edged and the trees need pruning. Jokingly, she considered putting a call into our landscaper Victor as there's a lot of work to be done here.

I wonder if it was the bus driver's first day driving this route. We got on the bus at stop six and plan to exit at stop 21. People in the bus, including Elsa, call out many times, "What stop is this? What stop is next?" No reply. The driver just keeps on going. When it appears, the next stop is the central train station, those passengers who want to disembark again call out to the bus driver asking what number the stop is. He finally *'gets the message;'* but what does the rookie do? He pulls out the bus route map which every customer receives, carefully *'like forever'* studies it, and says, "21!" It's the correct answer that the anxious passengers, including Elsa and I, want to hear. His prize for the correct answer is **NOTHING!** We get off the bus.

It's now just past 18:00, time to eat dinner before the journey back to the hotel. We spot a restaurant, *O'Malley's*, across the street and next to the train station. There's an international hockey game, Canada vs Finland, playing on a huge, wall mounted TV screen. It's the first live athletic event I have watched on the trip...if you don't count cycling, snooker, rugby, and football aka soccer. Our meals are fantastic and filling. Elsa enjoys a chicken quesadilla and a glass of red wine while I dig into baby back ribs and fries, a small side Caesar salad, and a cold Czech draft beer.

Full, it's time we head back to the hotel. While the transportation app is specific on which subway and bus to take, we **CANNOT** locate the T2 subway platform. We search in vain, walking from one end of the station to the other. Directional signs are no help. Finally, I ask a bakery counter cashier for help. She points us, *'hopefully,'* in the **RIGHT** direction; however, at the "T" intersection, we turn right even though the sign doesn't show the platform number we are looking for. Past frustrated and pissed, Bjorn ducks into a convenience store. The store person reads the platform number displayed on my iPhone and points out the door and right. Hopefully, we are getting close. Again, the signs fail us. So now, looking to cause an international incident, I ask a customer service person how to get to Platform T2. The agent provides **VERY SPECIFIC AND EASY TO FOLLOW** directions, *"Go down those steps and take any train on the platform on the **RIGHT**. Any of those subway trains will take you where you want to go to get on the bus."* Many thanks Sir. His instructions are **SPOT ON!**

Upon exiting the subway, we share an elevator with two ladies and a two-month-old baby sleeping in a carriage. Now, **MORE FUN OR MASS CONFUSION**,(pick one), begins. When we reach ground level, the agent's directions were to go to Bus Stand G at Slussen and take Bus 410 for two stops. Well, we see a bus stop clearly marked *'G Slussen;'* however, no Bus 410 is visible on the bus route map. When the first bus pulls up, Bjorn waits until all the passengers get on and, keeping his left foot between the open doors, asks the bus driver where we can catch Bus 410. In very clear and polite English, he points and says, "Go through **THAT** corridor, down one level and look for the **"G"** sign." He directs us to a large Bus Depot where numerous buses start their routes. He knocks it *'out of the park'* just like Bryce Harper and Aaron Judge, *'touch them all baby, it's **OUTTA** here, home run!'* Relieved and now removed from the *'how are we going to get home mindset,'* we board the bus and get off at the third stop.

After exiting, we immediately realize this is **NOT** where we got on the bus to begin today's journey! Why? We rode Bus 401 to town and return on Bus 410. We can clearly see the hotel at the top of the hill; however, walking up the street is **NOT** an option because there is construction **BETWEEN** the road and the hotel. There is **NO WAY** to cross. I remember this from last night when the cab driver Mike unsuccessfully failed to enter the hotel from this direction because the road into the hotel didn't exist anymore. I remind Elsa of this. There are two possible routes to the hotel — One, walk down the street to the left, then left up the hill using the street we walked down in the morning or two, take the dirt path up 200 meters to the hotel. Bjorn wants to protect Elsa's knee and take the longer, but safer route home while Elsa says, "No let's give the rocky, uphill dirt path a go." We slowly and steadily climb the hill which gets us to the *'promised land!'* Tired, we settle for a relaxing dinner, *'hang'* at the hotel, and enjoy what else — pizza, salad, and adult beverages.

Elsa retires to the room while I find a comfortable chair and outlet to charge my iPhone as I type today's storied adventure.

Until Sunday morning, it's *'over and out.'* Good night.

*****

Sunday, May 19 — Day 55
Touring Stockholm, Sweden

Our second morning in Stockholm mirrors Day One. The sun is out; it's a cloudless, blue sky morning. Don't ask what time the sun comes up. Let's just say it's very, **VERY EARLY!**

Elsa and Bjorn need to hustle to reach the dock for a waterway cruise. This tour is included in our *'Hop on Hop Off'* 24-hour bus ticket. There's another cruise to some outer islands on the agenda today, followed by a slow paced *'chill day'* in this vibrant city. Unlike yesterday, the breakfast room has plenty of seats. Many of the guests who attended the Taylor Swift concert last night are sleeping in as they relive and reminisce about attending her sold out event. Her last performance is tonight. I have no doubt many hotel guests will be attending her concert tonight.

For breakfast, I decided to have lunch again, just like yesterday morning. A lean, open faced pastrami sandwich, with hearty slices of bacon, sliced tomatoes, cucumbers, and two pieces of Brie cheese fill my plate. Dessert is a Swedish pancake covered in blueberries, raspberry sauce, and homemade, *'to die for,'* whipped cream. Hot tea, coffee, and a combo grapefruit/orange juice cap off the meal. It's just a little **TOO** early for a *'cold one'* that, no doubt, would pair nicely with the sandwich. Elsa eats light — Swedish meatballs, fruit, coffee, and juice.

We head out and walk down the nasty dirt and gravel hill for about 200 meters. Tram 30 pulls in. We think we are standing on the platform on the **RIGHT** side of the tracks. We get on. However, the lady tram driver chases us off. In no uncertain terms, she tells us because of the construction in the immediate area, she must pull forward and turn the tram around, then come back to pick up passengers on the **LEFT** side of the platform. Trams going in **BOTH** directions operate on the **SAME** track. Very interesting. Let's hope our tram does not meet a tram coming in the opposite direction. We board Car 3; however, there is no bar code reader to scan the tickets stored on our iPhones. Maybe it's free to travel on Sunday!

This is the first time we ride the tram to the Slussen transportation hub. Looking out the window, we see *'Bastard Burgers'* restaurant. Next door, there's another restaurant, *'Son of a Bitch'* fries and salads.

Bjorn *'feels'* the tram is going in the **OPPOSITE** direction of Slussen. But I soon conclude the tram is heading in the right direction. Despite the misdirection directions — "Yes, you go left versus right and then you get on the subway and go four stops vs two to the central train station. — **EVERYONE** knows you go left to go right!

It is standing room only on the subway out of Slussen. Elsa finds a seat next to a young man and his female companion. As the subway starts, the young man offers me his seat. Hold on sports fans. Am I really **THAT** old and feeble looking? I am not walking with a cane or mobility device. This is the second time this happens. Time for Bjorn to travel to Thailand for a neck and face lift! I decline the seat, saying to myself, *"I am **NOT** that old **YET**."* Maybe in a year or three!

When we arrive at the central train station, we stop at a drug store and then head to street level to find the *'Hop On Hop Off'* bus stop. Walking out of the station, I see a Red Bus, but (*hang onto your hats, here it comes fans*), it's the **WRONG** *'Hop On Hop Off'* bus company! Apparently, in Stockholm, there are **TWO** competing tour bus operators with the **SAME** bus name and color (red). You have to look very closely at the logos on the side of the bus to distinguish between them. Of course I didn't know this, nor did I look for the emblem — nothing new here. I take out my wallet and pull out what I **THINK** are the bus and boat ride tickets.(Now here comes an even **BIGGER BUT**.) **I show the bus driver tickets from yesterday's Royal Castle tour and receipt! To say the least, the bus driver is thoroughly confused. I FAIL to see the problem. I keep telling the bus driver these are the tickets I bought yesterday and INSIST we are, WITHOUT QUESTION, getting on this bus...period, paragraph, end of story!** It's apparent that our beleaguered and confused bus driver speaks no English. In despair and total confusion, he raises both of his arms up in air and *waves us on!* While illegally on the bus, Elsa strikes up a conversation with an American traveling from Minneapolis. Elsa has *'family roots'* there so the two of them *'talk story'* about the city.

We exit the bus at the boat docking area. Bjorn is 100% **SURE** he knows the boat we are looking for docks on the waterfront to the right. He sees a red flag; however, it's a competitor's boat docking area. Our boat is 400 meters **LEFT** up the river. Elsa is understandably **NOT** happy that I erroneously create extra steps for her injured right knee. Without question, I take *'another one'* for the team. When arriving at the correct boat dock, **I CANNOT FIND THE TICKETS.** I tear apart my wallet and back pack. No luck. **I can't find them!** I swear I put them in my wallet or backpack yesterday when I bought them. However, I remember emptying the backpack this morning in the room. I must have taken the tickets out of my belongings and put them in the trash can along with other nonessential things. Sebastian, the ticket agent who sold us the tickets yesterday, is standing nearby. He remembers this dynamic American duo from Las Vegas. I tell him our sad story. Sebastian comes through *'in the clutch'* and sells us two replacement tickets at a 10% discount. Not having any other option, I accept his offer and purchase two 24-hour bus and boat tour tickets. As you can imagine, I am **UPSET** and border on *'really pissed off.'* What a dummkopf Bjorn!! Elsa is **VERY** kind today, so no beating, just a very stern Hawaiian *'stink eye look'*! I deserve more. Why? The replacement tickets cost 70 Swiss Krona! *(Note – when we returned from the trip, I contacted our credit card company about the two charges (yesterday and today). They listened to 'my story' and 'made my day' by removing one of the charges!)*

Our canal tour boat leaves the dock at precisely 12:15. It's a beautiful, sun filled, cloudless sky day. Many locals are out and about enjoying an above normal, warm, spring day. There's a mild breeze to keep things *'just right.'* Shorts and a tee shirt are *'the order of the day'* for me.

We exit the boat at Stop 5 to visit the restored Viking ship *Vasa* Museum. The ship was built 400 years ago under the direction of the King of Sweden. Two Dutch brothers organized and managed the 400 worker job site. When the men were off fighting some battles, the town women took over the construction. The ship was 50 feet tall and was finished in two years, on August 6, 1628. Given the tools in place at that time, that's an *'extremely short time'* to build such a beautifully decorated **HUGE** fighting boat. And here comes the **BUT**.... on its **MAIDEN** voyage from dry dock to the Baltic Sea, it **SANK** a mere 1,000 meters after setting sail. Thirty crew members drowned.

According to museum literature, in the early 1950's, divers locate the boat in 30 meters of water. Experts are brought in to formulate a plan to raise the ship. On April 24, 1961, the ship that spent the last 333 years under water, is raised and eventually towed to a dry dock for restoration. Over 40,000 artifacts are found! Somehow, 15 full skeletal remains of the crew are preserved while partial body parts are retrieved for the remaining 15 drowning victims. The biggest restoration challenge was to prevent the wooden exterior from drying out. It took 17 years to slowly remove the water in the wooden hull. The 64-gun carriages are found in place.

Without a doubt, this was an arduous and amazing restoration effort. No other ship of that size had **EVER** been restored. Ninety eight percent of the original boat parts were reassembled. Today, the original wooden bolts were replaced with stainless steel bolts. The museum documents, in great detail, the ship's construction, restoration, and 800 plus wood carvings. Truly, this is another great museum tour for the traveling Americanos.

We finish the tour, exit the museum, and head for the *'Hop On Hop Off'* boat to continue the canal tour. We are playing with our iPhones and miss the boat by 30 seconds...... Bummer. We sit down on a grassy knoll along the water's edge, enjoying the sun's warmth, and wait 45 minutes for the next boat. Finally, we get on the **LAST** boat of the day and return to the starting point near the Palace. Elsa and Bjorn decide to walk towards the central train station and find a restaurant to eat dinner.

We pass four sidewalk cafes. Nothing looks good. Finally, we come across a small outdoor/indoor Italian restaurant *'Italian Cousins.'* Tatiana, a very pleasant and experienced waitress, greets us. She is from Argentina, makes small talk with us, answers our questions about the specials on today's menu, and recommends a sparkling red Italian wine for me. We start the meal by sharing a small salad that is **NOT** on the menu. The kitchen staff makes one for us. The salad is so good, I tell the chef that he should add this item to future menus. To thank us for this idea, the chef comps us an order of focaccia bread.

Elsa enjoys a glass of Chardonnay. The homemade pasta, sauce, and ingredients are cooked perfectly and served in round bowls. The dynamic duo thoroughly enjoys their meals. I also down two servings of extra-large green olives from Sicily and two glasses of the outstanding red Italian sparkling wine. Ice cream and a pastry dessert finish off the meal. Prior to heading out, we compliment the chef, and vow to return to try their made-from-scratch homemade pizza.

Stuffed, and ready for the luxury of our hotel room, we head to the train station to take a subway to Slussen and a bus to the hotel. Being this is our first full day in Stockholm, we are **NOT** 100% familiar with the public transportation system. The subway we look to ride departs on Track 2. I double check with a customer service rep; **BUT** (here we go again), Elsa heads down one level to **TRACKS 3 & 4**. We go back up the escalator one floor and take a quick **LEFT** to the escalator down to tracks 1 & 2. Two stops later, we exit at Slussen. Ninety eight percent of the exiting passengers go **LEFT** to leave the station. I, however, think I am **Yogi Bear** — *'smarter than the average bear'* — and lead Elsa up the steps to the **RIGHT**. This becomes a **FATEFUL** decision. Despite Elsa's pleas to retrace our steps and go out the other way, I feel I can get us to the bus junction by going around the block...another **FATEFUL** mistake.

The **WALK AROUND THE BLOCK STARTS** with an extra-long, 220 degree, **UPHILL** climb. With every step, Elsa sends another visual dagger directly at Bjorn. At the top of the hill, I admit I *'screwed up big time.'* I ask a police officer sitting in a two person patrol car how to get to where we need to be. Before pulling away, the officer points go back **DOWN** the hill, turn right, go two blocks, and turn right. By now, Elsa's knee is barking so loud she almost gets a *'citation for excessive noise'* in a residential area! **RIGHTLY, SHE IS PISSED**. I sense this, and for a moment, think of doing something *'stupid and illegal'* hoping the policemen will look the other way and give us a free, backseat ride to the bus terminal. But, before I decide, the police car heads down the street leaving us to *'hoof it'* back down. Elsa and I **FINALLY** arrive near our destination. We spot an elevator that we **THINK** will take us down to the bus terminal level. However, **TODAY** is just **NOT** our day. Four people in the elevator hold the door open for us. **BUT** this elevator is **NOT** going **DOWN**. It's going **UP** five nonstop floors to a rooftop restaurant! What else can go wrong?? We reverse course and go down five floors, returning to the start of this misstep. We walk a little bit further down a corridor, locate the correct elevator, go down to where we need to be, and walk over to Stop H to get on the bus that takes us to the hotel. Now, all we have to do is navigate the 200 meters **UP** the dirt and gravel path to the hotel entrance. To say Elsa is **PISSED** at me is clearly an *'understatement of epic proportions.'* She's tired, sore, thinking hard about shooting me, and resuming the trip solo. I know I am in *'big trouble'* and *'camp out'* in the hotel lobby for three hours writing and avoiding Elsa's wrath.

The day is over. Tomorrow **CANNOT** start or end as badly as today did. At least I hope so.

Until tomorrow, let's keep our fingers and legs crossed and get a good night's sleep.

Nighty, night from Stockholm!

*****

Monday, May 20 — Day 56
Stockholm, Sweden Archipelago

Bjorn is beat from yesterday's seven hours of sleep and a full day of activities – visiting a museum, sitting out in the warm sun waiting 45-minutes for a boat, and enjoying a great Italian dinner washed down with two outstanding Italian sparkling red wines.

Originally, I woke up at 06:00, checked the MLB and PGA golf scores, and fell back to sleep. Before I know it, the clock reads 09:00 — time to get up, get *'shaking and baking'* and ready for breakfast. The breakfast room is crowded today, full of *'Swifties'* who attended her final Stockholm concert last night.

This morning, I go *'American'* enjoying eggs, bacon, chicken sausage, one spoon of baked beans, pastrami, and a slice of the multigrain bread and butter, a cup of hot tea, and a glass of grapefruit/orange juice. Sadly, there are **NO** Swedish pancakes on the buffet today. Elsa goes yogurt with granola, fresh fruit, and coffee.

It's time to plan our journey to the boat dock to catch the 2 ½ hour tour of the *Stockholm Archipelago*. We use the **WAZE** navigation app on our iPhones to plan our route to the dock. The app provides multiple ways to get there which could take from 38 to 90 minutes!! That's a huge difference in travel time. After evaluating and studying the multiple routes, we decide to take Bus 414 to *Slussen* and take the M14 Subway three stops to *Östermalmstorg*. Upon exiting, we have a 500-meter walk; however, it's time for potty and a coffee stop. The subway drops us off on the exclusive shopping streets in Stockholm. You name the brand, it's here...*Zara, Prada, Monclar Tuvi, Oscar Jakobson, Louis Vuitton, Tiffany,* and *Gucci.* We enter a coffee shop in an upscale hotel and sit at a counter by the window watching the cars and people go by. We are seriously *'under dressed'* for this establishment. **BUT** we are on holiday! It is what it is! Today the weather is much cooler, more like a typical spring day in Stockholm. Most people are bundled up; however, some locals dress like its *'sunny and 75, whatever floats your boat!'* This timeout gives me time to write about the morning happenings.

The sky is cloudy with just a hint of blue sky peeking through. It seems like we can almost reach up, touch the white clouds, and blue sky. It's now time to walk to the **SPECIFIC** boat dock meeting place. Elsa plots the route. We are soon ready *'to roll.'* Question, *"Why is the restaurant playing American oldies songs?"* It makes me feel like I am home working out at the gym listening to oldies on my iPod (My iPod was part of the items that were in my backpack that was stolen in Milan on Easter Sunday. It's time to search eBay and purchase a new one.)

Elsa gets a **HUGE** navigator **PLUS**, **PLUS**. She plans the route to the boat dock and *'nails it'* without delay or any hiccups. When we arrive at the dock, we run into Sebastian, the red *"Hop On Hop Off"* bus and boat ticket seller. He is the agent who gave us a **HUGE** (**NOT**) 10% discount yesterday for the 24-hour *"Hop On Hop Off"* bus and canal boat replacement tickets.

Here's some important, **MUST KNOW**, information about the area from some of the tourist brochures and our observations:

- The boat ride is on the Baltic Sea. There are no tides.
- The archipelago consists of 14 main islands and 30,000 islands scattered throughout the enclave. Eighty-eight percent are privately owned; however, the laws in Sweden give anyone the right of entry for walking, picnicking, and camping.

- This group of occupied islands reminds us of the many islands in the Seattle area.

- The boat we are traveling on today is a former steam boat built in 1906.

- Low white clouds dot the sky.

- The countryside is lush green. There are many mature trees.

- On the numerous islands, there are homes which are occupied full and part time. Folks use ferry and roadway transportation modes to reach Stockholm.

- Closer to town, residential high rise condos are under construction.

During the ride, the weather *'changes for the better.'* The sun comes out and the clouds disappear. Without a doubt, the last 2 1/2 hours are a fantastic experience for us.

After exiting the boat, we walk across the street and sit down at a table at an outdoor bar that's part to a very high end hotel and restaurant. The waiters and waitresses are wearing sporty blue uniforms with white shirts and blouses. Again, we are *'well underdressed;'* however, we've *'been here before'* and know just how to act. Among the *'rich and famous,'* we enjoy beer, wine, potato chips, olives, and peanuts. Hey Dale, remember the time we secured tickets to get into the UNLV booster club seating area at Sam Boyd Stadium to watch the football game against BYU? I said, *"Dale, just act like we belong here and have been here before. Let's not embarrass ourselves or our families."* It worked to a charm!

Elsa's knee is feeling much better. We choose to walk to the central train station and catch the M14 subway to the Slussen bus depot and take one of four buses back to the hotel. **The journey is flawless** — no wrong turns or no going out the wrong exit. After the walk up the hill, Bjorn suggests that he head over to the mall just down the road from the hotel and pick up something for dinner. Elsa supports this decision 100%. I walk over to *Sabis Firar Grocery Store*. At the extensive salad bar, I create two salads and grab a bag of crackers, an orange, apple, a small pack of blueberries, and a non-alcoholic *Carlsberg* beer. (Beer, wine, and liquor sales are monopolized by the Swedish government similar to Pennsylvania's state controlled adult beverages model.)

The salads *'hit the spot.'* All the ingredients are fresh. We settle in and watch an old *NCIS* episode, in English with Swedish subtitles, and *Erin Brockovich*, an outstanding Julia Roberts movie.

Today's step count of 9,249 is slightly under our 10,000 steps a day goal. It's midnight — lights out. Tuesday is laundry day so I must get up early. So, until Tuesday morning...

*****

Tuesday, May 21 — Day 57
Laundry and Pizza Day

Today, it's my responsibility to take the dirty clothes to, now catch this, *'the one and **ONLY** laundromat in Stockholm!'* When Googling *'laundromats in Stockholm,'* you quickly learn there is only **ONE** because *'most if not all homes have a washer and a dryer.'* Very interesting, I see this lack of competition as a *'business opportunity'* especially for a location close to the hotels near the central train station. When you stay in any of the hotels in Stockholm, your only alternative for clean clothes is using the ultra-expensive hotel laundry service. Guests *'going that route'* may find it cheaper to toss their dirty clothes and buy new ones!

Bjorn begins the day with a quick shower and a light breakfast. I head down the hill to take either a bus or tram to Slussen. There, I will board the T18 Subway and ride four stops so I can be dropped off within one block of the laundry. I miss a bus by 12 seconds and wait patiently for another of the four bus lines that stop here and go to the central bus depot and subway at Slussen.

I am energized and alive today as I am *'gaining the upper hand'* navigating the public bus, trolley, and subway transportation system. I continue to witness the quiet, confident nationalism of Stockholm residents. Citizens are proud of their country.

Arriving at the laundromat, I meet the owner, Erika. She is a diligent worker, a great conversationalist, and uses F-bombs to emphasize her points. She charges 200 Swedish Krona for a wash and dry. She does the work. You pay **CASH ONLY** when the clothes are dry and ready for folding. I have two loads so the service will cost 400 Swedish Krona (about $37 US). Erika says the clothes should be ready in 90 or so minutes and recommends a walk around the area. I need some cash to pay her. She directs me to an ATM a few blocks away next to a '7-11'. (Yes, they have them here!) As I start out on my journey, the neighborhood '*feels*' like I am walking in the Upper West Side of New York City.

I stop at a coffee cafe for a cinnamon bun and a cup of coffee. The bun is '*to die for,*' possibly the best in Stockholm. Bjorn strikes up a conversation with Sebastian, the baker/manager and possible owner. Sebastian is very engaging and explains the Swedish government is transitioning the banking system from cash to cashless. He offers me an '*on the house*' coffee refill, a first on this trip! With a takeaway cinnamon bun for Elsa in hand, I cross the street, withdraw 500 Swedish Krona from the ATM machine, and begin the journey circling the neighborhood like Erika suggested prior to my returning to the laundry.

After the coffee and cinnamon bun, I need a potty stop. Sebastian's cafe did not have one. I spot a cafe nearby and ask to use the restroom. "Customers Only," replies the counter person. So, I buy a cinnamon bun to gain access to the restroom. This establishment's bathroom looks like it was built in the early 1900's, with a pull-cord, flushing handle and separate hot and cold water knobs on the sink, both a first on the trip.

I walk by a number of women's hair salons and manicuring locations. I take photos and text them to my granddaughter Dakota, who will graduate from cosmetology school on May 22. On each text, I add her name to the salon's name, signifying that someday she will have her own location!

Bjorn comes across a unique sign, *'Utfart.'* I'm not sure what their business is; however, our eating choices on the trip create frequent *'Utfart band practice!'*

Mature trees that line both sides of the street keep the sidewalks cool. I hear American music, *'The Rhythm of the Night,'* a 1994 hit song by Corona, blasting from a sidewalk speaker outside *Millers Men's and Women's Clothing Store.* With every step I take, I get that *'Upper West Side New York City vibe'* again as I walk by cafes and small retailers. Across the street, I see a green turf field lined for soccer play. Middle and high school boys and girls are playing soccer and a *'dry land'* version of water polo. There's a nine-hole, relativity difficult, grass putting course in the park where I sit on a bench under a large shade tree. Getting the ball *'up and in for par'* looks challenging.

Bjorn's return to the laundromat is perfectly timed. The clothes have just come out of the dryers. It's time to fold, pack up, and pay Erika 400 Swedish Krona.

Before heading out, Erika explains Sweden's banking system in greater detail than Sebastian earlier today. The country **IS** going **CASHLESS.** There will be very few physical bank locations. None will handle money similar to what I experienced in Italy and France. The Swedish system is designed to know your financial history and business. An electronic *'Big Brother'* surveillance camera system will be mounted at the ATM's watching everyone. She mentions that if someone is making a large deposit, say over 3,000 Swedish Krona (or about $275 US), the bank **WILL** ask you where you got the money! If they don't like your answer, they may not take your deposit!

I bid Erika a *'Danka'* and start the journey back to the hotel. I retrace my route, walking down the steps to Track One to take the M18 Subway four stations to Slussen. Arriving at Slussen, I walk across the street and down one flight of stairs to the Bus Depot and get on Bus 422 that will take me back to the hotel. **NO** missed steps or getting on the wrong subway or bus today! I am really getting the hang of the Stockholm public transportation system.

After a three-hour rest for Elsa and a writing afternoon for Bjorn, the kids head to *Cousins* Italian restaurant. It's a warm 65 degree, cloudless spring day, similar to yesterday. The sun is out in full force. We just miss Tram 30 by 17 seconds and walk over to the bus stop and hop on a bus to get to Slussen. Bus 414 arrives first. We exit at the end of the line with everyone else and walk across the street to the subway. On the walk over, Bjorn sees a young man carrying a golf bag that's *'home'* to 8 to 10 clubs. Maybe he is coming from the putting green I saw earlier today when sitting in the park waiting for the laundry to finish.

Arriving at the subway station, we descend to Platform 2 and take the M13 Subway to Stockholm's Central Train Station. We exit and walk two blocks to *Cousins* Italian restaurant where we've eaten before. Tatiana warmly greets us and seats us at a two person, intimate table. *Bonanza*, a 1970's cowboy TV series about a family who was living in Virginia City, NV in the 1860's, is playing on a wall TV screen with English subtitles. Elsa and Bjorn order a margherita pizza, adding olives, mushrooms, and basil. It has a very thin crust with edges that are soft and chewy.

Tatiana brings us small, individual size salads. She brings me a dish of the *'to die for'* green olives. She remembers. The small dinner salad is currently not on the dinner menu. Bjorn asks Tatiana to remind the owner to **ADD** the side salad to the dinner menu and call it *'The Turzer.'* Just like our last visit here, the pizza was outstanding. I washed it down with a cold draft beer. I give her my business card and tell her I will be watching their *'on line dinner menu'* to make sure they add it and spell our last name correctly, plus of course, *'10% for the big guy'*.

It's time to find the Radisson Hotel by the Sea where we will meet the tour guide for a Viking History, Fika & Countryside 9-hour Tour to *Sigtuna & Uppsala*. Location found; it's now time to return to the hotel. We head to the subway, go two stops to Slussen, and catch one of the multiple buses that take us to the hotel. The Slussen Bus Terminal Depot is the starting and end point for 19 bus routes to and from many communities and other locations throughout Stockholm.

This time, we catch a double long Bus 422. After we get off the bus, we walk up the dirt and gravel path to get home. It's time to *'chill'* and then hit the sack early. We have to leave around 08:00 to meet up with the all-day tour group.

Good night from Room 111 at the *Profil Hotel* in Nacka, Sweden. Despite a slow paced, and relatively unremarkable day, Bjorn gets in 10,830 steps.

*****

Wednesday, May 22 — Day 58
Viking History, Fika & Countryside Tour to Sigtuna & Uppsala

Today, we are going on a 9-hour Viking History, Fika & Countryside Tour to *Sigtuna & Uppsala*. I booked the adventure through *Viator*. At the Radisson Blue Waterfront Hotel at 09:00, we are supposed to meet the tour leader, Gabriel.

The tired couple is slowly up and about doing the normal shower and dress routine. We head to the breakfast buffet for morning nourishment. At 7:53, we set out to catch a Tram to the central train station. We board the M30 Tram and **THINK** we are heading in the right direction. However, Bjorn panics. We get off at the first stop. After double checking the route, the **PANIC** was not necessary. So, six minutes later, we jump on the next M30 and exit at the end of the line. There, we board the T17 Subway and go four stops, exiting at the train station. While on the subway, Elsie starts a conversation with a female pediatrician doctor from Kenya. She's in Stockholm for a three-day conference exchanging ideas and treatments with doctors from all over the globe.

One of the unique things we see in the central train station is three sizes (s/m/l) of pay lockers. People can store suitcases, bags, and other items. You will **NEVER** see this setup in American train stations anymore.

After exiting the subway, we retrace the route scouted yesterday to get us to the Radisson Blue Hotel. The journey is successful; however, we miss a turn that would have gotten us directly to the hotel entrance. Instead, we exit the train station, cross the street, walk one block right, ½ block left, and reach our destination. The tour leader texts me saying because of heavy traffic, he is running 15 minutes late.

The very basic white van (we later learn it's a rental for the day) and tour guide, Gabriel, arrive. There are six people going on the tour: two young ladies traveling from the Canadian province of Quebec and a young brother and sister traveling from Delaware. The young lady is a 2017 graduate of Penn State, my alma-mater.

Today's journey includes three stops at historic sites that date back to 900 to 1100 AD. At each stop, Gabriel describes what happened there and explains how the Vikings and citizens communicated via their version of *'social media.'* They used symbols and letters to describe what was happening. *'Conversation'* was etched on large 2 plus meter flat rune stones rising up from the ground. Much of the history centered on the religious (Christian or pagan) beliefs of the people and the battles where one group would overtake another. Stones were placed to mark property lines. Viking governance took place at the historic *Arkils Tingstad* assembly site. Here, laws were enacted, decisions made, and disputes resolved, similar to arbitration. All decisions were final. Appeals to a higher court **DID NOT** exist. Gabriel's presentation is informative and sheds light on early Scandinavian communication and governance.

Gabriel discusses the pagan burial procedures of burning bodies on a ship and the Christian procedures of burying people in graves. Kings and queens were buried in monuments called mounds. When a king was buried, personal items of wealth and a living wife, mistress, or female slave joined him in the grave. At *Broby*, a Viking graveyard, we learn about *Estrid*, the only identified Viking woman's skeleton in Sweden.

During the drive from one location to another, Bjorn sees his first golf course. Players are pushing hand carts in lieu of riding in a motorized cart or carrying their clubs.

We stop at *Valentina*, a small village for lunch and free time to wander about. Bjorn orders from the expansive salad bar while Elsa goes *'Swedish,'* ordering Swedish meatballs and buttery mashed potatoes smothered in *'fat free to die for'* brown gravy. Bjorn washes lunch down with a Carlsberg draft while Elsa enjoys a glass of Chardonnay. The salad, meatballs, potatoes, and gravy are outstanding and more than filling. I go *'piggy'* and *'inhale'* a slice of homemade blueberry cake for dessert.

The next stop is *Sigtuna*, Sweden's oldest town which was founded in 980 AD. We walk along the cobblestone streets, enjoy lakeside views, and listen to Gabriel discuss its rich heritage, including the site of the original cathedral of Sweden. After a quick tour, we are treated to coffee and a *'select your own'* pastry. Elsie enjoys a brownie while I stay with a different, but just a good, blueberry cake with whipped cream.

At *Old Uppsala*, Gabriel explains the *Royal Mounds of Gamla Uppsala* which have been traditionally linked to legendary Swedish kings. He told us the Royal Mounds of Gamla Uppsala, dating back to the 5th and 6th centuries, have been shrouded in mystery for generations. And according to AtlasObscura.com, some believed the three large mounds to be gods *Thor, Odin,* and *Freyr*, others thought them to be the burial sites of legendary kings, while some people believed them to be, well, simply natural lumps of dirt. The latter speculation angered Swedish King Karl XV, and in 1830 he commissioned a widely publicized excavation to settle the matter once and for all.

Headed by Bror Emil Hildebrand, the first archaeological dig of the Eastern Mound confirmed that it was indeed a burial site, though findings were less than spectacular: A clay pot of burned bones and some burial gifts. They believed it to be a grave for either a young woman or a young man and a woman. The second excavation in 1874 of the Western Mound yielded more impressive findings of warrior equipment, luxury weaponry, as well as a prominent man dressed in a suit of golden threads. This grave was confirmed to date back to the 6th century.

Though archaeologists were unable to identify the bodies of the mounds, they are quite certain the mounds belonged to a royal dynasty. As Sweden's oldest national symbols, the Royal Mounds have retained their significance, especially emphasized by a trip from Pope John Paul II in 1989. The three mounds are known today as the Eastern, Middle, and Western Mounds.

The final stop is *Uppsala*, where history and academia entwine. We tour the *Uppsala Cathedral* which is located between the University Hall of Uppsala University and the Fyris River in the center of Uppsala, Sweden. A church of the Church of Sweden, the national church, in the Lutheran tradition, Uppsala Cathedral is the seat of the Archbishop of Uppsala, the primate of Sweden. It is also the burial site of King Eric IX (c. 1120–1160, reigned 1156–1160), who became the patron saint of the nation, and it was the traditional location for the coronation of new Kings of Sweden (Source: Wikipedia).

It was relocated from Sigtuna to this college campus around 1270. New construction was completed in the early 1500's. In the first room on the left after entering, there are three original tapestries that tell the *'story'* of the numerous church leader discussions about the Cathedral's design. The back and forth decision making processes are depicted on the tapestries that ultimately led to the construction of the structure that is seen today. The church is very large, as most cathedrals are, and is held up by numerous four-five story marble columns.

On the drive back to Stockholm, Gabriel provides some statistics about the Stockholm Archipelago. There are 97,000 islands in the chain; 30,000 are occupied with 20,000 full time residents and about 10,000 additional inhabitants during the summer.

The one-hour drive back to Stockholm takes us through dreaded rush hour traffic. Four of the guests exit the van near the central train station. Gabriel tells us he must return the rental van in *Nacka*, which is very close to the Profil Hotel. We gladly accept his offer to take us to our hotel and avoid fighting rush hour commuters on the subway and bus. We get a chance to learn more about Gabriel. He is originally from Iran but left the country in 1989 at the end of the Iran/Iraq war. He has never returned. Not only does he lead tours here, but he also researches, organizes, plans, and manages group and private trips all over the world including the Far East, the geographical region that encompasses the easternmost portion of the Asian continent, including East, North, and Southeast Asia. This service is something we would like to learn more about and possibly participate in a group travel trip one day. Gabriel and I exchange business cards.

Our bellies are full from the large lunch, adult beverages, pastries, and brownies. A full dinner is **OUT** of the question. Plus, it's time to pack up and get a good night's rest for tomorrow's early departure to *Oslo, Norway*. So, at the hotel restaurant, Bjorn orders French fries, a Carlsberg draft beer, and Chardonnay while Elsie boils water in the electric tea pot for two cups of chicken bouillon soup. Our *'in-room picnic'* also includes an apple and buttery crackers.

Bags packed, teeth brushed, and lights are out. Tomorrow, we continue our historic journey to Norway, adding another country to our travel list and getting closer to the start of the 14-day Viking Mars Cruise through Norway which will end at *Reykjavik Iceland*.

The sun comes up at 03:55 so we make sure to close the window curtains tight. Until the morning, nighty night!

*****

Thursday, May 23 — Day 59
Stockholm, Sweden
to Oslo, Norway

Today, we say, "**GOODBYE** Stockholm" and "**HELLO** Oslo, Norway." It's just a one night stop arriving at 18:02. The weatherman forecasts temperatures around 76 degrees, about 22 degrees above normal! From there, we travel to *Bergen, Norway*, board the Viking Mars Cruise Ship, and spend 14 days sailing up the western Norway coast and eventually docking in Reykjavik, Iceland. For now, back to today's adventures.

The iPhone alarm wakes us from a sound sleep at 07:15. The sun has been up since 03:55. After doing the normal morning things to get ready to face the world, we head down, one last time, to the breakfast buffet. For my final Stockholm breakfast, I go American with eggs, bacon, juice, fresh fruit, a pastry, and coffee. Elsa enjoys her yogurt, fresh fruit, and coffee. Both of us are about 63% awake (or not fully awake?).

We return to the room and finish packing. It *'seems'* strange that mostly clean clothes take up so much room in our suitcases. Two hard Bjorn *'push downs'* on the suitcases allow Elsa to close them shut.

We say goodbye to Annika, the front desk lady, grab a takeaway coffee, and two fresh *'just out of the oven to die for'* cinnamon buns. I see lumps of white sugar next to a bottle of milk and coffee stirrers. (Is Mr. Ed, the talking horse, staying at the hotel?)

Our cab arrives on time at 09:15. Gustavo loads our luggage and drops us off at the train station main entrance. We have 45 minutes to kill. I purchase drinks for the ride. We both make one last potty stop. When I arrive at the coed potty room, the line to pay and enter is ten deep and not moving. I *'almost'* go to the cashier and pay the entrance fee for me and the 10 men and women ahead of me in line. Entrance problem would be solved, but I decide to save my Kronas.

On the way back to Elsie, I unsuccessfully look for the train station ticket office. Not finding it, I ask a shop clerk for assistance. I hear a surprising answer, "There is no train ticket office in the Stockholm Central Train Station!" "Really," I mutter and thank the young lady for making me confused but smarter today. I try to determine which of the four reserved seats purchased for this trip are *'active.'* I remember cancelling two reserved seats and receiving credit; however, was it for seats 14 and 15 or 32 and 33, both in car one? While waiting for the train on Track 10, I need to determine if car one is the **FIRST** or **LAST** car on the train. I spot a display sign listing the seven car numbers; however, I still don't know if car one is the first or the last car. Bjorn sees a local gentleman holding a Calloway golf club bag on his right shoulder and silently thinks to himself, "I bet he knows the correct order of the train cars." **BINGO**, the gentleman explains the train car order shown on the message board and points to the right side of the platform indicating car one will be at that end. Now, the only remaining question is which seats are valid and which ones are not.

It's my lucky day! While heading back to Elsie with the good news about the car one location, I see a lady wearing a green vest with the city's transportation system logo on the left side of her vest. I explain the predicament about which seats are valid and which seats were cancelled. She speaks very good English, pulls out her hand held electronic information device, finds our reservation, and confirms the assigned seats are 32 and 33 in car one. That's another **BINGO** today for Bjorn. I am *'on a roll.'* Should I buy a few Swedish lottery tickets?

The Swedish high speed train appears to operate on the Honor System. During the three-hour ride, no conductor walks the aisle checking tickets. At all departure stops, a conductor announces, in Swedish and English, the stop's name, the departing platform number, the side of the train to exit, and the destination, time, and track number for passengers exiting at this stop but continuing onto other destinations.

Elsie discovers there are free coffee, tea, fruit, and candy at the front of our car. I walk forward and bring back coffee, a banana, an apple, and four pieces of delicious, Swedish chocolate candy.

The train pulls into *Goteborg, Sweden* at 13:35. Of course, it's right on time. The soon to be *'Norwegians'* have 45-minutes to kill. The first priority is potty. Nothing is free. According to the sign on the potty clerk's counter, the entrance fee is 10 Krona. I put 10 Krona on my Citibank MasterCard. Love those American Airlines' frequent flyer miles I earn with **EVERY** purchase!

The departure clock is ticking. We grab takeaway salads, small wooden forks, knives, napkins, and one bottle of Corona beer and hop on the middle car of our train to Oslo. With lunch behind us, Elsa settles into a book while Bjorn cranks out yesterday and today's *'hot off the press'* things happening while traveling. There's always a, **BUT** however, you won't believe *'this happened story'* waiting to be described in entertaining detail. **'Shit really happens'** when traveling with these two (everyone just fill in what you think occurred, no right or wrong answer _____).

Our conductor is an older gentleman who is wearing the official light blue, male train conductor dress shirt with two top pockets (just like my Las Vegas bestie, Dale, who likes these kind of shirts because he can place pens and paper in them). The top two shirt buttons are undone. Black pants and black shoes finish off his official uniform. His grey beard dangles four to five inches below his lower lip. He looks tired and worn out as he *'shuffles'* from car to car. A fragrant odor indicates he could also use a hot shower and a clean shirt to replace the tired looking one he is wearing. He places inexpensive, over the counter sun glasses on his thinning hairline. His ticket scanner, cell phone, and keys (for whatever locks on the train he is responsible for) are attached to his belt. In summary, it's a disheveled look.

He inspects our Eurail QR codes on my iPhone but doesn't scan them to verify we are legit passengers traveling on the correct day at the correct time on the correct train to Oslo, our destination. Why doesn't he check the QR code? He doesn't have a QR code scanner on him!

From Goteborg, it is a 15-stop, 2 hour and 45 minute *'local train'* to the Oslo Main Train Station. At roughly 15:35, the train crosses into Norway at *Kornsjoe*. Our Swedish lassie, Elsa, will become Anna. Bjorn will become Viktor, in honor of PGA professional Viktor Hovland. At 15:35, the train crosses the border. Welcome Anna and Viktor to Norway, the 23rd county to which we have traveled.

The *'New Norwegians'* have reservations at *Clarion Hotel The Hub* in Oslo. We contact the hotel via the Booking.Com App and learn we should see the hotel when exiting the **FRONT DOOR** of the Oslo Central Train Station. Viktor has no clue which of the many doors is the front door. I see an exit door and lead Anna out what turns out to be the **SIDE DOOR** onto a plaza. A few large outdoor restaurants grace the plaza. I can't see the hotel. So, Anna *'stands pat'* by a large fountain to save precious steps for her right knee. The Google Maps App leads me down a walkway past the outdoor restaurants. Now, I clearly see the hotel! I call Anna, direct her down the sidewalk past the outdoor restaurants, and wait for her to reach me.

Once we unite, we cross the street, enter the hotel, and check-in. We take turns using the lobby floor potty. The entrance code is 2021. There is *'no charge'* once you have the secret four digit code. Our room is on the 10th floor. There are five elevators. We press our digital room key against a touch screen to call an elevator. The system displays the elevator letter (A to E) above the doors. Within seconds, an elevator arrives. We get on, press the button for floor 10, and the systems takes us to the 10th floor. This elevator system is ultra-high tech. *'Big brother'* is watching and knows where we are going.

There are 48 rooms on floor 10. Room 1043 is down the hall, turn left into another hall, make another left, and head down the backstretch straightaway. There are **ONLY** five more rooms past our room. Our room location provides a great way to build our daily steps count.

Remember, we are only here overnight. In the morning, we will visit the breakfast buffet at 07:00 and head out by 07:45 to catch the 08:25 train to *Bergen*.

In the elevator, Anna reads there is a rooftop bar and restaurant on floor 13, an unusual floor number usually not seen in hotels. We head up, take seats at one of the creatively decorated tables, and order drinks; a Chardonnay for Anna, and a *'special'* Bourbon Manhattan on the rocks for Viktor. I also order a bowl of olives and a bowl of mixed nuts. This ultra-high end 13th floor bar and restaurant overlooks Oslo. The lounge area is decorated with chairs, couches, accent pillows, and other *'fufu,'* and has the Christy Griffin *'I decorated this'* touch.

For dinner, we decide to try the lobby restaurant. We order Fish and Chips to split; however, the young waitress returns and tells us it's a minimum 20-minute wait until we get our food. The head waiter comes over and apologies for the delay. The kitchen is backed up handling a large group dinner party in one of the conference rooms. We tell the wait staff we don't want to wait and head across the street to a large, outdoor patio and two story indoor seating restaurant, *Egon Byporten*. We trust the food is very good because the restaurant, unlike others in the same area, is crowded. That's a good sign!

The restaurant relies heavily on guests to order their food and pay with a credit card. This method reduces labor costs and makes the operation run smoothly when customers are technically savvy. Patrons start the process by using their smart phone to activate the menu screens. Once logged in, the guest enters their table number and selects the items he/she wants to eat from screens which display pictures of each food item. Should you want to eat at the bar, each food and beverage item also has a corresponding number. I give it *'the old college try'* twice; however, the lack of an internet connection kills our order.

Option two for technically challenged *'old farts'* is to head to the bar, stand in line, give the bartender your table number, food, and drink choice numbers, pay, and return to your table. A server delivers the food when it's ready. I head to the bar and stand in line with what I believe are five other technically challenged people. I order a bacon cheeseburger, fries, and a draft beer, pay, and return to the table with the beer and wait for our food delivery. We split the fantastic burger and fries. You always know a burger is great when it's messy. This cheeseburger is **SUPER** messy. (Staff needs to hose us down before leaving.) On the table is a menu. l successfully order two scoops of ice cream using the menu QR code. When the receipt says it will arrive in 30 minutes, Anna flags down a young delivery waiter, requests someone *'shake a leg, hurry* *it up'*, and deliver the ice cream. Magic, within a minute, the ice cream arrives. **That gal can make stuff happen pronto, quickly!**

We J-walk across the street, over multiple trolley car tracks, and arrive back to the hotel. J-walking seems to be a popular sport in Baltic countries. The big brother elevator operating system assigns Elevator E for the ride up ten floors. Tomorrow starts very early, with a 06:15 iPhone wake up alarm already set to wake us up. So, from floor 10, room 1043 at Clarion Hotel The Hub in Oslo, Norway, good night now!!

*****

Thursday, May 24 — Day 60
Oslo, Norway to Bergen, Norway

The 06:15 iPhone alarm goes off but neither of us thinks the sound is an alarm. So, for about three minutes, the wake up sound Anna selected keeps going off. Finally, a prerecorded '*AI*' voice on the iPhone says, "Hey dudes, **GET UP** and turn off the damn alarm like **NOW!**"

Anna, with one eye open, is first to get up. Then, Viktor staggers to the shower. We hustle to get ready and abandon the room. With bags in tow, we head to the second floor for the breakfast buffet. Now, throughout the journey, every hotel we stayed at except Melina Milano in Milan and Le Bouclier D' OR in Strasbourg includes a buffet breakfast in the nightly room charge. Well, hungry traveling groupies, this hotel's buffet **TOPS** all of the others by at least 20 kilometers. (At first, I thought it might be impossible to describe what we feasted on, however, since we are on a 6 hour, 35 minute train ride from Oslo to Bergen, I thought I'd give it the old university (college) try.)

There are at least a **DOZEN** food stations. The basic refreshments are coffee, tea, and juice. Next, there's a large selection of cold cereals and yogurts, a fresh fruit bar with slices of oranges and grapefruit, blueberries, apples, bananas, tangelos, oranges, and some local fruits with which I am not familiar. That is followed by an extensive salad bar that has everything imaginable to create a custom, healthy meal. There's a station with lox and chilled salmon, various cheeses, and food choices I believe only '*locals*' would enjoy. I have no clue what some of the delicacies there are and I have no interest in tasting them. The best station, which, unfortunately, we did not have time to visit, is the '*create your own omelet bar.*' The tired, traveling Americanos eat a '*little bit of this and a little bit of that,*' most likely **NOT** a nutritious breakfast, but '*things*' that fill their bellies.

Before we head to the train station, Anna decides to stop by the ladies room. The buffet admission person directs her to the bathroom on floor 2. In a few minutes, Viktor gets a phone call from Anna. What could be wrong? Is the toilet out of toilet paper? Did she go out the wrong door and wind up in some small, rural Norwegian town? Did she split her slacks? Did she flush her iPhone or wallet down the toilet? — No fans, it's **NONE** of the above. **HOLD ONTO YOUR HATS.** Anna says she is **LOCKED** in the handicap bathroom and **CAN'T GET OUT!!! ARE YOU SHITTING ME?** (No pun intended.) She asks me to have the breakfast buffet check-in person return and free her from captivity **PRONTO, QUICK, LIKE A BUNNY NOW!!** Well, there are eight couples in line waiting for the buffet check-in person to validate their room numbers before they can enter. These hungry guests apparently are **PRIORITY** number one.

Finally, Victor interrupts him and says, "Sir, my wife and I have a train to catch! She is trapped in the ladies room!" Mr. check-in man lets the last couple enter to enjoy breakfast and makes a 180-degree turn to rescue Anna. At the same instant, my iPhone rings again. It's Anna. **SOMEHOW,** (and she has **NO** clue how she did it) she '*FREES HERSELF*' from the handicap potty.

We gather our bags, head down stairs to check out and head to the train station. **BUT**...let's say that's **NOT** how the story ended! My creative brain came up with this '*story*' which I hope you enjoy. Let's begin.

*Unfortunately for us, the buffet check-in person is **NOT** happy with us. He's afraid of any 'blowback' should Anna report him to the hotel general manager. Frantically, he calls the front desk and tells the three guest services agents about 'his side of the story' moments before we check out. He explains 'just the facts' like Dragnet's Sergeant Joe Friday always said when taking someone's statement. A front desk clerk promised their beleaguered co-worker he will document the incident in a Word file to 'cover his ass' in case human relations and guest services get involved. He plans to CC 'just the facts, no pictures or video' report to everyone, including full, part-time, and on call staff, and anyone else remotely connected with this hotel in the entire hotel chain.*

*When we check out, the front desk clerk lets us know the investigation about Anna being trapped in the handicapped bathroom is underway by hotel security, the local and national police, Interpol, the international office of the FBI based in Brussels, the CIA, and of course, the European Union security and anti-terrorist division. Hotel management places a 'do not allow them to book' red flags in their worldwide reservations system and alerts Expedia, Hotels. Com, Booking.Com, Kayak, and every other on-line or in-person reservations system where people book hotel reservations to not, under **ANY** circumstances, allow them to book a hotel anywhere worldwide. We are understandably embarrassed, shocked, and confused. But there's nothing we can do or say, so I belt out, "Screw it, let's roll Anna!" I trust you got a chuckle or two out of this. If not, I'll try harder next time!*

It's now time for the sprint to the Oslo Central Train Station, located just across the six-lane main street to our left. We use the skills and techniques we perfectly mastered last night to *'cross the street including J-walking, crossing against red traffic lights, and **DO NOT WALK** electronic signs.'* So far, our record is perfect. We carefully avoid getting hit by bikes, scooters, cars, trucks of all sizes, buses, and trolley cars. We arrive at the train station safe and sound without falling, suffering an injury, or heated *'Do you know where you are going?'* comments from Anna!

We grab a coffee, a cappuccino, and a pecan cinnamon bun and head to Track 3. We will soon board Regional Train 63 to *Bergen*, a 14-stop, 6 hour and 35 minute journey. Our reserved first-class seats are in Car 8, seats 25 and 26. When we hear the *'time to board'* conductor whistles, and walk towards car eight, a large herd of travelers on the platform rush by us looking for their car numbers. This train has nine cars. Of course, car eight is almost at the end of the platform and very close to the next Norwegian town. We do our normal best to get to our train car. I climb up three steep steps onto the train, balance on my surgically repaired left leg, and use all my strength to lift the two heavy suitcases, two carry-on bags, the fully loaded heavy backpack, and two takeaway cups of hot coffee, as well as Anna, onto the train. Success!

I secure our bags in the luggage racks. A few drops of my coffee spill. Apparently, I did not secure the *'hard to put on,'* no spilling lid. Anna gives me a quick smack on the back of the head and calls out, "You dummkopf." (Clearly, I did it the old fashioned way, I earned it.) We single file march — left, right, left, right — through Car 8 to seats 25 and 26. Of course, our seats are at the opposite end of the car! When we arrive at our assigned, reserved seats, there's a strapping young man sitting there. In 6.9 seconds, Viktor *'mulls over'* the situation. Did we get on the wrong car? (We did that once on this trip.) Do we have the correct seat numbers? (Yes we do.) I pull out our seat assignment tickets to confirm. Come to find out, the young Norwegian man is looking for a *'freebee'* first-class seat. Not today sir, now move out before I call Stien, the Car 8 conductor. Stien reminds me *'of/looks like'* a *'Billy.'* So, for the rest of today's story, Stien will be known simply as *'Billy.'* We check to see if other reserved seats are occupied. All of them in this car are sold out.

So, I guess the stowaway has to move to the rear of the train and sit with the commoners or chill and *'look cool'* standing at the bar in the food and beverage car.

Flashback — Years ago, when traveling from Lake Como to Paris, our train was overbooked due to an airline strike. On that trip, our names were Juliet and Pierre. I didn't have a seat thanks to an old Frenchie who occupied two seats next to Juliet and refused to give up one. So, I went with Plan B. Eleven years ago, Pierre thought he was a *'cool Euro.'* I chilled at the bar looking ultra-sporty wearing my Euro scarf and beret. Sure beats sitting on a jump seat between two high speed moving train cars.

Back to today's trip. Apparently, there's a major reservations computer seating glitch. Some passengers have the same seat assignments! Is this similar to an American Air Lines preplanned overbooking situation? Are some of these people on the wrong train or in the wrong car? Are there enough seats for all passengers in Car 8? Are all the Car 8 passengers going to have to stand in the aisle, *'move'* their bodies as the music plays over the loud speaker, and *'dive'* for a seat when the music stops, just like playing musical chairs? Billy, the young athletically built, big biceps conductor sees the seat assignment problem and asks everyone to take an open seat while he determines what happened and how to fix it. Is he going to hold a random drawing to kick some people off the moving train if there are too many passengers and too few seats? Will he send some passengers to the other cars to sit with the commoners? Will he create a 15-minute seat rotation system where some sit, some stand, and rotate locations when he blows his ear piercing train whistle? No, the **ANSWER** is *'none of the above.'* He is confident that despite some double seat bookings, *'it will all work out.'* Billy says, "No one will have to stand or change cars. Everyone will have a comfortable seat in Car 8. It is just a mix-up with the seat number(s) on the tickets. But for now, everyone please take any seat," he says. The train is pulling out of the station in 14-seconds....Tick, tick, tick.

When Billy asks us to see our tickets, I show him the printed reserved seat tickets. It was mailed to us in Nevada prior to the trip and the two month Eurail train travel passes on my iPhone. After examining our tickets, Billy has that perplexed, *'who are these Americanos and why are they sitting in reserved seats in Car 8 look'*? Translated, he can't find any record of our tickets on his handheld electronic thicket checking device. *'Houston, this is our **LAST** train ride, do we have a problem?'* Billy asks to see the paperwork from the tickets we ordered. I use my iPhone to locate the order and payment information in my account on the Eurail website. All the documentation is there: my order, confirmation, and payment receipt. Whatever, Billy decides, we are definitely sitting in our two legally purchased reserved seats and will **NOT**, under any circumstance, give them up. Possession is 9/10ths of the law, right? Later, Billy stops by and lets us know *'all is good'* with our seats.

As the train cruises through the countryside, outside the left windows we see evergreen, white birch, and a variety of deciduous trees, bright green grass, and fallen trees in areas *'cleared out'* by flood waters that had previously cascaded down the mountains. On the right side of the train, colorful buildings, homes, and trees reflect off on the glass-like lake. The scenes are *'one of a kind'* spectacular. Unfortunately, Viktor and Anna are sitting on the wrong side (left) of the train. Maybe it's time for Billy, the conductor, to organize rotating passengers left to right and right to left to share the views on both sides of the train.

The train quickly glides down the track, provides glancing, but spectacular, views of lush green, rolling hills and snow-capped mountains. We pass by horses and cows, fields planted with grains, sheep and goats grazing on steep hillsides, farm houses, lakes, granite mountains, and a waterfall or two. The beautiful Alpine-style homes along the lake shore and on the hillsides all have fireplaces. Firewood is neatly cut and stacked near the homes.

Billy doesn't need to rotate seats with everyone in first class: the lake and waterways switched to our side of the train. There are places where the lakes are narrow and create rapids for white water kayaking and rafting for those who may be high-risk adventurous seekers. Better wear waterproof outfits and a strong helmet or *'shit is guaranteed to happen!'* We notice the sky and clouds appear to be very high. Finally, as the train climbs higher, we spot frozen lakes on the opposite side of the train. Rain and fog create cold, winter scenery.

During the early part of the ride, Anna asks for the bottle of water Viktor purchased prior to their boarding the train. Most likely it's bounced around in my backpack side pocket. They think it's *'still'* water. **WRONG** travel reading fans. It's water *'with gas,'* also known as sparkling water. As Anna removes the cap, an *'old faithful like geyser of water'* covers the aisle, her coat, and anything on her tray table. Fortunately, it was just sparkling water and not anything that could leave a stain.

Our journey on the train is long; however, time flies because the scenery keeps getting better and better. Granite mountains are chiseled and shaped with steep, flat vertical sides. I suspect rock climbing them would be a challenging and dangerous sport, even for experienced climbers who attempt to scale these **VERTICAL** mountainsides to reach the top.

One question keeps popping up in my mind. How, and why, do the river waters roll along slowly and calmly, then, all of a sudden, turn into challenging waterways to navigate, followed by out of control roaring rapids for white water rafting and kayaking, and then revert back to being slow and calm?

Car 8 needs some maintenance. The motion sensors that activate opening the doors between Cars 7 and 8 need replacement.

In many instances, the sensors fail to open the doors unless you move around or tap on the doors. Behind our seats, there's a noise like a ringing cell phone that frequently *'goes off.'* The ringing does **NOT** come from a suitcase or bag. We are glad it appears to have nothing negative to do with train operations or the braking system! The digital messaging board in the car shows it is 48 degrees Celsius. Really!!! That's 118 degrees Fahrenheit! That's nearly impossible. It's **NEVER** going to be that warm in Norway!

The train pulls into Bergen on time. The hotel manager of *City Box*, Gracjana, emailed me simple directions to get to the hotel. "Just walk out the front door of the train station and look left. From there, you can clearly see the hotel name "City Box," on a building 3 1/2 blocks down the street."

City Box's check-in procedures are vastly different and unique to anything we experienced during our holiday. The system is 100% electronic, self-check-in. Of course, Viktor struggles with the process. I do not have the payment code the screen is prompting me to enter. Another guest sees the problem and mentions the hotel should have sent me an email today with the required code. *'Son of a gun,'* he's right. With check-in payment code in hand, I complete the check in process and take the two room keys the system creates and spits out of a special slot.

Room 201 is a junior suite on the second floor. This is the first European hotel we have stayed in where second floor room numbers start with a *'2'*. Most European hotels call the lobby street level "Floor 0". Floor 0 rooms normally start with *'1'* and Floor 1 rooms start with a *'2'*.

Thanks for our junior suite, even though it was at the end of a long, four left turn hallway to Room 201 (just like yesterday in Oslo). The room is quite large for a junior suite. There is more room for us to spread stuff out *'all over the place,'* unlike many of the other shoebox size European hotel rooms. It even has dual '*his and her showers*' in the bathroom.

Viktor needs to head out and locate the post office and a restaurant for dinner. Anna stays behind to rest and chill. I stop by the hotel office. Gracjana is on duty today. She prints out a walking map to the post office and tells me the post office is located in the **CO-OP** grocery store about 800 meters out the front door. She instructs me to turn left, walk towards the central train station, then just across the street from the station's main entrance, bear left down a cobblestone walkway. Her directions are '*spot on.*' Small retail stores and restaurants line both sides of the cobblestone walkway. I find a Norwegian bar and restaurant whose menu looks good.

Anna took off to the four-story shopping mall two blocks before the train station. I head in that direction. We rendezvous, walk around the mall, and head to dinner. The local Norway bar and restaurant is set up like a cafeteria. After reviewing the menu, we place our order with the cashier/waitress, pay, and take a seat. We decide to split the homemade fish soup, chili, and chips. A cold, draft beer, and a not-so-good white wine wash down the meal. For the record, it's around 17:30/18:00. This is the earliest dinner we have eaten in months. In the walk back to the hotel, Anna needs ice cream. We stop at *Narvesen,* a 7-11, Circle K type store in the mall. We order medium size vanilla soft ice cream on sugar cones. Anna coats her ice cream with crushed nuts while I say '*no*' to her inquiry of my wanting a similar coating.

Returning early to the hotel, Anna and I decide to take advantage of the hotel's washer and dryer located on our floor. It's my job to save Anna steps and do the wash. First, we access Netflix on the TV and start a movie. Whenever I leave the room for the laundry, Anna pauses the TV. On my first trip to the laundry, I find the washer in use. Someone has 30 minutes remaining on their cycle. So, I park our laundry on the table to alert anyone interested in using the washer that *I'm next.'* Thirty-one minutes later, I return, remove someone's clothes from the washer, place them in the dryer, load our dirty clothes in the washer, and make the wash payment with my credit card. Fifty minutes later, I return to dry the clothes. The other guest has 15 minutes left on the dryer. So, 15 minutes later, I return. The dryer is empty. I load our clothes, pay, and return 30 minutes later to check the status. Some clothes are dry while others need more time. The dry clothes go back to the room. Thirty minutes later, the remaining clothes are dry and ready for folding. Anna is in charge of folding.

The *'no brainer'* Class "B" movie is over. It's time to turn out the lights, get to sleep and be ready for an exciting day tomorrow. We will board the *Viking Mars* cruise ship, unpack for the first time in 60-days, and begin an ultra-exciting 14-day Norwegian cruise from Bergen, finishing in Reykjavik, Iceland!

Good night from Bergen, Norway.

*****

Saturday, May 25 — Day 61
Welcome Aboard The Viking Mars Cruise Ship

Goodbye Bergen City Box Hotel. Thanks for our junior suite even though it was all the way (just like yesterday in Oslo) at the end of a long, four left turn hallway on floor two to Room 201. After a good night's sleep, the traveling dynamic duo shower, get ready to hit the breakfast buffet, and head to the post office to mail the remaining *'just gotta have'* souvenirs and junk. Anna opens the window and is surprised the streets are virtually **EMPTY** of people and vehicles. It's so quiet outside. I remind her it's Saturday.

(Before I delve more into today's theatrics, May 25 is a difficult day for John. Forty years ago on this day, John's first son Chuckie, aka *'the freckled face kid,'* died after falling off an ATV and landing on his right temple. Back in 1984, time was a healer; however, no parent should ever have to endure burying their child. Chuckie was a great kid — full of life, a very good student, and athlete. He volunteered to work with autistic children. Chuckie my man, we love you and miss you tons. Please continue to look down on us, keep us safe, and make sure we make more good decisions than not.)

We take the elevator down to the ground floor and enter *Nedre Nygaard Cafe*, the restaurant adjacent to the hotel. We **ASSUME** (you all know what assume means) that *'breakfast is included in the room rate'* just like all but two of the hotels on the trip.

The Bergen City Box Hotel does not have a restaurant. After chowing down on granola, an Italian Prosciutto or Parma ham, (pick one) and a sliced chicken open faced sandwich, cucumbers, tomatoes, red bell pepper slices, a chunk of Brie cheese, apple and orange slices, seedless red grapes, orange juice and coffee, we start to leave the restaurant. Anna engages in conversation with restaurant personnel and learns we **MUST** pay before leaving or the staff will call the Bergen Politi (police). (This is not a United Nations or NATO free breakfast!) Our *'but, but, but'* fails to register with the hostess. We are **CONVINCED** by the hotel's information found on Booking.Com that states *'breakfast is included'* in our nightly room charge. Our pleas fall on deaf ears and do nothing but make the exasperated hostess reach for her cell phone and start dialing 911 or whatever the Bergen 3 digit distress number is. This is a very huge *'ah shit'* moment. Really, it's the first breakfast *'hick-up'* in 60 days of traveling. Sadly, it just wiped out 147 plus *'atta boys'* we earned for making good decisions since March 26, the first day of our holiday. The *'atta boy'* counter was depleted very quickly, like .00748 Nano seconds, immediately reset to 0. We must now start the count all over again. There are only 17 days left on our adventure.

It's time for me to head to the post office in the CO-OP grocery store. Anna neatly packs the large CO-OP, .40 Swiss Francs grocery bag with *'our just gotta have'* souvenirs. I gather the bag in my arms for safety reasons, (i.e., I do **NOT** want the bag bottom to tear open with our most precious *'gotta have things'* in it and create a mess on the streets of Bergen.) It's a comfortable, warm spring like morning. Just a few cars and motor bikes are about. Some Bergen locals are out and about. Many are wearing tee shirts and shorts. Why? Today's weather will be 20 degrees above normal!

Viktor completes the 800 meter walk to the grocery store. Morton is a CO-OP grocery store employee and post office clerk. He's a very pleasant, customer service man on duty this Saturday morning. He's pulling *'double duty'* as the post office **AND** grocery checkout clerk. (Is this an oxymoron, customer service oriented post office clerk?) I select the correct size box for our non-breakable *'treasures.'* Morton does the rest. He assembles the box, (most likely I would tear it apart trying to put it together), adds packing material to fortify the contents, tapes it shut, checks the paperwork, places it on the scale to calculate the shipping cost, runs my credit card, and hands me the receipt and tracking information.

On the way back to the hotel, I see the *'just right gift'* for my sister Barbara. The shopkeeper checks his inventory and locates the correct size. I purchase a handmade hoodie and a universal lady's cover-up dress suitable for wearing to the swimming pool, beach, or just lounging around the house. I pay the bill and head back to the CO-OP store to mail the items to Barbara in Ocean City, New Jersey. I anoint Morten *'postal employee of the trip.'* His service and personality far exceeds that of the overweight, angry old postal clerk lady in Strasbourg, France who tore me a new asshole for selecting the wrong country mailing box and tearing it up to use for packing material.

The package I sent from France took a lot longer than expected to reach home. Diane, our Illinois based part-time house sitter and former **all pro** spoiler of our late tabby cat Tee, along with husband Tom, reports two of the beer glasses inside the box from France broke. I suspect the *'bad attitude French postal worker'* put the box in the back room for a week or so and tossed it around like the gorilla in the Samsonite luggage commercial and drops it on the ceramic tile floor for extra measure. (To refresh your memory, go back and read the Day 47— May 11, 2024 story for my interactions with the French postal worker.)

Originally, I have Morten tied for first place *pleasant customer service agent* with the young female postal clerk in Interlaken, Switzerland; however, Morton did *'just a little bit more'* than she did (the Swiss postal system is more automated and requires the customer to enter the sender's and recipient's information electronically) because the Norway postal system requires manually prepared shipping documents that you have to press your pen hard, the third copy is your receipt. Morton went *'just a bit further'* by assembling and packing the two shipping boxes for me.

Before heading back to the hotel, I use my remaining Norway Krone currency and purchase two, three Krone scratch off lottery tickets. Unfortunately, my tickets only show two matching numbers. You need three to win something. Two out of three is close but *'no cigar'*. At least I gave it a shot.

I head back to City Box Hotel, gather up the suitcases and Anna, and head to the lobby. The front desk clerk calls a cab and checks us out. Two minutes later, a white, four-door Tesla taxi cab rolls up. Inge, a portly man most likely in his 60's, has a seven inch grey beard. He loads our *'stuff'* into the expansive trunk. Anna is very impressed with the all-white leather seats. It's a quick 10-minute ride to the dock where the *Viking Mars* cruise ship awaits us. Boarding opens at noon; however, other passengers have checked in. Unlike our two-hour outside wait to board a Holland America cruise liner in San Diego last November, we **BREEZE** through the check-in process on the Viking Mars and the security briefing in record time. We then take the elevator to Deck Seven where lunch is *'waiting for us'* in the open seating buffet restaurant. From cab drop off to lunch, we are talking less than 30-minutes, a boarding record!

The lunch buffet is better than outstanding. It makes the Holland America lunch buffets look like a second rate Las Vegas casino spread. Let me share some of the items on the buffet. It includes rolls, bread for a sandwich, and add a variety of cheeses and lunch meats. There's a *'make your own'* salad bar, hot Asian fare choices, baked wild salmon, vegetables, potatoes, wings, pasta, and other items that just wouldn't fit on my 24" dinner plate. The dessert bar offers a variety of *'sugar and fat free'* (**NOT**) cakes, pastries, cookies, and ice creams. A 12" dessert plate allows for sampling one of each. The professionally dressed wait staff offers coffee, tea, cold drinks, champagne, beer, wine, and every adult beverage imaginable. We have the *'all you can drink beverage package'* giving us a *'free run'* to try one of each! The staff is very attentive and polite, offering water and clearing dishes without being *'in the way.'*

Sue and Tony, from Perth Australia, join us at an eight-person window-side table. They have been traveling by air for three days to reach Bergen, are in their 80's, and have traveled extensively both throughout Australia and the world. They are great storytellers. We banter back and forth discussing mostly non-political topics. Sue was an operating room nurse whom the hospital would sometimes *'ring up'* in the middle of the night when emergencies happened, forcing Tony to prepare the children's breakfast and school lunch sandwiches. We exchange business cards and hope to spend time with them at one of the many *'watering holes'* on the ship. Tony wants to talk American politics. Viktor will have to leave Anna in the room for that *'conversation.'*

The restaurant management staff wears matching company suits, shirts, ties, shoes, and name tags, and they welcome passengers with a friendly smile that makes you *'feel special.'* Our first impression of *Viking Cruise Lines,* and the three-year old cruise ship Viking Mars, is extremely favorable. We anticipate the next two weeks will provide experiences and opportunities where we might consider switching our cruising allegiances from Holland America to Viking.

The ever impressed dynamic duo stroll the Deck 7 outside perimeter. The views of Bergen are spectacular on this near cloudless, warm sunny day. I find a comfortable chair and couch in the *Explorer's Lounge* on Deck 7 to relax and write while Anna heads to the room. Suddenly my phone rings. We have **ONLY** been on the ship for less than two hours! Anna cannot find her all-important ship card key that not only opens the stateroom door, but also contains the entire cruise itinerary, shore excursions, upgraded dinners, unlimited drink package, on and off the ship access, and anything else needed to get around the ship. I check my wallet, my man shoulder purse, and all eight sections in my navy blue backpack....**NOTHING, ZIP, ZERO, NADA NO** *'most important card'*! Anna goes to the customer service desk on Deck 1 to hopefully get a new card. I hope there is no charge for a replacement card or else I will recommend the ship's staff cut her loose and remove her and her belongings from the ship!! (LOL). Anna is **NOW** actively participating in the *'Shit Happens'* game. She is contributing *'events and stories for the book'* by doing *'just Anna things.'* Good news reading fans...Anna gets a new card, customer service disables her old card so no one else can use her benefits, and there is **NO CHARGE**! They informed her she is now #1 in the ship's record book for the quickest time any guest has lost their guest card in the ship's three year history with a time of one hour and 47 minutes! You go Anna.....you are now #1!!

I spend my afternoon relaxing in the *Explorers Lounge* on Deck 7 writing about today's events. Numerous roving bar waiters ask if I need a drink. I thank all of them; but I am still full from lunch. While sitting and writing, Shauvik Chaufhuri, the ship's General Manager, welcomes me aboard. Small talk leads to a *'Cliff Notes'* summary of our current 60-day holiday. I mention I am authoring a book about our daily happenings. Shauvik would like to chat with me during the cruise and invites me to stop by his office on Deck 1. I make a note to stop by. Who knows what such a meeting could lead to!!!

Around 17:00, Anna joins me at the Deck 7 Explorer's Lounge. She enjoys red wine while I have a double Jack Daniels Bourbon Manhattan on the rocks.

We're a little tired and decide to **NOT** dine at 20:00. Instead, we head to the buffet at 18:00. The buffet dinner is just as good, if not better, than lunch. For openers, there's shrimp, oysters, scallops, cold slices of salmon, small pieces of crab, ceviche, octopus, and various sushi items, including ahi and salmon. A *'select your own green salad and fixings'* includes anchovies for a Caesar salad, providing something *'green'* for the pallet and meal. Main dishes feature Korean salmon, pork chops, pork loin, and seafood along with a variety of potatoes, rice dishes, and breads. I am sure I missed a few dishes. Maybe I'll bring a camera or note pad tomorrow to be more specific.

And let's not forget the all-important dessert bar with a choice of ice creams, cakes, cookies, puddings, and pastries. Put it this way, if you can't find something to eat on this expansive buffet, you are either *'very picky'* or just *'not hungry.'* I am proud to report that I sample a variety of items on the buffet and savor a Riesling white wine. I complete the mini feast with two small pastries (*fat free, sugar free offerings*). Anna, on the other hand, chooses pork roast, a baked potato, salad, and two glasses of red wine, and finishes it off with ice cream and decaf coffee.

After dinner, we stroll Decks 7, 8, and 9. The sun sets around 22:30. So, there's plenty of daylight well into the evening. Anna heads to the room to sit outside on the balcony and read while I remain at the front of the boat on Deck 9 chilling and reading articles on the ESPN App. My iPhone is down to 8% battery life. I go back to the room, sit with Anna to get familiar with our shore excursions (Viking offers guests a no-charge shore excursion at each port stop in addition to more extensive, costlier pay jaunts). We also discuss the dates and times of our two specialty dinner reservations, the spa and workout room, and other activities onboard the ship which are available during our 14-day cruise.

Before retiring we decide that breakfast on the balcony sounds great for Sunday morning. We make our selections and hang the order outside on the stateroom door knob. *'Living large is the only way to go.'*

We have a 10:30, two-hour tour of Bergen for Sunday. Just as Dandy Don Meredith would sing at the end of Monday Night Football in the 1980s, alongside his unforgettable and unabashedly outspoken sidekick, Howard Cosell, the message was clear: 'Turn out the lights, the party's over!' So, good night from room 6041 on the Viking Mars cruise ship docked in Bergen, Norway.

*****

Sunday, May 26 — Day 62
Bergen, Norway

May 26, today's date, and the trip's Day 62 are reversible. Don't remember this happening on any of our journeys before. And just how many loyal readers notice this? Maybe, just maybe that's a good omen for things to come today. I should buy a few Norwegian scratch-off lottery tickets.

Anna wakes up at 07:30, 30-minutes before the wake-up *"Revelry"* bugle alarm blasts from my iPhone. We have a two-hour bus tour of Bergen this morning, departing at 10:30 sharp. So, breakfast in the room makes perfect sense. Are we *'living large'* on holiday and taking full advantage of this special, *'being spoiled luxury'*? Are we bragging about *'the way'* to enjoy breakfast, or are we being prudent to maximize our morning routine? Pick one, only one please, and leave your comments in the space below.

Breakfast will arrive between 08:30 and 08:45. This gives both of us ample time to shower and get dressed. It's another beautiful sunny, 20 degrees above normal spring day in Bergen. Light clothes are the order of the day.

At the allotted time, the doorbell rings. A short female staff member delivers our breakfast (yes Kristy, the mother of grandchildren Brady, Tanner, Dakota, and Hunter, there is someone out there that's closer to the ground than you!) She's a stocky, strong young lady. She had to be to lift the overloaded tray of breakfast goodies we ordered before turning in last night. While I hold the door open, there's **JUST** *'enough room'* and I mean **JUST** for her to wiggle her way in the very narrow room entranceway and set the tray on the coffee table. She quickly returns with the coffee. I make an executive decision, voting 1-0, a unanimous majority in Room 6041, and carefully move the breakfast items outside to the veranda table. So, what's on the Day One menu? Anna has a ham and cheese omelet, a 1/2 order of bacon, a blueberry muffin, grapefruit juice, and coffee. Viktor enjoys scrambled eggs with corned beef hash, the other half of the bacon side order, a blueberry muffin, coffee, and orange juice. We split the cantaloupe, watermelon, honeydew melon, and banana fruit tray. We are ready for today's tour.

We head to Deck 1 to disembark the ship and board a tour bus. We are in Group 25. Barbara, a young, tall, slender world traveler from Kosice, Slovakia is today's Group 25 tour leader. (Considering my lineage is part European, is there a chance we are fifth cousins on father's side of the family?) This is Barbara's second season leading tours. She claims to be an adventurist just like the snowbirds who flock to the greater Phoenix area during the winter from colder parts of the U.S. Barbara *'disappears'* during the mostly dark (4-5 hours a day of sunlight) and very cold winters to warmer European and Southeast Asia climates.

Today's participants connect listening devices to a left ear piece to listen to Barbara's presentation. Here's what we learn about Bergen:

- Bergen is the second largest city in Norway.
- There are 300,000 residents living here and 600,000 in *Oslo*.
- It normally rains 240 days a year. Recently, the weather has been 20 degrees above normal with no rain.
- Oil and gas are the number one export, fishing is number two.

- An 11th century Church is the second oldest building in Bergen.

- A wooden fire station was built in 1903.

- Many homes were built during the 19th century.

- Rhododendrons thrive in the humid weather.

- Bergen has seven mountains around the city. However, there are nine mountains. Once a month, residents walk all seven mountains. It's a *'Bergen'* thing to do.

- Cross country skiing is a popular winter sport.

- Norway is the second largest market for Tesla electric cars. Charging stations are strategically located throughout the city.

- During World War II, on April 14, 1944, a German freight ship, the *Voorbode*, which was used for military transport, travelled from Oslo to *Kirkenes*; however, it docked in Bergen for repairs because it had mechanical problems. Normally, a ship like this would not be allowed to stop in a major port. Why, you ask? It was carrying 136.5 tons of explosives! A lack of proper control allowed the ship to dock in Bergen. On the morning of April 20, the ship exploded in the harbor killing 160 men, women, and children and wounding nearly 5,000, mostly civilians. The explosion created a 700-meter high water column resulting in a tsunami that swept through the harbor. The air pressure from the explosion and the tsunami that followed flattened whole neighborhoods near the harbor; then fires broke out and further destroyed the wooden houses. The force of the water tossed sand, mud, stones, iron plates, timber, and steel from the ship crushing everything in its path. Houses fell apart, brick buildings suffered damage, and windows two kilometers away were smashed.

Voorbode's anchor was later found on the 417-metre-high (1,368 ft) mountain *Sandviksfjellet,* almost two miles from the blast area. Norway declared Bergen a disaster area. The town's children were forced to evacuate to prevent illnesses from spreading. Important cultural buildings were severely damaged but were later restored.

From Wikipedia: "The Germans initially tried to conceal the extent of the catastrophe, probably because it exposed their failure to maintain security regulations. Because the explosion occurred on Adolf Hitler's birthday, there was some suspicion of sabotage, but investigations revealed that the explosion was an accident caused by self-ignition. Rescue efforts after the event were extensive and have been well documented."

- Witchcraft was practiced from the 15th to the 17th centuries. Women who *'thought differently'* were considered witches and were burned at the stake.

- Bergen is Norway's biggest and busiest port. Every year, 350 cruise ships dock here. The harbor can hold up to four cruise ships a day.

- From April to October, the city buzzes with tourists.

- Many houses in the older section of town are just a short step or two from the roadway. Don't run out of the house fast and without looking...you could quickly become a hood ornament. Homes are built very close together (like zero lot line properties in Woodbridge, Irvine, CA) and have small, if any yards.

- On Sundays, all non-tourist related stores close.

- Norway was under Denmark rule for 400 years. In 1905, Norway gained independence.

- In 1850, Ole Bull, a famous violinist, founded the Bergen Theater.

- Bergen has the second oldest philharmonic orchestra behind Vienna.

- Edward Griegs was a famous Norwegian composer and pianist. His mother was his first teacher. Ole Bull recognized his potential and convinced Edward's mother to send him to Germany and Denmark to further his musical education. He is widely considered one of the leading Romantic era composers. was an artistic and intellectual movement that originated in Europe towards the end of the 18th century. The purpose of the movement was to advocate for the importance of subjectivity, imagination, and appreciation of nature in society and culture in response to the Age of Enlightenment and the Industrial Revolution. Griegs' music is part of the worldwide standard classical repertoire. His use of Norwegian folk music in his own compositions made Norway's music famous.

- Bryggen is located along the waterway in the old Bergen historic district. It is a series of Hanseatic heritage commercial buildings lining up the eastern side of the Vågen harbor. Bryggen has been on the UNESCO list for World Cultural Heritage sites since 1979. In the 14th century, the Hanseatic League[a] was a medieval commercial and defensive network of merchant guilds and market towns in Central and Northern Europe. Norwegians traded dried stock fish for raw materials, grains, and other food stocks. The Norwegian climate makes it difficult to grow vegetables and grain. Two thousand strong German men lived in this area. A red light district prospered here. Local Norwegian military placed their cannons facing Bryggen to send a message to the Germans to *'don't cause trouble'*.

- In this designated UNESCO historical district, some of the buildings along the waterway are leaning slightly due to the unstable, moist ground they were built on. Throughout history, Bergen has experienced many fires since most of its houses were traditionally made from wood. This was also the case for Bryggen, and as of today around a quarter were built after 1702, when the older wharf side warehouses and administrative buildings burned down.

Well fans, that's what the old Americanos learn today and felt *'compelled'* to share with our *'hundreds'* of valued followers. If you zoned out, fell asleep, or went back to watching mindless, brain destroying TV or videos, you missed some excellent Bergen history and most likely will fail the post Bergen portion of the trip test. You still have time to backtrack and read it.

At the completion of the two hour tour, Anna and I decide to remain in Bergen, do some shopping, and take a leisurely one mile stroll back to the ship. We have to be back on board by 15:00. The ship leaves port at 16:00 whether you are onboard or not. We have learned that Viking Mars **ALWAYS** stays on schedule.

I pick up some baseball caps for the grandsons and buy Anna a white Norwegian sock hat. Most likely, she will need this as we approach colder climates and finish the cruise in two weeks in Reykjavik where's it's **NOT** sunny and 75! We finish our shopping and head to the ship. The pathway to Viking Mars is dotted with uneven brick size stones.

Arriving at the ship, we head to Deck 7 for lunch at *The World Cafe*. Viktor samples a 1/2 sandwich, fries, salad, dessert, and washes it down with a Coke Zero while Anna enjoys a bowl of soup and some salad but, shockingly, **NO** dessert.

After lunch, we go forward on Deck 7 and *'chill'* in the expansive Explorers Lounge. Anna finds a comfortable chair while I choose to *'stretch out'* on a leather couch. For the next few hours, we *'hang out.'* Anna reads and I write. I also spend some time chatting with a couple from New South Wales, Australia. They took a number of long flights to get to Bergen and will be on this ship for 28 days. When we depart the ship in Iceland, it will continue onto Greenland, Nova Scotia, Northeast Canada, and south along the United States' Eastern seaboard. The cruise ends in New York City. I momentarily thought about extending our cruise by two weeks; however, we really want to spend three days in Reykjavik before heading back to Henderson on Tuesday, June 11. At 16:00, the ship departs the harbor. We are on our way to explore Norway and Iceland!!

We reunite at 17:00. I meander over to Anna's sitting area. We enjoy a few adult drinks (remember, we have the unlimited adult beverage package), and chat with a Reno, Nevada couple about world travels. It's a small world out there. They tell us about a great wine area in Mendoza, Argentina.

It's now 18:15. We head to the rear of Deck 7 for dinner at The World Cafe. I try a very small serving of a variety of Norwegian prepared dinner items including venison rolled in a puff pastry, tenderloin steak, lamb, one Norwegian meatball, one mussel, three shrimp, one Norwegian dumpling, one small potato, and a medley of fresh broccoli, carrots, and cauliflower, I cap my dinner with my favorite non-alcoholic beverage...Coke Zero. I commit a mortal sin by having small, but very tasty slices of two Norwegian cakes and decaf coffee. Anna goes more conservative choosing lamb, shrimp, veggies medley, snow crab, and water, and finishes her meal with — you guessed it — ice cream and decaf coffee. It's time to return to Room 6041, fill out our room service breakfast order, hang it on the outside door knob, and check the time for Monday's shore excursion. We need to get off the boat and head to the designated tour bus by 08:50 for a 09:00 departure. Our first day aboard the Viking Mars ocean liner and the Bergen city two hour tour amounts to a great start for the next 13 days and nights. Good night from Room 6041 on the Viking Mars Cruise Ship.

*****

Monday, May 27 — Day 63
Geiranger, Norway and Geirangerfjord

It's Monday morning at 07:15. We wake up and open the balcony curtains to witness our ship slowly moving through a Fjord! We have never, ever seen, up close and personal, this spectacular view of nature. Hearty, green trees grow out of the sheer granite hillsides. An occasional 1,000 foot or so waterfall majestically cascades down through indentations in the mountains created by millions of years of falling water.

This morning's *'on the veranda'* breakfast is a light fair. We share everything - scrambled eggs, coffee, fruit, orange juice, and a croissant. The anxious cruisers can't wait to start the 09:00 tour.

At 08:30, we meet our fellow explorers on Deck 1. The Viking Mars anchors off the coast of Geiranger, so we board a boat tender that takes us to shore. Once there, we will climb aboard a tour bus that will take us on today's excursion.

At 09:00 today, we assemble with fellow explorers and take a three-hour tour of the area. Don't worry; the excursion is **NOT** a three-hour *'Gilligan's Island'* adventure. The Howells, Mary Anne, the skipper, the movie star, the professor, and of course Gilligan himself, didn't book this cruise...maybe next time.

Time out!!! Anna cannot find her ship ID card!. This is the **SECOND** one she has **MISPLACED** in three days of being on board! I hope someone on the ship is **NOT** running up a huge tab on our nickel. She rushes off to Guest Services on Level 1 to request a new card. Anna is told *'in no uncertain terms'* that if she loses one more card, she will be in **BIG TROUBLE** with customer service. A third lost card triggers being unceremoniously tossed overboard with her belongings into a small rowboat without oars. She better *'up her game'* on ID card security or *'face the music.'*

After a few minutes, I follow her and learn from Guest Services personnel that Anna **WAS** there but, after receiving her new card, she **TOOK OFF**. The agent points **RIGHT** indicating *'she went that way.'* I spot a herd of travelers heading down the steps to Deck 1. That's where travelers get onto the tenders to reach the dock and their excursion group. I assume she was in the crowd. (But we all really know what *'assume'* means, right?)

There's one seat left on a tender that's leaving. Viktor, being a solo traveler at this time, boards. But he can't locate Anna. He calls her; she answers. However, the cell phone service is *'worse than poor.'* We can't hear or understand each other. I hang up and send seven texts updating Anna on what's transpired. Anna does not reply. Has she decided **NOT** to go on the excursion? Has she booked all day spa services? Has she decided to hit the gym for a workout? Has she grabbed a book and headed to the Deck 7 Explorers Lounge to read and drink cappuccinos? Or, has the staff removed her from the ship by tossing her and her belongings overboard for just losing her third ship ID card?

Finally, after numerous *'where are you texts,'* she replies and tells me she's on the next tender to shore. She texts me about her morning *'adventure'* after leaving the room with me. After going to Guest Services and procuring a new ID card, she tries to call me while she follows the crowd to the theater looking for me. She goes down to Deck A where the tenders depart from and instead of following the herd of people heading to the tenders to go ashore, she makes a **WRONG TURN** and **winds up in the ship's Medical Center on the other side of the ship! She's lost.** A ship employee directs her up the Deck 1, then over to the other side of ship, and then down the steps to the departure area on Deck A. This is just another *'go up, go down'* Anna journey.

The dynamic traveling duo reconnects on shore. We walk to Tour Bus 18, the last bus at the end of the line! It's just like our hotel rooms in Bergen and Oslo.....all the way at the end of the hall.

Stollen is our bus driver today. He's in his 60's, has thinning white hair, and is very friendly and professional. He has a great personality, is always smiling, and is a great storyteller. He tells us about his **BIG** family. He has six children and 25 grandchildren. During the short days of daylight in winter, even though he stays busy fishing, he also does *'lots of snuggling'* with his wife, hence the large family. Today's guide, Alex, hails from Spain. He leads seasonal spring and summer tours in this area. Off we go on a three-hour bus ride that will consist of 11 hairpin, 180 degree turns on a well paved 1 1/2 lane wide, two-way road. Well-constructed guard rails that *'MIGHT stop a bike'* are placed along the side of the road to prevent cyclists from falling thousands of meters to *'meet their maker.'* If you have been to Maui, it's similar to the 300 plus turns and switchbacks on the *Road to Hana*. When taking the Road to Hana, one drives over numerous one-lane bridges on a roadway that, in some places, *'needs attention.'* Also, whenever drivers approach a blind left or right turn around a mountain, they are supposed to honk the car horn to alert oncoming vehicles to **STOP** as you are barreling around the turn. Here in *Geiranger*, drivers **DO NOT** honk their horns on blind turns — they just *'go for it, play chicken'* and attempt to beat oncoming traffic to the impasse and **FORCE** them to back up. Stollen's aggressive driving works well without incident. So far, he has clearly won **EVERY** battle. He forces cars and busses to back up and let us pass as he fearlessly and nonchalantly motors around the blind turns.

Today's tour will include three picture taking stops. Two will include souvenir buying opportunities and potty.

Below is a little information about Geiranger, Norway courtesy of Viking Cruise Lines:

- Nestled amount the towering peaks of *Geirangerfjord*, the small village of Geiranger is the gateway to some of coastal Norway's most magnificent natural treasures.

- Nearby, the *Seven Sisters Waterfall* tumbles 1,000 feet into the fjord's water, while directly across the fjord, the *Suitor* waterfall also plunges down a steep face.

- The overlook known as *Eagle's Bend* towers 2,000 feet above the village, accessed via a winding mountain road with 11 hairpin turns.

- The *Norwegian Fjord Center* puts this entire natural splendor into perspective with fascinating exhibits.

- Closer to shore, the village's octagonal church is a delightful gem, resting on tranquil pristine shores with wonderful views of the fjord.

Here's what the 75-year old adventurous duo learns about the area on today's tour:

- The mountainous soil is poor, making it very difficult to grow vegetables.

- We pass along, and over, roaring rapids and tumbling water-falls that bring fresh water to the local residents.

- When stopping for photo opportunities along the rocky terrain, **NEVER, EVER** listen to the person taking your picture if he/she says to *'take a step or two back.'* The result of listening to this request will definitely **NOT** turn out good for you and will **NOT** create a better souvenir photo.

- The cold, windy darkness in winter has a negative effect on year round residents. The lack of sunlight makes their bodies deficient in Vitamin D. Residents fish, hunt, ski, and take Vitamin D during dark winter.

- Beer is sold in stores until 20:00. Whiskey and wine sales are controlled by the Norwegian government, similar to the Pennsylvania Liquor Control Board system. Norway imposes these laws to prevent children from being exposed to alcohol consumption. Norwegian laws prohibit outdoor drinking, even on balconies or at picnics.

- Visitors and locals can pitch a tent and camp **ANYWHERE** in Norway, for free.

- Stollen, our bus driver, owns a remote *'man cave'* cabin. To reach it, he must walk 90-minutes thru the woods and rocky terrain. There's no electricity at the cabin. He uses the remote cabin retreat to rest up, *'clear the cobwebs between his ears,'* hunt, and fish.

- Both Norwegian men and women hunt. Equality of the sexes is ever present in all workplace opportunities.

- We look at impressive, sometimes indescribable, views. I take videos. (Hopefully, when we get back, I can find someone to merge the many short videos into one video that will provide great entertainment for our five ardent vacation followers).

- Fjords don't freeze because of the salt water. Rain water creates a frozen lake or two. Locals won't drive on the roadways until the ice melts.

Our second stop is a souvenir store and rest area in Djupvasshytta, Geiranger. I select a collection of '*just gotta have stuff*' and head to the check-out counter. When I pull out my credit card to pay, the clerk informs me their credit card processing machine is **DOWN**. Cash is the only form of payment today. Having adapted to the European cashless society model, I do not have any cash on me to cover the $65 charge. I unsuccessfully try to borrow cash from fellow travelers. Next, I offer the checkout lady a compromise — extend me credit for this purchase and email me information on how I can direct deposit or wire transfer the money into the business bank account. She makes my day by accepting my latter proposal! **THAT'S CUSTOMER SERVICE!** I hand her my business card that has my email address on it. About a week later, she emails me. Immediately, I wire her the money.

Every friend at home asks us the same question, "What did you like best on the trip?" My standard answer is "The last place we visited." Today's three hour tour thru the fjords confirms my answer.

This morning, the tour started on a cool, windy, overcast day. During the trip, the sun tries to peak its head out of the clouds. At stop three during the last 40 minutes of the tour, the wind dies down. There's a few high, white clouds sprinkled on the blue sky background. We take many photos and videos of the surrounding area. And I take a selfie or two as I stand very close to a waterfall as it cascades onto the roadway. By 11:30, the sun is out in full force and is shining on the surrounding mountains, boats, and shops.

The bus returns to the Geiranger Village Center and boat dock. We have no cash. I hustle around the village looking for an ATM machine. Shopkeepers point straight down the pathway on the left. Unfortunately, the ATM is '*no worka, out of commission.*' I learn there is another ATM further down the path towards the grocery store. Success, I withdraw 400 Norwegian Krone (about $36 US) and hustle back to the bus to tip and thank Stolen and Alex for their excellent presentations.

Viktor has *'misplaced'* Anna. Or has she gone off in whatever direction, doing whatever it is she is doing, or looking for. Clearly, she is an independent spirit (or completely lost). She is nowhere to be found and does not answer my numerous calls and texts. Finally, I text my location and alert her I am going *'buying.'* Come find me!

I go on a souvenir buying spree. I **NEVER** *'shop,'* I just buy. Today I am *'on a roll'* buying *'stuff'* for friends. Most likely, after I give them a local souvenir, they will toss it in the trash. No need to list the stuff I buy, including refrigerator magnets, decals, ball caps, an ear cover-half hat, and extra thick Northern Lights - half way up the calf socks.

I am *'geared up'* to replace my stolen Las Vegas pullover golf, rain jacket, **BUT** — Here comes the, **BUT** — this Mafia controlled shop wants the equivalent of $300 for a not so fancy, basic, quarter zip, blue pullover raincoat! **Are you shitting me????** It only rains about four inches a year in Vegas! The price is outrageous and way over my budget. So, I tell the cashier to *'keep it.'* I desperately want to tell the young lad where to *'put it'* **BUT** — (here we go again with a **BUT**) — it's not the time or place, and it's not the kid's fault. He just works there. Knuckles, Leftie, Little Al, Mean Joe, and Fat Gonzo set the prices and make sure **EVERYONE** pays full price, no discounts!

I move on down the road to another souvenir establishment. Anna finally catches up and tosses a few *'real special gifts'* onto my *'pile of stuff.'* Today's cashier is Matilda. She's a young lady from Sweden. Her name brings to mind *'Waltzing Matilda'*, a song developed in the Australian style of poetry and folk music called a *'bush ballad'*. It has been described as the country's *'unofficial national anthem.'*

While Anna gets lost again, I sit outside *Fiskekaka*, a take away sandwich joint. The lady sitting to my left is chowing down on their fish sandwich special. I *'think'* about it; but don't *'ask her for a bite.'* When Anna surfaces from shopping, she orders the fish sandwich. We split the grilled, fresh fish sandwich that includes shredded lettuce, a special sauce, and onions inside a warm, soft pita bread. *'It's the bomb.'* I wash it down with a local Norwegian *Friaran Pilsner* bottled beer. The sandwich turns out to be, without a doubt, the **"BEST EVER"** fish sandwich I have eaten and exceeds my former **"BEST EVER"** fish sandwich served at the *Paia Fish House* on Maui.

Refreshed and finished contributing to the local economy, we walk over to the dock to catch a tender back to the Viking Mars cruise ship. The boat's name, Mars, reminds me of Spike Lee's, *Michael Jordan Nike Air Jordan* shoe commercials created in 1991 during Jordan's time with the Chicago Bulls. The sneakers became a global craze thanks, in part, to ads featuring Jordan and filmmaker Spike Lee, who played *Mars Blackmon*, a character created for his directorial debut, ***She's Gotta Have It***. Mars was featured in the commercials and uttered the famous tagline, ***"It's gotta be the shoes!"***

Back on board, Anna plans to read, hang out, and watch the ship's departure from the Explorers Lounge on Deck 7. I place my bathing suit and workout gear in my backpack and head to the gym, jacuzzi, steam room, and ice room to work out and reinvigorate my body. Even though I've averaged over 8,000 steps a day, my body craves a 50-minute, 9-mile recumbent bike cardio ride, stretching, and light weights workout. I follow that up with 20 to 25 minutes of steam, 5 minutes in the ice room, and 20 minutes in the jacuzzi. While in the steam room, Victor chats with Dale, a retired lawyer and Jeraldine, a retired doctor and phycologist from New South Wales Australia. He's originally from Michigan and she is from

Scotland. After marrying, they relocated to Australia. They travel extensively and maintain residents in Australia, Michigan, and Scotland. She's a work-out aficionado having tried all the hot and cold facilities from steam and jacuzzi to ice room, ice water plunges, and ice water buckets dumped on her head (ice bucket challenge). It's time to hit the showers. The ship provides a terry robe, towels, lockers secured with your ship ID, and showers with shampoo, conditioner, and shower gel. I may have found a second home on the ship. The facilities are outstanding and provide numerous options that I thoroughly enjoy. Anna, you know where to find me.

After almost three hours of fun and three bottles of water, I return to the room and place my wet workout clothes and bathing suit on the veranda to dry.

Viktor finds Anna at the bar at the Explorers Lounge on Deck 7 fully engaged in *'chit chat'* with Adrienne, her best new bar friend. They are both drinking white wine. I order two Pilsner beers. Information on the canned beers compares this Norwegian beer to Czech Republic Pilsner beers. I engage in small talk with the ladies and Bill, Adrienne's husband. Anna started drinking with Adrienne around 16:30 at the Deck 7 lounge when the ship left port and maneuvered through the fjords and I was in the gym. Anna tells me the views were impressive, highlighted by spectacular waterfalls.

Adrienne's name brings back South Philadelphia memories for me. I recall several classic scenes from the movie **"Rocky One"** where Rocky chases chickens to quicken his foot movement. To build up his endurance, he ran through the Italian Market and ran up the Philadelphia Art Museum steps, finishing with his arms raised in triumph. He was also seen walking home one night screaming for **"Adrian."** Anyway, that sets the scene for *'Drinking 403'* today. Thank goodness we have the unlimited drinks package. If not, our bar tab would be close to *'three figures.'* Anna lost count of the drinks she has consumed. Did she have four or five? No matter, she will continue indulging at dinner with more wine.

After getting a good buzz, the foursome decides to eat dinner at the sit-down dining room. The dress code requires we upgrade our wardrobe to gain entrance. After a quick trip to the room to put on the required garb, we meet up and pass the dress code test to secure a table for four. The wait staff wears their ship provided uniforms. The Maître d' wears a suit. We place our food and drink orders, then continue the *'get to know each other banter,'* including how the couples met.

All the good that I did in the gym *'went out the door tonight.'* I order two beers, two Riesling white wines, scallops wrapped in bacon, and a Caesar salad with anchovies for starters, salmon and a small potato main course, and lemon meringue pastry and decaf coffee for dessert. Anna orders the scallops and bacon opener, lamb chops, veggies, the lemon meringue pastry, and decaf coffee.

Bill is sitting directly across from Adrienne, his wife, and romantically says, "I have the most beautiful view on the entire ship" as he looks left at **ME** and **NOT** directly across at Adrienne. It's the sentence of the night! Adrienne has a blank stare on her face. Her mouth is open, shaped like the letter 'O.' She's silently thinking, "So, when were you going to tell me?"

Adrienne and Bill are 20 to 25 years younger than Victor and Anna. They are just *'warming up'* and decide on more adult beverages, going to listen to music, and dancing. Ah youth. Anna and I are fortunate we *'left the car home today'* and grab an Uber from the restaurant on Deck 2 to our room on Deck 6. We are almost *'dead on arrival'* with faint pulses and irregular heartbeats as we stagger back and into Room 6041. We are simply old and *'out of adult beverage drinking shape.'* To say the least, we are light weights, "Class A" rookie baseball players.

Anna falls into bed mumbling, "Why did I drink so much?" Victor shows no sympathy as he hands her three Rolaids for heartburn and indigestion. I plant myself on one of the two comfortable room chairs and spend an hour relaxing and watching a Facebook video featuring Don Rickles and Rodney Dangerfield during a 1980's performance on Johnny Carson. Those two, along with many other great performers like George Burns, Bob Newhart, Bob Hope, Ray Romano, Jack Benny, Robin Williams, Flip Wilson, Phyllis Diller, and Joan Rivers (ok she could get a little salty) defined clean, slapstick comedy storytelling that I still enjoy today.

It's midnight; however, it's still partially light outside. The sun sets around 21:00 and rises at 03:30. We are nearing the Arctic Circle and the land of the Midnight Sun.

Until Tuesday, our first travel day at sea, good night!

*****

Tuesday, May 28 — Day 64
Day At Sea

Today is an *'at sea'* day. This means we can explore things on the ship, such as listening to guest lectures and walk the quarter mile lap four times around the outside of Deck 1 so we can say, "We walked a mile for a Camel". We can also:

- sit and chill in the Deck 1 Viking Living Room area and play with our phones or read.

- eat and drink to our hearts content.

- hang out by the swimming pool on Deck 7 and catch some rays.

- stay in bed and do *'squat'* to recharge the body batteries which have been working at 120% on this holiday.

- hit the gym for a cardio workout, stretch various body parts, pump some iron, and use the various upper and lower body exercise machines, or

- spend time in the steam and ice rooms, take the cold water bucket challenge, soak in the jacuzzi, then enjoy a refreshing shower.

For my day, I choose to chill in the Deck 1 Viking Living Room in the a.m., get a 50-minute Swedish massage at 13:00, hit the gym for a workout, spend time in the steam and ice rooms, do the cold water bucket challenge, and enjoy a refreshing shower. Anna decides on an 11:00 massage. Both massages are excellent. The massage tables are top of the line, and so are the masseuses and they earned a nice tip from both of us!.

Prior to leaving Room 6041, Anna cannot open the in-room safe. After numerous failures, she calls Guest Services for assistance. Questions run rampant thru my head; Did someone sneak in and change the code? Did Anna forget the code she entered to lock it? Did someone break into our stateroom, open the safe, and walk off with millions of dollars of Anna's jewelry and other irreplaceable, one-of-a-kind, items? Remember, Anna has already lost two room keys needed to enter our state room, exit and re-board the ship at every port of call, enjoy unlimited drinks at every bar on the ship, unlimited purchases at the high end jewelry stores on board, and unlimited treatments at the Deck 2 Spa. Maybe the perpetrator(s) saw Anna drop her card, picked it up, and nonchalantly followed her to Room 6041. Now that they had the room number, did the perpetrator(s) enter when our room was unoccupied and break into the safe? Is it time for Columbo, Joe Friday, Hawaii Five-0's Steve McGarrett, the Miami Vice duo of Rico Tubbs and Sunny Crockett, and NYPD Detective Andy Sipowicz, to get involved, solve the case, and bring the perpetrator(s) to justice? (One could only wish!)

Within minutes, a highly trained, 20-year veteran of ship operations and opening safes (that won't open due to foolish mistakes made by inebriated or forgetful guests, both young and old), uses his 'magic' or 'some trick' he learned at safe cracking school to open the safe and reveal that the contents have not been disturbed. Anna must sign numerous forms and statements of facts to confirm it's our safe, the contents are in-tact, and if it happens again, there is a 500 Norwegian Krone fine, payable only in cash, no credit cards, or room charge to avoid being unceremoniously tossed overboard onto a rubber raft without oars. In my fantasy mind, I think to myself...her only saving grace, besides me, is there's almost round the clock sunshine. Perhaps a passing ship could spot her floating aimlessly on the sea. Or maybe the tides will bring her to shore. Or I'll jump into the freezing water, use my superhuman breath to *'whoosh'* us to shore. Either way, she'll be rescued and I'll gain some bonus points with her. Anyway...

Gasp!!! Our in-room TV remote is not working. Most likely the batteries are close to death. "G," our 24/7, 14-day lead cabin person, brings us new 'AAA' batteries. The remote now works a little better, however, Viktor asks for a new one. "G" contacts the engineering and audio visual department to secure a new remote. Later in the day, a new, still in the plastic packaging, made in China, remote is placed on the bed for us to easily spot. I hope we don't get charged for the new batteries and for the new remote. I plan to check our room charges statement later today. I can display it on the TV. Ah, technology.

Viktor hits the gym and enjoys a cardio and stretching work-out. I also spend time in the steam room, ice room, and jacuzzi. Refreshed and showered, I join Anna on Deck 7 at the front of the boat to watch as the ship crosses the Arctic Circle.

Around 18:30, there's a definite **BUZZ** aboard ship as we approach *'Crossing the Arctic Circle.'* The ship's passengers, of all nationalities and ages, gather at front of the ship on Decks 7 and 8 and wait anxiously to see this momentous occasion. According to Wikipedia, "The Arctic Circle marks the southernmost latitude at which, on the winter solstice in the Northern Hemisphere, the Sun does not rise all day, and on the Northern Hemisphere's summer solstice, the Sun does not set. These phenomena are referred to as *'Polar Night'* and *'Midnight Sun'*. The further north one progresses, the more obvious this becomes. For example, in the Russian port city of Murmansk, three degrees north of the Arctic Circle, the Sun stays below the horizon for 20 days before and after the winter solstice, and above the horizon for 20 days before and after the summer solstice.

At 18:37, the ship slowly passes a **VERY SMALL OBJECT** marking the **EXACT SPOT** where the ship crosses the *'whatever longitude and latitude'* of the Arctic Circle. There's no fanfare, no fireworks, no band or music, and no cheerleaders to celebrate this *'once in a lifetime'* event .....all we see is a round metal marker with a bird sitting on it! If you blink twice, you'll miss it. This bird is going to be in many pictures. However, when the ship crosses the Arctic Circle, a digital sign with multi-colored blinking lights, displays *'Congratulations! You have just crossed the Arctic Circle!'* Quick, take a picture, Anna!

After passing the *'tiny, significant, but not life changing'* land-mark, we go to the buffet, enjoy dinner and desert, and mosey on back to Room 6041. Time to catch up on some well needed sleep in preparation for tomorrow's 11:00 assault on *Narvik*, Norway.

There will be no more sunsets and sunrises as we are in the midst of the Midnight Sun. It's now 24/7 daylight for the duration of the cruise, or at least the Norway segment. Glad, the room has thick curtains to keep the round-the-clock daylight from entering the room and disrupting our sleep.

Until tomorrow — From north of the Arctic Circle on the Viking Mars cruise ship, good night!

*****

Wednesday, May 29 — Day 65
Narvik, Norway

It is another day docking at another Norwegian port. The Viking Mars moors in Narvik, a 19,500 person seaport city with an abundance of World War II history.

Pulling back the curtains in our stateroom, the sun is out in full force at 07:30 and blinds us! Today's excursion starts at 11:00, so last night before bed, we placed our room service order on our exterior door handle. Our continental breakfast order of fruit, juice, coffee, a side of bacon, and two croissants arrives promptly at 08:30. It is very pleasant outside, so we sit on the veranda and enjoy our first breakfast above the Arctic Circle. Narvik is experiencing another above normal, warm, sunny, no wind, mid-60's day. After breakfast, we do our normal *'morning routine'* and get ready to attack Narvik.

At 09:29, Viktor bolts to the buffet in the back of the ship. It closes at 9:30. I sneak in **JUST** ahead of staff who are getting ready to shut the doors until lunch time. Anna follows a few minutes later, emphatically raps on the door, and gains the attention of the armed, 6'6", 237-pound, young security guard. He is decked out in a full riot gear uniform, helmet, and face shield. He has a 28-round semi-automatic magnum hand gun on his right hip and a fully loaded, and ready to use with a half second's notice AK47 strapped over his right shoulder. After a full body pat down and an X-ray machine scan, he checks Anna's identity through the international criminal security database where agencies like Interpol, CIA, FBI, and every other worldwide law enforcement agency has access to. After passing all the intelligence and criminal data base checks, and correctly answering their 178-questionnaire, she is allowed to proceed and locates me. (OK, this really didn't happen, but my imagination would have enjoyed watching Anna go through these paces.) Next time, we should leave together to hit the buffet at the same time. After finishing breakfast, we head to the departure ramp on Deck One.

At the end of the 250-meter pier, the tour excursion person verifies our reservation for the two-hour city bus tour. We are directed to Bus 18. Today's driver is Geir. Our tour leader is Sonya.

Sonya is a matter of fact, bubbly, *'raw meat and straight whiskey,'* mid-60's, retired grandmother. Many moons ago, she migrated from Western Canada. She adds her pleasant personality to *'tell it like it is.'* Her *'off the cuff'* humor makes everyone laugh. Her opinions on everything are conservative and very refreshing. She follows an informational script which lets everyone know what they are looking at. When the group exits the bus at the first of our three stops, she reminds us to follow along and watch for her #18 *'lollipop tour sign'.*

Here's some important information about Narvik, Norway courtesy of the Viking Mars Daily Newsletter:

- Narvik is situated on the innermost shores of the Ofotfjorden within the Arctic Circle.

- The small town enjoys a dramatic backdrop, encircled by mountains in every direction and the glacier that spills right to the water's edge.

- One version of the town's name, Knarravik, approximately translates into "good, natural port." It served the Vikings well as they were among the first to settle here.

- Much later in the 1870's, the discovery of iron ore in the nearly Swedish town of Kiruna forever shaped Narvik. Kiruna needed a year-round, ice-free port to ship its new discovery. So, a rail link was built directly to the water. Today, Narvik is a major exporter of iron ore.

Below are some other interesting things the traveling Hendersonites learn today:

- Norway declared its independence and adopted a constitution in 1814 after being ceded to Sweden by the Treaty of Kiel following the Napoleonic Wars. The Constitution of Norway was signed on May 17, 1814, establishing a Union between Sweden and Norway. However, it was only in 1905 that Sweden recognized Norway as an independent constitutional monarchy.

- The city proper is noticeably clean.

- While it snows in Narvik, the city uses snow making machines to keep the ski slopes operating for visitors and locals. The ski slopes peak as high as 640 meters (almost 2100 feet.).

- Their waterfront location receives plenty of rain which turns snow, then into mush, and ice. Residents attach ice cleats to their shoes and boots to safely navigate the icy streets.

- The Port of Narvik, which never freezes, is a huge exporter of Swedish iron ore. A railway line runs 10 daily trips, 24/7, from the Swedish owned company, *LKAB* in Kiruna, Sweden to Narvik. Iron ore is loaded onto ships and shipped worldwide.

- Original homes located in Narvik are classified as *'Class 2'* homes. City redevelopment laws forbid owners from altering the home's exterior.

- The midnight sun (no darkness) runs from May 22 to July 18 each year. The city operates in significant darkness from

November 18 to January 22. The Northern Lights appear from September to April.

- There are three main religions in Narvik - Lutheran, Catholic, and Buddhist.

- The city's main source of goods and cargo comes from Oslo through Stockholm via train.

- 1,900 students attend college in Narvik. The primary majors are nursing, engineering, and satellite communications.

- Norway provides excellent childcare starting at one-year-old. The children learn social and other skills at an early age.

- Ladders are secured on rooftops to allow access to annual chimney cleaning.

- Along the waterfront, businesses are constructed on landfills because there isn't much available flat land. Most houses are built on inclines.

- As our bus rolls through a 1 1/2 kilometer tunnel, Anna commented on how nice *'the bridge is'*!

- At Stop 3, we visit a Lutheran Church which was built in 1842. Eight ladies, dressed in local custom attire, sing four Nordic songs to the group.

- The World War II invasion by the German Nazis left many *'hard to forget'* scars on this city. The Germans arrived on April 9 1940, bombed, and burned parts of the city.

- They defeated the Norwegian Navy because they coveted the never frozen seaport location. The Nazis blew up two Norwegian naval ships in the harbor, killing 300 sailors. The citizens could hear the dying sailors' screams and cries. The sea water turned red with the blood of the dead men. The sunken ships remain buried in Narvik harbor.

- The Nazis transported 900 Yugoslavian and Russian prisoners of war to the city, where they walked ten kilometers to the *Beisfjord Concentration Camp*. They were given shovels and ordered to dig trenches near the camp. Residents were ordered to stay inside and keep their blinds closed. The guards then used machine guns to slaughter the young men and bury them in the trenches.

- The Germans were finally removed from Narvik on May 8, 1945 at the end of World War II. However, the scars of war remain, especially for the elderly Narvik residents who lived through that period of time. Reconstruction of the city was completed during the 1950's. There's a World War II museum in town.

- During World War II, the Lutheran Church was hit by nine bombs. Two exploded and damaged the building. In 1947, repairs were completed. The pews are painted in a historic Norwegian color, *Farmers Blue*.

- The Lutheran Church, like many older homes in Narvik, is constructed of wood. The structure and roof are held up by four thick wooden support pillars. The wooden roof is supported by four cross beams, two in each direction. The balcony contains the organ and is held in place by eight round pillars. Two sets of wooden steps lead up to the balcony.

- Various Scandinavian Nomadic languages spoken locally make communication difficult at times. The dominant languages are Norwegian, Swedish, Danish, and Finnish.

- The Norwegian language is difficult to listen to. It sounds like you have a mouth full of potatoes. Three vowels are AH, YH, and OH.

- The Norwegian word "**FART**" means speed. The Norwegian word "**STUMP**" means speed bump. So, the Politi can pull you over for *'Farting and recklessly driving over Stump.'*

- Norway sends its garbage, via rail to Sweden where the Swedes convert it to fuel to heat homes.

At the conclusion of the two-hour tour, the bus drops us off at Viking Mars. We decide to walk the 1.5 kilometers to town. Unfortunately, it's all **UP HILL**. However, Anna's knee is functioning better than usual — no brace, no cane, just a 95%+ normal stride.

Apparently, the intermittent rest and relaxation has calmed down what is going on in her knee. I do some souvenir shopping while Anna window shops. We Google a good burger/fish sandwich restaurant near us and locate one a mere two minutes away. Unfortunately, Google Maps assumes you know where you are, you know all the street names, and you can locate street name signs. We walk in four different directions and finally locate the restaurant, just 60 meters (65 yards) from where we were originally standing.

We enjoy lunch at *Fiskehallen*. We split fish and chips, a very thick vegetable soup, and a Norwegian *Lofotpils* Draft Pilsner Beer. The food is outstanding. The fish is perfectly deep fried and is so fresh it almost bit me. According to the waiter, the fish was caught either last night or today! When the coast is clear and no one is paying attention, I **ADD** the beer glass to my European beer glass collection.

Anna decides that we should walk to the Mall, about 200 meters across a busy, 'no crosswalk' intersection and traffic circle. Despite her pleas of, "***NO**, don't cross here, there's traffic,*" I spot an opening and get us half way across to our destination, and spot another opening to the sidewalk near the Mall entrance. Success! Jaywalking is a European sport I am mastering.

Anna finds nothing to buy, while I buy a pair of casual pants, a matching long sleeve, quarter zip shirt, and a Norway black tee shirt.

It's time to safely cross the street. Fearless Anna jaywalks between two stopped cars to reach her destination. Viktor heads in the other direction to place two postcards in the Red Post Box across the main, four-lane street. I walk towards a marked crosswalk; however, I spot an opening in the traffic, jaywalk across four lanes, stop half way across a narrow sidewalk traffic divider, and finish the journey when *'the coast is clear'* of oncoming traffic. I deposit the postcards in the Red Post Box attached to the side of a building and walk three blocks to meet up with Anna. This time, I use the *'Walk/Don't Walk'* electronic pedestrian crossing signal to safely catch up to her.

A Viking sponsored shuttle bus takes us back to the ship. I *'dilly dally'* taking those last *'just gotta have pictures'* while Anna disappears onto the ship. I find a lounge chair at the outdoor swimming pool, under a protective roof, and begin composing today's story. I text Anna and let her know where I am hanging out. An hour later, she stops by but, after chilling with me for half an hour, she *'disappears'* once again. Maybe she found a sugar daddy on board and slips away for drinks and small talk. Or she went to the room to take a nap, or she headed to the Explorers Lounge on Deck 7 Forward and orders a glass of wine. I text her to learn where she is; however, I get no reply. Is it time for me to call the Guest Services Desk on Deck One, report her missing, and ask a staff member to make an announcement over the ship's public address system asking for help locating her?

Meanwhile, I gather up my backpack, my purchases, and my shoulder purse. I put my shoes on and head back to the room for some quiet time provided Anna is not there! Columbo and Sergeant Joe Friday are now on the *'missing Anna case'* working in conjunction with Viking Mars ship security and Narvik Politi to locate her. Success! Ship security locates her aimlessly wandering the passageways. Whatever...

Glad I was hungry for dinner tonight. From the buffet three mini-lobster tails, Beef Wellington, sushi, and sashimi, one slice of pizza, and a green salad *'flew over the counter'* and jumped on my plate. All I did was *'look'* at these items. The next thing I know, the food is stacked high on my plate. I need both hands to carry the plate to the table on the Deck 7 outdoor sitting area. Anna was *'good.'* She chose one lobster tail, a slice of Beef Wellington, and some veggies. Viktor promises to *'cut back tomorrow,'* on his food intake — maybe skip a meal or three.

For the past few days while walking around the ship and in the gym, I keep seeing some men that not only look like Griff, but also have his short, clippers only, hair style. I've almost gone up to them and shout, *"Hey Griff, its John Boy. When did you get here bro?"*

Anna and Viktor can't believe we are above the Artic Circle sitting outside in 70 plus degrees, sunny, no wind, clear blue sky *'nighttime'* weather on the Viking Mars cruise ship. We are on the stern, Deck 7, eating area at 19:23. We finish a spectacular dinner, drink a glass of wine, and gaze at the water and shoreline, where a few houses dot the tree-lined hillsides. Life is way, way better than great. We feel truly blessed.

Time for Viktor to give *'big shoutouts'* to my Saturday golfing buddies — Ed, Mike, Dave, Dan, Girard, and Doug H. Sadly, gentlemen, there are no slots, keno, or video poker machines on the Viking Mars. It's a smaller ship with less than 1,000 guests. Every stateroom comes with a veranda. There are, however, numerous watering holes throughout the ship. With the unlimited daily drinks option guests purchase prior to embarking, the six of you could aggressively compete for most drinks per day, per week and for the 14-day cruise. Ed, there are many bottled beer choices, all imported. There's no *Bud* or *Bud Light*. Mike, you can calm your nerves and stay balanced by starting and ending the day gargling with top shelf vodka, scotch, and bourbon, *Makers Mark*, or *Fire Ball*.

Dan, you are a man of all adult drinks so there's plenty of imported beer, red and white wine, *Prosecco*, champagne, and the hard stuff listed under Mike above. Now Dave, as a lawyer, you could start a class action lawsuit against Viking to get them to add video poker and keno machines so you and your bride could feel right at home on a Viking ship. Let's not forget Girard. He could hire on as an independent contractor to offer financial and business planning seminars while getting a free cruise. The only drawback I see is there is no cigar smoking lounge on board. You may have to hang off your stateroom veranda by your ankles to enjoy a stogie. Just don't fall overboard! There's no way the Captain can quickly stop the ship, do a 180 degree turn, and attempt to locate you in the foggy ocean.

Mr. Doug is a strapping 6'4" hunk of a man who is willing to pour a great *'JT style'* Makers Mark Bourbon Manhattan on the rocks when we visit Green Valley Ranch's *Sidebar*! He always has a smile on his face! It is because the regulars Mike, Dave, Dan, Girard, and Ed are tipping the maximum after Doug *'manipulates'* the video poker machines at the bar so that every now and then, (i.e., two to three times per night) someone catches a Royal Flush or manipulates the Keno machines so that Dave, his wife, Mike, or Ed catch an '8' number, huge Keno Win!

Ben Labrador, my Hawaiian friend, with your entertainment organization background, you could manage the musical acts on board while telling *'Hey Brah'* Hawaiian stories at the bar as you sip on a Diet Coke or Diet Pepsi through a certified California paper straw. Finally, Dale, my longest tenured Las Vegas friend, you are the best. When you sold your bad ass speed boat, my grandson

Hunter and I almost ended our relationship with you; however, Anna and Culleen kept the families together by bribing us with Culleen's Mexican delicacies and Anna's excellent selection of top shelf, '*not the cheap shit,*' Chardonnay and Pinot Noir.

Dale, you saved us from the baby bunny that avoided our killer cat, 'Tee' and made a new home under our bottom kitchen cabinets. You always have the necessary tools and experience to fix anything. There is very little, if anything, you cannot repair. A few years back, Dale singlehandedly built, from scratch, a 16' by 12' man storage shed. However, his wife Culleen liked his creation so much that she moved most of her '*stuff*' into the shed while Dale was out running errands or playing golf. When he returned, he found Culleen had taken 99.5% possession of the shed. She only left half of one shelf for his '*stuff*' and added a sign on the door announcing, "Culleen's She Shed". That's a real "Shit Happens" moment.

I, on the other hand, am very good at calling a repair man and writing checks or plopping down a credit card whenever something breaks. Anytime I attempt to fix something, it ends up bad, and it is more costly to fix or put back together. At least I know my limits. And yes Dale, I still don't have a shovel, and I never plan to purchase one. Dale is an 81-year-young, dear friend and a solid Trump conservative. He still wears the '*Make America Great*' hat I bought him in 2015. He is fine-tuning his golf game by playing three times a week and is also anticipating he will be kicking my ass when I return from this trip in late June.

Our late, great friend, Marty, aka Martino, left us almost three years ago. We miss him and his '*tell it like it is*' attitude. A great golfer and former boxer, Marty was always looking for ways to '*mix it up,*' never taking a back seat to anyone. He was a true friend, a warrior, and teetotaler who had a quick, colorful whit. Marty had the ability to '*say things*' that **ONLY** Marty could get away with! Griff and I frequently cry out, "*Marty, where are you, we need you!*" He was a fair sports bettor who hated parlays. Marty bro, we miss you. Keep looking down on us and telling us to "Go Fuck Yourself"— your signature saying.

I can't forget "Mr. 300 Bowler of the Year", Dennis 'Griff' Griffin, a pal's pal. He's the most solid, rational, fair, and caring conservative man I know. He **ALWAYS** has a good word to say about anything or anyone and *'reels me in'* when I go *'off on one of my rants or hit one of my numerous errant golf shots.'* Griff addresses me as *'John Boy,'* something that only Griff can get away with. Griff nursed me back to good walking health when I had my right hip replaced a few years ago. He'd take me for daily walks, gradually increasing the distance to over two miles a day. He starts everyday by reading the Bible, followed by feeding his totally spoiled and enabled dog, Bandit, and enjoying coffee while reading the Review Journal sports and editorial sections. Sometimes his next door neighbor, 'Pops' a retired raging Cajun who never saw a beer he didn't like, joins Griff for morning coffee. During the NFL season, Pops whips up one of his unique and special Cajun dishes for our Monday night football get togethers at his home.

Griff bowls twice a week at the Southpoint Hotel and Casino. He anchors both teams he's on, carrying a strong and fairly consistent *'107 average'*. Griff has an extensive network of college fraternity brothers that he gets together with four to five times a year for various outings including a three-day golf experience. One of his *'brothers'* is my favorite all time baseball player, Michael Jack Schmidt, a Major League Baseball Hall of Fame third baseman. Griff is on the phone seven to ten times a day with Dick, his 81-year-old *'big bro'* to get updates on Ohio sports teams. That includes the "Indians" or "Tribe" (not the Guardians), the Brownies, Cavaliers, and 'The Ohio State' athletics programs, especially football and basketball. Griff is also an avid, serious fantasy football player. In the fall, he squares off with his sons and several friends for year round bragging rights. Thanks, Griff, for always being there to keep me, *'most of the time,'* on the *'straight and narrow'* and for being there for me rain or shine.

For the rest of the Saturday Las Vegas golfers who may remember me, after all it's been almost 22 months since *'I teed it up'*. I don't have enough info on each of you to write something about. But I do know that Butch, doesn't understand how his weekly, notoriously low scores give him a very high *'nut'* that makes it nearly impossible for him to win any serious money. Then there's *'The Judge'*, another Dennis, who has homes in Henderson and Utah.

Doug Bradford, one of the regular Saturday golfers, is another *'solid citizen'* who is very close to his son, daughter-in-law and his young grandson who suffers from a heart condition. When I returned from this trip, I spent many an afternoon getting to know Doug while golfing. When I learned about his professional background in broadcast journalism, I asked him to edit this book. Doug took up the challenge and has done an amazing job making the book *'sound good.'* On the flip side, his friends may not recognize Doug because after 550 plus pages, he has picked up my colorful vocabulary and sarcastic phrases!

Let's not forget about Tommy, Valley High School's Athletic Director, and history teacher. On February 25, 2024, the local group of the *St. Jude's Cancer Research Center* was holding a fund raiser on the 4th hole at *Wildhorse Golf Course* in Henderson. For a $20 donation, golfers got **ONE SWING** to win $10,000 for a *'Hole In One'*. Standing on the tee box 147 yards from the hole, Tommy hits a *'thin'* 7 iron that lands just short of the green, bounces up onto it, rolls towards the cup, and **BINGO**, the ball is in the **HOLE!** Tommy's wallet is instantaneously $10,000 **HEAVIER** (minus the action the IRS will take). He will be forever known as **"Mr. $10,000"**. The shot also got Tommy into a $1M, one shot *'Hole In One Challenge'* on a 186-yard Par 3 hole at Chimera golf course.

With 25,187 spectators, ESPN, The Golf Channel, family, and friends, including Griff, JT, Mike, and Butch looking on, Tommy hit his shot just left of the green, pin high, and instead of watching the ball trickle 25-feet downhill into the hole, the ball hung up in the four inch rough and came to a sudden stop. **BUT**, unlike the rest of us, he had a **SHOT**.

Lastly, there is Ben Campbell. He moved about three years ago to the red neck hills of Kingman, AZ. He lives off the land, hunting and growing organic vegetables, and sells survival gear and related *'stuff'* to extreme right wing radicals who live in the back country of the western United States. I clearly remember the first time we played golf together at Chimera, with Dale and me. On the 14th hole, he aced the 148 yard par three by hitting a thin 7-iron about 120 yards. We watched the ball roll over the gravel in front of the green, onto the green, and then into the hole! Marvelous shot and memory!

In sections of this book, I have recognized Thom Metcalf, a long-time friend from Maui who along with his bride, Marie, moved to Henderson a few years ago. He is a masterful painting artist, a Mr. Fix-It former home builder, a great cook, and an avid golfer. He has tried on many occasions to fix my *'back foot Johnnie'* golf swing. But, as many people have said, I have a great practice swing but when I get over the ball, I have *'issues'* with the ball and my brain says *'kill it'* versus making a good swing and letting the ball get in the way. I keep trying — maybe someday I will *'get it.'*

All, it's time for bed. We set the alarm for a 06:00 wake up, followed by our in-room breakfast, before heading out at 08:00 on another touristy adventure into parts unknown of Norway. Until tomorrow, out!

*****

Thursday, May 30 — Day 66
Lofoten Islands, Norway

At 07:00, Viking Mars arrives at *Lofoten Islands,* Norway, and docks at *Leknes Cruise Port.* Roads, bridges, and tunnels connect the eight main islands.

Viktor and Anna are up before the 6:30 iPhone alarm goes off. Today's tour of three of the eight main islands departs at 8:30. Breakfast arrives at our room at 06:45 promptly. We enjoy oatmeal, eggs, a side of bacon, two blueberry muffins, a fresh fruit plate, OJ and V8 juices, and fresh brewed coffee and milk.

After showering and getting dressed, we head down to Deck One, exit the ship, and arrive at Bus One at 08:20. Zebe is today's bus driver and Veronik is today's tour guide. Our land and sea tour is scheduled for three hours...another *"Gilligan's Island three hour tour."*

Before we continue on today's adventure, here's what the Viking Mars Daily Newsletter says about *Leknes* (Lofoten), Norway:

- Home to breathtaking jagged peaks, a temperate summer climate and sheltered bays, the Lofoten Islands stretch 118 miles into the Norwegian Sea from Norway's coast. Ships in the archipelago's cozy fishing harbors are dwarfed by the hulking massifs rising from the waters. The setting was ideal for Norse settlements in the early Viking Age. Cod has long been harvested from these waters as the fish come here to spawn. More recently, the fish have been caught from traditional *rorbus* — charming cottages that hover above the waters on stilts. The Lofoten Islands are beautiful any time of the year, but the summertime midnight sun illuminates their magnificent glory around the clock.

Today, we learn many *'little tidbits'* about this remote area of islands in Norway.

- Lofoten Islands, in Northern Norway, have been voted by National Geographic as one of the most appealing destinations in the world. Located just above the Arctic Circle, at the 68th northern parallel, Lofoten basks in the ethereal Midnight Sun during summer and witnesses the magical Northern Lights from September to April.

- After World War II, Italy quickly built four large fishing ships, side by side, in Ancona Italy. Four ship building companies completed the project. Norway needed the ships to catch cod. Italy was one of Norway's largest buyers of fish. Forty to sixty per cent of the cost to build the ships was paid in fish.

- Wooden fish drying racks dot the coastline.

- Fish heads are exported to Nigeria where the locals use them to make soup.

- Ninety-seven per cent of aluminum cans and plastic bottles are recycled. As the local saying goes, "Consumers borrow the packaging" and get money back when they recycle cans and plastic bottles.

- Bird watching brings many summer tourists. Over 250 species of birds call this area home.

- There is a horse racing track that is used only three times a year.

- The white tailed eagle has a nine foot wing span.

SH?#! HAPPENS AGAIN! - TRAVELING WITH JOHN AND LESLIE

- Approximately 4,700 people call Leknes home. The town employs five policemen and has no stop lights. Round abouts are placed at intersections to keep traffic moving.

- The *'Circle K'* convenience store is a top attraction in town.

- Two - 39 passenger propeller planes periodically take off and land at the local airport.

- Ferries run from island to island. Cars mostly use the ferries to get back and forth from the islands.

- Rain and snow storms, accompanied by strong winds, will close the roads and the bridges between islands.

- From October to April, the area can experience violent storms. Hurricane force winds can reach 270 km or 170 mph.

- "Dim fart," in Norwegian, means you are speeding while driving. (Maybe I'll use that when I get pulled over by one of Henderson's finest. "Sorry Officer, I didn't know that I was dim farting!!"

- School buses take students who live in remote areas to school. The public can also ride these buses. There is no remote area bus transportation during the summer months when schools are closed.

- On February 1, 2024, *Ingunn*, the strongest storm in the 2023-24 European season, slammed into Norway and was the most powerful storm in more than 40 years. The storm developed from a very powerful, low-pressure jet stream and raced across the Atlantic. It heightened avalanche risks, left residents without power, forced them to remain indoors until the tempest passed, tore paint off houses, destroyed some homes, and shut down roads and the airport.

- The Norwegian Flag is a combination of the Swedish and Denmark flags.

- In December, the lakes freeze in a clear, crystal form.

- Prior to World War II, many of the main travel routes were gravel roads and dirt trails. After the war, the main roads were paved. This project was completed in 1953.

- In olden times, ferries took people from island to island. Today, five of the eight large islands are connected through a tunnel under the sea or over bridges while only three require ferries to reach them.

- *Lufortin* is the highest bridge connecting the islands. Bad weather including snow, ice, and excessive winds, close the roadway, sometimes for days at a time. Once the bridge is closed, there is no way off the island. It's good to have a Plan B when traveling in poor weather, especially in the dark, winter days.

- It's a four-hour drive to Narvik. This road connects Norway to Sweden.

- Remote island residents rely on access to fresh water and the sea to fish and remain independent. They grow vegetables to remain self-sustaining.

- Some 25,800 Norwegians live throughout the eight large islands — 10,764 live on Vestvagoy. This island has a big moose population which can be seen near roads and swimming from island to island in search of food. While Anna and Viktor were driving around this island, Victor thought he saw Bullwinkle, the Moose and his sidekick, Rocket J. Squirrel.

- Despite being inside the Arctic Circle, the Gulf Stream creates elevated temperatures relative to the Lofoten Islands latitude.

Winters are mild while summers are warm. However, the weather changes quickly. Locals wear layered clothing.

- The surrounding area is dotted with hundreds of small islands in the north western part of Finland, southwest of yesterday's Narvik stop.

- During the 24/7 hours of summer daylight, golfers play at *Liufortin Links* Golf Course. A round of golf costs $250 during summer months.

- Otters, red foxes, and mink farms are present on the island chain. In 1860, the last bear was shot. Wolves have also left the area. Sheep freely walk over large tracks of land and hills. Cows produce milk which is used to make cheese. Sheep and cows are housed inside in barns during the harsh winter months.

- There are 24 (count them) types of mosquitoes that call this area home. As long as the wind blows, they are not a problem because mosquitoes don't like wind. Inland however, flies and mosquitoes are a problem and just love taking a bite or three out of people.

- The difference between low and high tide is about nine feet.

- The water rarely gets warmer than 54 degrees. Our guide told a funny story about *'white as a ghost'* visitors skinny dipping up to their knees. On our trip, some adventurous people provided a unique *'viewing experience'* for the two passing tour buses.

- The local fishing season runs from January to April during some of the harshest times of the area's weather, especially during the dark, not sunny days of January and February.

- When you take in all the coastlines of the numerous islands, Norway has the second longest coastline, next to Canada.

- During the dark winter season, residents take vitamin D and watch whales frolic in the surrounding waterways. I wonder if they sit in their cars to watch '*underwater submarine races*' too?!?!

- Cruise ship tours can be cancelled from the end of May to the end of August because of bad weather. Lucky for us, today's weather was sunny and warm with temperatures in the low 60's.

Our two-hour bus ride ends in the village of *Henningsvar*. A boat ride will complete the remaining 90 minutes of the tour and take everyone back to the cruise ship dock. But first, we have 35 minutes to roam through the village, grab a snack, and purchase those '*just gotta have one of a kind*' souvenirs. I sprint to town to make an '*investment*' at the local souvenir store. I also purchase and write four postcards to family and friends that I hope will '*get there*' by Labor Day.

The boat ride out of Henningsvar provides a good look at the village. I find a seat on the uncovered top deck in the first row at the back of the boat as it enters the open seas. However, it is just '*too cold*' for this old fart. So, I head down one flight of stairs to the enclosed sitting area. Here, cushioned chairs and tables provide a warm and relaxing place to sit and enjoy the views, sip on hot chocolate, and munch on a cinnamon bun with Anna.

Returning to the ship, I grab a quick workout, sit in the steam room, jacuzzi, and ice room, shower, then journey up to the Explorers Lounge on Deck 7. I join Anna, Billy, and Adrienne for drinks. The four of us travel to the dining room for a four-course meal with wine pairings. The chef really knows how to create a special meal and the sommelier really knows how to select the appropriate wines that bring out the best in the food offerings. Adrienne and Billy want to venture back to Deck 7 Explorers Lounge. We pass on '*more fun*' tonight. We've had enough adult beverages for the evening. Anna retires to our room. I spend an hour or so sitting on my favorite leather couch in the Viking Living Room, on Deck One, recapping today's events. My body is saying, *'No Mas.'* So, I head upstairs to our Deck Six room and place our breakfast order selections on the exterior door handle. We have another tour in the morning. Nighty, night from Viking Mars, Room 6041!

*****

Friday, May 31 — Day 67
Tromsø, Norway

Well, if you crash and burn because you can't run with the *'big dogs'* the night before, it's best to sleep in for 12 hours and attempt to restore the body batteries to a consistent positive charge. After spending an hour on Deck 1 writing yesterday's happenings, my *'battery'* died at 22:30 last night. A 911 call to AAA for a jump is fruitless. AAA doesn't have member services available in Norway. So, I do the next best thing —I bury myself in bed, curl up in the heavy blankets, and tightly close my eyes. Anna has already beaten me to the punch. Not feeling 100%, possibly due to a cold coming on, she buried herself in bed after dinner at 20:30. When I arrive at the room, she is locked in a deep sleep that even an earthquake, or emergency siren from ship security, wouldn't budge her.

Their day starts at 10:31. When the traveling senior Americanos open the curtains, we are greeted by a sunny, blue sky with a wisp of white clouds. Early this morning, the ship docked in *Tromsø*, Norway. Anna and I are amazed at what we see, a large city with major hotel chains, local businesses, and houses. Snow covered mountains provide a stunning background. Are we really above the Arctic Circle?

Anna's not feeling 100% due to the quartet of excuses: lack of sleep, a cold coming on, too much playing tourist, and too many adult beverages. So, she does the wise adult thing, she cancels her shore excursion for the day and attempts to move our upgraded special dinner at the highly acclaimed Italian restaurant from tonight to another night. While staying behind for some rest and relaxation, Anna might walk to the other side of Deck 6 and toss in a load of laundry in the no charge, ship supplied, washer and dryer.

Let's take a look at what Viking Mars Daily Newsletter has to say about Tromsø, Norway:

- Tromsø has long been considered the gateway to the Arctic.

- From the late 18th to the early 20th century, housing construction boomed, and today the city's historic center boasts the largest concentration of wooden houses in northern Norway.

- With a rich array of French Empire, Swiss, and neoclassical architecture also spread throughout the city, Tromsø exudes an air of sophistication which rivals that of some of its southern European neighbors.

- The *Arctic Cathedral*, a stunning structure of soaring while rooflines and triangular peaks, has been compared to the *Sydney Opera House*.

- For panoramic views of the city, ride the cable car up to Mount Storsteinen or get there by climbing the 1,200 stone steps up the Sherpa staircase.

- The city is also home to the northernmost botanical garden in the world, a rare collection of alpine and Arctic plants, and the northernmost brewery.

- Tromsø has achieved the certification *'Sustainable Destination'*. While this doesn't mean that Tromsø is completely sustainable, it has made a commitment to reduce the negative effects of tourism, while strengthening its positive ripple effects.

Today's adventure is a three hour bus ride starting at 12:30 to see the sites of Tromsø. Our tour leader is Victor, a 6'10" German. He studied photography at a college in Rhode Island. The basketball coach asked him to come play for the team. Victor's pre-NIL answer was, "How much you going to pay me?" The answer was $0. Victor said he made a wise decision to focus on his studies. It was a smart move for many reasons including that he does not have the NBA body-type, and a 6'10" white guy is rarely NBA material.

Victor (not be confused with me, Viktor) focused his education on photography, human conditions, and people. Recently, he says he spent two years hitchhiking more than 16,000 miles through 41 American states while learning, and studying, how Americans live and vote.

The bus driver today is Per. Victor related that the long, 24/7 sunshine and great weather is an opportune time for midnight mountain hikes, like the one he did last night.

Here's what Victor taught us today:

- The tour starts on Tromsø Island where the cruise ship is docked. It will take us over a bridge to the main part of the city and return through a six kilometer long tunnel.

- The midnight sun is two months long, from mid-May to mid-July. It is very important to have a set of strong curtains to keep the sunlight out at bedtime.

- The opposite of 24/7 sunshine is the polar nights of 100% darkness, from the end of November to end of January.

- When the sun first reappears, even for one minute, the locals rush out to feel the warmth of the sun's rays hitting their cheeks. Vitamins D3 and K are daily *'must take'* supplements during dark winter.

- Winter sports participation is a **MUST**. Even in the dead of winter, unless there's a huge storm, the darkness is no excuse not to jog, bike, cross country ski, or participate in any outdoor sporting activity.

- On clear, dark winter nights, the Northern Lights provide an exciting nightly show, no two of which are ever the same! But, when you go out, watch out for ice and snow. Slip and falls are a *'real downer'* and broken bones ruin a tourist's holiday.

- The city has 60,000 residents and 10,000 university students representing 130 worldwide countries. With the influx of people relocating to the area, rapid economic and real estate development has things happening fast in Tromsø.

- The current infrastructure is maxing out. A new airport that is under construction will hopefully operate efficiently to bring more tourists to the area.

- The excursion's first stop is the local *Nordlysplanetariet (planetarium)*. While here, I watch *"Extreme Auroras,"* an informative and impressive movie from the Science Centre of Northern Norway that is projected in the planetarium's full-dome format. With this technology, you **FEEL** as if the Northern Lights surround you...nature's own visually delightful light show. Each night, natural appearance comes with a different intensity of speed and color. No two *'Aurora Borealis Northern Lights live shows'* are ever the same.

- The Gulf Stream brings warmer water from the Gulf of Mexico into the North Atlantic Ocean and keeps the coast warm in the winter with temperatures ranging from -10 to -18 degrees Celsius while inland temperatures reach -30 to -40 degrees Celsius.

- Despite the cold dark days and nights, hotels always run 100% occupancy in the winter months. Tourists pay around

$800 a night to witness the Northern Lights and experience 24/7 darkness.

- Last year, travelers who failed to book accommodations wound up sleeping in the uncomfortable airport. While driving on the bridges, I saw many new waterfront apartments and condos under construction. These new units will cost approximately 4M to 5M Krone to purchase ($384,000 to $460,500 US).

- Men and women with young families flock to this area for academics and employment opportunities. They also choose to raise a family where education is priority number one. Tromsø offers a safe living environment with clean, healthy air to breathe and a variety of outdoor sports and activities for everyone. The average age of the 80,000 residents is below 30 years of age.

- The top employment opportunities are tourism, education, and healthcare (doctors and nurses). Residents in outlying areas must arrive by plane to reach the largest hospital in Northern Norway to visit specialists and get advanced medical care.

- The magic of the area causes many one-year visitors, who come for either educational opportunities or to live the northern lifestyle, to stay for longer periods of time. As a local saying goes, "If you sit too long on the toilet, you will miss the summer!"

- Tromsø is the home of *Urnes Stave Church*. Built in 1200, it's the largest wooden church in Scandinavia.

- The Arctic Cathedral was designed by Architect Jan Inge Hovig. The cathedral is a community landmark, visible from the Tromsø Sound, the Tromsø Bridge, and when landing in Tromsø by aircraft. It was built between 1964 and 1965 and was dedicated on November 19, 1965. The 11-aluminum-coated concrete panels on each side of the roof provide the cathedral's form. The main entrance on the western side is surrounded by a large glass façade with a pronounced cross. In 1972, a fantastic glass mosaic on the eastern side was added. It's the largest stained glass window in Europe. The glass work contains many symbols and generates considerable attention among visitors. The padded oak pews, the large prism chandeliers, the altar rail, and pulpit are the most significant fittings, all of which are in a style that agrees with the cathedral's severity and simplicity. Because of the church's distinct look and situation, it has often been called **"The Opera House of Norway"**, likening it to the famous Opera House in Sydney, Australia. There's an artificial white tree in the back of the church that holds white bird ornaments with the name of every child baptized during the current calendar year.

- Viktor (me) almost starts a fire in the church while lighting two candles requested by his sister Barbara.

- The *Tromsøysund Tunnel* runs under the *Tromsøysundet Strait*, connecting *Tromsøya* island (and the city of Tromsø) with the mainland suburb of *Tromsdalen*. The two-lanes in each direction tunnel opened on December 4, 1994. It is 3,500 meters (11,500 feet or 2.2 miles) long and is 123 meters (about 400 feet) below the water surface. Too bad Anna is not on the bus today as it drives through the tunnel. She would most likely say something like "It's a nice bridge"...just as she did yesterday while driving through another long tunnel on our bus tour.

- Construction of the Tromsø Bridge cantilever road bridge that leads directly to the city center of Tromsø began in 1958.

The bridge opened in 1960. At the time of its opening, it was the longest bridge in Northern Europe, with a length of 1,036 meters (3,399 feet). At a cost of 14.5 million Krone ($2M US), it crosses the Tromsøysundet Strait between Tromsdalen on the mainland and the island of Tromsøya.

- The bridge replaced an inefficient ferry connection between the two sides of the strait, and it helped boost the growth and development of Tromsø. Prior to constructing the bridge, ferries referred to as *Black Coffins,* because of their color, were used to shuttle people between the islands. A ferry system is still in operation from the outer islands. Prior to the ferries, in the 1920's, residents used row boats to cross.

- There are no ski lifts in this area. Skiers must climb to the top of the mountain while carrying all their gear before skiing down. The mountainous region has a high risk of avalanches.

- The town has a new 21 engine fire station that supports the surrounding area. There's also a new police station.

- The area's crime rate is low. Normally, there is nothing to worry about. However, times are changing with the influx of foreigners moving to the region.

- Drugs are also becoming a problem. Illegal substances like amphetamines, cannabis, cocaine, and ecstasy enter the country through the uncontrolled land border with Finland and Sweden. Drugs also enter the area by planes, container ships, and cruise liners. In the old days, illegal drugs entered the country on snow scooters and were transported to cars.

- On an outer island, one man has lived alone for 50 years. During severe storms, he cannot leave his cabin for two to three weeks. The fierce strong winds can blow so hard you can land on your butt.

- Winter storms with extremely fierce strong winds can tip over a tour bus. Hence, when storms get bad, everything, including the roadways, shut down.

- The city has a nuclear bomb shelter that holds 40,000 people.

- Northern indigenous people called *Sami* live in the northern parts of Norway. Between 80,000 to 100,000 Sami call the Baltic Region home. Originally, there were 10 Sami languages. Today, four are still in use.

- Americans living in North Dakota and Minnesota today may have some Sami DNA in their genetic makeup as a result of Sami migration into the Americas.

The weather has been great with above normal warm temperatures. Today, I see *'locals out and about'* wearing shorts and tee shirts while I am bundled up to stay warm in the 50 degree weather.

The tour bus returns to the ship area at 15:30. I have roughly just short of an hour to get back on board before the 17:00 scheduled departure; if you are not on board at the scheduled departure time, *'tough tullies'*. You are *'on your own nickel'* to catch up with the Viking Mars at the next port of call.

Viktor walks quickly through the island village snapping pictures of everything within sight, including the small boats, the marina shops, restaurants, and streetscapes. There's an old Catholic Church up a slight 90 degree incline that catches my attention. Arriving at the church doorsteps, I enter, light a few candles, and take a handful of photographs. Next, I spot a souvenir store with large, colorful, blinking lights that *'draw me in'* with little, if any resistance. After making two laps around the store, I gather up half an arm full of those *'I just have to have stuff or my trip is not complete'* items, including a cute, stuffed reindeer for ailing Anna. Just like many other places along the trip, I make another hefty contribution to the local economy.

I finish the jaunt around town with a stop at the pharmacy for drugs for Anna and I enjoy a cold one at a local *Rathskeller* bar. As I am about to leave, the fancy beer glass magically and carefully jumps into my backpack without breaking. Another *'just have to have'* beer glass souvenir to add to the others *'collected'* on the journey to share a cold one or three with friends when returning home. I anticipate spending three to four days telling numerous trip stories. I'll also share the 25,392 pictures and videos with friends clambering, "Victor that's hilarious, please tell that story again!"

As I am near the ship, I call Anna and ask her to step out on the veranda so I can wave to her and take a few pictures of her on our Room 6041 veranda. Out of nowhere, the calm windless afternoon is suddenly and violently interrupted by a 65 mph gust of wind that nearly tosses her overboard, forcing her to hang on for dear life. Tragedy averted; Anna sees me walk away from the ship. Is he disembarking and moving to Norway? Is he just lost and can't tell a cruise ship from a local pub? Is he looking for free potty? Are Norwegian maidens calling out to him to follow them to sea? No, I spot an ATM machine behind the local tourist office. I just have one Norwegian Krone on me. I anticipate needing a few bucks to tip the local guides on our remaining Norwegian excursions. With just seconds to spare, I make it back on board.

Tonight, we grab dinner at the buffet and enjoy adult drinks while sitting on the stern (outside rear ship deck).

Anna retires to the room while I head to the Viking Living Room on Deck 1 to relax in *'my corner leather couch'* next to an electric outlet to keep my iPhone charged. I enjoy the quiet retreat and listen to cello and violin musicians play soft, classical, and relaxing music followed by a classical piano player making soft music on the 88 ivory keys. I also catch up on my daily writing.

As the clock strikes midnight on another 24-hour, no dark day, I head to Room 6041 where I find Anna *'out like a light'*. I quickly fill out the room service breakfast order for tomorrow, hang it on the outside door handle, and retire for the day/night. Until the morning...oh wait, it's already Saturday...nighty, night!

*****

Saturday, June 1 — Day 68
Honningsvag and North Cape, Norway

We wake up at 06:30, look outside, and see....thick, dense *'San Francisco like'* fog. The ship is moving **VERY SLOWLY**. The fog horn is being **BLOWN LOUDLY** to alert other vessels, who may be in the ship's path, to **GET OUT OF THE WAY**, the Viking Mars is coming thru and **NOT STOPPING**. Just, *'get out of the way'* because our ship is most likely larger than yours and can't stop on a dime. The fog soon dissipates and the shoreline becomes visible. Land ahoy! However, in this part of the Baltic world, the weather is known to change rapidly and, after turning our attention to the TV for a few seconds, the *'San Francisco like'* fog rolls back in! The half-awake Viktor and Anna enjoy listening to seagulls singing as they welcome us to port and dive at our veranda door begging us to toss some food overboard. However, according to ship rules, that's a big **'NO-NO'** illegal activity that will result in your being unceremoniously tossed overboard without your belongings or a boat or raft. Clearly, one would be in survivor mode before succumbing to the cold Baltic Sea and becoming fish food.

While waiting for breakfast to arrive, we watch a video on the history of *Honningsvag,* today's port of call. The Viking Cruise line's informative and educational videos are well done and very educational.

Breakfast arrives. We share the scrambled eggs, bacon, and fresh fruit plate. We each have a muffin; mine is blueberry and Anna's chocolate. I enjoy a V8 and coffee while Anna drinks orange juice and hot tea. She's still a little *'under the weather'* and like yesterday will be sending me out solo on today's excursion.

The high today is a **BRISK** 46 degrees and the low a **BRISKER** 42. The ship's staff warns that the weather changes rapidly. I *'go Nordic'* today. I'm wearing calf high extra thick socks, my over the ankle hiking boots, a long sleeve Foot Joy black compression shirt, a red, long sleeve 1/4 zip pullover, and a black zip up jacket. In the backpack, I have a heavy Rio Secco rose colored golf vest, my Euro grey and black scarf, gloves, and a beanie hat. My bestie, Griff, had a normal senior moment and forgot to send me off with hand warming packets he uses when golfing in Henderson's extremely harsh, cold, and windy winter days. For the record, I know he's **NOT** going to need them mid-summer as temperatures reach triple digits in June, July, and August.

Prior to boarding the excursion bus, I stop by the buffet and then go to the Deck One departure area trying to scalp Anna's ticket as the excursion is currently sold out. Despite my best efforts and shouts of "Tickets, who needs a ticket for today's sold out bus ride to North Cape?," I fail to find a taker. My ticket hustling skills are definitely rusty as all events around the world for the past five years or longer use paperless bar coded tickets. Plus, as I head to customer service to return Anna 's ticket, I am unceremoniously pulled into a soundproof, small back room by four, 6'6", 295 plus pound, retired, All-Pro defensive linemen. My shoes and socks are removed, and my feet are placed in a large bucket of ice water. A hood is tightly wrapped over my head making it very difficult to breathe. The over-zealous, very strong, undercover ship security guard handcuffs me to a rickety chair connected to four large electric car batteries. I am interrogated and threatened with corporal punishment (kick the shit out of me within an ounce or two of death) and multiple electric shocks unless I immediately reveal my motives for trying to hawk Anna's ticket.

Viktor explains it's just an *'old American thing'* to do when one has an extra ticket or two for an event, like an MLB game. Thankfully, they *'buy'* my story (not my ticket), release me, and makes notes in my file about the incident, resolution, and future action to be taken should this ever happen again on this or any future Viking river or ocean cruise. I have been added to Viking's "Top 10 Most Watched" passenger list for the remainder of my time on earth and possibly into the hereafter! Later in the day, the ship's captain and general manager disavow any knowledge of my harrowing incident. Sounds like a "Mission Impossible" line if you ask me. Viktor is rightly shaken, stunned, and woozy from this harrowing experience; but he's now back in line to exit the ship and board the bus. Anna instructs me to take lots of pictures, videos, and bring her back a gift, like yesterday's stuffed Reindeer or else!

I mosey down to Deck One, wait until 10:25 to disembark, and locate the tour bus for the 10:30 excursion around Honningsvag and the spectacular North Cape viewing area. Today, I am directed to Bus 14. Daisy, a young German lady, is today's narrator and Sara is the chariot driver. Norway's laws require all riders to fasten their seatbelts or be subject to steep fines and possible jail time. Accordingly, I *'buckle up.'*

Here are some *Honningsvag* facts I learn on today's excursion.

- Honningsvag is a town of 2,400 year round residents. It's Norway's most northern town, 1,300 miles from the North Pole. It was named by an explorer in the 1400's as the *'bay below the horn shaped mountain'*. This area is over 10,000 years old. The original inhabitants survived living off sea resources.

- Honningsvag is dotted with quaint, colorful houses that overlook the peaceful bay of the Barents Sea.

- Honningsvag is located on the ice free Bering Sea. From mid-May until late July, there is 24/7 sunlight. From late November until late January, the area is in total darkness as the sun disappears and goes on an extended *'paid holiday.'* The clear, dark winter skies offer a great viewing venue to witness the magical green, red, yellow, and violet Northern Lights. Forecasters predict more intense solar flares will happen in the future.

- Honningsvag is situated at a bay on the southeastern side of the large island of Magerøya. The famous North Cape and its visitor center are located on the northern side of the island. Honningsvag is a port of call for cruise ships, especially in summer months.

- Though it was named by the Vikings, nothing in the main town, Honningsvag — apart from its whitewashed church — predates the Second World War. Retreating Nazi occupiers, facing defeat, burned everything but the 19th century sanctuary to the ground.

- The North Cape is the point where the Norwegian Sea, part of the Atlantic Ocean, meets the Barents Sea, part of the Arctic Ocean.

- The North Cape was discovered in 1553 by British sailors attempting to find a sea route through the Northeast Passage. Our tour excursion bus is taking us there. It's a unique, natural opportunity to witness firsthand the stunning Magerøya

Island. The North Cape is the furthest north one can travel by land in Norway.

- The drive up to North Cape passes by stark, rocky, unattractive landscape devoid of trees. The grass is dead; but the guide says it *'comes back'* for a few months in the summer. Along the route, we see numerous reindeer, some nursing recently born babies.

- Every year, Sami families from *Karasjok*, about 250 kilometers (156 miles) south, bring their reindeer herds north and allow them to scatter throughout the island.

- You must travel 46 miles inland to see trees and mosquitoes.

- The plateau is accessed by Route E69. It's an 80-mile, or 129 kilometer long road that includes driving through five tunnels. This roadway is the northern most network of roads in the world.

- Considered the northernmost point of the European continent, Knivskjellodden can only be reached by hiking nine kilometers (5.6 miles) in about six hours from the North Cape parking lot. This is as far north as one can travel on Magerøya.

- Explorers located the northeast passage Arctic shipping route connecting the Atlantic and Pacific Oceans. It provides a 10% to 40% quicker alternative route to China and India. While dangerous, icy waters made the early years' journeys challenging, the reduction in sea ice has increased the shipping lanes and made the journey much safer.

- The fishing villages specialize in catching salmon, cod, and red king crab, many are 6' long and weigh 22 pounds.

- Ocean fishermen use fishing line tied to a piece of wood to catch fish in the ocean Fly or cast fishing is popular when fishing in rivers in the Fjords.

- Sami indigenous people still live a nomadic lifestyle in the high Arctic villages hunting, fishing, and trading.

- *Gjesværstappen Nature Reserve* is a group of three high, steep-sided, grass-covered islands that come together and create an ideal location with the sea rich in nutrients. It's a bird watchers paradise and nature reserve. The grass-covered islands are home to large colonies of sea birds such as puffins, razor-billed auk, kittiwake, gannet, cormorant, guillemot, and sea eagles. Visitors ride boats to observe the birds living on the cliffs.

- On today's excursion, Viktor sees many almost bald *'Mike Gardner and Griff haircuts'* on the bus. He almost taps a few guys on the shoulder and says, "What are you (Griff or Mike) doing here?"

- During the winter, the government cleans the roadways every 12 hours.

- June, July, and August summer visitors fill the hotels, some of which were formerly used for housing during the 1994 Winter Olympics.

- Signs along the road indicate *'Stop For Reindeer.'* Traffic comes to a halt when reindeer cross the road. If a reindeer decides to take a nap on the roadway, a major traffic jam occurs.

- Reindeer fir is the warmest of all animal firs.

- Eagles aggressively attempt to steal newborn reindeer up to three months old. Mother reindeer carefully watch over their babies.

- Red poles placed along both sides of the roadway mark the location of the edge of the road for drivers when it snows. A similar system can be found in America's Yellowstone National Park.

- In 1664, *Andrew Terrill*, an Italian author, completed an epic 7,000 mile journey on foot and cross country skiing from the southernmost point on the Italian mainland, *Melito di Porto Salvo*, to the northernmost point in Norway, North Cape.

The higher the bus takes us up to North Cape, the fog rolls in, thereby decreasing visibility.

So far on our Norway excursions, Viktor learns many things about Bears, Eagles, Vikings, and Dolphins. Rumor has it the NFL plans to schedule an outdoor regular season game in 2026 near North Cape in Norway. NFL field construction personnel will be arriving soon to mark off the field, hire locals to remove the rocks, and level the location prior to installing a synthetic field. Old wooden fish drying racks will be converted into temporary bleachers and team benches. Lift style cranes will be shipped in from somewhere to hoist wooden pallets high above the field for the offensive and defensive coordinators to observe game action and use smoke signals or spears to send plays to their team's bench. Enough room will be left around the playing field for cars to park very, very close to each other. Drivers will keep their high beam lights on to illuminate the playing field, especially if it's a late season game during dark winter.

The game-cast will be bounced off Norwegian 1970's, AOL, dial-up satellites back to New York City for an eight hour time delayed broadcast. TV announcers will be based in Los Angeles and they'll call the game while watching the grainy delayed telecast. FOX, ABC, CBS, and NBC will be bidding on the exclusive TV rights to the delayed broadcast, starting at 4:00 AM EST. At the present time, there will be no Sirius Satellite Radio, Prime Video,

Apple TV, ESPN, or Paramount streaming accounts or live broadcast of the game. But remember, money talks and the NFL, a cash cow in its own rights, loves money!

Teams will stay in two-man, wind resistant tents that max out at 34 degrees so players can get the feel of the nomadic Sami lifestyle in this remote part of Norway. Norwegian nutritionists and cooks will use local delicacies to create meals for both teams. Air Force One and Two will fly both teams to Norway 36 hours before game time and return the teams home 72 hours after the game is '*in the books*' to allow a day or two for local sightseeing and provide ample time for both teams to game plan for their next games the following Sunday.

It takes about an hour to reach North Cape. Everyone must get off the bus. Viktor has 45 minutes to check out the sites. The Visitors Center is located in the main (and only) building. Located three floors down, there's a theatre showing a short movie about this unique area. I don't go inside. Instead, I walk to the right towards the Fjords and ocean. The rocky, gravel landscape makes walking slow lest one trip, fall, and tears their pants or breaks a wrist, arm, ankle, or leg. To denote that they were there, previous visitors created rock artifacts that obviously meant something to them. I stop, gather up about a dozen, various shaped stones, and create a rocky coat of arms or an ancient Chinese symbol letting others know that I was there, too.

At the edge of the Fjord, there's a steep, long drop off to the rocks and water below. While it's a '*gotta take lots of pictures, videos and a selfie or three,*' it is **NOT** prudent, wise, or safe to stand close to the edge while having a picture taken, especially if the photographer says, "Just take a few steps back." The results would probably lead to a horrific, life-ending accident.

While walking back to the main building, I see a one man tent set up next to a bike. Who the hell is camping in this god forsaken cold, damp, rocky, foggy, and desolate location and why? I venture over and speak with the brave, carefree camper whose name I forget and learn about his adventure. It's simply a personal challenge to ride the bike 34 kilometers **UP** from town to North Cape and hang out **ALONE** for a few days. When asked what's for breakfast, the young man points to a small pot heated with propane to make oatmeal. We didn't get into the sleeping or hygiene practices; but it was clear to me that this early 30's man has his *'shit together'*.

Just before entering the main building, I spot a man in his late 50's, early 60s, wearing **SHORTS** and sitting on his non-electric bike packed with camping gear on both sides of the back tire. The weather is in the low 40's. It's cold, damp, and windy. The fog is rolling in. Rain is forecast. What was he thinking when he got up today, most likely after spending the night camping outdoors? *'Let's take a 34 kilometer bike ride down the hill to town on a cold, damp, windy, foggy, and rainy day on a 1.5 lane road!'* Are these Norwegians nuts, crazy, fearless, or a combination of all three? It wasn't in my nature to ask him.

Inside the visitors center, I find an expansive souvenir store and load up on *'I just gotta have one of this and that,'* along with a few stamped and ready to mail postcards, and a gift for Anna. I am *'old school.'* I invest a small fortune in stamps to mail the postcards back to family and friends in America.

The time is nearing 12:45, the bus departure time. Being from Las Vegas where nothing, squat, zero, starts on time, I hustle down three flights of stairs to watch the video. It is an outstanding production shown in a room filled with North Cape history. The clock shows 12:49. I hustle up three flights of stairs hoping the bus has **NOT** left without me. As I scan the parking lot for Bus 14, a tour guide sees me, calls out and says, "You are late! You will have to perform an act of contrition; write every passenger a personal apology note after verbalizing a heartfelt apology when entering the bus and sing the Norway national anthem." When I get on the bus, **EVERY** seat is occupied except for my assigned seat in the last row. Every passenger has their heads down. No one wants to make eye contact with me...all this over being a mere 4 minutes, 36 seconds late! Whatever!

We have a new team taking us back to the ship. Margot, a French National, is our tour guide and Tony is our bus driver. Tony has a tough job. It's raining. Dense fog creates low visibility. Let's hope he can see the asphalt road so we can all return in one piece. Margot has it easy peasy. Thanks to the fog, there's nothing to see, so nothing to describe. Plus, we took the same road up. I seriously doubt the scenery on either side of the road has dramatically changed. Margot adds few tidbits of information not mentioned on the ride up.

- The Greenland shark lives 500 years and reaches full maturity at 150 years of age.

- There are reindeer, seals, and a variety of bird species living here. There are no predators, like wolves or polar bears.

- During dark winter, from 11:00 to 13:00, there is less darkness than the rest of the day. If there are no storms or clouds, the Northern Lights, or Aurora Borealis, put on a fantastic and unique show nightly.

- There is a dark green house located at the intersection of the roadway from town to the left hand turn up to North Cape. This 'house' marks the location where cars and buses assemble in winter to safely convoy to the top.

- There are three supermarkets on the island. Fish caught in fresh and ocean water provide protein for local diets.

- When the lakes freezes, ice fishing is popular. Salt prevents ocean waters from freezing.

- Red king crab is a delicacy. It's shipped worldwide and contrary to what one thinks, it's very expensive for local consumption.

- Berries provide a good source of Vitamin C. *Tamsøya* is the lush berry growing island near the North Cape. Locals pick and preserve berries for year round consumption.

- Blueberries from Morocco are sold in local grocery stores.

- The area is very safe. There's little if any crime. People respect each other and their belongings. It's not necessary to lock house doors or cars at night. The local police department is open from 10:00 to 14:00 on Mondays and Thursdays. Legend has it that a lady stole someone's car but brought it back the next day because she *'felt guilty'* for her dishonest actions.

- Locally, there's no hospital. It's a four-hour drive should someone need an X-ray. It's a 20-hour drive or 15-minute helicopter ride to the closest hospital. Patients needing immediate medical attention are airlifted to the closest hospital. Norway's government medical insurance covers all travel costs.

Once the bus arrives back at port, I quickly head to the nearby souvenir store to buy a few last minute goodies. I am back on board at 14:00. I head to the swimming pool area on Deck 7 and enjoy an All American lunch consisting of a Costco size, perfectly grilled hot dog, fries, salad, pickles, olives, and coleslaw, all washed down with Norwegian Pilsner beer.

Catching up with Anna, I review the day's journey and show her the videos and pictures I took. After a quick workout and shower, it's time for dinner. Tonight, we decide to dine at the sit down restaurant and are assigned table 68. Sitting to my right, Anna's left, are two elderly ladies, one who is turning 86 years old next month.

They have traveled the world for over 20 years. Anna and I engage in traveling *'shit happens'* stories with them. For some strange reason (**NOT**) our stories top their stories by 4.5 kilometers.

I order a Caesar salad, extra anchovies, light dressing with no extra parmesan cheese, the Norwegian fish stew, and two glasses of a smooth Cabernet Sauvignon. Blueberry cheesecake and decaf Americano coffee complete the meal. Anna orders a half chicken roasted in beer, veggie soup, a local dessert, coffee, and wine. Satisfied and nourished, Anna heads to the room to rest. She's still fighting a nasty cold. I head to the Viking Living Room on Deck One, find *'my corner leather couch,'* plug in my iPhone, listen to classical piano music, enjoy an adult beverage, and author more stories. As the clock strikes midnight, I'm reminded that it's 24/7 daylight outside. I leave the living room area and retire to Room 6041 where I find Anna fast asleep. What can I say other than it was another extraordinary Viking Mars cruise day. Can't wait to see what Sunday, an *'at sea day,'* will bring! Until the A.M., good night!

*****

Sunday, June 2 — Day 69
Day At Sea

Today is an *'at sea day.'* The ship is swiftly cutting thru the cold North Sea waters for the 450 plus mile journey to *Svalbard and Longyearbyen.* Tomorrow, Viking Mars will dock there. We will spend Monday and Tuesday nights in port.

After a long night of writing, I woke up at 08:15, checked the sports scores on the ESPN App, and the latest news on the Fox News App. Prior to retiring last night, I used the ship's four-page Daily Briefing newsletter to plan our Sunday. Speakers will be presenting detailed information about the next port stop, *Svalbard and Longyearbyen.* Plus, they will present the history of the brave and adventurous Viking Explorers who sought new lands and shipping routes. There's also a *'sales pitch'* about future Viking Ocean and River Cruises. Needless to say, we are both very happy with Viking Cruise Lines.

The first lecture starts at 09:30. We rush to put on our *'Sunday best cruising outfits,'* grab a takeaway cup of coffee and a cappuccino, and head to Deck 2 to learn about the next port stop. We hope to be smarter and better informed about the upcoming two days in port. When the presentation ends, we take the elevator to the Deck 7 Explorers Lounge for breakfast. We enjoy fruit, a waffle, orange juice, pastry, coffee, and cappuccino.

Our next stop on today's agenda is Deck 2 to learn about *Futures River and Ocean Cruises*. Viking uses a slick, Hollywood produced 4K video to entice traveling cruisers to pull out their credit cards and place a mere $50 deposit on each and every future cruise. The ultra-slick, professionally produced videos show smiling, well-dressed men and women having *'the time of their lives'* enjoying a cocktail or wine (never shots and beer) and dining on lobster, a medium rare filet, a mixed green or Caesar salad, and sharing a baked potato at one of the exclusive restaurants on their understated and elegantly decorated cruise ships. The scenes are produced to *'suck you in'* especially if you only have a .004% interest in a future cruise(s).

The video shows couples enjoying one of the many exclusive Viking excursions that are included in the cruise price. The unspoken sales pitch ends with *'getting the audience excited'* by showing cruise ships and riverboats slowly cruising on bright, sunny days. The sky is **ALWAYS** bright blue and cloudless. The ships cruise in dark blue water or on beautiful rivers. In the background, viewers see inviting and enticing ports of call cityscapes. After 15 short minutes, here comes the brief, five-minute *'subtle sales pitch'* that includes **ALL** the benefits of booking future cruises before disembarking. Some of the benefits, with the mere $50 deposit include selecting your dates and room type for your next cruise. Potential cruisers see the regular room price and the *'on board'* discounted room price displayed in 14" colored letters. But one must book **BEFORE** the cruise ends to get the preferred price. Once signed up, you also get an immediate $100 credit per guest credit on your current cruise. Are we participating in the *'Deal Or No Deal'* game show? We look at each other and say, **"It's time to make a deal!"**

The traveling seniors book two future cruises. Cruise 1 is a September 2026, 12-day journey starting and ending in Milwaukee, Wisconsin, thru the Great Lakes and into Canada.

Cruise 2 is a ten-day, late March 2025 river cruise through Portugal on one of Viking's newest riverboats. We have an appointment on Tuesday, June 4 at 16:00, with the cruise consultant to learn about the Antarctica adventure and future cruise(s) on Viking Mars.

After *'bringing out the credit card'* and *'committing'* to the Great Lakes cruise, Anna heads to the room for a nap. I go down to the Deck One Explorers Lounge and find a seat on my favorite couch in the living room sitting area. I sit there for a while, then head back to my room.

It's time for dinner. We look at the sit down restaurant menu and the buffet dinner choices and decide to eat at the sit down restaurant. I order a Caesar salad, extra anchovies, light dressing, and no extra parmesan cheese. For my entrée, I select roasted duck breast with vegetables. I add a glass of Cabernet Sauvignon. For dessert, I go with blueberry pie, two scoops of vanilla ice cream, and an Americano decaf coffee. Anna goes prawns cocktail, medium rare beef tenderloin steak, and baked potato with butter and bacon bits. She selects two glasses of wine: a Cabernet Sauvignon and a Coppola red wine. For dessert, she orders — you guessed it — vanilla ice cream topped with whipped cream and a side of chocolate sauce and an Americano decaf coffee. The food is excellent and *'hits the spot.'*

After dinner, we walk to the theater to listen to lectures about Monday and Tuesday excursions in Longyearbyen and Svalbard.

Here's what we learned from lecturer Corey Sandler:

- *Spitsbergen Island* is part of the Svalbard archipelago. The town of Longyearbyen is located on this island.

- The Svalbard archipelago is located very close to the top of the world, approximately 1,000 miles north of the Arctic Circle. Svalbard means *'cold coast.'* The area covers 24,000 square miles. There are five resident settlements and only 32 miles of pothole paved roads. The residents are *'alive'* and surprisingly very happy to live and work in this unique environment. Sixty percent of the land mass is covered with snow and ice year round. Many of the mountains have flat peaks.

- The average residency is six to eight years. As of December 2023, approximately 2,900 people call this area home. Most residents range in age from 25 to 44. Very few locals are over 65. Most residents rent homes and apartments from the *Pryamiden* coal company, the university extension, or the Norwegian government. All shopping is *'Duty Free'* for both locals and tourists.

- Locally, there is very limited healthcare. Residents needing medical attention, surgeries, or other care for life threatening emergencies are evacuated via helicopter to the mainland for medical care. The cost is covered by the Norwegian medical system.

- In the summer, the top six to eight feet of the ground is dirt. Below that, the permafrost layer extends more than 1,500 feet down. The ground remains frozen year round. Hence, dead bodies cannot be buried here for fear of skeletons being pushed up by the thawing permafrost.

- Both being born and dying in Longyearbyen is highly discouraged as a matter of policy, according to Norway Today. In fact, this policy applies to Svalbard in general. People who are gravely ill should fly to mainland Norway for treatment and well just in case the treatment doesn't work. If you do happen to die in town, it's possible to be cremated and the ashes buried, but this requires a license and lots of paperwork that could take a month.

- Read More: https://www.grunge.com/436842/ heres-why-this-town-forbids-the-burials-of-bodies/

- The Gulf Stream keeps the west side of the islands climate relatively mild while the east coast side remains frozen year round. For this reason, the cruise ship will travel southwest to Iceland.

- Greenland is the nearest land that's 430 miles away. Tromsø, Norway is 730 miles south.

- The sun rises on April 19 and sets on August 24, providing 24-hours of daylight. From August 27 to February 29, the area is in **TOTAL DARKNESS**; but on clear nights, the locals enjoy the Northern Lights show. The intervening days remain grey and cloudy as the region transfers from 100% light to 100% darkness. Legend has it that when a resident was asked. "What's it like to live in total darkness?," the reply was simply, "We turn on the lights!" Another unique occurrence that makes you crazy occurs during the summer when a friend calls to go for a walk at 03:00.

- Svalbard Mountains are snowy and ice covered year round. It is also classified as an *'Artic desert.'*

- Polar bears are a natural predator. There are about 1,000 polar bears in the area. There are signs warning residents and tourists **NOT** to go out of the city proper without a guide who is carrying a rifle. Polar bears present a clear and present danger. Guards' rifles use three inch long bullets to ward off and, if absolutely necessary, kill attacking polar bears.

- An elaborate system of transporting coal from mines to ocean vessels was designed and built in the early 1900's. The system could transport 120, one-ton buckets of coal in one hour. It was an engineering feat that is still visible today. The system was shut down in 1987 when the coal company switched to trucks to transport coal.

- In 1596, Dutch explorer *William Barentsz* found this uninhabited land while searching for a faster shipping Northeast Passage lane to the Far East.

- Whaling was the main occupation when the area was first settled in the 1500's.

- Whaling was a popular business. Over 300 ships from numerous nations would descend on the area. Thousands of whales were killed and processed. The blubber was cooked in whaling pots that produce whale oil. The whale fluids were nicknamed *'blubber cement.'* It held the whaling pots that cooked blubber into oil together. The pots are still visible today.

- In 1607, explorer *Henry Hudson* landed. Unfortunately, after three years, he didn't find a Northeast Passage to China. In 1612, 130 whalers and explorers were buried as deep as the permafrost would allow.

- During the 17th and 18th centuries, most of the remote whaling and sealing outposts went quiet.

- The region was repopulated in the 19th and 20th century when explorers discovered there were business opportunities to make money from mining coal.

- In 1891, Hamburg America Cruise Line passengers first visited the area. In 1901, industrialist John Munro Longyearbyen, who created his fortune in Michigan via theft from insider information gained during his surveying career in mining and lumber businesses, arrived in Svalbard. He studied the land and returned in 1905. He purchased most of the land and named the town Longyearbyen after himself. He was instrumental in creating the coal mining industry. In 1917, he liquidated his positions. From 1918 to 1969, a Norwegian coal company controlled the mines and owned the land. Today, only one of the original seven mines is in operation.

- In 1905, the Swedish and Russian Svalbard alliance ended. In 1920, Norway gained sovereignty over Svalbard. Even today, military installations are prohibited. From 1925 to 1928, explorers tried to reach the North Pole from Svalbard. On May 7, 1926, an explorer used a blimp to reach the North Pole.

- Svalbard played an important role in World. War II. In 1941, the Germans came to Svalbard and erected a weather station. In 1943, allied forces bombing eliminated the weather station.

- Coal mining operations were scheduled to close in 2022. Today, one mine remains open. There is a rumor that Russians still mine coal for steel production in their war against Ukraine.

- The Svalbard or *SvalSat* is a satellite ground station located on *Plataberget* near Longyearbyen in Svalbard, Norway. It opened in 1997. The *'farm'* has over 100 white mushroom caps. It's the largest ground station for low orbit satellites circumnavigating the planet. The satellites travel North to South at 17,000 miles per hour and capture non-military data from the entire world in a mere 90 minutes as the earth rotates left to right around the sun. SvalSat and KSAT's Troll Satellite Station in Antarctica are the only ground stations that can see a low altitude polar orbiting satellite. Data is transmitted to partnering agencies worldwide, including NASA, via 2 high-speed 850 miles under water cables.

- In 2008, Norway opened a 500-foot deep Global Seed Vault in Svalbard. All nations can store precious seeds used for food growth and production. The seeds belong to the country who stored them. The vault is immune from any manmade or weather related events. Almost one million seed samples from all over the world are stored here, with a total capacity for up to four times that.

- Finally, here are two unique Norwegian laws. The government has alcohol rationing cards in place to prevent excessive alcohol consumption especially during dark winter.

- Law two requires carrying indoors and outdoors shoes to prevent tracking coal dust into homes.

Hopefully, every reader now has a great understanding and appreciation for this remote and challenging outpost where hearty, outdoor loving, and friendly people call home.

Around 22:30, while standing on the Room 6041 veranda, prior to climbing into bed, I see snow-capped mountains partially obstructed by a low bank of clouds. Courtesy of former Monday Night Football announcer and Dallas Cowboys quarterback Dandy Don Meredith, it's time to "Turn out the lights, the party is over." It's time to turn in for the night in anticipation of tomorrow's docking in Longyearbyen Svalbard, Norway.

*****

Monday, June 3 — Day 70
Svalbard, Norway

We rise at 07:11, in port, at Longyearbyen Svalbard, Norway. It's a *'crisp'* 41 degree cloudy day. At 07:30, we turn on the television and listen to the daily announcements, including today's safety briefing of **"DON'T go outside the city limits ALONE without an armed escort to protect you from polar bears."**

We pass on in-room dining, choosing instead to enjoy breakfast at one of the many places aboard that are offering a variety of breakfast options. Anna is still not feeling 100%. She decides to stay on the ship, order room service, rest and read. Given today's weather forecast, it's a smart decision. I see a *'business opportunity'* to make a few *'sheckles'* by scalping her excursion ticket for today's sold-out siteseeing adventure. I head to the buffet area on Deck 7 in the rear of the ship, hold up the ticket in my right hand and loudly call out, "Ticket, who needs a ticket for today's two-hour site-seeing tour of Svalbard?" No takers. I repeat the message in the Viking Living Room on Deck 1 and the Deck 7 Explorers Lounge. Again, I just get a bunch of *'nasty looks'* but no takers. Finally, I *'give up'* and return the very valuable excursion ticket to Guest Services on Deck 1. The Guest Service agent informs me that returning the ticket two hours or less before the excursion starts results in a $200 fine for failure to adhere to the ship's three-day cancellation policy.

The agent says, "Sorry, no exceptions, I just charged your on board account $200. And thanks for cruising with Viking!"

Two hundred bucks lighter in the wallet, I stop by the General Manager's office to chat with GM Shauvik Chaudhuri. We met at the Deck 7 Explorers Lounge on May 25 shortly after I boarded the ship. We spend about twenty minutes exchanging career and traveling stories. He told me what *'closed the deal'* for him to join Viking. Shauvik was *'sold'* on Viking's Operating and Guest Services Mission Statement that emphasizes *'you never get a second chance to make a good first impression.'* Viking focuses on *'the little things'* for guest enrichment. Staff go *'out of their way'* to do *'whatever is necessary'* to ensure every guest enjoys the cruise and the *'Viking Experience.'*

I mention our excellent experiences with the ship's staff. Every onboard employee clearly *'lives up'* to the company's Mission Statement and greets all guests with a friendly, cheerful smile. As Shauvik pointed out, Viking's operations are **NOT** focused on *'the glitz and milking every last nickel'* out of their valued guests. The ship's 500 team members look sharp in their uniforms and appearance. They all exhibit *'superior customer service skills'* and don't push the *'extras'* like spa treatments and jewelry purchases. There's no loud noise, no slot machines, and no **"I WON"** or **"I LOST"** screams from people playing blackjack, poker, or craps tables. There's no *'I had too much to drink' bravado'* and *'rabble rousing'* at bars, loud music, bingo, or silly games. Viking Mars projects an *'understated elegance'* (Anna's favorite saying) throughout the ship. Everything is in its right place. I promise Shauvik to mail a copy of my 2013 first edition book **"SH?#! Happens, Traveling With John and Leslie"** and when it's finished, I'll mail a copy of my 2024 book about our current 78-day journey. Shauvik has *'ship things'* to attend to. Before leaving, I ask if it would be possible to get a *'behind the* *scenes tour'* of the three-year old vessel. Unfortunately, that's *'not going to happen'* this time around.

It's time for breakfast. I head to the breakfast buffet on Deck 7. Unfortunately, the room closed a mere 11-minutes ago. Breakfast Plan B takes me to the Explorers Lounge on Deck 7 forward. There's a small food counter offering breakfast items including oatmeal, fruit, pastries, and fresh bread. I select oatmeal, a mixed fruit bowl, and a Danish pastry with blueberry jam. On the bar adjacent to the food counter, I grab a cup of coffee and a glass of freshly squeezed OJ.

Around 10:00, the sun is *'trying'* to peak out. I head to our room to gather up my back pack and appropriate warm clothing. I knock on the door; however, Anna does not answer. Apparently she has *'skipped out,'* must likely hanging out in the Explorers Lounge on Deck 7. When I reach into my pocket for the room key card, I cannot find it. Luckily, *'G'* our room steward, is nearby and lets me into the room. I toss the room in vain; however, I cannot find the *'gotta have with you'* key and identification card that allows access to our room and exiting and re-boarding the ship. I just joined Anna as a member of the card carrying, dues paying member of the *'lost room entry and exiting, e-boarding the ship card club.'* She's still in the lead by a two to one margin. I need the card to exit the ship prior to joining today's tour. The clock is ticking — it is almost time to exit the ship for today's excursion. I sprint down five flights of stairs to the Deck One Customer Service Area, explain my dilemma, and obtain a new card in less than 45 seconds. The representative confirms my room number and reminds me there will be a $250 fine added to my onboard account since Anna and I passed the "no charge limit" of two lost ship cards.

The customer service area has four agents sitting at four large desks. Each desk has two comfortable side chairs for guests. One of the male of representatives reminds me of a Maui basketball referee associate and friend named 'Romel.' I almost say, "Romel, when did you start working for Viking?"

It's time to leave the ship and board the tour bus. Andrea, today's tour guide, is from Sweden. The 30 mph wind makes for a very cold day. The unyielding, fierce winds cut through my 15 or so layers of clothing and leave red marks on my exposed cheeks. However, it's warm sitting in the back row of the bus. I am on the left side of the bus. The good news is the window next to me was recently washed, allowing for clear photos.

The landscape is stark and barren, like a picture from the 1920's *"Oklahoma"* dust bowl. Most of the apartments, condos, and single family homes are within a stone's throw of the Svalbard Mall and CO-OP grocery store. A few adventurous souls live in the surrounding hills, isolated from a majority of civilization.

The permafrost layer creates an unstable foundation for homes, apartments, and commercial and retail buildings. Depending on the depth of the annual thaw, older homes and buildings will *'shift'* and may require rebuilding. Newer homes are built on poles a minimum of three to four meters high to prevent shifting as the ground thaws.

Scooters and snowmobiles outnumber the number of people living here and are the favorite mode of transportation, just like bikes in Amsterdam.

The tour first stops at the Visitors Center for a 45-minute detailed *'show and tell'* experience about the history of Svalbard and the surrounding area. Our guide, Andrea, warns everyone that this is a **'45-minute'** not a **'46 or longer'** minute stop. Andrea plans to keep this tour on schedule. The bus waits for no one. So, if you are not on time, the bus will leave without you. You will be left to fend for yourself.

Andrea is very confident, articulate, and well versed in local history. She explains the history of the artifacts and small scale models representing the area's development and history. I can't resist making a small investment in Svalbard souvenirs, including a book about the area.

The second stop is the famous "Polar Bear Warning Sign." Andrea takes everyone's picture standing next to, while pointing to, the unique warning sign.

On the third phase of the tour, the bus uses the *'pothole two lane roadway'* to take us around the town's perimeter. We get to see everything there is to see, including the stark hillsides and mountains, the mall, housing units, local businesses, coal mine buildings, the discontinued coal transportation system, the airport, two cruise ship docks, the vast damp wasteland, and the river.

Below is the information Andrea shares with the group today.

- Coal mining took root in the late 1800's. In the 1920's, the Norwegian government took over mining operations.

- Most of the residents in this tiny Arctic metropolis are Norwegians, but there are residents from around 50 other countries. In all, around 2,100 people call this place "home", and they enjoy a strong sense of unity and fellowship.

- There's a local police force but no military presence. Norway has a coast guard fleet.

- The mountains are 90% coal seams. Many have north/south folds like an accordion. Mountain tops are mostly flat.

- There are no trees or bushes. Cold mining operations go 120 to 150 meters horizontally versus traditional vertical mine shafts.

- Most of the village residents live within a few kilometers of the Mall. There are only 48 kilometers (32 miles) of roads in the area. Driving off road is strictly prohibited. Most areas of Svalbard are inaccessible due to its remote location and climate.

- In this remote, isolated region, mortal danger is ever present all the time. It either breaks you down or builds you up.

- If you live in this region, you have to love outdoor exploring, sports, and activities or Svalbard is not for you, especially during dark winter months.

- Ninety percent of housing stock is rental condos and apartments in two to three story buildings that are mostly owned by the Norwegian mining company or the Norwegian government.

At the end of the 2 1/2 hour tour, Viktor takes a Viking provided shuttle bus (local cab vans) to the Mall. First, I join a line and look for a bus. Not finding one, I wander around the dock area, trying to say reasonably warm as the cold temperatures and 25 mph plus winds pass thru my numerous layers of clothing and nip at my cheeks. Finally, the line I first started out in is in fact the **CORRECT LINE** to catch a van to the Mall.

Arriving at the Mall, my first stop is the local post office. I purchase four postcard stamps. Two postal workers explain the cost and time (about one month give or take) to mail a package from this remote location to the United States.

The exterior of the Mall is stark and unattractive; however, once inside, you notice the stores display very colorful clothing and souvenir items. There are three restaurants and a sporting goods store. The CO-OP grocery store, the only grocery store in town, is brightly lit and offers a complete array of grocery, dairy, meat, fish, produce, bakery, frozen foods, and cleaning products as well as souvenirs, household items, men, and women personal grooming products. It's about 75% the size of an American grocery store and a smaller version of a Walmart Superstore.

At the CO-OP store, I buy a polar bear stuffed animal for Anna and a suitcase to haul my stash of souvenirs home in lieu of mailing them and waiting for their arrival, hopefully before Labor Day.

For lunch, I visit a local deli restaurant and enjoy a fabulous tuna fish sandwich on a large round, very thin wheat roll. I wash it down with a local Spitsbergen Pilsner beer. Willpower prevents me from trying the *'to die for'* desserts.

While walking through the Mall, I am pleasantly surprised when one of the stateroom staff on Deck 6 recognizes me, addresses me by name, and warmly greets me!

I notice children riding bikes home from school. Some are wearing helmets. There's a large, challenging skate board park near the Mall.

Svalbard has a small, 250 student university. The school offers a variety of elective courses. Students usually stay for two semesters and intensely *'dig into'* specialty courses such as *Survival Skills at -20 Celsius; Survival Hiking Skills Without a Guide or Rifle to Avoid Being Eaten by Polar Bears; How to Survive Swimming in the 50 Degree Ocean and Live to Tell About It; How to Avoid Becoming a Coal Miner's Daughter; Snowmobiling Down Steep Slopes While Being Chased by an Avalanche; Two-day, 48-hour Cross Country Skiing During Dark Winter; Exotic Recipes for Bear and Reindeer Burgers and Stews; Camping Skills on the Frozen, Rocky Tundra; and Starting a Fire and Outdoor Meal Preparation in -20 degree Celsius Weather After Little or No Sleep.*

The smart students study geology, biology, physics, weather, communications, and native living. Some of the tour guides are former students. When students leave Svalbard, they are ready to take on the nomadic Svalbard, Norway lifestyle for at least a few weeks before losing their sanity and focus on real life.

No one misbehaves here. The village is run like Las Vegas when the mob **RAN THINGS**. If someone *'crosses the line, local enforcers'* take a shovel and the person for a *'ride out of town to the coal mines,'* dig a hole, and start a fire. The body is gone forever. After being unaccounted for a few days, locals assume the missing person must have wandered off and was eaten by a polar bear. The story at the local bar goes like this: "I told him not to go out alone at night, past the restraint ropes and sign indicating don't pass this point without an armed guard with big rifle for protection." **That's the story and the boys in town are sticking to it.**

After a fun filled day, I head to the gym for a quick work out and hit the steam room, ice room, ice bucket challenge, jacuzzi, and ice bath (to soak his feet). After a refreshing shower, I join Anna and new friends Billy and Adrienne for drinks and dinner.

Today was great fun-filled, learning, and exploring day. The ship remains in Svalbard overnight. So, tomorrow is another exploration day in this very remote and very unique part of the world. Good night from the Viking Mars docked in Svalbard, Norway!

*****

Tuesday, June 4 — Day 71
Longyearbyen - Svalbard, Norway

This morning, Viking Mars **MUST** abandon its shoreline berth to allow another cruise ship to dock *'in the front row.'* Did someone screw up and not reserve a two-night docking pass or did the other cruise line *'pull rank'* on Viking? Around 07:00, the Captain and navigator deftly maneuver the Viking Mars into the bay. Her passengers hardly notice the position change. Today, tenders will ferry guests from the ship to the dock and back again.

Today is our final day in Norway. We get up at 07:15, just in time to listen to an important announcement from the Captain. Rough seas are projected for the next two days while we're at sea. The Captain tells us the ship will be departing one hour earlier today, at 14:00. This change allows the Captain to increase the ship's speed later today and tomorrow. He will slow the ship down when we encounter rough seas on Thursday. The *'rough seas'* may turn out to be a ***'Disneyland E ticket ride.'*** Better get the Dramamine and sea sickness bags out! There will be **NO** hanging over the verandas to relieve sea sickness. Why, you ask? Someone's sea sickness could rain down on unsuspecting guests on lower floors.

Breakfast arrives at 07:45. It's our normal unimaginative breakfast of scrambled eggs, bacon, muffins, fresh fruit, fresh squeezed orange juice, V-8 juice, and coffee with cream. Anna is still not 100% and plans to stay on board again today. She makes a really good decision since it is very cold and extremely windy outside. I need to *'rock and roll'* and head to Deck One. Time is of the essence. I skip the shower, throw on numerous layers of warm clothing, hustle to Deck One, and add my name to the *'going ashore'* tender boat list.

Getting on the tender becomes an exciting, dangerous, and *'what the hell am I doing'* moment. The ocean is rocking and rolling. Waves send ice cold ocean water into the narrow ten inch gap between the ship and the tender. Three elderly men and women, who are carefully being assisted onto the rocking tender *'are in the wrong place at the wrong time.'* A huge wave drenches them from head to toe with the icy cold ocean water. Instead of getting on the tender, the crew members assist the *'cold and soaking wet guests'* to the Medical Center on Deck A. They are evaluated for frostbite, the onset of a bad cold, and pneumonia. Viking compensates them for this *'life altering experience'* with free first class room cruises for the rest of their natural lives. I hope I am lucky enough to get soaked when it's my turn to board the tender. When it's my turn to leave the ship, I carefully watch the ocean wave patterns and allow other passengers to go ahead of me until I'm 263.7% sure I will get an unpleasant, but very rewarding soaking and compensation package.

My *'solid gold'* plan fails. I get a command from the crew manning the tender "Get on **NOW** or wait 30-minutes for the next boat to take you to shore". I **MUST** go to the CO-OP grocery store to swap out suitcases. The suitcase I purchased yesterday was *'way too small.'* I need a much larger one to hold all of my *'just gotta have, why did I buy all of these shit souvenirs.'* Then, I **MUST** return to the ship and deliver the new suitcase to Anna and return to the dock prior to today's 11:00 shore excursion. Surprisingly, today's five minute ride to shore is relatively smooth. Occasionally, the tiny transport boat sways up and down, left to right and back to front in five foot swells. However, no one gets sick. That's a **PLUS!**

Upon exiting the tender, I am rudely smacked in the face by 47 mph gale force winds. My left leg is not 100% strong. Remember, one year ago, I had surgery to repair the Achilles tendon I tore **TWICE**. The high winds and rocking cause me to lose my balance and almost unceremoniously tumble into the cold, rough seas. Using the cold metal hand rails, I fight the wind **UP** the 10 meter long semi-icy metal ramp, reach solid ground, and walk a few steps to the waiting shuttle bus. It will depart at 9:30 and will take me to the CO-OP grocery store in the Svalbard Mall. Unlike yesterday, the sun is *'trying its best'* to come out of hiding from behind the clouds. It is 38 degrees Fahrenheit. Add in the 25 to 35 mph winds, it's closer to five to ten degrees Fahrenheit. If you don't believe me, you should feel my face and hands.

I arrive at the Mall at 09:35. I am 25-minutes early. All of the stores, including the CO-OP grocery store, open at 10:00. I stroll to the post office and mail four postcards. I notice an open door into the Mall. Inside, I locate a warm waiting area and get out of the fierce wind. The CO-OP opens exactly at 10:00 so I walk to the counter on the left side of the store to exchange the suitcase. The first clerk I encounter is **CLEARLY** new. It might be her **FIRST** day. She has **NO CLUE** about how to issue a refund and ring up the new purchase. An experienced clerk takes over, processes the refund, adds the price of the new suitcase, and graciously accepts my MasterCard for the price difference.

Quickly, or as quickly as a 75-year-old body can move, I board the shuttle bus to take me back to the dock and tender transportation area.

This shuttle bus is transporting three ship guests back to port. I walk quickly to the tender loading dock. Carrying my backpack and new suitcase, I carefully head down the icy metal ramp. As I attempt to step onto the small boat, a very strong gust of wind knocks me off stride. I lose my balance, go flying to the right, stagger, and regain my balance. Fortunately, *'I do NOT go face down'* on the dock (unlike Joe Frazier's second bout with Mohammed Ali as Howard Cosell screams out in his raspy nasally voice, **"Down goes Frazier!"**)

I text Anna and let her know I am on my way back to the ship. I plan to meet her on Deck One and hand off the new upgraded suitcase. At least that's the plan for the next 27 minutes, 19 seconds. Unfortunately, today's excursion leaves the dock area minutes after my projected return to the ship. *'Houston, we have a problem!'*

Anna understands the plan; however, she realizes I won't have time to return to the ship, hand her the new suitcase, and return to the dock for the 11:00 excursion departure. What should I do with the suitcase? Should I return to the ship, give Anna the new suitcase, and return to shore for another excursion? I approach one of the tender's staff, explains the situation, ask if a Viking tender staff member can take the suitcase back to the ship, and have one of the employees loading and unloading the tender drop the suitcase off at Guest Services on Deck 1? The tender supervisor seems confused by my request but offers to secure the suitcase on the dock where I can pick it up after my tour. I **ALMOST** *'buy into this alternative;'* however, what if it rains? So, I climb aboard the tender and ask a gentleman if he would take the suitcase to Guest Services on Deck One where Anna will be waiting. He graciously agrees to help me out. I call Anna and explain **PLAN B** for getting the new suitcase to her.

Today's excursion leaves at 11:00. Our group will learn all about raising and training sled dogs. But for now, I have 30-minutes to kill. The Viking tour excursions clerk suggests I wait in a nearby building until the tour bus arrives. **GREAT** idea, it's not getting any warmer. The wind continues to howl and continues to penetrate my 15 layers of clothing and create frost bites on my exposed cheeks.

I hang out inside a small office lobby with other guests waiting for the sled dog tour. A few minutes later, 6'6", 287 pound **Gunnar** shows up and uses his gruff voice to unceremoniously kick everyone out of the lobby — "Get the hell out of our office **NOW** or **ELSE!** I don't care **HOW** cold it is outside. **JUST** get out of here!" He is definitely a no nonsense, *'read my lips'* kind of guy. Fearing bodily harm for not complying, **ALL** of us frantically rush out the door, creating a stampede, and banging into each other. Four elderly people fall to the ground; but luckily avoid being trampled to death. Apparently, the lobby is an extension of the one and only important local dock office. In the office, we clearly see three young employees sitting at their desks, drinking coffee, eating Norwegian pastries, playing video games, and watching garbage, no brainer videos on their iPhone 3's. I assume Gunnar didn't want the tourists to see just how hard the locals run the all-important port operations. In my humble opinion, after observing *'this local talent pool,'* it's a wonder just how the huge cruise ships manage to enter the harbor area, not collide with each other, and dock in their assigned berths.

The 11:00 *'Learning About How Local Husky Dogs Pull Sleds'* bus arrives. The shortage of tour buses in this small island requires *'bus sharing'* to get guests to their tour destination and back. Today's tour guide is Stanislav. He is from Slovenia and has lived in this area for eight years! This is truly an amazing feat as most people only last two to three years is the desolate outpost. He provides us with a brief history of the Svalbard Longyearbyen area.

Stanislav shares the following information with us:

- In 1906, Norway acquired control of the region and in 1925, Norway was granted sovereignty over the region.

- Currently 2,597 people representing 60 nationalities live here.

- Homes **WERE** heated with coal. Today, they are heated with cleaner diesel fuel.

- *'On the rock,'* there's one gas station at Circle K. There is also just one grocery store.

- The Longyearbyen River runs down from the mountains into the ocean. It's not deep and it freezes in the winter.

- A University extension opened in 1993. About 250 students attend and live in student housing quarters. They must all learn to use firearms because of the polar bears. The University offers special courses geared towards the environment. Potential students apply and upon acceptance, come from all over the world for one to two semesters of study.

- There are 14 fenced-in dog yards. Some 600 spirited sled pulling dogs call Longyearbyen Svalbard home.

- People arriving here **CANNOT** secure long term housing if they don't have a job. Many of the local employers own housing.

- The bus passes by the sign warning about polar bears. Occasionally, someone *'borrows'* the sign. The last missing sign incident occurred two years ago.

- Graduating high school students are allowed to party and do *'stupid things'* for three days. Someone in the group *'gathered up the courage'* to remove the sign. Three days later, the sign was found in the Governor's car! He proclaimed, **"I didn't take it!"**

- There's a manmade lake between the mountains and the narrow two lane road. When the roadway was constructed, it created a barrier where the mountain runoff created the lake. The 14-kilometer long lake provides the town's drinking water.

- The town's first airport was removed from this desolate area. In 1975, the current airport opened a few kilometers down the road just past where cruise ships dock.

- The Northern Lights observatory was moved out of town because the area's growth created light pollution.

- During winter months when the roads are covered in snow, residents use snow mobiles to get from Point A to Point B.

- Remotely located cabins are visible in the distance. By law, all cabins **MUST** be connected to a public road. Gravel roads provide access to the cabins.

- Individuals must live and work locally for six months before buying a cabin.

- Local reindeer have short legs, move slowly, and are generally fat. Locals are used to living next door to reindeer.

- The terrain has no vegetation or trees. It's a desolate, unappealing landscape; however, those who live and work here love the area.

- A weather observatory was constructed in 2007 to gather weather data about the surrounding area.

- During winter darkness, locals wear headlamps on their way to work.

As we near the location of the sled dogs, Stanislav gives us a safety briefing. Once everyone exits the bus, an armed guard will escort us to see the sled dogs. We are told, *'in NO uncertain terms'* to **NOT** wander off, just **STAY** together. Not wanting an outside chance of becoming a polar bear's next meal, the group stays in a tight formation.

I definitely have *'gone to the dogs.'* I thought about abandoning the tour, trying to attract polar bears, sacrificing myself by taking *'one for the team,'* and leaving Anna all of my $11.73 worldly possessions.

Mia is a seven year resident who lives on a remote hill alongside a dog kennel. She is our *'everything you want to know about the construction and operation of dog sleds, and the training and care of sled pulling dogs'* speaker. She has a rifle slung over her left shoulder. She **NEVER** places it on the ground. Mia is extremely energetic and lives year round in this harsh environment. Without a doubt, she clearly loves her job talking to tourists, training dogs, and making wooden sleds. It's really cold and windy, enough for many to seek shelter inside a small building. Mia, however, acts like it's a *'normal, cool, comfortable day.'* Her body language projects, *'what are you people bitching about? It's not that cold!'* Clearly, I totally disagree with her assessment of the weather conditions. The wind is blowing at least 25 mph. The temperature is in the low 30's. Even though I am bundled up, I am **COLD!** But I *'gut it out'* and remain outside listening to her spiel.

She is wearing thick pants designed to keep her warm to -30 degrees and is also wearing a warm jacket but no hat or scarf. Even though her cheeks are rosy and red, she's clearly *'comfortable'* in these weather conditions.

Mia tells us the Greenland inspired sleds are constructed locally and are *'very travel functional'* and easy to repair. The sleds are held together by ropes instead of metal bolts that can snap in harsh, cold weather. Mia trains the dogs starting with the two leaders. The dogs come from Alaska and Greenland. All of the dogs **LOVE** to run. She teaches commands in Norwegian, including go left, go right, and stop. Sometimes, the dogs **ARGUE** with her, wanting to offer **THEIR** opinions on where and when to go or stop. The dogs who are part of the dogsled team, are paired with dogs that *'get along'* and *'like'* each other. After all, who wants to spend any time next to someone they don't like. Or for that matter, staring at their butts while in transit.

After seven to eight years, sled dogs are retired and put up for adoption. Young puppies are constantly in training and learning mode; but they are never sent to pull a sled without experienced dogs. Gradually, they work into the sled pulling rotation. Mia trains and runs dogs daily. She tells us dogs will eat most everything, including dirt.

Gabriella, a young woman from Mexico, is our assigned security guard. She is *'packing.'* There is a holstered gun on her right hip and a loaded rifle on her left shoulder. She is a sharpshooter from Mexico City who has claimed numerous pistol and rifle awards for being the *'Annie Oakley of both Mexico and Longyearbyen Svalbard.'* She works as a tour guide in many Baltic areas. Just like Mia, she's well versed in local history. She has that *'special quality and glow'* that *'screams out'* from her words, smile, and body language. Without a doubt, she is fully engaged in this area, belongs here, is happy with herself, and really loves what she is doing.

Today's guides are *'very special people'* not just hearty souls who live the Baltic lifestyle. Their smiley and expressive faces, voices, body language, and expressions convey they love what they are doing. This comes across *'loud and clear'*!

Should a tour group these women are protecting engage with a polar bear, they first fire two warning shots to scare the bear. They then contact the helicopter security support team. When the helicopter arrives, someone will shoot the bear with a tranquilizer gun and remove the incapacitated animal back into the wilderness. They would use four bullets if they ultimately needed to shoot the animal. The goal is **NOT** to kill the bear unless absolutely necessary.

Our hosts serve the group coffee, hot tea, and fresh pancakes with jam. Stanislav narrates a polar bear video presentation. Below are some details.

- Polar bears are very aggressive and dangerous. Their diet consists of calorie rich blubber and skin from seals. They need to eat 50 to 75 seals annually to survive.

- Polar bears have an incredible sense of smell. It is so good that they can sniff out prey from up to 16km, or about 10 miles, away.

- Polar bears can go for eight months without eating and are active year round. Skinny, female bears are the most dangerous.

- Just one out of three baby polar bears survive past three years of age.

- Female bears give birth to cubs in snow dens (in November or December) and are about 30cm long or about the height of a standard 750ml bottle of wine.

- Polar bears can swim very fast.

- Polar bears primarily eat ring seals, but they may occasionally hunt and kill adult reindeer.

- Reindeer are quite friendly and will allow you to take a selfie with them.

Once the guides finish their presentations, everyone heads back to the bus. On our ride back to the dock, it's clearly evident that **EVERY** vehicle in town is covered in coal dust and dirt from the stark lands. Clearly, because of the ever present coal dust, it might appear to be a great business opportunity to open a car wash. However, it's clearly too cold!

At the end of the excursion, I am about 20th person from the back of the line that's getting onto the **LAST** tender returning to the ship before the captain sets out for Iceland at 14:00.

Back on the ship, I head to the swimming pool snack bar area for an All American hot dog, fries, coleslaw, olives, pickles, and a cold Norwegian Pilsner. Anna has already eaten lunch; but she joins me at a poolside table to look at the pictures and learn about today's excursion.

We *'chill'* for an hour and head to our 16:00 meeting with the future cruise consultant. I am *'dead set'* on booking the 13-day Antarctica Cruise which starts in Brazil in February 2025. Anna feels this journey is *'not her cup of tea'* so she acquiesces and says it's ok for me to fly solo on this *'bucket list excursion'* and hopes a friend or family member can *'pony up big bucks'* and join me. After 30 minutes, we select a 2025 Portugal River Cruise and a 2026 Great Lakes Cruise and we fork over the $50 deposit for each cruise. I booked the Antarctica cruise; however, when I return home I cannot find a traveling companion and refuse to pay *'big bucks'* for a double occupancy room. I cancel the trip and get a full refund. Maybe sometime down the road, we can tackle this excursion. Sadly, a bout with pneumonia and acid reflux requires us to cancel the 2025 Portugal River Cruise. Hopefully, my health will improve and permit cruising in 2026!

After committing to the future cruises, we head to the Viking Living Room on Deck 1 and listen to the classical piano player. It's now 19:00, time for dinner. We venture up to the buffet on Deck 7. I enjoy a cup of soup, one piece of veal, broccoli, one scoop of fried rice, wine, desert, and decaf coffee. Anna chooses the soup, roasted chicken breast, wine, ice cream, and decaf coffee.

The boat is *'rocking and rolling'* as it speeds through the four to six foot swells on our two day, no darkness journey to Iceland. Rough seas are forecast for the journey and will slow down the boat's speed.

I walk Anna back to Room 6041. Tonight, we cross a time zone that requires that the clocks be rolled back one hour, thus giving the tired travelers an extra hour of shut eye. I return to Deck 1

Viking Living Room, finish today's story, listen to some classical violin and upright bass guitar live music. At midnight, the music stops, the bar closes, and the lights dim. It's time for bed so I return to Room 6041.

The seas are getting rougher. As I stumble about the room, holding onto anything to prevent my falling, I am afraid I'm making too much noise. However, Anna is *out like a light.* She's not moving. I place a mirror under her nose to make sure she is *among the living.* Success, moisture appears on the mirror - she is *still with us.* The ship is rocking and rolling as I jump into bed. I **FEEL** like I am sleeping in a water bed. Luckily, the *rocking motion* quickly puts me to sleep. Good night and sweet dreams from Room 6041 on Viking Mars.

*****

Wednesday, June 5 — Day 72
Day At Sea

Day 72 is a sea day, a chance to chill, sleep in, catch up on writing, veg, or just do squat 0 nothing. During the night, we cross a time zone and gain one hour to either sleep in or enjoy a 25 hour day. Unfortunately, we must manually reset the time on our iPhones as the phone **CANNOT** detect the current time zone. The ship must be way, way out in the middle of nowhere. If you think about that long enough, it can be quite nerve racking. Exactly where the hell are we?!! And please don't give me that latitude - longitude *'mumbo jumbo.'* Please be much more specific like xx miles north, south, east, or west of _____ (fill in the blank). Just tell me something that makes sense. After all, who are we to question those in charge, allegedly *'in the know,'* much more informed, and *'allegedly'* smarter than us?

Before I get started telling today's stories, let me first say I **ANTICIPATE** a relaxing day at sea with **NOTHING** happening. But, and we all know that there's always a **BUT**.... Here are a few stories to hopefully brighten your day.

I wonder if the breakfast room service delivery men and women play a daily game called *'Can You Top This?'* Here's how I think the game goes…At the end of serving the meals, each room service team member tells the group what the most *'INTERESTING'* thing they witnessed that day. Points are awarded for clarity of presentation and content, such as observing naked body parts of men and women: score triple points for that! Reporting that room occupants appeared to have just woken up would get two points. I surmise that the winner gets a 24-hour break, a 90-minute massage, and a facial at the spa. The decision of the five panel, supervisory judges is final. There is no appeal process. Simply just try harder next time.

I wonder how a room service staff member would handle this make-believe scenario. It's Anna's turn to open the room door for room service. Lying motionless in bed, with the blankets pulled over my head, there is a strong, odiferous smell that permeates the room causing the server to cough loudly and tweak his nose. Clearly, something is **NOT RIGHT** here. He asks Anna if she need some assistance. She declines and tells him her husband expired a few days ago. Not about to miss the next two days at sea, Anna told the serve she decides to cover his body and sprays the room with a lavender air flesher to smother the odor of the decaying body. Tomorrow, Anna says, she planned to call guest services, have the body moved to the ship's morgue, and then call the cremation service back home that we both have. A worldwide cremation service contractor will pick up the body at the next port of call in Iceland. Case closed...game won by our bewildered room service team member.

Now, let's go back to the *'real world goings on.'*

After our traditional room service breakfast, I take advantage of the extra hour today by watching a video presentation of the history of Svalbard from 3 million years ago to present. I hope to learn how the mountains were created by tracing the history of the mountain's geologic development. Different rock formations make up the flat mountain tops. The hillsides rocks formations and colors appear to fold like an accordion.

It's time for some interesting geological history. Going back millions of years, Svalbard developed from a tropical sea to a desert to rivers. At some point in time, North America's and Svalbard's tectonic plates collided and crumbled the rocks, creating coal. A thick ice sheet moved Svalbard north from the equator to its current location. Want to know more?—Google *'Svalbard History.'*

I need to wire transfer 510 Krone to a souvenir store from a previous excursion stop. I accumulated my normal array of stuff. The store's credit card processing system was down. I had no cash on me. The sales lady *'bought'* my tears, begging, pleading, and agreed to email me an invoice. l use the Wells Fargo Bank App on my iPhone to wire the money to the Norway souvenir store.

While looking for a comfy couch or chair on Deck 1 in the Viking Living Room, I discover someone's room card lying on a chair. I pick up the card that has the guest's name; however, for security purposes, there is no room number on the card. I walk through the entire lounge area calling out the name on the card and hoping to receive a generous tip should the person still be nearby. After no one steps up to claim this valuable asset, I walk the room again trying to solicit bids to sell the card. No one took the bait because without the room number, everyone recognizes the card is useless.

Hey, at least I gave it a shot. It would have only taken one sucker to close the deal.

I do the proper thing. I head across the room to Guest Services, turn in the key, and ask for the $300 reward. The four staff members rise from their chairs and fall down in stitches on the carpeted floor, laughing their asses off before asking for my stateroom number to post the $300 reward. Sports fans, this is **NOT** what happened. My request was met with a sternly delivered message, *'get out of the Customer Service area **NOW** or we will call security.'* Remember these guys man the small, soundproof room with every bell and whistle, legal and illegal, interrogation tool used on me the other day. Not wanting to experience their *'methods of customer service'* again, I gladly verbally, and in writing, agree (a three-part form press hard, the third copy is yours) to accept the two day ban from the first floor Viking Living Room and Customer Service areas.

Around 16:30, I head to my room and gather up my stuff to hit the steam and ice rooms, the jacuzzi, and the ice bath tub to soak my feet. A quick shower completes my body revival.

Anna and I have 18:00 dinner reservations at the ship's Italian restaurant on Deck One forward. Anna enjoys calamari and shrimp appetizer, a steak with potatoes, a glass of red wine, chocolate cake topped with vanilla ice cream, and a decaf coffee with cream. I ordered the seafood pasta appetizer, a variety of grilled fish, two glasses of red wine, and two tiramisu desserts (piggy, but it was **SO, SO** good), and decaf coffee with cream.

Anna retreats to the room while I head to Deck 7 Explorers Lounge for some last minute writing and an hour's worth of *All In The Family, George Burns, Rodney Dangerfield, and Don Rickles videos.*

As the clock strikes midnight, and after two sparkling waters, I close the lounge bar. I return to the room to find Anna fast asleep. I check the MLB scores and news and place the room service order on the outside door handle. Until 08:00 when breakfast is expected to arrive, it's nightie-time, lights out, and pleasant dreams.

*****

Thursday, June 6 — Day 73
At Sea Somewhere In
The North Atlantic

Today is day two of two at sea. Our last port of call is scheduled for Friday. On Saturday morning, the ship docks in Reykjavik, Iceland, and our 14-day Norway and Iceland cruise ends. Today's room service breakfast fare is our normal, traditional continental breakfast. I plan to head to the buffet and order an omelet. Anna wants to do one final load of wash so we have clean clothes for the balance of the holiday. Trip groupies and readers today is a learning day. I will be writing about the history of Iceland and the *'behind the scenes'* aspects of Viking Mars, presented by the Chief Engineer.

Yesterday, I missed the history of Iceland lecture. So before heading to the buffet, I watch a replay on our stateroom TV.

Below are important historical facts about this remote North Atlantic island nation taken from the Iceland lecture:

First, there are **EIGHT** important dates in Iceland's history:

1. Irish Monks settle Iceland in the 8th century.
2. *Gardar Svavarsson*, a Vikings explorer, settled in Iceland around 860 AD. *Flóki Vilgerdarson* settled around 868.
3. *The Althing*, an annual parliament, is created in 930 AD to make laws and resolve disputes. Sessions were conducted at Law Rock and ended in 1262. In 1874, Iceland was given

limited autonomy. The Althing Parliament had power over internal affairs.

4. The *Age of the Sturlungs* rule was from 1200 to 1262. The King of Norway was recognized in 1262. Iceland was under Norwegian Rule from 1262 to 1380 under *Kings Haakon and Skule Bárdsson*.

5. In 1380, Denmark ruled Norway and Iceland. *Olaf Il* of Denmark and *Olaf IV* of Norway ruled. Danish kings took little interest in Iceland, a remote, windswept North Atlantic island, frequently ravaged by epidemics, volcanic eruptions, earthquakes, cold spells, famines, and pirate attacks.

6. From 1402 to 1404 and from 1494 to1495, pneumonic plague hits Iceland. Only 50% of the population survived.

7. In 1783, the *Laki volcano* eruption killed 9,000 people. Lava flows obliterated 200 farms and villages.

8. On June 17, 1944, Iceland dissolved its union with Denmark and the Danish monarchy. Iceland became an independent republic, which it remains to this day.

Other important dates in Iceland history taken from the video:

• In 1000 AD, *King Olafur Tryggvason* forcefully reintroduced Christianity. Osleifur Gissurarson was the first bishop of Iceland.

• The *Akureyri Church* is located in Reykjavik. The cathedral has stain glass panels depicting scenes from Icelandic religious history. They were created by the British firm Wippell Mowbray in 1973.

• Iceland is the land of *'fire and ice.'* The *Fagradalsgjall volcano* eruption started in 2024. This volcano is active today.

- *The Little Ice Age* occurred from 1275 to 1300, followed by *'substantial intensification'* from 1430 to 1455. Iceland suffered shorter growing seasons and colder winters.

- In good times, farmland was *'marginal.'* Climate change created acute hardships for early settlers.

- The Christian church *'no meat fast days'* increased the demand for dried cod. The cod trade became important to Iceland's economy.

- In 1904, Iceland attains home rule. Rules by parliamentary majority is introduced.

- In 1918, Iceland achieves full self-government under the Danish Crown. Denmark retains control over foreign affairs only.

- In December 1918, the Kingdom of Iceland was formed. At the beginning of World War II, Iceland was a sovereign kingdom in personal union with Denmark. *King Christian X* was head of state.

- On May 10, 1940, the quiet island of Iceland was abruptly thrust into the global conflict of World War II. *Operation Fork*, a code name for the British military occupation of Iceland, was launched to prevent Nazi Germany from using the island as a base for air and naval operations against the British Isles.

- On July 7, 1941, the defense of Iceland was transferred from Britain to the United States, which was still a neutral country until five months later. However, 50,000 American troops were involved in defending Iceland.

The Icelandic Flag consists of the white cross which represents the frosty chill of the mountainous glaciers. The red represents the rich abundance of lava fields, volcanos, and geothermal springs. The blue represents the ocean and Iceland's seafaring culture.

The *Cod Fishing Rights Wars* involved Iceland versus Britain. There were three Cod Wars:

1. September 1958 to March 1961
2. September 1972 to November 1973, and
3. November 1975 to June 1976.

Over time, the fishing limits started at two miles from Iceland shores. Later, the limits moved to 12 miles, then 50 miles, and ultimately 200 miles, the current universal fishing limits.

THE ICELAND BANKING COLLAPSE OF 2008

- The 2008 global financial crisis shut down bank lending, precipitating the bankruptcy of Iceland's banks.

- Iceland nationalized *Kaupthing Bank, Landsbanki,* and *Glitnir Banks* after they defaulted on $62 billion of foreign debt.

- The Icelandic Krona value dropped 50% in one day and the Icelandic stock market dropped 95% in a week.

HOW ICELAND RECOVERED

- In February 2009, voters elected *Johanna Sigurðardóttir* and her Social Democratic Alliance coalition. She served as Iceland's first female Prime Minister from 2009 – 2013 as well as the world's first openly LGBT head of government.

- Capital (money) was barred from leaving the country. The government raised taxes and prohibited citizens from buying foreign currency or foreign stocks.

- People invested in local businesses, real estate, and private equity.

- Tourism boomed when the Islandic currency exchange rate fell.

- Volcanic eruptions in 2010 and 2011 further enhanced tourism, as did the *Game of Thrones* television series which had some scenes filmed in Iceland.

ICELAND'S GREEN CREDENTIALS (taken from the video)

- Iceland is the world's largest green energy producer per capita and largest electricity producer per capita, with approximately 55,000 kWh per person per year.

- Iceland's Hydro-Electric Power comes from over 100 waterfalls including *Dettifoss, Goõafoss, Skogafoss*, and other power waterfalls.

- Geothermal power heats 87% of the county's houses. Iceland is a leader in using geothermal energy for space heating, with geothermal water heating around 90% of its homes. Iceland's geothermal power comes from magma plumes that heat reservoirs to temperatures over 750°F (400°C), as well as naturally pressurized geothermal fields with potable water at temperatures less than 300°F (150°C).

- Icelanders have been using geothermal energy for home heating since farmers began using pipelines to connect hot springs to their homes in the early 20th century. By 1930, Reykjavik's first geothermal district heating system connected a school, hospital, swimming pool, and about 60 residential buildings to geothermal energy. Today, hot water from springs is pumped from boreholes that can be 200 to 2,000 meters deep directly into homes, eliminating the need for hot water heating. Geothermal energy is also used to heat greenhouses, which contribute to Iceland's high levels of local food production.

- Iceland's geothermal energy is a vital part of the country's clean energy model, which also includes hydropower sources. In total, Iceland's geothermal power plants generate about a quarter of the country's electricity and two-thirds of its home heating. Iceland is one of the top 10 geothermal generating countries in the world, with a total installed geothermal power generation capacity of 755 MW.

- Geothermal energy has been used by Icelanders since the Viking Age, with initial uses including washing and bathing. Later, it began to be used to heat homes, greenhouses, and swimming pools, as well as to keep streets and sidewalks free of snow and ice.

- Currently geothermal power heats 89% of the houses in Iceland. Over 54% of the primary energy used in Iceland comes from geothermal sources.

- Iceland's geothermal energy is a vital part of the country's clean energy model, which also includes hydropower sources. In total, Iceland's geothermal power plants generate about a quarter of the country's electricity and two-thirds of its home heating.

- Iceland is able to produce clean, inexpensive energy from the waterfalls and underground pressurized geothermal fields where the water reaches 300 degrees Fahrenheit. The water is also purified and cooled to provide cold drinking water.

- The North American Plate and the Eurasian Plate fault crack runs through thru Iceland. The crack moves apart at a rate of 2.5 cm per year. The ridge passes directly through Iceland, creating a crack in the Earth. You can go into the crack and touch Europe and North America at the same time.

- Iceland has the clearest water on earth.

- The Aurora Borealis Northern Lights reign supreme on clear nights during dark winter.

- Iceland's land mass is 11% glacier and 30% volcanic.

- Iceland covers 40,000 square miles, about the size of Kentucky. During World War II, American and British troops represented 50% of the country's population. Iceland ranks third worldwide behind Finland and Denmark as the happiest place on earth.

- Phone books in Iceland list people by their **FIRST NAME**, not their last name.

- The country has a variety of animals including horses, cows, sheep, goats, artic foxes, dogs, cats, and 20 species of whales. There are no ants, snakes, or mosquitoes.

HULDUFÓLK: ICELAND'S HIDDEN PEOPLE

Iceland has a rich history of folklore and legends.

LANDVAETTIR – THE FOUR GAURDIAN SPIRITS OF ICELAND

1. *Mionesheidi* – The Bull Grioungur
2. *Bolungarvik* – The Vulture/Griffin Gammur
3. *Langanes* – The Dragon Dreki
4. *Hohn* – The Giant Bergrisi

ICELAND: WORLD'S MOST LITERARY COUNTRY

Saga academic Sigurur Nordal described Icelandic medieval literature as follows:

- "No nation in Northern Europe has medieval literature which in originality and brilliance can be compared with the literature of the Icelanders from the first five centuries after the settlement period".

- Literature is the only constant cultural activity since Iceland's settlement in the 9th century.

- They started writing prose narratives, Icelandic sagas, and historical narratives in the 12/13th centuries.

- Snorri Sturluson was an Icelandic historian, poet, and politician from 1179 to 1241.

- Iceland is a nation of authors. With around 300,000 people, Iceland has more writers, more books published, and more books read per head, than anywhere in the world. In 1944 after independence from Denmark, literature helped define Icelandic identity. One in ten Icelanders has published a book. In Iceland, books are exchanged on Christmas Eve. Families spend the rest of the night reading. They generally take their books to bed along with hot chocolate. How cozy and wonderful does that sound?

- Iceland publishes more books per capita than any other country.

Here are some facts about the Svartsengi volcanic system that started erupting in 2020 and continues today.

- The system is on the *Reykjanes Peninsula* in southwest Iceland, north of Grindavík and southeast of Keflavík International Airport. The Icelandic name for the system is Eldvörp–Svartsengi, which translates to *"fire cones–black meadow"*.

- Composition - The system is made up of volcanic craters, fissures, and cones.

- Activity - The system was relatively inactive for centuries until 2020, when a series of magmatic intrusions began. The most recent eruption, on May 29, 2024, began on the *Sundhnúkagígar* crater row. The initial fissure was over one kilometer long, and lava flowed at a rate of 1,500 to 2,000 cubic meters per second, covering roads. The eruption also caused significant ground uplift and gas emissions, with lava fountains reaching heights of 60 to 70 meters.

- In December 2023, as part of the *Sundhnúkur* eruptions, some craters began to erupt. On 14 January 2024, a second eruption began following seismic activity associated with the area of the *Sundhnúksgígar* craters. As of November 2024, there had been seven eruptions.

- History - During the Holocene, the system has erupted more than 15 times, producing basalts and lava flows on land, as well as explosive activity offshore. The last eruption before 2020 was around 1240.

- Iceland is a founding member of NATO. While Iceland does not have an army, its strategic geographic position in the Atlantic makes it an invaluable member. NATO bases track Russian submarines.

Around noon, the captain updated everyone on our location. The ship is 250 miles from Iceland and is heading southwest. The ocean is 4,600 feet deep and swells are 11 feet. Around midnight to 04:00, the ship will encounter 60 to 70 knot wind speeds and

18 feet seas. However, the ship is scheduled to dock tomorrow at 08:00 in *Isafjordur*.

After lunch, and spending a few hours on Deck One Explorers Lounge, I attend a one hour Power Point presentation by the Viking Mars Chief Engineer Ivar Arthur Skogvang.

Here's what I learned about ship's history and its operations above and below deck.

- Viking Mars was commissioned in 2022. The ship was built in Fincantieri Ancona, Italy.

• Gross Tonnage	47,842 Tons
• Overall Length	748 Feet
• Overall Width	103 Feet
• Height Over Water	144 Feet
• Maximum Speed	18/20 Knots
• Power Production	2 6,720 KW 12 Cylinder Diesel Engines
	2 5,040 KW 9 Cylinder Diesel Engines
• Propulsion	2 7,250 KW Propulsion Motors
• Fin Stabilizers	Fincantieri Hydraulic Stabilizers
• Number of Guests	Maximum 930
• Staff	Maximum 489

- The Power Management System is a complicated combination of functions monitored in the Engine Control Room. System monitoring is manned 24/7 to make sure all systems are properly operating.

- The diesel engines consume most of power created by the ship's power management system.

- Power is needed to operate all functions within the ship.

- When in port, the ship is plugged into a local power source.

- The Electric Propulsion System is a complicated system to manage power.

- Tunnel thrusters control the steering.

- Fin Stabilizers balance the ship.

- To minimize Sulphur oxide emissions, effluent and discharge, the closed loop *Alfa Lavel MultiScrubber DeSOx* is connected to various sources such as boilers and power generators. Water mixed with alkaline (Caustic Soda) is pumped into the scrubber, reacts with the flue gas, and neutralized the Sulphur Oxides. This process reduces emissions by 80% to 90%.

- Local environmental regulations do not allow the ship to burn or have heavy oil in places like Svalbard, Norway. The ship emptied the tanks of heavy oil while in port in Tromso, Norway.

- The system recycles heat energy to heat the ship's hot water.

- Reverse Osmosis System produces 1,000 tons a day of fresh water.

- The ventilation Air Handling System keeps the ship's temperatures comfortable.

- Effluent water cleaning system filters and cleans waste water. When in port, the cleaned waste water is pumped from the ship.

- The Ultrafog fire extinguishing system releases water by the heat measured at various locations on the ship like a guest room, the kitchen, the laundry, and the engine room.

- Galley equipment receives regular maintenance at night.

- All of the ship's numerous components are built to the manufacturers' safety standards.

- A planned maintenance system is in place to ensure all systems and equipment are maintained to manufacturer's safety standards.

- Viking is testing a Hydrogen generator for power production as environmental regulations and restrictions on regular fuel usage are happening worldwide.

While the presentation was in many instances very technical and *'way above my pay grade,'* the chief engineer is extremely knowledgeable. He presents the information so everyone present can understand just how the ship operates and stays compliant with environmental laws. After listening to the Chief Engineer, I have greater appreciation for everything the Engineering Department does to enhance traveling guests' experiences and to keep everyone safe.

Outside the ship, the wind is howling and the ocean swells are increasing. I tried to step outside; but a strong, cold wind greets me and almost knocks me down. I guess I will not be heading outside to check the temperature and watch the waves. It's time for a workout. I return to the room, gather my bathing suit, clean clothes, and toiletry bag and head to the gym. My daily executive workout consists of 15 minutes in the steam room, five minutes in the snowy cold room, the ice bucket challenge, and time in the jacuzzi. After a quick shower, I am ready to *'take on the world'* and enjoy dinner with Anna, Billy, and Adrienne, our Reno travel friends.

At 19:17 on Thursday night, we are in the main dining room enjoying dinner with Billy and Adrienne. Over the ship's intercom system, Captain Erik Saabye makes a chilling but important announcement. Viking Mars has encountered very rough seas with

18 foot waves while heading to tomorrow's port stop in Isafjordur, Iceland. Strong winds from Greenland, 400 miles to the west, are blowing large chucks of ice into the ship's planned route. Consequently, the Captain decides to turn the ship around, head northeast, and go **AROUND** the ice to avoid a *'Titanic moment.'* Tomorrow's docking at Isafjordur is cancelled.

The Captain sets a course to Saturday's departure stop, Reykjavik, located on southwest side of Iceland. All doors leading to the outdoor decks are locked and barricaded with furniture to prevent anyone from going outside and, most likely, getting unceremoniously tossed overboard by the strong winds. Guest room attendants **LOCK** all veranda doors preventing *'daredevil and adventurous guests'* from going outside to take pictures, observe the 18 foot plus rolling whitecaps, and run the risk of falling overboard into the icy cold North Atlantic.

A Colombo and Sergeant Joe Friday investigation reveals what *'really happened'* on the bridge prior to the ship's *'changing course'* announcement. The navigator notices the navigation system *'going bonkers'* indicating the presence of ice in the ship's path. The system can't determine the number of ice sightings or the depth and size of underwater icebergs. However, when the alarms go off, this is **NOT** a situation to ignore.

The Captain reviews the data and summons his management team. He's responsible for almost 1,400 lives, and follows procedures in the 632 page, three ring binder Viking Mars Operating Manual, Chapter 26, Section 52, Paragraphs 32 to 87. The **BEST** and **ONLY** course of action is to quickly, like **NOW**, turn the ship 360 degrees around and head back towards Norway. He issues a *'point blank, no questions'* order to Chief Engineer Skogvang. Ivar stares at Captain Erik and says, "Erik, you want **ME** to turn the 986 foot long cruise ship around **NOW** and head back towards Norway? Have you been drinking again? What are you smoking in that pipe of yours? Do you know how much time, manpower, and precious fuel this will take? And what happens if this maneuver doesn't get the ship out of troubled icy waters? Huh? Are you **REALLY** sure you want the crew to do this? And how are you going to explain to the *'suits'* why you issued this order and spent hundreds of thousands of dollars **NOT** in the ship's 2024 operating budget? Don't you realize your decision will affect our expected hundreds of thousands of dollars semi-annual bonuses payable July 15?" General Manager Shauvik Chaudhuri joins the conversation and backs Captain Erik. The score now stands at two to one in favor of turning back. The beleaguered Captain looks Ivar in the eyes and says, "Read my lips. **NO** more discussion or comments from the peanut gallery. Turn the fucking ship around like **NOW!**" So, the Chief Engineer walks over to the navigation control center, logs in with his user name and emergency situation 39-digit password, and presses **ONE** button to automatically turn the ship around in 5 minutes, 14 seconds. That was easy!

At 01:27, the Captain sounds the **General Alarm** waking up all guests and crew. Over the ship's loudspeaker, the message is **CLEAR**, get to your *'abandon ship'* location on Deck Two, put on your life vests, and test the *'here I am light'* located on the vest near your right shoulder. The half-awake crew is instructed to put their vests on **FIRST.** Crew members are much more valuable than a majority of the 79 year-old and older guests, many in the final 4 minutes 23 seconds of the fourth quarter in the game of life, down by six points, out of timeouts, and lifesaving drugs.

The ship's *'all religions'* Chaplain is an 87 year-old man with two artificial knees and hips, a pacemaker, hearing aids, and is hooked up to an oxygen tank. He tells **EVERYONE** to say their last act of contrition and send texts to family and friends updating them on the current situation, telling them how much you love them, and hope to see them either soon or in the afterlife.

The ship's 272 band members sharply dressed in their 1910 style ship band uniforms and hats, play *'Nearer My God To Thee'* as if nothing is happening. The most junior *'abandon ship personnel'* haphazardly load the guests and release the lifeboats. During this process, three boats fall into the icy waters but luckily, they are empty. This means there are 105 less seats available. Finding no volunteers to remain behind, the crew hastily conducts a *'drawing straws'* contest. The 105 souls who drew the short end of the straw were sent back to Deck Two to await further crew instructions. The most experienced senior crew and staff will remain behind should the situation improve. They continue to operate the ship as if nothing happens for the 27 guests who chose **NOT** to abandon ship and stay behind and the 105 guests who drew the short end of the straw.

We are among the 27 souls that stay on board and enjoy a five course gourmet meal and a glass of fine red wine with our two friends from Reno. If we are *'going down with the ship,'* it's going to be with a good meal in our bellies and a glass of wine in hand. Stay tuned for Friday's update on the harrowing overnight adventures.

Finally, the *'situation'* returns to normal. The unlucky 105 passengers who drew the short end of the straw and the 27 volunteers who chose to stay behind resume the cruise as if *'nothing happened'*. The passengers, who were placed in the lifeboats and cast into the 36 degree cold, dark, and icy North Atlantic, were picked up by three fishing trawlers heading to Greenland. Hopefully, they can *'figure a way'* to join the cruise in Reykjavik before the Viking Mars departs on Saturday night. Viking Cruise Lines sends out a blast email, texts and prerecorded phone messages claiming **NO** responsibility or liability for this unfortunate incident. Let's see what the *'ambulance chasing'* attorneys will say about the facts surrounding this ***'incident.'*** (Ok, now that I got your attention, this really didn't happen but makes for a good story. I can only imagine this is what it was like on the Titanic!)

After dinner, Anna heads to the room for R & R while I head to my favorite leather couch on Deck One in the Viking Living Room to enjoy a night cap and complete some writing. Walking back to the room, I felt like a person who had way too much to drink. The ship's rolling left to right violently thrusts me left and right into the hallway handrails. Can't wait to strap into our *simulated water bed* and experience the *'rock and roll'* ocean lulling me to sleep. So, until our breakfast arrives at 08:15 on Friday morning, good night.

*****

Friday, June 7 — Day 74
At Sea

Last night's ten to eighteen foot rolling seas rocks us to sleep like babies. The constant *'rocking and rolling'* made the bed **FEEL** like a waterbed on steroids. Thanks to wearing Viking's *'don't fall out of bed seat belts,'* we **NEVER** fell on the floor. By 07:14, the sea is calmer, thank goodness.

Today's docking at *Isafjordur* is cancelled due to delays resulting from rerouting the ship yesterday. Thus, today we will be *'at sea'* on our last sailing day. We were really looking forward to spending time in Isafjordur; but as Leslie's friend Marie, back in Henderson often says, "That's safari!" Better safe than sorry.

Our last in-room breakfast is another basic continental. No need to restate the obvious. Anna convinces me it's time to pack our *'souvenirs'* and clothes and be ready for our early morning departure in Reykjavik. We pack the souvenirs in Anna's blue suitcase. We plan to carry it off the ship to avoid a *'gorilla baggage handling experience.'* We will check three bags and carry off a small duffel bag, backpack, and the blue suitcase stuffed with souvenirs when we depart the ship in Reykjavik.

When the packing ordeal is complete, I watch a short Viking video about today's cancelled port of call, Isafjordur. While we will not be stopping, here's what we missed. Info provided by the video and Wikipedia.

Isafjordur, which translates to '*Ice Fjord*,' is home to 2,600 residents. *Skutulsfjorour*, as it was originally named, was first settled by *Helgi Magri Hrolfsson* in the 9th century. It is the oldest and most remote, breathtaking region in Iceland.

For centuries, it was mind-blowing how people struggled to survive in near total isolation. Isafjordur has a Sub-Artic climate with cool summers and cold dark winters. In the summer, temperatures will top out at 50 in July. During dark winter, the Northern Lights are on full display in the clear, dark sky.

Isafjordur is best known for its dramatic landscapes, which were created by a series of ancient volcanoes and ice age glaciers. Three sides of the oceanfront fishing town are bordered by stunning mountains. It's the center of trade and tourism for the region. Some of Iceland's oldest and best preserved buildings are found here. The old town has wooden houses with corrugated tin roofs built by fishing merchants in the 18th and 19th centuries. Despite its size, small population, and historical isolation from the rest of the country, the town has a relatively urban atmosphere. There is a school of music, a hospital, the University of Akureyri of the Westfjords, and a cultural center with a library and showrooms. The small town is known as the center for '*alternative music*' outside of Iceland. Fish processing is the main economic engine supporting the area. The artic fox is a protected species. Bird Island has the only windmill in Iceland. Only one family lives on the island. The island has the smallest post office in Europe. Enthusiastic bird watchers flock to Bird Island in the summer.

At 08:49, Captain Erik comes onto the ship's communication system and announces a medical helicopter will be landing on Deck 8 to transport a passenger with a medical emergency to Reykjavik. All facilities in the back of the ship on Decks Seven and Eight are closed. Access to these decks is '*off limits*' until the passenger is successfully on his/her way to the hospital. Around 11:00, the helicopter arrives, picks up the sick passenger, and transports him/her to the hospital.

Around 12:03, the Captain alerts the passengers that the ship is back on schedule to dock in Reykjavik on time Saturday morning. We notice the sun is trying to peak out. The seas are much calmer.

I pack a copy of the room service breakfast door hanger menu to use at home. I sure hope our Henderson staff collects it when we retire for the night. We look forward to breakfast in bed at the requested 15-minute time window.

The rest of the afternoon, I hang out in the Viking Living Room on Deck One. The bar serves small finger sandwiches. They *'take the edge off'* without spoiling my dinner appetite. Anna *'shows up'* for her favorite roast beef finger sandwich.

Around 16:30, I head to the gym for my daily executive workout. After a shower, I am ready for a beer, or three, and dinner.

The traveling seniors have reservations at the Italian restaurant at 18:00. Seating at a window table, we watch the ocean pass by as the ship cuts through the North Atlantic. We enjoy linguine, soup, fish, and Argentine red wine. For dessert, we order decaf Americanos with cream. Anna selects, what else, vanilla ice cream with chocolate sauce and whipped cream while I *'pig out'* on **NOT** one but two *'to die for'* tiramisu cups.

Anna retires to the room while I settle into my favorite leather couch in the Viking Living Room on Deck One. I notice the sun is still out and shining brightly at 20:30. It's time to retire for the night and anticipate Saturday's 09:00 disembarkation in Reykjavik.

*****

Saturday, June 8 — Day 75
Reykjavik, Iceland

Well, traveling fans, after 14 glorious days and nights, we disembark Viking Mars. Our cruise started in Bergen, Norway and covered 3,026 nautical miles. When I booked this trip 11 months ago, I envisioned it as a *'nice, relaxing, 14-day, no brainer cruise'* after 61 exciting days traveling thru Europe. Boy was I surprised! Our first experience with Viking Cruise Lines was fantastic. We boarded the ship and settled into our room in less than 20 minutes! Viking Mars is a three-year-old cruise ship that accommodates 900 passengers. The understated elegance of the ship, our room, and the amenities, including the gym area, the Explorer's Lounges on Decks One and Seven, the various dining options from buffets to sit down specialty restaurants exceeded our expectations. The onboard staff is extremely professional, friendly, and hard working.

We are so pleased with the Viking *'Experience'* that we booked a September 2026, 14-day Great Lakes USA and Canada cruise. But now, let's get back to Saturday's Viking Mars departure and settling into Reykjavik for three days and three nights prior to heading back to *'reality'* in Henderson, Nevada on Tuesday, June 11 via Icelandic and Southwest Airlines.

The anticipation of getting off the ship has us up and about at 06:30. The ship is docked and undergoing the normal *'end of cruise things,'* like unloading departing passengers' suitcases, trash, and restocking the ship with everything to set sail Sunday for a trip around Iceland and onto Greenland, Nova Scotia, Northeastern Canada, and finishing up 14 days later in the Big Apple, New York City.

We have about 90-minutes to get ready, stop at the breakfast buffet for our last onboard meal, bid ado to Adrianne and Billy, two of Reno Nevada's solid citizens, and say thanks and good bye to "G" and his team of outstanding room stewards. They took great care of us.

We placed our luggage in the hallway at 22:00 last night. Staff collects the departing passengers' belongings, stores them overnight in the ship's bowels, and delivers them to the dock in the morning for departing passengers to pick up. We take our final elevator ride down to Deck Two and walk down the semi-steep walkway to the pier. We pick up our luggage in the large tent area, walk 150 meters to the taxi cab area, and jump in a cab for a 15-minute cross city ride to our new home for the next three nights, The *Center Hotels Plaza*. The cab driver's name is Siggi. For the next three days, my name will be Siggi and my traveling partner will be known as Joanna.

The cab drops us off just across the street from the hotel. We notice many couples pulling suitcases heading towards the Center Hotels Plaza.

Two cruise ships docked this morning. Access to the hotel is through a circular revolving door. As Joanna enters the revolving door, she trips over a 1 1/2" metal lip that's part of the door frame. She lands like someone doing a belly flop and face plants in one of the four revolving door entry ways. She lands **HARD** hitting her forehead, arms, elbows, stomach, and legs on the cement ground. Her legs extend outside the door frame and stop the revolving door! I rush to her aid. I wedge myself into the door to comfort her and check for injuries. Obviously, she is stunned and although she did not *'pass out,'* she is clearly dazed, sore, in shock, and understandably upset. After a few minutes, another gentleman assists me getting her back on her feet. Hotel staff opens a side door so we can get her inside and seated. I go back and round up our suitcases and belongings. For the next few minutes, Joanna just wants to be *'left alone, cleaning out the cobwebs,'* and determining her injuries.

Front desk staff witnesses the incident. I approach Gosia, a front desk clerk, and ask to speak to the manager. We don't know yet if she needs medical attention. What I hear next is seriously **UNBELIEVABLE, "There is NO manager on duty until Monday morning at 08:00 and no one working today can make a decision on what to do, including providing medical attention."** You have GOT to be kidding me! Forcefully and in no uncertain terms, I **DEMAND** Gosia check us into a room **NOW!!**

Another clerk fills an ice bucket so Joanna can ice body parts that hurt. Gosia assigns us an upgraded room on the sixth floor and gives me the keys to Room 662! Joanna is up and moving **VERY SLOWLY**. I put her into the room and place more ice in the plastic bag. She gets into bed, sits up, and places the ice bag on her sore body parts. I retreat to the lobby, gather up our belongings, and bring them to the room. After a few hours of icing and a few Aleves, she is feeling a little better. I think she **DODGED** a potential serious injury. Come Monday at 8:00, I will be in the lobby hunting down the front desk manager and having a stern, one way *'conversation'*!

The clock strikes 12:00. It's time for lunch. Joanna wants to get out and eat lunch. Her recovery from the fall is amazing! She is a trooper, that's for sure. We walk across a small plaza to *101 Bistro* and share an order of **outstanding** fish and chips and a cold local beer. The aroma of perfectly fried fresh fish fills the tiny sit down restaurant. The coating is crunchy but not oily, and the fish is **SO** fresh, it tries to smack me in the face. How fresh was the fish.....it was caught less than 24 hours ago.

The weather has changed from mostly sunny at 06:30 to overcast and cool. There's a slight wind and dampness hanging in the air. The weather app shows it will be 48 degrees all day; however, that doesn't *'hold water'* with us. I am wearing four layers of clothing, including a hoodie and jacket. Joanna has three layers, including a heavier jacket. We both wear something on our heads to prohibit warmth from escaping through the top of our heads.

After lunch, we do the *'first day in a new city thing.'* We slowly roam the streets, window shop, buy a few souvenirs, and despite the *'cold'* weather, we walk 6,400 steps. Joanna finds an inexpensive pair of gloves with an Iceland patch to replace my misplaced left glove that's been *'missing'* for two days. No store offered a left hand only glove for sale. At the top of the gradual one way uphill roadway, we enter the *Hallgrimskirkja Church*. From the church's website, below is some of the church's history.

- The church is named after the Icelandic poet and clergyman, Hallgrimur Petursson (1614 to 1674), author of the Passion Hymns.

- State Architect Gudjon Samuelsson's design of the church was commissioned in 1937. He is said to have designed it to resemble the basalt lava flows of Iceland's landscape.

- *Hallgrimskirkja* is a Lutheran Parish Church. At 244 feet tall, it is the largest church in Iceland and among the tallest structures in the country.

- Known for its distinctively curved spire and side wings, it has been described as having become an important symbol for Iceland's national identity since its completion in 1986.

- It took 41 years to build the church. Construction started in 1945 and ended in 1986; however, the landmark tower was completed long before the whole church was finished.

- At the time of construction, the building was criticized as too old-fashioned and as a blend of different architectural styles.

- The church houses two large pipe organs. The first, a *Rieger-Kloss* organ was installed in 1946. This organ was moved to the South Wing when it opened. A new pipe organ was commissioned from *Frobenius* in 1985. Soon after, in 1988, the church council decided that the Frobenius pipe organ wasn't big enough and commissioned another from the German organ builder *Johannes K*lais of Bonn. There are 102 ranks, 72 stops and 5,275 pipes. It is 49 feet tall and weighs 25 tons. Installation finished in December 1992.

- The church has a nine story steeple and viewing area providing a spectacular 360 degree view of Reykjavik.

We invest 20 Icelandic Kronas, take the elevator up eight floors, and climb 32 steps to take in the view. While there, I make various videos of the cityscape.

Returning to the church's large patio, we observe a group of men and women dressed in colorful, expensive 1900's clothing standing next to a variety of 1900's bicycles including a bike with a 5-foot high front tire and an elevated seat for the driver. I talk with some of the riders and learn they are a local club that enjoys history and gets together to dress up and ride their bikes thru cities and the countryside.

The weather changes again. It's now a partly cloudy day with temperatures in the low 50's. We head down the pathway towards the hotel. Along the way, we continue window and souvenir shopping. It's 16:15. Just up the street from our hotel, a local hotel bar sign displays **'Happy Hour.'** *'Being thirsty and happy,'* we enter and settle into a table. The bartender brings a glass of the house red wine and a local Icelandic draft beer. The beer's logo is etched into the glass...Is the glass another *'potential in the back pack souvenir'* for me? However, the bar is not crowded. Slipping the glass into the backpack proves to be challenging and difficult. So, Joanna suggests, "Just ask the bartender if you can purchase it." The bartender pulls a clean glass off the bar's shelf and says, "Enjoy, no charge." Siggi is more than happy and gives the bartender a nice tip. For the first time on our holiday, this beer glass does not have to '*disappear*' into my backpack like the other 11 glasses acquired so far in the journey.

We walk to our hotel, drop off our '*just had to buy treasures,*' and rest for an hour. Around 18:00, we search out a nice local restaurant for dinner. One block from the hotel, we enter *Apotec*, a high-end restaurant. The Matre'd asks if we have reservations. In unison, we reply, **"NO, BUT DON'T YOU KNOW WHO WE ARE?"** The Matre'd is **NOT** impressed and informs us the next available table is at 21:30. He suggests we dine in the crowded and unappealing waiting area. Neither alternative works for the hungry and tired travelers. Joanna spots three open seats at the three seat bar and asks, "Can we eat at the bar?" "Yes," he answers. He leads us to our seats and provides menus. Here is a little history about the restaurant. The building formerly housed a large pharmacy. *"Apotec"* is the Icelandic name for pharmacy.

Siggi and Joanna order adult beverages and engage the bar staff in '*small talk.*' Bjarturis, a 6' 4" good looking, young male bartender, is an experienced mixologist who is taking classes to learn about wines. Joanna provides a five minute, three credit course on various wines and orders a red. I order a local draft beer. After studying the extensive menu, Joanna orders lamb chops and carrots. I order a shrimp salad and a large appetizer size bowel of olives. Next, the staff places a basket of warm, freshly baked bread in front of us. The fragrance of freshly baked bread fills the air and our nostrils. The bread with, of course, butter is '*to die for.*' We could easily make a meal on bread, butter, and drinks.

Tattoos are popular in Iceland as evidenced by the *'abundance of ink'* on the bar staff. We freely engage with the young 20's something, five person bar staff, swapping life and travels stories. They are polite, friendly, professional, outgoing, and hard working men and women. It's funny. People say Icelandic people are very reserved and hard to get to know. However, our strategy is to always engage and *'see what happens.'* Tonight, we succeed and make five new friends. (By the way, as a side note, Joanna's lamb chops were three double size chops with bones in place, enough for both to share.)

On the way back to the hotel, we stop at the local grocery store and buy fruit for a pre-breakfast, in-room snack to get the day going. Joanna then does her best *'Eve imitation'* and leads me into the gelato store adjacent to the hotel. She goes two scoops while I show restraint and order just one.

Back at the room, Joanna chills with a book while I retreat to the hotel lobby for *'quiet time and writing.'* The sun sets at 23:49 and rises at 03:04. So, it *'never gets completely dark'* this time of year. Every time I look out the window, it looks like 15:00. It's hard to imagine it's time for bed. As the clock strikes midnight, it's nighty, night time. I retire to Room 662 to rest up for tomorrow's exploration of Iceland.

Let's finish up today's story with some history of Reykjavik.

According to Wikipedia, Reykjavík ("Bay of Smokes") was founded in 874 by the Norseman *Ingólfur Arnarson*. According to history, he decided on the location of the settlement using a traditional Norse method: when land was in sight, he cast his high seat pillars overboard and promised to settle where the gods decided to bring them ashore. Two of his slaves then searched the coasts for three years before finding the pillars in the bay which eventually became the site now known as *Reykjanesskagi*. There he settled with his family around 874, in a place he named Reykjavík or "Smoke Cove", probably from the geothermal steam rising from the earth.

This place eventually became the capital and the largest city in modern Iceland.

The site of the modern city center was farmland until the 18th century. In 1752, *King Frederik V of Denmark* donated the estate of Reykjavík to the *Innréttingar* Corporation. The leader of this movement was Skúli Magnússon. In the 1750s, several houses were built to house the wool industry, which was Reykjavík›s most important employer for a few decades and the original reason for its existence. Other industries were undertaken by the Innréttingar, such as fisheries, Sulphur mining, agriculture, and shipbuilding. Until the 20th century, it was a small fishing village and trading post. It was granted municipal powers and was designated the administrative center of the Danish-ruled island often referred to as the *"Land of Fire and Ice"* on August 18, 1786.

Reykjavík is the commercial, industrial, and cultural center of the island. It is a major fishing port and the site of nearly half of the nation's industries. An international airport *Keflavík*, is 20 miles west-southwest. Reykjavík's manufactures include processed fish and food products, machinery, and metal products. Strikingly modern and clean in appearance, the city is largely built of concrete and is heated by hot water piped from nearby hot springs. Its many public outdoor swimming pools are also geothermal. Buildings of note include the *Parliament Building* and the *Church of Hallgrímur*. Among the city's cultural highlights are the *National and University Library of Iceland*, the *University of Iceland* founded in 1911, the *Iceland Symphony Orchestra*, and the National Gallery of Iceland. Bessastadhir, the residence of the president of Iceland, is outside the city. 140,000 people call Reykjavik home. There are 240,000 residents in the greater Reykjavik area or 63% of the 378,000 people living in Iceland.

Reykjavik is the northern most capital city in the world surpassing Juneau by 400 miles. A mild climate aided by the North

Atlantic current keeps the weather sub polar. Temperatures rarely reach 65 degrees or drop below 32.

The Reykjavík summit of 1986 was held on October 11 and 12, 1986, between U.S. President Ronald Reagan and Soviet Premier Mikhail Gorbachev. The meeting, the second between the two leaders, was intended not as a summit but as a session in which the leaders explored the possibility of limiting each country's strategic nuclear weapons to create momentum in ongoing arms-control negotiations. The Reykjavík Summit almost resulted in a sweeping nuclear arms-control agreement in which the nuclear weapons of both sides would be dismantled. Although no agreement was reached, many historians and government officials, including Gorbachev himself, later considered the Reykjavik summit a turning point in the Cold War.

During the exchange of proposals, the leaders agreed that nuclear weapons must be eliminated, and they nearly produced an agreement to eliminate Soviet and American nuclear weapon stockpiles by 2000. The space-based missile defense system, known as the Strategic Defense Initiative (SDI) *and derisively nicknamed the "Star Wars' program which was* being considered by the United States, prevented such an agreement. President Reagan refused to limit SDI research and technology to the laboratory. Gorbachev, however, would not accept anything less than a ban on missile testing in space. Despite the failure to reach an agreement on that issue, both sides felt that the meeting was a success and opened the way for further progress.

*****

Sunday, June 9 — Day 76
Waterfalls and Black Sand Beaches

Mother Nature calls at 03:30. Looking outside, there is a pink line of light stretching across the horizon. The sun was rising! The sky is cloudless blue. Our home for the next 2 1/2 days is Reykjavik, Iceland, an island 400 miles east of Greenland in the North Atlantic Ocean.

Today is Day 76, a very significant number. Can anyone guess what the number '76' represents? How about Joanna's 76th birthday coming up just around the corner on July 29! Please make a note of the date. She loves cards (and presents—lots of them.) Our 78-day European adventure is an early gift to commemorate the occasion. All I have to do now is buy a birthday card or send a few electronically from American Greetings.Com where I have an account.

Sadly, tomorrow ends our journey. The way I look at it, the cost of this trip and its importance covers birthdays, anniversaries, and Christmas presents for at least 10 years! Not sure Joanna will agree but...that's my story and I am 10,000% sticking to it!

Johanna's internal alarm goes off at 07:15 which means *time to rise and shine Siggi.* Gazing out our 6th floor window, there's just one, puffy white cloud spoiling the 99.9% cloudless sky. Right now, like this second, it's a clear sunny day; however, we are in

Iceland where the weather can change without warning in a *'New York minute.'* And it has. Close to the hotel, a series of wispy white clouds are lightly brushed into the blue sky by famous artist Thom Metcalf. However, some start to fade into never-never land.

Joanna brews two cups of coffee to kick-start our day. We are scheduled to pick up our two-day Thrifty Rental Car at 09:00. Let's get this *'show on the road'* for an exciting day of driving thru the area and witness *'up close and personal'* the many wonders Iceland has to offer.

At the breakfast buffet, I expect an Icelandic Viking array of pickled herring and whale, cod fish heads, whale blubber sauce, roasted goat, goat's milk cheese, and dark, almost black, *'hard as a rock'* bread. I am pleasantly surprised that the only local fare is pickled herring and some funky grains. I load my plate with freshly baked bread, scrambled eggs, bacon, and fruit. Unfortunately, the orange juice is so watered down it is almost clear and tasteless. The coffee is perfectly brewed and hot. The aroma of freshly brewed coffee fills the breakfast room. Joanna arrives at the breakfast room just as I am leaving.

I return to the room and tell housekeeping the light over Joanna's side of the bed is out. The housekeeping lady does not understand nor speak English. I point to the light in question and signal *'out, no worka.'*

I gather up 17 layers of clothing for today's adventures, grab the iPad, coat, hoodie, and backpack and head to the lobby to pick up some important papers I emailed last night to the front desk. Unfortunately, the young front desk clerk Amalia, my new bestie, has zero record of receiving them. She politely asks me to resend.

Joanna and Siggi could both use a day or two to rest and recover. However, with just 2 1/2 days left before heading home, we set out and march on to explore the sights of Iceland.

We grab a cab to take us to the Thrifty Car Rental office to pick up our vehicle. Saad, our cab driver, is from Togo in Western Africa. He's lived in Europe for the past nine years. After meeting and marrying an Icelandic lady, they relocated to Reykjavik. When we arrive at the car rental facility, I ask Saad if he prefers payment in cash or with a credit card. Being an entrepreneur who understands the 'cash economy,' he says, "I prefer cash." I am 20 Icelandic Kronas short; however, Saad says, "Deal".

The rental vehicle is a Mazda CX 5 - just like my car in Henderson. As we pull out of the parking lot, the low tire pressure light flashes on the consul. I stop and tell the attendant who says, "Nothing to worry about. The sensors are always broken given the quality of some of the roads, so don't worry." Okay then—off we go as we drive east to see waterfalls.

Our first stop is the N1 Convenience Store for potty, drinks, and a fresh tuna fish sandwich. Along with the gasoline pumps, this store has 20 or so electric car charging stations. (Hey Mayor Pete, how many did your administration construct in the USA with that ungodly pile of Covid relief cash Biden bestowed on you?)

The speed limit on the six lane divided highway through the city is 60 kilometers per hour (KPH). Red light enforcement cameras are strategically placed to capture the license plate number and driver(s) face when anyone runs a red light. We pass by the area's largest shopping mall, numerous apartments, houses, and office buildings. Once outside of town, the roadway drops to two lanes in each direction. The speed limit increases to 90 KPH. Most 'locals' drive in the right hand lane and obey the speed limit. A few people rushing to their destination fly by us at well over 120 KPH (this reminds me of some drivers in Las Vegas).

Once outside of town, old, barren lava fields from previous eruptions line both sides of the highway. Thirty or so minutes later, the roadway descends to sea level. We stop in the small town of

Hveragerdi, a small city of well-maintained single family homes, apartments, small businesses, greenhouses, and a nine-hole golf course. (Read tomorrow's story to learn about the course.) Once outside Hveragerdi, the terrain is flat farmland. Lava rocks have been removed. Horses, cows, sheep, and goats roam the hillsides enjoying their *'24/7 week'* of eating and sleeping. The climate is mild and perfect for spring and summer growing seasons.

Joanna's excellent navigational skills get us to the *Seljalandsfoss Waterfall* without a hiccup. Guests must purchase a two-hour parking pass. I drop Joanna at the entrance and find a parking space. I walk over to the parking pass kiosk, but when I got there to purchase the pass, I don't have my wallet on me. So, I head back to the car to grab it. Just before I purchase the ticket, I see a young lady and her friend pulling out of a parking spot. Hmmm, I wonder if... so I gently knock on the driver's side window, point to the parking pass on her dashboard, and use pantomime to ask for the pass. Surprisingly, the driver rolls down her window and hands me the pass. I smile, shout out two **"Danka's,"** head to my car and place the pass on the dashboard.

The *Seljalandsfoss Waterfall* is extremely tall and spectacular. It gives off a misty and moist water spray which gets us slightly wet. At this waterfall, travelers can climb on the slippery, wet rocks and go **BEHIND** the falls. Siggi's Achilles is not 200% strong so I only go *'halfway'* to get soaked by the spray, listen to the deafening, strong force of water crashing to the bottom, and witness *'up close and personal'* the *'full force'* of this natural wonder. To the left of the main falls is a narrow waterfall that lacks the power and force of Seljalandsfoss.

While observing this marvel of nature, we run into Billy and Adrienne. After taking selfies, pictures, and videos from all angles, we walk about a mile down the path paralleling the hillside to marvel at four additional waterfalls, including *Merkjarfoss/*

Gluggafoss, a powerful waterfall that is hidden **BEHIND** a mountain. To reach this thunderous waterfall, I must **CAREFULLY** walk on a narrow, rocky, wet walkway and through a narrow tunnel and into a small stream that leads to the powerful waterfall. Again, I use common sense and stop halfway into the tunnel for fear of losing my balance, slipping, and falling. However, I smartly extend my iPhone to capture pictures and videos of this dramatic site. On our one mile trek back to the car, I take more videos and pictures of three less spectacular waterfalls.

Along the road to these spectacular waterfalls, we split the tuna fish sandwich. Our stomachs are reminding us it's time for lunch. A few miles down the highway, in the town of *Eyjafjallajokull*, we stop at the *Faxi Bakery and Restaurant* for lunch. Billy and Adrienne join us. Lunch is delicious - homemade mushroom and tomato soups, a grilled cheese sandwich, a cold one and wine. After lunch, we '*bid ado*' to Billy and Adrienne and continue our journey to locate other waterfalls and tourist spots that are listed on the tour map. We pass by the *Skogarfoss Waterfall*; however, the day is getting long so we settle for a long range view from the highway and continue our journey to the black sand beach.

Before we assault the beach, we stop in *Vik*, a remote seafront village in southern Iceland. Vik is home to roughly 350 residents. Perched on a hill overlooking the village and ocean is the wooden *Reyniskirkja Church*, which was built in 1929. The church's parking lot provides excellent, long-range views of the ocean and surrounding area.

We leave Vik and drive a mile or so down the road to the *Black Sand Beaches*, called *Reynisdrangar* and *Reynisfjara,* and park. The beach area offers breathtaking views of the hillside in front of us and the ocean, including a natural arch that spans the shoreline and 120 meters out into the ocean. At the Black Sand Beach, the waves are deceiving prompting the placement of numerous warning signs along the shoreline designed to prevent tragedies. Multiple thin rock formations rise out of the ocean. The most spectacular site Joanna and Siggi see is the basalt columns that look like giant, uneven steps with uneven landings set against the hillside. Young and agile children and adults test their climbing skills to reach the top and improve their ocean and surrounding hillside views. Siggi employs *'common sense'* and only climbs up about five feet to improve his view and take more pictures and a selfie or two. Joanna remains at sea level. Tourists use flat black rocks they find around the beach to build small *'monuments'* on the black sand beach. I gather up numerous small and large rocks and create *'Casa Turzer'* to mark today's visit. I also fill a cup with black sand and select five, perfectly shaped, flat black rocks that I bring home to display in my **'Henderson Man Cave.'**

After leaving the beach, we decide to drive up the road to the ocean side of Vik. I stop the car and Joanna jumps out to shop in the village store while I drive to the beach to get a closer look at the natural rock arches jutting out into the ocean. After snapping more pictures, I stop and gaze at the seagulls majestically gliding against the green mountains. The area is so peaceful and quiet, allowing me to listen to the sounds of seagulls communicating with each other *(where are we eating dinner tonight?)* as they slowly glide around, ever thankful they live here.

The parking area is soft sand. Slowly and carefully, I drive away without spinning the car's wheels and go pick up Joanna. There is **NO** souvenir store that I can't pass up. Spotting one, I enter, make an investment in Vik, Iceland *'stuff'*, and join Joanna for a beer in the adjoining *Halldirskaffi Café*. Reykjavik and Baltic country stores, cafes, restaurants, and bars play *'American oldies'* music. *'Mombo Number Five'* is playing in the café.

It is time to head home. Traffic is flowing nicely on this late Sunday afternoon. Suddenly, the traffic in the right lane comes to a **DEAD STANDSTILL!** I notice the left lane is still moving so I change lanes and pass 50 or more cars while the majority of drivers are satisfied to *'sit and wait'*. When this situation happens in the USA, most drivers pull into the left lane. The two mile backup suddenly ends when two lanes of traffic merge into one lane outside Reykjavik.

After passing through the main center of town, I locate an open parking spot two blocks from the hotel. The instructions for the machine that reads the credit card and issues a parking ticket are in Icelandic. Somehow, by pressing all the buttons, I navigate the screens and purchase a parking pass. Later that night, I learn paid parking ends at 21:00. Overnight parking from 21:00 to 9:00 is free. So, how many kilometers did we travel today? Today's journey covered 390 kilometers (242 miles).

After unwinding at the hotel, Joanna and I make an executive decision to eat a light dinner. We take Billy and Adrienne's recommendation and walk two blocks to *Tres Locos* Mexican Restaurant. Joanna orders a chicken quesadilla and a *'house special'* margarita. I order chicken enchiladas, beans, and rice, the *'special'* margarita, and a draft beer. The bill is outrageous, $130 US or 17,307 ISK, almost as much as Billy and Adrienne spent last night; however, they ordered much more food and adult drinks than we did. Someone got a *'deal'* and someone (i.e., us) *'got screwed.'*

It's time to head back to the hotel. I stop at the local grocery store and purchase fresh fruit for our pre-breakfast in-room *'get the day started'* snack. Joanna settles into bed to read. I head to the lobby to do what else? — write more stories. The 21-hours of sunlight plays *'games with my mind'*. At midnight, I finally realize its past my bedtime. Tomorrow is our last day in Iceland and our **LAST** full day on holiday. So, let's make the most of it! We plan to put the *'pedal to the metal.'* Today, while sightseeing, we walk 8,346 steps. Nighty, night, and sweet dreams from Reykjavik!

*****

Monday, June 10 — Day 77
Gullfoss Waterfalls and Strokkur Geyser

We plan to start our final day, day 77, by getting up at 06:30 and be on the road by 07:30. But, we wake up at 07:37 and start today's adventure at 10:00. Our bodies needed *'just a little more shuteye'* and time to wake up for our final day of exploring Iceland. Today's plan calls for visiting waterfalls and geysers outside Reykjavik.

The morning sky is similar to yesterday's light blue background with thin, *'Metcalf'* wispy white clouds painted on the blue canvas sky using quick, light, upward brush strokes. Looks like Thom either cleaned yesterday's brushes or purchased new ones.

Before eating breakfast, I stop at the front desk and locate the front desk manager. I take a few minutes to update him on *'what happened'* Saturday morning. I tell him about Joanna's fall in the revolving front door and the front desk staff's reply, *'no hotel employee is in charge that can authorize medical attention if your wife needs it!'* Further, I suggest the staff paint the 1.5" raised piece of metal on the base of the revolving front door **YELLOW** or place yellow safety tape on the metal. I also suggest placing signs on the outside of the door and building to alert guests to **'WATCH THEIR STEP'** when entering the revolving door. Joanna is **NOT** the first person to trip and fall when entering the hotel. I listen to his 'story' about how the city, who owns the sidewalk, is dragging their feet to allow the hotel to build a ramp. **Whatever dude.... Send someone to Home Depot, Lowes, or the local hardware store to get yellow paint or tape ASAP.** Later that day, he emails me a 'sorry this happened note.' I made a mental note to contact the hotel manager and corporate office when I return home.

After a quick breakfast, we head to the car. (I sure hope our rental car is where I parked it last night.) The instructions for buying a parking permit were in Icelandic. I used my weak linguistic skills to 'guess' which buttons to push to buy the correct amount of time to park the car overnight. Last night, I asked the hotel front staff to translate how many hours I purchased. They couldn't interpret the Icelandic language receipt. Fortunately, the car was where I left it last night.

After entering the car, Siggi says to navigator Joanna, "You got the map?" She replies, "No, do you?" Siggi says, "No. I guess it must be in the room." I drive to the front of the hotel and pull into the taxicab parking area. Joanna 'darts' to the room, locates the map, and returns. We are now down another 15 minutes schedule wise, but hey, it's the last day on holiday! Or maybe it's time to go home. You think?

The first planned stop today is the *Gullfoss Waterfall*. It's about a two hour ride through the Icelandic countryside. As described yesterday, the terrain varies from mountains to farmland, with various sizes of volcanic rock, marshy wetlands, streams running thru the landscape, and farmland cleared of rocks and ready to plant. Horses, sheep, goats, and cows enjoy the 21 hours of daylight and 'living the dream' munching on grasses as far as the eye can see.

Most Iceland drivers obey the posted speed limit. Occasionally, I come across an aggressive driver who thinks he is on the Formula One race circuit. Traffic cameras looking for speeders and red light runners are mounted on the busy southeast section of Highway One in town.

Roadway lane markings leave *'a lot to be desired.'* In many cases there are no painted lines separating lanes and marking the left and right roadway shoulders.

About 40 kilometers out of town, we drive by a police car parked at the top of a hill looking for speeders. I *'dodge a bullet'* because I *'jam on the breaks'* and bring the car's speed down to the posted limit. Here's a conversation that **COULD** have taken place between two police cars. "Gunnar, this is Stefan at Mile Marker 73. A grey Mazda CX-5 is headed your way. There are two old Americano tourists pushing the speed limit." "Got you, 10-4 Stefan, I will keep an eye out for them. I'm setup in Hvolsvollur at Mile Marker 89." "Gunnar, the car's plate number is 123 FA." "Thanks Stefan. If my brand new high tech radar gun catches them a mere .5 kilometers over the posted limit, they're mine!"

The traveling Americanos make a pit stop at 10:39 at OB, one of the four Circle K, Wawa, and AM/PM gas station and convenience stores in Iceland. We both use the restroom facilities. Joanna alerts the cashier than there is no *'most important paper'* (i.e., toilet paper) in the ladies room. The cashier tells her it's *'bring your own TP Monday.'* "Just grab some off the shelf, no charge." After a potty stop, coffee, a tuna fish sandwich for later, and a soft serve ice cream cone dipped in chocolate sauce and rolled in finely cut nuts (Joanna not me), we are back in the road. At 10:37, Joanna's eating ice cream and loving it! What's wrong with that picture?

When we entered the store, there was a teenager aggressively scrubbing the sidewalk by the entrance door trying to remove coffee and soda stains. I tell him, "Nice job, you are a hard working kid." When we exit the store, the bucket and scrubber are there; but the kid is gone! He must have taken his talents elsewhere after my comments.

Around 12:30, we roll into the Gullfoss Waterfalls parking lot. We join hundreds of other travelers and walk one mile to the falls. The route takes us down 123 sturdy metal grate-like steps to a path leading to an *'up close and personal'* look at the power and force of Iceland's Number One waterfall. This waterfall is **WAY PAST SPECTACULAR!** Carefully, we walk to the edges where the falls begin and take selfies, videos, and lots of pictures. You can *'feel'* the mist and force the waterfall creates. Capturing the energy produced by the waterfall is one of the ways Iceland creates some of its electric power. Niagara Falls is spectacular; but Gullfoss is a close second.

Back at the souvenir store and restaurant, the food line is long, so we head to the car, split the tuna sandwich, an apple, and go to *Strokkur*, Iceland's equivalent of Old Faithful. I call ahead and leave a message to let the geyser know we will be there in 20 minutes. *"Please save your fury so we can witness a spectacular show."* Joanna is tired. She *'passes'* on the walk to the geyser and heads into the store and restaurant. I hoof it 3/10 of a mile to catch a glimpse of the geyser doing its *'sprouting water thing'*. After a few minutes, the geyser blows its stack, sending hot water and steam into the air. A few minutes later, it goes off again; but this time with less force. Possibly the guy hidden underground who triggers the eruptions is on break or left for the day. The last eruption is a dud. The geyser said, *"I've done this enough today. I'm tired. That's all I have left in me. Come back tomorrow."*

Below is important information about *Gullfoss Waterfalls* from one of its brochures:

- Gullfoss (translated to Golden Falls) is one of Iceland's most iconic and beloved waterfalls, found in the *Hvítá River Canyon* in Southwest Iceland.

- The water in Hvítá River travels from the *Langjökull Glacier* before dramatically cascading 32 meters (105 feet) down

Gullfoss' two stages in a dramatic display of nature's raw power.

- Because of the waterfall's two stages, Gullfoss should actually be thought of as two separate features. The first, shorter cascade is 11 meters tall (36 feet), while the second drop is 21 meters (69 feet). The canyon walls on both sides of the waterfall reach heights of up to 70 meters (230 feet) and descend into the great Gullfossgjúfur canyon. Geologists believe this canyon was formed by glacial outbursts at the beginning of the last ice age.

- In the summer, approximately 140 cubic meters (459 cubic feet) of water surges down the waterfall every second, while in winter that number drops to around 109 cubic meters (358 cubic feet). With such energy, visitors who *'get too close'* should not be surprised to find themselves drenched by the spray from the powerful waterfall.

Let's get back to today's excursion. Slowly and carefully, I head back to the main building and look for Joanna. After entering the building, I do what I always do, buy a few mementoes. Strokkur is Iceland's most visited active geyser. It is one the three major attractions on the world-famous Golden Circle **sightseeing route, along with Gullfoss Waterfalls and Pingvelir National Park.**

From Wikipedia, here is what makes active geysers rare:

- Active geysers, like Strokkur, are rare around the world, because many conditions must be met for them to form. They are thus only found in certain parts of highly geothermal areas.

- The first condition that is necessary is an intense heat source; magma must be close enough to the surface of the earth for the rocks to be hot enough to boil water. Considering that Iceland is located on top of the rift valley between the North

American and Eurasian tectonic plates, this condition is met throughout most of the country.

- Second, you need a source of flowing underground water. In the case of Strokkur, this comes from the second largest glacier in the country, Langjökull. Meltwater from the glacier sinks into the surrounding porous lava rock and travels underground in all directions. Flowing water evidence is found in Þingvelir National Park, where many freshwater springs flow straight from the earth.

- Finally, you need a complex plumbing system that allows a geyser to erupt, rather than *'just steaming'* from the ground like fumarole. Above the intense heat source, there must be space for the flowing water to gather like a reservoir. From this basin, there must be a vent to the surface. This vent must be lined with silica so that the boiling, rising water cannot escape before the eruption.

That's enough about Strokkur Geyser. Let's get back to today's excursion.

I locate Joanna, who was seated at the restaurant, and show her the videos and photos of the Strokkur Geyser. We share a bowl of mushroom soup to *'take the edge off'* before heading back towards *Hveragerei*, located at the base of the three kilometer hill about 45 kilometers outside Reykjavik. The two lane country road takes us past vast stretches of land sitting on volcanic rocks and covered with a green mosey ground cover or just devoid of any growth. We see homes, farms, horses, sheep, goats, and cows enjoying 21 hours of daylight while enjoying a buffet of green grasses.

Many farms remove the volcanic rocks and create vast fertile areas to plant a variety of grasses. We also drive by a sod farm where the work crew is removing and rolling the grass for delivery to customers. For miles and miles, mountains surround the vast flat terrain and remind us of driving through Wyoming, Montana, and North and South Dakota.

We drive by a large horse farm. In a large corral, the horses are *'milling around and hanging out.'* One of the chestnut brown horses is on the ground, lying on its left side with its head in the dirt. It doesn't appear to be moving. Other horses walk by and ask, "What happened? Were you out late last night and had too much to drink? What did you eat? Were you hanging out with that light brown floosy horse again? Are you breathing? Shall we call the vet or call your family? What's up?"

As mentioned on a few occasions, we drive past fenced in areas where all sizes and ages of sheep graze. As we pass by, I blow the car horn. Some of sheep stand up and wave while others look at us and mumble "like why are you honking the horn? What are you thinking? Are you trying to disturb our 24/7 eating?" Some of the younger sheep are skittish. They leave their mothers and start a stampede. Now, sensing danger, the older, laid back sheep join the stampede and race across the field back to the barn area.

One of the unique things we observe are strategically planted birch, pine, and poplar trees that create wind breaks to protect homes and farm buildings that must experience periodic and unannounced strong winds.

Joanna wants to stop in Hveragerois and look for some small decorative vases. After three stops at flower stores and greenhouses, the search ends unsuccessfully.

I notice a sign for a local golf course just over the hill. The drive takes us to Hveragerois Golf Club, a nine-hole links style course that weaves through the local terrain set against a mountain background. There are no golf carts. Everyone walks and pulls a two wheel golf bag cart. These are hearty Icelandic men and women. The sun is out and beats down on the course and golfers. The temperature, however, is in the mid 50's. There's a slight breeze just enough to add *a 'chill in the air.'* Some of the men and women are wearing shorts and short sleeve shirts! I ask a hearty, stocky gentleman in his late 40's about wearing shorts and a short sleeve golf shirt in this weather. He says, "We are Vikings. We are hearty and strong. And tomorrow we will be sick and not go to work!" Other players are slightly more bundled up with long pants and a long sleeve golf shirt or a ¼ zip pullover jacket.

One of the unusual course hazards is the steam rising out of the ground. Very hot underground water under pressure creates steam. If a player's golf ball lands in a steam spouting area, the player cannot retrieve his/her golf ball; however, the player gets a free drop two club lengths away from the hazard without penalty. Joanna and I share a beer while looking out over the course. There's a foursome on each of the nine holes. There is no backup on the tee box or in the fairways. We leave the course with another souvenir beer glass. It's time to head home. About an hour later, we arrive in Reykjavik, park the car in our favorite parking lot, and drop our *'stuff'* in the room.

Let's digress for a few moments. Some towns have long, 15 to 20 letter names, such as *Kirkjubaejarklaustur, Myrdalssandur, Brautarholt* and *Hvolsvollur*. Please don't ask me to pronounce them...just not gonna happen. Street names can be equally challenging. Try saying **"I'll meet you on the corner of Skolavoroustigur and Bergstadastraeti"** fast, three times.

The Reykjavik Leiden public transportation buses are bright yellow and run on electric power. Kamala Harris would *'drool and cackle like a hyena'* if she witnesses this. One cannot forget her glowing remarks about how she *'loves yellow school buses!'* She's an ultra-far left radical who the Democrat back room powers to be (Pelosi, Obama, et al) *'selected'* to replace Biden on the Democratic presidential ticket. She's got nothing better to do than *'flip flop'* her political positions, call Republican presidential candidate

Donald Trump every name in the book and *'a threat to democracy,'* lie like a rug, and scare women into thinking their reproductive rights and abortions will be severely restricted if Trump wins the November 2024 Presidential election (Spoiler alert—Trump won.)

As President Joe Biden's *'Border Czar,'* Harris failed to secure our southern border and, without **ANY** concern for Americans safety and local governments' finances, permitted millions of unvetted illegal immigrants to freely enter our country and, in many cases, commit serious crimes on innocent Americans without consequences. Maybe she can send FBI missing persons' agents, the United States Marshall Service, and the CIA to locate Department of Transportation Secretary Mayor Pete Buttigieg and update him about the electric school buses and the abundance of electric car charging stations scattered around Iceland.

In 2021, President Biden signed the bi-partisan infrastructure package into law with $7.5 billion specifically directed towards building tens of thousands of electric vehicle charging stations across the country to appease anxious drivers and New Green Deal environmentalists. As of June 2024, seven EV charging stations were built! Possibly, Mayor Pete could be out riding his bike thru the racist inner city streets he loves to talk about or get his bike out of the back of his Black government issued SUV vehicle two blocks from his office and *'jump on'* his bicycle, thus fulfilling his commitment to the environment.

Before dinner, we walk to a clothing store near the church to exchange a sweater I purchased for my sister, Barbara. On the way back down the pathway, we run into Amalia, the experienced and knowledgeable front desk person who was pushing her young son in a stroller while walking with a friend. We continue to stroll down the street, eliminating all restaurants for a variety of undisclosed reasons and settle into our favorite local establishment, Bistro 101, for a cheeseburger, fries, fish and chips, a glass of very nice red wine, and a local draft beer. The wine is so good. We will buy five individual sized bottles of this wine at the Duty Free Store in the airport so we can enjoy when we return to Henderson. Before retreating to the hotel, I make my final run to the grocery store for pre-breakfast fruit.

Joanna heads to the room and shows great restraint by **NOT** stopping for a gelato. I hang out in lobby for the last time reading and writing until after midnight. It's finally time to turn in and get a good night's sleep. In the morning after breakfast, we check out and head to the airport. So, for the last time on our 77-day journey, good night! But wait, we still have one more day, Day 78, of traveling before we head home.

*****

Tuesday, June 11— Day 78
Reykjavik, Iceland to Henderson Through Denver

Going to bed last night at a reasonable hour was *'not in the cards'* knowing today, Tuesday is the **LAST DAY** of our fabulous 78-day holiday thru Europe. Siggi crawls into bed at 17 minutes past midnight. At 04:19, *'mother nature'* wakes him up. After a quick pit stop, I turn on the iPad and my cell phone to retrieve the Southwest Airlines record locator codes for our Denver to Las Vegas flight later tonight. I check us in and download our boarding passes. We are in Group A, boarding passes A51 and A52.

At 08:00, Joanna's iPhone alarm *'rattles our minds and bodies.'* No sense in rushing. The only activity for today is packing, returning the rental car, and getting to the airport with plenty of time to spare. We have First Class Seats, C3 and A3, on Icelandic Air Flight F1671 direct to Denver at 16:55. It's roughly an eight hour flight.

Siggi showers and dresses; however, he cannot find his black Reebok sneakers. Did I leave them in Room 6041 on Viking Mars? Did Joanna toss them out because she thinks they're ugly? Did the housekeeper need new shoes for someone at home? Whatever, my Reeboks are *'missing in action.'* However, it does *'lighten the suitcase load.'* I send an email to the Viking Mars General Manager asking if housekeeping may have found them in Room 6041. Later I learn they could not find them.

Before heading to purchase additional parking time, I stop at the front desk to request a late checkout, until noon. The clerk asks, "What's your room number?" Immediately, and who knows why, I have an embarrassing *'senior'* moment. I can't remember our room number! All that flashes through my mind is Viking Mars Room number 6041! "I can't recall. I know it's on the sixth floor. I'm having a senior moment." The front desk clerk asks my last name and locates the room number. Her body language screams out loudly, *'Who am I dealing with? Can't he remember his room number??? What about your name, cell phone number, and mother's maiden name?'* Should she call the *'meat wagon'* to take me to a mental hospital where the staff dresses from head to toe in white uniforms, where all the rooms are double locked and include padded walls and electric shock treatments are the *'soup de jour.'* The young front desk clerk makes an *'executive decision'* and gives me a pass. Clearly, she doesn't want to complete the company's 18-page, legal size, Incident Report Form to clearly document the reasons why she ships me off. Case closed.

Next, I ask the young lady for directions to the closest post office where I can mail a package. She grabs her iPhone and uses fingers on both hands to *'allegedly'* find a location. She indicates it is near the Cathedral. I *'know better'* and say, "I have been up that road twice. Unless I am blind, there's no post office there." She brings up Google Maps to show me the location. "Young lady, that's a **Red Post Box** hanging on a wall. That's where people drop stamped letters and postcards. I need a post office to mail a **PACKAGE!** And by the way, young lady, there's a Red Post Box out the front door, turn left, down the street one block, and left at the next street. It's hanging on the wall, on the left side. Can't miss it," I curtly tell the clerk.

"Do you get out much and walk around the local neighborhood? There's a whole world out there."

Confused, she asks the clerk to her left for assistance. Four hands, on two iPhones, click away trying desperately to locate a **REAL** post office. It's 08:57. I kindly tell the ladies, "I've got to run, but I'll be back. Take care of the eight or so unhappy check-ins standing behind me." They remain perplexed. You think I was asking for directions to the moon or Hawaii.

At 08:58, I hustle up the street to the parking lot and buy three more hours of parking. Overnight parking is free from 21:00 to 09:00. However, from 09:00 to 21:00 daily, everyone pays to park. I buy the maximum allowable, 3 hours. Parking is paid for through 12:00.

Returning to the hotel, I ask the two confused clerks if they have solved the mystery of the post office's location. Do I need to put Columbo or Sergeant Joe Friday on the case? They look up from their iPhones and simultaneously shake their heads right, left, left, right. So be it. "Thanks for trying." At the end of the reception desk, I turn right towards the elevators. Looking to my right, I see a tall blonde front desk employee apparently watching over three front desk employees *'like a mother bird watching her newborns.'* She is sitting on a high-back stool, legs crossed, and intensely playing with her iPhone. Maybe she's using some new "AI" software to track and evaluate each employee's real time job performance. Or is she watching some mindless video, playing a game, checking email, writing a story, or just *'acting busy.'*

I get her attention by clapping loudly, jumping up and down, and using the first two fingers on my right hand to signal her from my eyes to hers back and forth indicating *'let's talk.'* I have a question. I explain the post office location question. After about five minutes of pressing every key on her iPhone and using Google to locate a **POST OFFICE,** she locates one in the next village 45 kilometers away! Google indicates it's **ONLY** a 15-minute drive so I guess it's on the *'unlimited speed expressway'* out of Reykjavik. She touches her iPhone to mine, transferring the address to my iPhone. Magic! To be on the safe side, I take a screen shot to preserve the location. I say, "Thanks." Within seconds, she's back in her *'queen bee position'* on the high-back stool intently returning to whatever she was doing before I interrupted her. Whatever...

It's time for breakfast. I take the elevator down one floor to the breakfast room. I grab two takeaway cups of coffee, two granola bars, some fruit, and bacon before the breakfast room closes at 9:30. I head to our room and share the goodies with Joanna. When I arrive at the room, I'm pleasantly surprised. Joanna has **EVERYTHING** packed! Plus, it will **NOT** be necessary to stop at the post office to mail a sweater to my sister Barbara.

It's almost noon — time to hit the road. Siggi retrieves the dark grey Mazda CX-5. I park across the street from the hotel entrance, gather up Joanna, load the suitcases and travel bags into the car's rear storage area, and begin the journey to the Thrifty Car Rental location. I fill the tank and after some slight confusion, locate the Thrifty Rental Car office. There were 50,376 kilometers on the odometer when we rented the car. On Sunday, we drove 390 kilometers. On Monday and today, we drove an additional 285 kilometers. When returning the car, the odometer reads 51,051. Not bad for two days of driving through the countryside.

I take the keys and the odometer reading into the office. Next, I ask the counter lady what time the next airport shuttle van leaves. To my dismay, utter surprise, and **WHAT THE HELL, YOU HAVE GOT TO BE KIDDING ME!!!,** the counter lady says, "We don't offer shuttle service to Keflavik International Airport (KEF)! It's 45 to 50 minutes away!" "Hold on young lady, when I **ADDED** the additional one day rental, the gentleman in **THIS** office who processed the rental **ASSURED** me

THIS location provides a *'no charge'* shuttle service to KEF. Why would I pay a one day rental fee for only 2.5 hours over the original 10:00 check-in time without the ride to the airport?" I show her the email from the office employee. She understands the situation and asks the manager to join us. At first, I mentally prepare for a potential confrontational conversation. However, to my surprise, the manager clearly understands the employee's mistake. First, we negotiate waving the extra day rental fee, and I pay the cab fare to the airport. But the young lady knows the fare for the 45 to 50 minute cab ride will be more than the one day rental refund. The manager calls the local cab company to confirm the cost. It's now back to the bargaining table. I suggest Thrifty waive the 50 Euros airport drop charge. I will drive the car to the Thrifty location at KEF. It's a done deal. The manager documents the arrangement in the rental contract file, provides a map to the Thrifty KEF location, and bids us safe travels. I thank the manager and the counter clerk for their professionalism and excellent customer service.

After the extra-long delay, I return to the car, shut the rear hatch, and get into the driver's seat. Joanna asks, "What's up?" I explain the situation and the resolution. She's good with it. For the past two days, first class navigator Joanna did a fabulous job getting us from Point A to Point B. She didn't miss a beat or a turn. For that successful service and *'job well done,'* it earns her an "A" and six college credits for Navigation 203, using the Waze App to get us from Point A to Point B.

The road to KEF is a four lane divided highway constructed through massive lava fields. The lava fields and rocks of all sizes and shapes line both sides of the highway as far as the eye can see. Many, many years ago, lava flowed from the volcano towards the ocean, creating an additional land mass extending into the North Atlantic. Great engineering and construction skills were needed to build this highway to the airport. Building the highway and airport opened up this side of Reykjavik to construction of single family homes, apartments, as well as commercial and industrial buildings, effectively creating a new section of town.

The Thrifty Car Rental check-in is effortless. Within minutes, we are on the van to the airport terminal. Riding with us are two, early 20's USA college graduates. They just spent two weeks driving the entire coastline of Iceland and camping! (As a side note, while I would love to return and take the trip these young ladies took, **BUT**...camping for us is, at a minimum, either Holiday Inn Express, Hampton Inn, or Best Western.)

Our van driver parks in a bus unloading area and draws *'nasty words'* from the bus driver right behind us. A few long and loud horn honks, the first heard in months, and *'back and forth hand gestures'* solve nothing; but it appears the two drivers now know each other. Maybe they can get together for a cold one or two after work and resolve their differences.

KEF is a very large, international terminal. Icelandic Air is the major local airline. Siggi and Joanna arrive at the Business Class baggage check-in station, check three bags, no charge (we are allowed 4 bags), stow the boarding passes and luggage tags, and head for security. Just as we turn right onto the main corridor, the Icelandic carry-on baggage patrol unceremoniously pulls me over and asks to see if my carry-on suitcase fits in the *'shoebox size box.'* It fails the test. The officers politely, but in no uncertain terms, tell me to go back and check the bag. I explain, to **NO** avail, the contents are fragile. *'No cigar, too bad, no exceptions today.'* I am, unequivocally, instructed to return and check the bag **NOW**. If I fail to follow their explicit instructions, I could be kicked out of the airport for creating an international incident. I point and tell them, "It's **ON YOU** if anything breaks!" They instruct me to have the check-in person place a **FRAGILE** tag on the bag. Begrudgingly, and without any other choice, I head back, check the bag, and ask the clerk to please put a **FRAGILE** tag on the suitcase. This checked bag is **FREE** since our flight status covers four checked bags at no charge. She understands, *'handles business,'* and tells us to enjoy today's trip.

Next, we stop at the KEF Duty Free extensive shopping area to turn in our Iceland Duty Free shopping receipts. We expect a small refund to hit our credit card sometime before Labor Day 2025. Why so long you ask? Government moves very slowly in Iceland. We spend about 15 minutes *'shopping'* for last minute items including candy, *'local spirits'* for my golfing friends, and five small bottles of the red wine Joanna enjoyed last night at dinner.

The security line for First Class passengers is very short. Iceland doesn't have a TSA-type airport security check-in system. We place our belongings, including two small duffel bags, Joanna's purse, shoes, belts, coats, everything in our pockets, watches, iPad, and backpack in bins that pass through security X-ray machines. Our bodies contain numerous replacement parts, including new knees and hips. Without a doubt, we fail the full body X-ray machine security check. Failure sets off the alarms indicating that security personnel *'better pat down and carefully wand the two very suspicious looking old travelers.'* We get *'full body pat downs'* and *'full body wand scans.'* We pass these tests without incident and proceed to retrieve our belongings.

After security clearance, we head to customs. Federal agents check our boarding passes, passports, and stamp our passports. Nothing irregular pops up on their computer screen indicating *'hold, detain, handcuff, and interrogate.'*

With First Class boarding passes in hand, we gain access to the Icelandic Air Executive Customer Lounge around 14:00. Here, we enjoy lunch, a beverage or two, and settle into comfortable chairs to wait for our 16:55 departure. Later, we meet up with Billy and Adrienne who are travelling on a different flight bound for Chicago. We exchange goodbyes. Shortly thereafter, we head to Gate D24.

The boarding process already started. The area is **VERY** crowded. It's a full flight. Travelers patiently wait to get on the plane. Joanna flags down an Icelandic employee and tells him we have First Class seats. Immediately, he *'jumps into action,'* leads us past the hoard of *'back of the plane coach passengers'* to gate personnel who quickly direct us to the front of the line. However, there is **NO** jet-way to board the flight. Airline personnel herd passengers onto buses that transport everyone to the Boeing 757 plane parked in a passenger loading area.

On the bus, I sit next to a young lady from Denver. She's wearing a *'**Phillies'*** baseball cap. She is originally from Doylestown, PA, a 30-minute drive north from Willow Grove where I grew up. The young lady is flying home after attending Game Two of the Phillies/Mets two baseball game *London Series*. Now that's a dedicated Phillies fan flying *'across the pond'* to watch a game. She has no clue as to why Icelandic Air is routing her from London to Reykjavik to reach her final destination of Denver.

It's time to *'que up'* to board the plane. Everyone walks up a 19 step staircase to enter the plane, just like in the old days of air travel prior to the 1960's. Thankfully, no one has a *'Joe Biden frequent stumbling and falling moment'* by falling *'up'* the staircase.

We settle into seats 3A and 3C. For both of us, a glass of chilled champagne goes down smoothly before take-off. Siggi gets into, what else, composing today's story while Joanna watches a movie. Approximately 90 minutes into the flight, the first class cabin attendant serves us a seafood dinner and wine.

After dinner, we resume our pre-dinner activities. Joanna leans over and whispers to me, "I just took off my shoes. Please let me know if you can smell my feet." Siggi immediately *'feels woozy and almost passes out.'* The flight attendant senses trouble and activates a switch that immediately drops down my oxygen mask. This action sets off an alarm throughout the plane causing hysteria and confusion for the 287 passengers on board. Flight attendants jump into action, calm everyone, and inform the passengers *"There is* **NOTHING** *to worry about. It's* **JUST** *a mechanical malfunction causing an oxygen mask to deploy."*

Gradually, my breathing, blood pressure, and heart rate return to normal. The flight attendant leads Joanna into the lavatory, hands her a wash cloth and hand towel, and instructs her, *in no uncertain terms,* to use the soap and wash those size 11's **NOW** or she won't be allowed to return to her seat. She tells Joanna to put on her shoes and **DO NOT** remove them until you get home. The Captain sees a **RED LIGHT** blinking on his screen indicating an oxygen mask deployed in first class. He leaves the cockpit to investigate and listens to the first class flight attendant supervisor explain what happened. She reassures the Captain the situation is well under control; there's nothing to worry about. He's satisfied that things are back to normal; however, he tells her to contact him if this passenger causes another disturbance. After returning to the cockpit, he uses the intercom system to advise the passengers *"everything is under control... there's nothing to worry about."*

Icelandic Air flight 444 touches down at 6:57 P.M., Denver time (Mountain Standard Time). We have until 9:22 P.M. to reach our Southwest Airlines connecting flight to Las Vegas, leaving from Gate C51. First, we walk well over 1 1/2 miles to reach Customs. Our step count reaches 9,277 steps today. Seventy-five percent or more of the steps are walking through the Denver airport. Customs clears us in less than two minutes. It must be our *'good looks and innocent, smiling faces.'* We get two laminated cards indicating to the next security checkpoint to *'just let them through, do not stop them, check their belongings, or interrogate them.'* Our next stop is baggage claim. Here, there's a **MAJOR** 30-minute delay. On the plus side, luggage carts are **FREE**. We grab two luggage carts to transport our three suitcases, two small duffel bags, backpack, and plastic bag holding the booze purchased at the Reykjavik Duty Free store. After locating our three checked bags, we quickly pass through the final Customs security checkpoint and hand over the *'get out of jail free cards.'*

Our one and only **PRIMARY** goal is boarding tonight's Southwest flight to Las Vegas. Originally, it is scheduled to take off at 9:00 P.M.; however, the departure is first changed to 9:22 P.M. and is now re-scheduled to depart at 9:50. Without this 50-minute departure delay, we would **NEVER** make the Las Vegas flight.

Next, we must check our bags. After clearing Customs, we get into the Southwest Airlines *'Recheck Your Bags Line.'* Unfortunately, we misunderstand what *'Recheck Your Bags'* means. It **DOESN'T** mean *'here are our bags, please check them in for the flight to Las Vegas tonight.'* It means *'***IF** you checked your bags in Reykjavik **ALL the way through to your final destination,** you drop them off here.'* Personnel in Reykjavik had **NO CLUE** how to check our bags through to Las Vegas. Consequently, we **MUST** now walk down a long corridor, turn right, find the second bank of elevators, and go up to Level Six. Here, we check our four bags with Southwest.

The automated baggage check-in service requires each traveler to scan their boarding pass, follow the prompts on the screen, remove the machine generated baggage tags, place the new tags on each piece of checked bag, tear off the checked baggage receipt, and take the bags to agents standing behind the baggage drop-off counter. Six agents are standing there, laughing, and talking. Clearly, they are **NOT** busy. Why? Because each customer does **ALL** the work for them! I can't figure out where to scan my boarding pass. No instructions say, *'**Scan Documents Here.'** I ask one of the six *'just standing around agents'* to show me where the scanner is. She nonchalantly shows me, completes the task in seconds, and after my baggage tags print, helps Joanna get her luggage tags. The entire process took less than two minutes; so, why don't the agents get out from behind the counter, assist travelers, and speed-up the process? The baggage clerk puts the bags on the conveyor belt. They are now headed to the *'sort and process baggage area'* for loading on the Las Vegas bound airplane. At least we hope so!

Hang on travel *'groupies,'* we are **NOT** yet ready to walk to the gate. Next, we must go through TSA security. The *'TSA Pre-check'* security checkpoints are **CLOSED** for the night. So, we line up and wait 15 minutes to reach TSA personnel. They check our tickets and waive us through to the screening area. **EVERYTHING** but our shoes **MUST** go through the X-ray screening process. Of course, our metal body parts set off *'bells and whistles'* indicating *'check these people out, they may have implanted something illegal in their bodies.'* We pass the second check point with flying colors; **BUT** (it's really been a long time since we had a *'BUT moment,')* some of our carry-on luggage requires additional screening.

Our small bottles of booze and red wine trigger an additional search. We have no clue what the additional screening is all about. The agent informs us the booze could be confiscated. One at a time, each of the five wine bottles are placed into a machine checking for who knows what. Maybe they are examining the alcohol content percentage. The bottles pass the *'looking for liquid explosives test!'* Using official government issued TSA packing tape, the agent reseals the plastic bag containing the booze. Next, we search for Terminal C gates. Currently, we are in Terminal A. Signs direct us down one floor to the underground shuttle train that takes passengers to the A, B, and C Terminal gates. We board the next train and exit at Terminal C. Another long walk, this time assisted by moving electric sidewalks, finally gets us to Gate 51.

I park Joanna at the gate seating area. This plane is apparently just one-third full. I call *'Mr. 300',* Dennis 'Griff' Griffin to coordinate his picking us up at Pole 10 in the Las Vegas Airport Passenger

Pickup Area for our ride home. I then hustle to a take-out counter and buy a tuna sandwich on marbled rye bread. My second stop is a takeaway coffee location. I order a decaf Americano coffee with cream for Joanna. While waiting for the plane to board, we *'gobble the sandwich down like we NEVER saw food before'* and line up to board the flight. Since there are just 62 passengers on the flight, the flight attendants *'spread out'* the passengers to *'weight balance'* the plane. We never experienced that one before. The plane takes off on time. It's still hard to fathom we have been gone 78 days. Now, we are only one hour and twenty-four minutes from Vegas. If all goes well, we could be *'in the door'* at home before the clock strikes midnight.

When the wheels touch down and it's clear to make a phone call, Siggi follows the *'pick us up plan'* and calls Griff. I will call him again when we have *'bags on a luggage pull cart,'* and we're crossing the bridge to the passenger pick-up area, Pole 10. Success! (By the way, Griff is a great Uber driver, something to keep in mind for your next travel adventure. Plus, he charges little, just bring over a few beers to his house while he watches his beloved Ohio State Buckeyes football team!)

Griff and I greet each other with a *'knuckles bump and bear hug'* (no kissing), load the bags into the back of his Honda SUV, and head to1836 Hovenweep Street in Henderson. When we pull into the driveway, we *'hear'* the scratchy voice of former Boston Celtics announcer Johnny Most screaming, ***"It's over...it's all over!"*** *after the Celtics clinch another NBA championship in the 1970's.* For the past 78 days, traveling 17,455 miles, roaming nine European countries, visiting over 36 cities, staying in 16 hotels, and spending 14 nights on the Viking Mars cruise ship –it all comes to an end, but who's counting. Plus, counting the days on the cruise ship, we enjoyed 70 mornings of free breakfast included in the nightly hotel room rates.

Siggi and Joanna arrive home at 10:45 P.M. **Reality sets in… we are now simply John and Leslie.**

P.S. A few days after settling in at home, I email the Center Hotels Plaza Reykjavik hotel manager and the corporate office to let them know about Joanna's fall, my interactions with the front desk staff, and bring to their attention a number of critical issues. I reiterate my recommendations to paint the *'trip and fall hazard'* **YELLLOW** or cover it with bright **YELLOW** tape and post signs on the building and doors to alert guests to watch their step when entering. After a few days, I receive an email telling me the metal is painted **YELLOW**. Plus, the hotel manager processed a 50% *'Inconvenience Credit'* for our troubles and the poor service we encountered during our stay. That was nice of him — I just hope no one else trips and falls. Plus, we received a nice discount for out 4 night stay in July 2026!

Until our **NEXT** adventure—thank you for reading our book! We hope you enjoyed exploring the places we visited and laughed along with our *"Shit Happens"* moments that always seem to find us wherever we go!

*****